Beginning iOS Media App Development

Ahmed Bakir

Apress®

Beginning iOS Media App Development

ISBN-13 (pbk): 978-1-4302-5083-8

ISBN-13 (electronic): 978-1-4302-5084-5

Trademarked names, logos, and images may appear in this book. Rather than use a trademark symbol with every occurrence of a trademarked name, logo, or image, we use the names, logos, and images only in an editorial fashion and to the benefit of the trademark owner, with no intention of infringement of the trademark.

The use in this publication of trade names, trademarks, service marks, and similar terms, even if they are not identified as such, is not to be taken as an expression of opinion as to whether or not they are subject to proprietary rights.

While the advice and information in this book are believed to be true and accurate at the date of publication, neither the authors nor the editors nor the publisher can accept any legal responsibility for any errors or omissions that may be made. The publisher makes no warranty, express or implied, with respect to the material contained herein.

Managing Director: Welmoed Spahr
Lead Editor: Michelle Lowman
Developmental Editor: Russell Jones
Technical Reviewer: Gheorghe Chesler
Editorial Board: Steve Anglin, Mark Beckner, Gary Cornell, Louise Corrigan, Jim DeWolf, Jonathan Gennick, Robert Hutchinson, Michelle Lowman, James Markham, Matthew Moodie, Jeff Olson, Jeffrey Pepper, Douglas Pundick, Ben Renow-Clarke, Gwenan Spearing, Matt Wade, Steve Weiss
Coordinating Editor: Kevin Walter
Copy Editor: Sharon Wilkey
Compositor: SPi Global
Indexer: SPi Global
Artist: SPi Global
Cover Designer: Anna Ishchenko
Photography: Gheorghe Chesler
Graphics: Rafael Rodriguez

Distributed to the book trade worldwide by Springer Science+Business Media New York, 233 Spring Street, 6th Floor, New York, NY 10013. Phone 1-800-SPRINGER, fax (201) 348-4505, e-mail orders-ny@springer-sbm.com, or visit www.springeronline.com. Apress Media, LLC is a California LLC and the sole member (owner) is Springer Science + Business Media Finance Inc (SSBM Finance Inc). SSBM Finance Inc is a Delaware corporation.

For information on translations, please e-mail rights@apress.com, or visit www.apress.com.

Apress and friends of ED books may be purchased in bulk for academic, corporate, or promotional use. eBook versions and licenses are also available for most titles. For more information, reference our Special Bulk Sales–eBook Licensing web page at www.apress.com/bulk-sales.

Any source code or other supplementary material referenced by the author in this text is available to readers at www.apress.com. For detailed information about how to locate your book's source code, go to www.apress.com/source-code/.

Dedicated to my father, Mohammed Bakir, who brought home our first computer when I was four and always encouraged me to play with it, even after I broke it two days later.

Contents at a Glance

Contents

About the Author

Ahmed Bakir is the founder and lead developer at devAtelier LLC (www.devatelier.com), a San Diego-based mobile development firm. After spending several years writing software for embedded systems, he started developing apps out of coffee shops for fun. Once the word got out, he began taking on clients and quit his day job to work on apps full time. Since then, he has been involved in the development of over 20 mobile projects, and has seen several enter the top 25 of the App Store, including one that reached number one in its category (Video Scheduler). His clients have ranged from scrappy startups to large corporations, such as Citrix. In his downtime, Ahmed can be found on the road, exploring new places, speaking about mobile development, and still working out of coffee shops.

About the Technical Reviewer

Gheorghe Chesler is a senior software engineer with expertise in Quality Assurance, System Automation, Performance Engineering, and e-Publishing. He works at ServiceNow as a Senior Performance Engineer, and is a principal technical consultant for Plural Publishing, a medical-field publishing company. His preferred programming language is Perl (so much so that he identifies with the Perl mascot, hence the camel picture), but also worked on many Java and Objective-C projects.

Acknowledgments

There are so many people I would like to thank who helped me during this most challenging and rewarding period of my life that I could probably write a book about it (ha ha!). But, so I won't lose my readers' interest, I will briefly name just a few people. If I have forgotten anyone, please forgive me; I write apps to counteract my absentmindedness.

First, I would like to thank my family, Mohammed, Layla, and Roba Bakir, who always pushed me to explore my full potential.

Next, I would like to thank Michelle Lowman at Apress, who found me at Macworld and kindly asked me if I was interested in writing a book. I will never forget our conversations about sleep deprivation.

Kevin Walter, my coordinating editor, who had the unfortunate task of constantly reminding me to finish my chapters, but always brought positivity to every exchange.

Russell Douglas, my technical editor, and Sharon Wilkey, my copy editor, who helped me find my writing voice and caught all of my stray commas.

Gheorghe Chesler, my technical mentor, who taught me the beauty of clean code (and Perl golf). His input as the technical reviewer of this book helped me shape my thoughts into a work others could use.

Mike MacKenzie, my business mentor and one of my first clients, who has always provided me with invaluable advice and great times in Orange County.

Rafael Rodriguez and Viraphol Sengsourya, two of the first members of devAtelier LLC, whose constant hard work, diligence, and positivity have shaped the image of the company immensely. A dignified designer (Rafael) and an excellent engineer (Viraphol) who have been incredible partners and confidants.

Carol Miller, one of my first computer science professors at North Carolina State University, whose engaging lectures and stories of "critical chickens" made every class impactful and inspirational.

And finally, I would like to thank all of my friends, who have constantly supported me, encouraged me, and had the patience to listen to my crazy stories (most of the time). See you, space cowboys.

Introduction

Do you remember the first time you experienced multimedia on a computer? Was it the carefully orchestrated town music of The Oregon Trail on an Apple II? Or maybe it was a YouTube video of a talented feline playing a catchy tune on a keyboard?

What about when you started to get into programming? Was it to make a game? Or perhaps emulate the exact tone of the school bell so you could get out of class early?

For many people, multimedia has been one of the most exciting and personal aspects of computing. For some of us (myself included), it was an inspiration to learn programming. The lure of multimediat has not changed as computing has become mobile, but fortunately, it is now easier than ever to get started making your own multimedia apps.

iOS provides an incredibly deep set of APIs (application programming interfaces) that allow you to display and capture photos, videos, and audio within your apps. These APIs are built directly into Cocoa Touch, meaning you do not need to include any external libraries to use them. For many of the APIs, including the camera, the capture interface exposed in your app is the same one used throughout the system. This is a great improvement over the "good old days," when integrating a camera may have required talking to your component manufacturer for several weeks and porting sample code.

The goal of this book is to help you take what you already know about iOS app development and apply it to media app development. One of the great things about Cocoa Touch is how much Apple has abstracted low-level functionality for you. You can now build apps that let you play video without having to become an expert on video codecs.

By building apps that focus on specific APIs, and picking up new programming concepts along the way, you will make incremental progress and avoid being overwhelmed by the seemingly infinite set of APIs available in iOS. The units in this book (photo, video, audio) begin by showing you how to get started with the relevant APIs and then peel back the layers, allowing you to customize your apps beyond the basic features provided out-of-the-box.

You have already accomplished a lot to be far enough in your iOS development journey, and I'm glad you've decided to start looking into multimedia features. Let's go the extra step together and build some amazing media apps!

Chapter 1

Welcome to iOS Media App Development

What Is the Purpose of This Book?

This book is an in-depth guide to iOS media app development, targeted at beginning- to intermediate-level iOS developers. In this book, you will learn how to build apps that take advantage of iOS's programming interfaces, or APIs, for capturing, displaying, and manipulating still images (photos), videos, and audio resources. The last part of the book covers new functionality, including the Swift programming language, which Apple introduced in iOS 8.

In presenting these topics, I have taken some cues from tutorial-based guides, which introduce you to topics by providing you with code snippets. However, this book goes deeper than typical tutorials by introducing background information, presenting discussions on implementation challenges, and providing keystone projects to reinforce your new knowledge. These keystone projects frame each chapter by giving you a full-fledged application that takes advantage of the features covered, as well as lessons from other popular applications. By building a real application, you will gain a deeper understanding of the software design process, and more experience with tackling implementation challenges—often the hardest part of finishing an app.

You may have already tried developing an app but stopped, or have friends in the same position. One of the most famous complaints about iOS development is that it is too limited in what it allows you to do. Although there is some truth to this statement, in that the iOS platform forces you to develop apps "in a sandbox" and hides access to many otherwise common features, such as a global file system, many of these complaints come from having to develop for Cocoa Touch, an extremely platform-specific framework. Programming for a framework allows you to take advantage of many features for free, such as drawing a view or instantiating a media player, but the cost is the time required to learn the framework and its limits. Furthermore, the sheer number of frameworks iOS provides can be daunting to newcomers, who feel they need to become familiar with all of them before they can get started. This book will help you build media apps by focusing on the iOS media frameworks and the skills you need to use them.

Several guides to iOS development exist that briefly touch upon iOS media app development, but I feel that they provide only cursory glances at the material. Similarly, Apple provides excellent documentation for its APIs, but the wording and level of technical depth can be intimidating. This guide complements the two by providing specific information with an accessible approach.

What Makes Media App Development Different?

It can be hard to sum up all the skills required to be an app developer, but I define an iOS media app developer as a person with an in-depth knowledge of iOS's media features and the ability to apply this knowledge to create products. To be successful in this role, you need to be able to do more than just "make it work." You need to be able to use your knowledge to identify design approaches, point out problematic requirements, and debug problems in the field.

My goal is to build up your background knowledge without making the experience overwhelming. It is important to build up a large base of knowledge to draw upon, but it is equally important to present that knowledge base in a way that allows you to retain it or quickly return to it as a reference. Comprehensive API references and pure problem-solution approaches are extremely valuable for fixing specific problems, but do not provide a clear path for learning. As a media developer, you will be expected to master several frameworks, each with its own set of requirements and prevailing design patterns or suggestions on how you should write your code. Through the discussions in this book, which build in complexity, I provide you with a guide you can follow at your own pace, yet still use as a reference.

Although it is extremely important to understand everything a framework can do, is equally important to understand the limits of a framework. Many times, you will be asked to implement a feature, but upon further research you will realize that it is not possible or would require more effort than the project budget or time allows. You may also discover that you can cover 90 percent of your use cases with one approach, which is faster than the approach that would cover 100 percent of the use cases. To be successful as a media developer, you have to identify these problem areas and possible solutions quickly, and communicate them to the correct decision makers. One particularly challenging aspect of being a media developer is that the media frameworks are among the most complex frameworks in Cocoa Touch. They also place some of the strictest requirements on implementation. The discussion material and keystone projects in this book will expose you to these limitations and show you how to address them to build working products.

Depending on whom you ask, the most exciting part of any development cycle is debugging. Your video player may work great in portrait mode, but then suddenly start dropping frames as soon as the user rotates the device. To figure out the root of this problem, you would need to use tools to generate data points, and then tie those data points back to a cause. Throughout your career, you will notice the same problems repeated in many projects. Having the experience of identifying the root cause of a problem enables you to quickly identify and fix it the next time it comes up. As you begin to debug media apps, you will notice that due to the sensitive nature of their operations (such as smooth video playback), they are the most prone to resource-based problems and strict configurations. More than anywhere, this is where you will get your real training on Xcode's Instruments. My goals with the advanced topics and discussion sections are to expose you to common root causes of problems, walk you through the process of using the tools you need to identify them, and explain how the data the tools produce will help you resolve such problems.

As a media developer, you may find yourself in the role of an "encyclopedia" for media programming topics—but that role also carries the responsibility of applying that expertise to the design process and being the "go-to guy" (or gal) for issues with the media-related code. This book will not only help you retain what you learn, but also make you aware of the pitfalls sooner rather than later.

What Do I Need to Know to Use This Book?

This book is both accessible to beginners and relevant for advanced programmers. Because the focus is on media app development, I am assuming you've had at least a cursory introduction to the following:

- Core programming concepts (object-oriented programming, pointers, functions)
- Core iOS development topics (Xcode, Interface Builder, Cocoa Touch)
- Objective-C syntax

Based on these assumptions, I use language from this core knowledge base as part of the natural writing style of this book. This will allow the experienced to feel right home, while also giving beginners valuable experience with the terminology used in the field. For additional help, I recommend the books listed in Table 1-1.

Table 1-1. Recommended References

Topic	Title and Author
Introductory iOS development	*Beginning iOS 7 Development* by James Nutting, Fredrik Olsson, David Mark, Jeff LaMarche (Apress, 2014)
Using Xcode and the debugger	*Beginning Xcode* by Matthew Knott (Apress, 2014)
Intermediate iOS development	*Learn iOS 7 App Development* by James Bucanek (Apress, 2013)
Objective-C syntax	*Beginning Objective-C* by James Dovey and Ash Furrow (Apress, 2012)

I also recommend referring to the iOS Developer Library (`https://developer.apple.com/library/ios/navigation/`). As Apple's official resource for iOS API documentation, the Developer Library is updated with every release of the SDK. You need to keep a constant eye on the SDK version, because methods are often updated or removed. Be sure to use the document version that matches your SDK. You can find the documentation for older SDK releases under the Retired Documents Library link, shown in Figure 1-1.

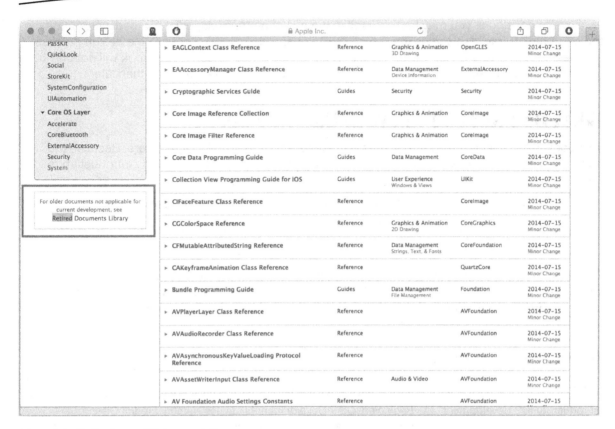

Figure 1-1. Finding legacy iOS documentation

> **Caution**   Apple also maintains prerelease documentation for beta releases of iOS. These are a good reference for bleeding-edge development, but are not recommended for production, as they are constantly in flux and their accuracy is not guaranteed.

In an effort to offer a streamlined, comprehensive experience, the book is divided into four units: images, audio, video, and advanced media topics. To make the content flow in a natural manner, I have organized the content using the following structure:

- Part 1: Background information and core frameworks

- Part 2: Intermediate framework applications

- Part 3: Advanced implementations (including lower-level code)

For beginning developers, I recommend starting with the first chapter of each unit and working your way into the later chapters as you gain more familiarity with the concepts. For intermediate and advanced readers, I recommend using the first chapter for a quick introduction to the unit and then diving directly into the topics you are interested in within the later chapters.

What Do I Need to Get Started?

As with traditional iOS app development, to get started in iOS media app development, you need an Intel-based Mac running OS X 10.9 or later (Mavericks) and the latest version of Xcode and the iOS SDK from the Mac App Store. As part of the App Store submission process, Apple checks to make sure your binary is compiled on a "valid" computer and SDK version. While it may seem like an annoying step, it helps ensure that applications are compiled against a common standard, eliminating crashes caused by the compiler. The easiest way to stay up-to-date on both is by downloading them from the Mac App Store.

> **Note**   You can find old versions of Xcode on Apple's Developer site, but keep in mind that you need to use a current version to submit to the App Store.

Unlike traditional iOS app development, iOS media app development places a strict requirement on testing with hardware devices. When you started in iOS development, you may have noticed that a lot of features you were trying to implement could easily be tested with the simulator alone. Unfortunately, many of the features we will be programming for in this book (for example, taking pictures and audio recording) are not supported by the simulator and must be tested with a physical device. Additionally, testing on the simulator will give you compatibility errors for some features.

The suite of hardware devices to keep on hand for testing depends greatly on the range of devices you need to support. In general, you should do your core development on a device that is in Apple's latest tick-tock cycle (for example, iPhone 5 or iPhone 5S) that is running the latest version of iOS. In your test cycle, you should also have access to a device running an older supported iOS version (for example, iOS 6.1), and a device with an older hardware specification (for example, iPhone 4S). I do my core development on an iPhone 5 and iPad Mini with Retina Display, and when I reach the testing phase, I use an iPad 3 running iOS 6.1 and borrow a friend's iPhone 4S. Having a mix of devices and system versions enables you to identify the widest range of compatibility issues before Apple does during the App Store approval process.

An Active iOS Developer Program Account Is Required to Use This Book

Many of the APIs you will need to use in this book (for example, for assessing the hardware camera on an iPhone) require you to tether a device to your development computer. Apple does not allow you to simulate hardware cameras or audio recording devices through the simulator. Attempting to call these APIs from the simulator will cause your samples to crash.

To test directly on hardware devices, you need to upgrade your Developer Program account to a paid tier (Individual or Enterprise.) You may already have a free account for access to the support forums and documentation library; however, you need a paid account for its device management features and ability to provide signing certificates. To protect users, Apple requires that all iOS applications be signed with a valid code-signing certificate in order to run on a device. A paid account gives you the ability to create these certificates and build a signed application you can run on a device.

You can sign up for a paid iOS Developer Program account by navigating to the Apple Developer Program site (https://developer.apple.com/programs/) and selecting the iOS Developer Program link, as shown in Figure 1-2. You will then be asked to continue by signing in with your Apple ID account.

Figure 1-2. Signing up for a paid iOS Developer Program account

> **Caution**   You need to create a new Apple ID for app development if you are already using your account for publishing content to iBooks. Apple does not allow accounts to be shared between stores.

Building Your First iOS Media App

To become comfortable with the style of this book and the depth of its content, you're going to start with an exercise: building a simple app that lets you alternate between two images. The focus of this exercise is to expose you to the kinds of problems you may see the first time you try to run one of your apps on a device. You will cover the media APIs used in the app in more detail further in the book.

In implementing this exercise, the focus will be on following a device-centric workflow. You'll explore how to set up a project, make provisioning profile requests, and cover the basics of running an application with a device attached.

> **Note**   The source code for all of the sample applications and keystone projects in this book is located on the Apress web site. For this project, you can find the source code in the Chapter 1 folder. The application is called ImageChanger. The project will run on any recent Mac that is able to open Xcode 5 or newer.

About the Application

To demonstrate iOS media app development, you will learn how to create an application that lets you do the following:

■ Load an image into a view in your project

■ Enable a button to change the image

■ Change the image based on the user's selection

The user interface is extremely simple, as shown in Figure 1-3.

Figure 1-3. Mock-up for ImageChanger app

As shown in the mock-up, our app contains one screen with a button and an image. When you click the button, the currently displayed image changes. The state toggles, meaning that clicking the button twice returns the app to its original state.

Setting Up the Application

This application uses a single view. Select Single-View Application as the project template (see Figure 1-4).

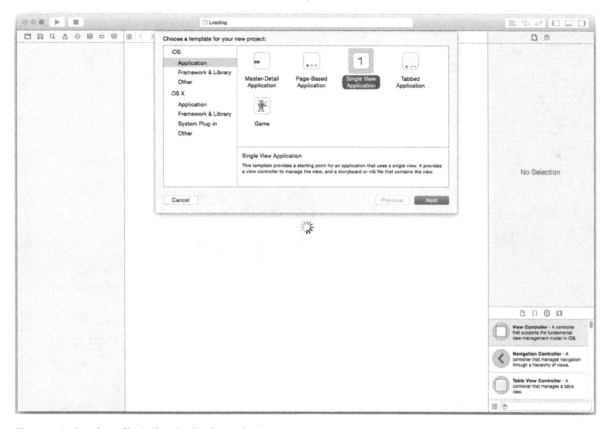

Figure 1-4. *Creating a Single View Application project*

After selecting the Single View Application template, you're asked to name your project and select a location in which to save it. After this is complete, you will start laying out the user interface.

You need to add a button and an image view onto your main view controller to make your storyboard look like the mock-up in Figure 1-3. You can find Interface Builder templates for a button, image view, and many other common user-interface elements in the Object Library at the bottom right of the screen. You add items to a view controller by dragging them out of the Object Library and dropping them onto the target view controller. The Object Library is highlighted in Figure 1-5.

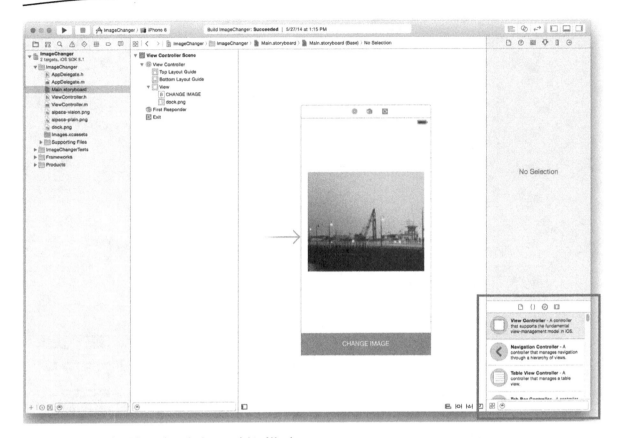

Figure 1-5. The Object Library is at the bottom right of Xcode

Adding Images to Your App

To toggle images, you first need to import them into the application. You can import images or any other kind of file by right-clicking any item in the Project Navigator (the left pane of Xcode.) Click the Add Files option and select your target files. For this app, select two image files (either PNG or JPG).

To make one of the images appear in the image view, select the image view from within Interface Builder, as shown in Figure 1-6. In the Attributes Inspector, navigate to the Image drop-down list and select the image you just added from the list of file names you'll see there.

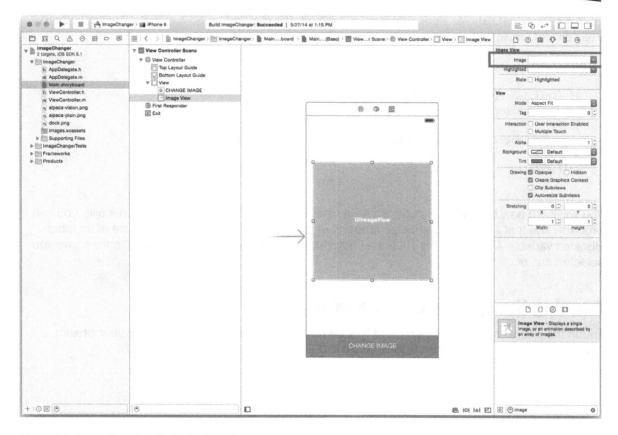

Figure 1-6. Image drop-down in the Attributes Inspector

Handling User-Interface Events

To make the active image change based on user-interface events, you need to tie the source code to the storyboard. The main view controller is represented by the ViewController class, so in ViewController.h, you would add the following properties and method signatures:

```
@property (nonatomic, assign) BOOL isActive;
@property (nonatomic, strong) IBOutlet UIImageView *imageView;
@property (nonatomic, strong) IBOutlet UIButton *changeButton;
-(IBAction)changeImage:(id)sender;
```

The imageView and changeButton objects represent the user-interface elements. The changeImage: method represents the method that needs to be called when the user presses the button. The isActive property allows you to track the state of the button.

To make the event handler work, you must implement the method by adding the following code to ViewController.m:

```
-(IBAction)changeImage:(id)sender
{
    if (self.isActive) {
        self.imageView.image = [UIImage imageNamed:@"alpaca-vision.png"];
    } else {
        self.imageView.image = [UIImage imageNamed:@"alpaca-plain.png"];
    }
    self.isActive = !self.isActive;
}
```

You will learn how this block of code works in Chapter 2, but from a high-level perspective, you can probably see that it changes the image property of the image view, based on the state of a global Boolean variable. Make sure the [UIImage imageNamed:] method exactly matches the file name you selected earlier.

Running the Application on a Device

To run the project on a device, you need to start by setting a development team for your project. Navigate to your project properties and select the Team drop- down (see Figure 1-7).

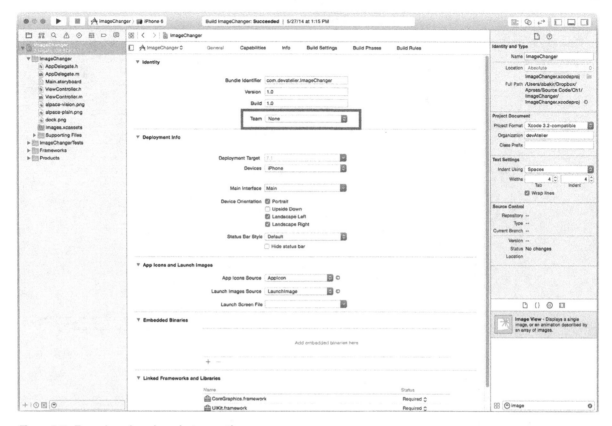

Figure 1-7. Team drop-down in project properties

Under the options, you can see all the development teams your computer currently has signing information for, as well as an option to Add an Account. If your drop-down menu is empty, select Add a Team to bring up the Xcode Account Manager, which will ask you for your Apple ID and guide you through the process of downloading a development certificate to use on your computer (see Figure 1-8).

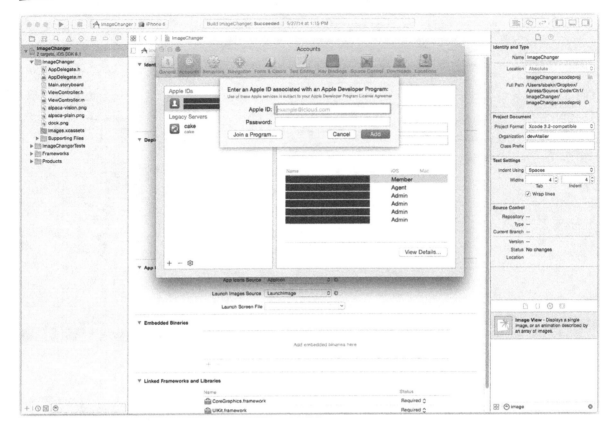

Figure 1-8. Xcode Account Manager

If the Account Manager finds that your iOS Developer account has not been set up with any development certificates, you need to log in to the site and select the Certificates, Identifiers & Profile link in the top right, as shown in Figure 1-9.

Figure 1-9. Finding certificates in the iOS Dev Center

From the Certificates link, select Add Certificate, and generate an iOS App Development certificate. The next page (see Figure 1-10) gives you detailed instructions on how to generate and upload a certificate signing request file to Apple.

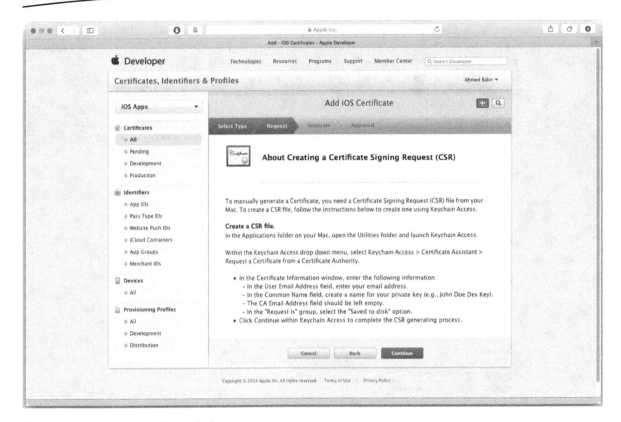

Figure 1-10. Generating a certificate signing request

> **Caution**   All your certificates will use this CSR file for identity validation, so remember where you store it, and protect the file. Attempting to generate a new CSR file will void all your existing certificates. Xcode provides an Export Developer Profile tool if you need to migrate to another computer.

After the CSR file is validated, a certificate file will be generated and automatically downloaded. After the download has completed, double-click it to install it on your computer.

Now that your development certificate is ready, bring up the Account Manager again, and it will successfully create a Wildcard Provisioning Profile. Provisioning profiles act like device access control lists; the wildcard provisioning profile allows you to sign and deploy an app to an Apple-registered, USB-tethered device. For this example, the wildcard profile is fine, but you will want to generate an App ID and development provisioning profile before you distribute your app for testing.

After Xcode recognizes your team, it shows the name in the Team drop-down. Next, plug an iOS device into your computer via USB. If your device is successfully recognized, it will be available in the device drop-down next to the Xcode Run button, and no errors will show on the project properties screen. If the device is not recognized, a Fix Issue button will appear under your team name. Clicking it triggers a wizard that will attempt to add your device to your iOS Developer Program account. Figure 1-11 shows an example of Xcode not recognizing the team.

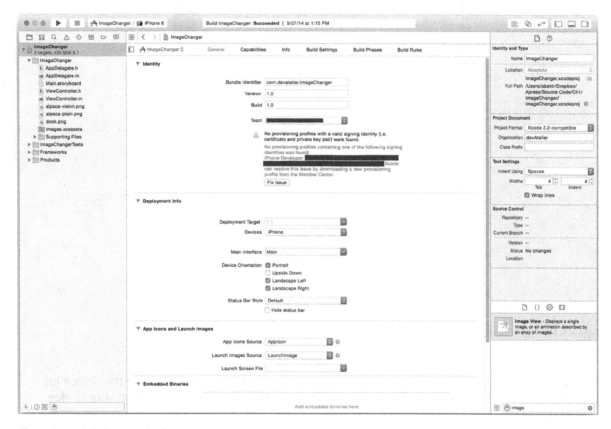

Figure 1-11. Failed team selection

If your device is still not recognized after clicking the Fix Issue button, open the Xcode Organizer and attempt to add the device by navigating to the Devices screen, and selecting your device, as shown in Figure 1-12.

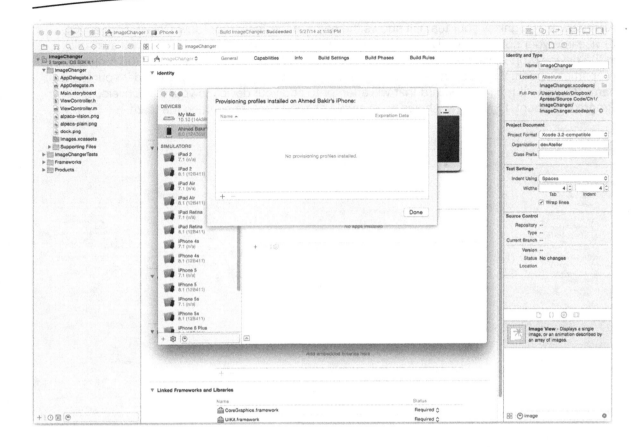

Figure 1-12. Xcode device manager

After you have resolved all of your device signing issues, your device will appear in the device list drop-down and you can click the Run button to compile and run your application on your device.

Debugging Common Problems

In a perfect world, everything works bug-free the first time you try to run an app. In the real world, however, it's common to miss something, at which point you need to figure out how to fix it. The most convenient way to get started with debugging is by setting breakpoints in your code. When you are running devices tethered to your development machine, they are running through an instance of the LLDB debugger, which allows you to add special diagnostic hooks for debugging that can then present debugging information in case of a crash. A *breakpoint* is a command that tells the debugger to stop running your application when it gets to a particular line you have marked. When code execution reaches a breakpoint, you can choose to continue running the program, to abort, or to inspect variables and the call stack.

The easiest way to set a breakpoint is to click the vertical bar right next to the line of code you want to stop on. Turning on the Line Numbers option in the IDE makes things a bit easier, because then you can simply click the line number. You can see an example of an enabled breakpoint in Figure 1-13. The line number has a blue arrow as its background.

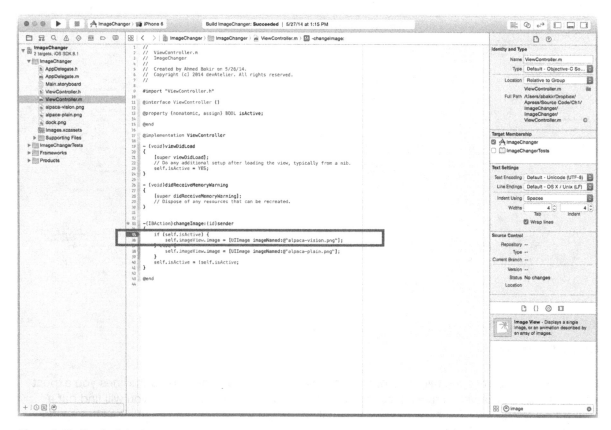

Figure 1-13. Breakpoint set

When the execution hits the breakpoint, the debugger information panes appear on the bottom of your screen, providing you with a variable inspector and a command-line interface to the debugger (see Figure 1-14).

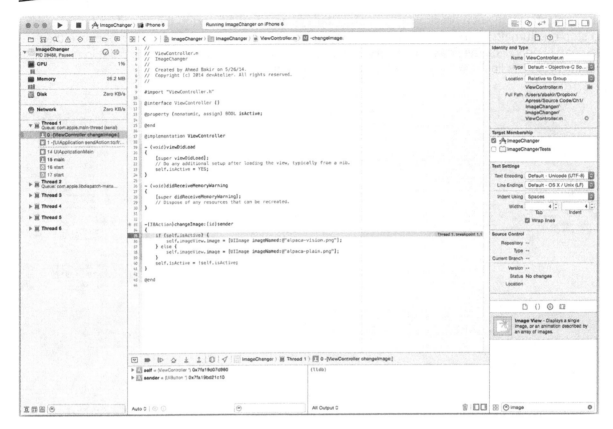

Figure 1-14. Breakpoint hit

By placing breakpoints carefully, you can check to make sure the code gets to the lines you expect it to, and check variables to make sure they are in the state you expect. Often, you will find out a method never executes because it never gets called, or you will see that a variable has the wrong value because of a logic error.

Table 1-2 shows a list of common problems and solutions you may see when trying to implement this sample application. While you can download the application from the Apress web site and run it that way, we highly recommend trying to build it yourself, so you'll become familiar with the process.

Table 1-2. *Common Errors When Trying to Build ImageChanger App*

Problem	Common Solutions
Application will not run on device	Make sure your team is set correctly and that your device is registered with the iOS Developer Program.
Image view does not show correct image on launch	Make sure your image is correctly added to your project.
	Make sure your image view is correctly tied to a property.
	Make sure your view startup code does not reset your image view.
Button does not change image	Make sure your button and image views are correctly tied to properties.
	Make sure your button event handler method is correctly registered and that it can be reached via a breakpoint.
Image view is blank after pressing button	Make sure the image name in your button event handler method is exactly the same as the file name of your second image.

Summary

This chapter began by presenting the purpose of this book, what's different about media app development, and the requirements you need to get the most out of the book. You saw the basic goals for the book, and how it's structured so you can learn at your own pace, as well as the assumptions made about your prior programming experiences and knowledge. You covered some reasons that media development is different in terms of resources and developer expectations. Finally, by building a simple ImageChanger application, you began to explore some of the most essential workflows for building a media app and running it on a device.

Part 1

Images

Chapter 2

Adding Images to Your App

The best way to learn to draw is by studying still-life subjects. Similarly, the best way to get into iOS media app development is by starting with static images!

In this chapter, you will use Apple's `UIImage`, `UIImageView`, and `UIImagePicker` classes to represent, display, and import images into your applications. These classes abstract a number of useful features, from decoding files to providing in-app access to iOS's system-wide camera controller.

Using the UIImage Class to Represent Image Data

Unlike plain-text files, which store data in a human-readable format, images have a complex set of attributes that require them to be stored as binary data—including compression and color space information. All binary data requires a special class to decode it and represent it in a way that allows your program to use it. `UIImage` is the class Apple provides for representing image data. You can think of it as the common language for all operations that involve image data. For instance, `UIImagePickerController`, which you will use later to select images from the camera and photo roll, transmits your selections as `UIImage` objects.

In the next two subsections, "Loading Bundled Files" and "Loading Images at Runtime," you will see how to use `UIImage` to load images from various locations on the file system. To make this image data visible to the user by placing it on the screen, you need to use `UIImageView`, which you'll explore in the next major section of this chapter, "Using the UIImageView Class to Display Images."

Loading Bundled Files

One of the more common tasks when developing an iOS media app is loading an image from a designer-provided file, such as a background image, some clip art, or a custom button design. To become familiar with this workflow, you will build a single-view application that displays an image in a square frame, similar to the sample project from Chapter 1. If you need to review how to create a single-view application and add an image view to it, you should review the last section of Chapter 1.

The easiest way to start working with a desired image is to call the `UIImage` private method, `[UIImage imageNamed:]`, to create an image object from a file in your project bundle:

```
UIImage *myImage = [UIImage imageNamed:@"Flower.jpg"];
```

Project bundle may seem like a foreign term at this point, but it is a concept you are probably already familiar with, without knowing it. If you have ever performed a secondary click on an application in OS X, you've noticed a Show Package Contents option. On both iOS and OS X, .app files are smart containers that contain compiled object files and bundled resources, such as images, sounds, and precompiled data. When your app is compiled, all the source files are turned into object files, and any other static files you include are copied directly to the bundle.

The [UIImage imageNamed:] API works by searching through the project bundle for a file with the exact same name as the one you provided in the name parameter. The API is case-sensitive and does not perform any extra logic on the name, so make sure you pass the file name exactly as it appears in the bundle, or the returned object will be nil.

> **Note**   PNG files and asset catalog–backed image sets are the only exception to the rule requiring you to use the exact file name. You do not need to specify a file extension for either of these types.

You can confirm that a file is part of your project bundle by making sure you can find it in the Xcode Project Navigator (the left pane of the IDE), as shown in Figure 2-1.

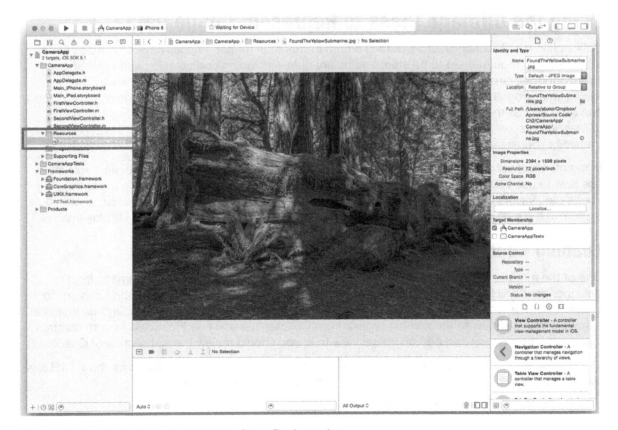

Figure 2-1. Xcode Project Navigator, highlighting image files in a project

In this example, you will see a Resources folder. To keep the project folder organized, it's best to create groups before importing files. I prefer to put all of my image files and other external assets into a Resources group. You can create a group via the New option in the File menu, or by importing a folder during the Add Files step. Groups and folders will not prevent you from using the [UIImage imageNamed:] API.

Using Asset Catalogs To Manage Images

Starting with the iOS 7 SDK, Apple introduced *asset catalogs* to the iOS development workflow. Asset catalogs simplify your workflow by providing a central location to store your image files, and a graphical user interface to manage these files. While it is easy enough to manage a handful of image files in the Project Navigator, the process quickly becomes unwieldy when you need to manage dozens of files, or multiple sizes of the same file—situations that asset catalogs are meant to alleviate.

Asset catalogs are an important concept because Apple places strict requirements on providing multiple resolutions of your image files. Apple will even prevent you from submitting your app to the App Store if you are missing a required resolution of the launch image or app icon.

In this exercise, you will learn how to use an asset catalog to manage files within your project, and how to modify your syntax to indicate that you are using an asset catalog.

Every project you create for the iOS 7 SDK or greater comes with a blank asset catalog file named Images.xcassets. Click this file in the Project Navigator, and you are presented with the screen in Figure 2-2.

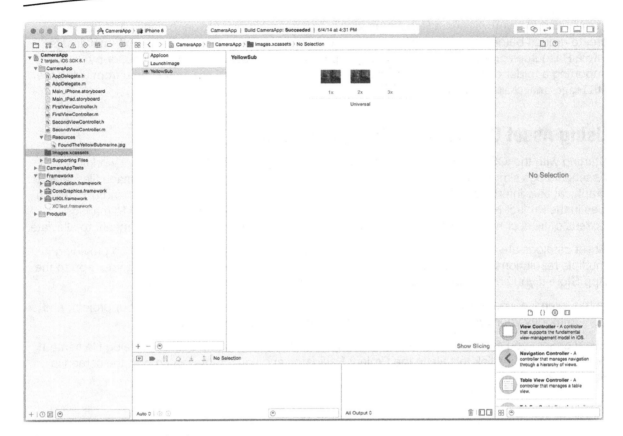

Figure 2-2. *Asset catalog user interface*

The asset catalog user interface provides two panes: the *set list* in the left pane and the *set viewer* in the right pane. To help you manage multiple resolutions of the same image, asset catalogs use *image sets* to represent image files. The idea is that you add every resolution of an image to a set; then in your code, you can refer to the set instead of the individual image file names. This places the burden of determining the appropriate file (for example, non-Retina or Retina) on the compiler, rather than the developer.

You can use the set list to navigate between image sets by clicking them. Similarly, you can use the Add and Remove buttons at the bottom of the pane to manage sets. When you click an image set, the set viewer will be populated with placeholders for all the resolutions you should provide for the set.

You can add images to a set by dragging and dropping from a Finder window onto the appropriate placeholder (for example, you would use the 2x placeholder to represent the Retina version of an image). You continue this process for every resolution of the image you need to include in the project. To update an image, simply drag the new version onto the appropriate thumbnail. Xcode takes care of everything else for you.

> **Note**   At the time of this writing, PNG files are the only file type supported with asset catalogs. You need to continue using the Project Navigator for JPG files.

To use an image that is managed by the asset catalog, change your syntax to use the image set name instead of the file name:

```
UIImage *myImage = [UIImage imageNamed:@"Flower"];
```

The compiler will automatically determine the correct version of the image to use on the currently running platform.

> **Note**   For app icons and launch images, the system will create compiler warnings for missing resolutions. Required resolutions are updated along with the SDK, so make sure you stay up-to-date.

Loading Images at Runtime

While [UIImage imageNamed:] is a convenient API, it is designed solely for images that are bundled with your app. When you are trying to load an image at runtime, such as an image that has been downloaded, you need to use a different API: [UIImage imageWithContentsOfFile:]. The key difference between these APIs is that at runtime, you need to specify the path of the image file, rather than its name within the bundle. Listing 2-1 provides an example of this process.

Listing 2-1. Loading an Image File at Runtime

```
NSArray *searchPaths = NSSearchPathForDirectoriesInDomains(NSDocumentDirectory,
                          NSUserDomainMask, YES);
NSString *documentFolderPath = [searchPaths objectAtIndex:0];
NSString *localFilePath = [documentFolderPath stringByAppendingString:@"DownloadedFlower.png"];
UIImage *myImage = [UIImage imageWithContentsOfFile:localFilePath];
if (myImage == nil) { NSLog(@"File does not exist!");}
```

As you can see, the majority of the work lies in finding the path for the documents directory. Every app bundle comes with a documents directory, which is meant to serve as your target for saving or creating files. You can use Apple's system macros (or shortcut methods) to quickly find the documents directory for the app. Each app installation has a unique directory path, so it is important to run this method at runtime.

Once you have the documents directory path, you can append your file's name by using the [NSString stringByAppendingString:] method. If your image has loaded successfully, your UIImage object will be non-nil.

> **Note**   You may be saying, "I thought iOS didn't have a file system!" While iOS does not provide a globally accessible, shared file system, as on a PC, it does provide a file system within your app's sandbox that you can use to store and retrieve files at runtime. It is called a *sandbox* because you can do (almost) anything you want in your sandbox, but no one else is allowed in your sandbox, and it is hard to take your work out of the sandbox (in other words, there are very limited APIs for inter-app communication).

SUPPORTED FILE FORMATS

Unlike a simple text file, which is stored as ASCII data and can be opened by any program, image files are encoded binary files and require special instructions (decoding) to be opened correctly. One of the most convenient features of UIImage is that it abstracts the decoding of the file formats shown in the following table.

Popular File Formats Supported by the UIImage Class

File Format	Extension(s)	Primary Use
Portable Network Graphic	.png	Modern, lossless raster image compression. Preserves alpha (transparency) layers.
Joint Photographic Experts Group	.jpg, .jpeg	Very efficient lossy raster image compression. No support for alpha layers.
Graphics Interchange Format	.gif	Legacy lossless image support. Primarily used for animated images on the Web.
Bitmap Image File	.bmp	Uncompressed image support. Popularized by early versions of Windows.
Tagged Image File Format	.tiff, .tif	Legacy low-compression image support. Popularized by early image-capture devices and desktop publishing packages.

While the system can load these file formats, it will not optimize their file sizes or density for you. An uncompressed, 10MB bitmap file will take much longer to access and draw than a compressed 100KB JPG file. Whenever possible, try to use compressed JPGs (or PNGs if you require transparency layers).

> **Note**   If your designer provides you with Photoshop files only (.psd), you will need to manually save the layers as image files yourself. The Photoshop file format is a resource-intensive moving target, so it is highly unlikely that Apple will provide system-level support for it.

Using the UIImageView Class to Display Images

To display images in your app, you need to use a subclass of `UIView`, the atomic unit for user interface elements in iOS. To bridge this gap, Apple has created `UIImageView`, which provides an area to place the image on the screen, methods to dynamically scale the image at runtime, and an outlet for touch gestures.

In this section, you will learn how to initialize `UIImageView` with images and will explore various ways to use it to handle dynamic content sizes.

Initializing an Image View

Initializing `UIImageView` is simple: all you need to do is initialize it with a source `UIImage` object, as shown here:

```
UIImage *myImage = [UIImage imageNamed:@"Flower.jpg"];
UIImageView *myImageView = [[UIImageView  alloc] initWithImage:myImage];
```

Although the `[UIImageView initWithImage:]` API does not specify a frame as a required parameter, you should provide one. Frames in Cocoa Touch specify the location and size of a user interface element. If you are building your interface with Interface Builder, the frame for your element will be created automatically. You can find an example of setting the frame programmatically in Listing 2-2.

Listing 2-2. Setting a Frame Programmatically

```
UIImage *myImage = [UIImage imageNamed:@"Flower.jpg"];
UIImageView *myImageView = [[UIImageView  alloc] initWithImage:myImage];
myImageView.frame = CGRectMake(10, 10, 100, 100);
[self.view addSubview:myImageView];
```

Note the addSubview call in the preceding code, which places the image view on the screen.

Note   You can change an image view's content at any time by setting the `image` property.

Setting Image-Scaling Options

You may have seen this problem before: you request an image with a resolution of 640×480 pixels, but receive an image with some other size, such as 637×480. To solve this extremely common problem, Apple builds dynamic scaling features into all `UIView` objects, which you can control with the `[UIView contentMode]` property. In Table 2-1, you will see a table of popular content modes and the behaviors they specify.

Table 2-1. Popular UIViewContentMode Constant Values

Constant Name	Specified Behavior
UIViewContentModeScaleToFill	Stretches content to fit the aspect ratio of the view's frame.
UIViewContentModeScaleAspectFit	Scales content to fit in the view's frame, while preserving the original aspect ratio. The rest of the frame displays the view's background color (transparent by default).
UIViewContentModeCenter	Centers content while preserving its original dimensions.
UIViewContentModeTop	Aligns content to the top edge of the frame, while preserving its original dimensions.
UIViewContentModeLeft	Aligns content to the left edge of the frame, while preserving its original dimensions.

The default contentMode for all UIView objects is UIViewContentModeScaleToFill, which stretches or shrinks your content to fit the bounds of the UIView. When selecting a contentMode, think about what your visual design references specify (or require for other elements). If you are centering an image in the middle of the screen and have no requirements on how the edges are aligned, UIViewContentModeScaleAspectFill is a safe option. When you need to preserve a specific edge, you may want to look at one of the edge-alignment options, such as UIViewContentModeTop or UIViewContentModeLeft. In the case where the content's aspect ratio needs to be exactly as specified by the view, explore UIViewContentModeScaleAspectFit, or manually crop the image before presenting it.

To specify a content mode, simply set the property on your UIImageView object:

```
[myImageView setContentMode:UIContentModescaleAspectFill];
```

Using the UIImagePickerController Class to Select Images

UIImagePickerController is Apple's UIViewController subclass, which provides access to the system-wide camera controller and saved images thumbnail browser. When you configure the controller to use the camera as its data source, you will see the basic camera interface you are familiar with from the system's built-in Camera app. When you configure the controller to use saved images, you will see the same thumbnail-based interface used in the Photos app. Through UIImagePickerController, Apple provides a quick way to import pictures into your apps, removing the burden of writing low-level hardware interfaces and letting you concentrate on high-level uses for photos.

In this section, you will see how to use the image picker to select images from the camera roll, take pictures by using the hardware camera, and export this data as a UIImage object. Along the way, you will also learn about some background concepts that the UIImagePickerController class depends on, and explore some of the class's limitations.

Throughout this section, you will be building the app illustrated in Figure 2-3. It is a camera app, which displays an image in a UIImageView and a Take Picture button, which brings up the UIImagePickerController. When the image picker has completed, the app should return to the main view controller and display the selected image. The completed code for the app is included in the

ImagePicker project, which is provided as part of the code bundle for this book, in the Source Code/ Download area of the Apress web site (www.apress.com). The ImagePicker project is in the Chapter 2 folder of the code bundle.

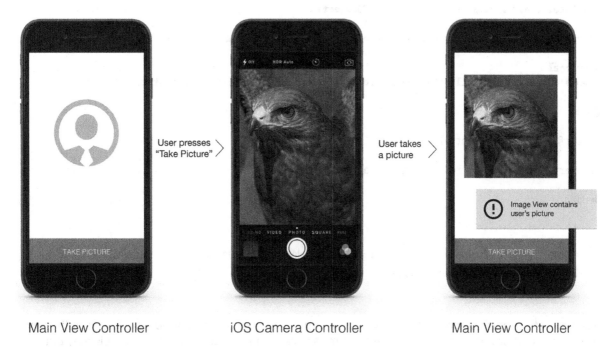

| Main View Controller | iOS Camera Controller | Main View Controller |

Figure 2-3. Flow diagram for a camera-based app

Working with Protocols and Delegates

When developing an app that uses the image picker, you are often expected to develop a workflow that looks like the one described in Figure 2-3.

For extremely simple classes, you can handle all the logic within one class. However, UIImagePickerController is a completely separate view controller; therefore, you need a way to pass messages between it and your class. Following the patterns of object-oriented design, you do not want to include information about your class in the image picker, because it needs to be a class that can be used by another class. Also, you do not want to duplicate features from the UIImagePickerController in your code.

The Objective-C language features that UIImagePickerController relies on for message passing are called *delegation* and *protocols*.

A *protocol* is a way of defining a limited interface for inter-class communication, which can be inferred by importing the header file of the class whose protocol you want to implement. A protocol specifies a name (for identification) and a list of methods and their parameters. You can also specify a priority level for a method with the block keyword optional. You define a protocol by placing an @protocol block containing the naming information and method signatures in your header file. Listing 2-3 shows a simple header file, which defines a protocol that is similar to the one the UIImagePickerController class uses.

Listing 2-3. Header File for Simple Camera Protocol

```
#import <UIKit/UIKit.h>

@protocol CameraViewControllerDelegate <NSObject>

-(void)cameraViewController:(UIViewController *)controller hasImage:(UIImage *)image;

@optional
-(void)cameraViewController:(UIViewController *)controller didCancel:(BOOL)state;

@end

@interface CameraViewController : UIViewController

@property (nonatomic, strong) UIImage *capturedImage;

@end
```

> **Note**   All methods that are not under the @optional block are considered required and must be implemented by the protocol's receiver.

You will notice that I did not include any code examples of how these methods work. This is the key advantage of a protocol: a protocol defines a means of communication between two classes but never implements the target logic. You can think of a protocol as similar to an abstract class in Java.

To tie this to a concrete example, the UIImagePickerController class defines a protocol that indicates it will send messages after the picker has been closed, and after it has taken a picture. It is up to you, in your presenting class, to handle what happens when it sends these messages.

The way to handle this data is through delegation. *Delegation* is the concept of passing a unit of work off to another class. In the case of the image picker, all the work of creating the camera controller instance, taking pictures, and presenting a data stream is delegated to the image picker class. When it is done, it will send the result back to us. The object that implements the protocol and receives its messages is called the *delegate*.

To implement a protocol, you need to modify the receiving class's header file to include the protocol definition, and modify the class definition to indicate that it implements the protocol. It's called the *receiving class* because it receives messages from the delegated class. Listing 2-4 shows an example of a header file for a class that implements a protocol. This header file is intended to be similar to your main view controller's header file.

Listing 2-4. Header File for Class Receiving Protocol Messages

```
#import <UIKit/UIKit.h>
#import "CameraViewController.h"

@interface FirstViewController : UIViewController <CameraViewControllerDelegate>
@property (nonatomic, strong) UIImage *selectedImage;
@end
```

The syntax for indicating protocols is to frame their names in angle brackets. You place these after the base class name. You are not limited in the number of protocols you can implement, but you need to make sure they do not have any conflicting method names before adding them!

In the implementation (.m) file, you define the behavior for the methods indicated by the protocol. As shown in Listing 2-5, this is where you can handle what to do with the picture when the image picker is ready, or what do when the Cancel button has been pressed.

Listing 2-5. Implementation File for Class Receiving Protocol Messages

```
#import "FirstViewController.h"

@implementation FirstViewController

- (void)viewDidLoad
{
    [super viewDidLoad];
        // Do any additional setup after loading the view, typically from a nib.
}

#pragma mark - CameraViewController delegate methods

-(void)cameraViewController:(UIViewController *)controller hasImage:(UIImage *)image
{
    self.selectedImage = image;
    [controller dismissViewControllerAnimated:YES completion:nil];
}

-(void)cameraViewController:(UIViewController *)controller didCancel:(BOOL)state
{
    if (state == YES) {
        [controller dismissViewControllerAnimated:YES completion:nil];
    }
}

@end
```

The #pragma mark in this listing creates comments that will appear in the Xcode method navigator drop-down menu. It is a good idea to use comments like these whenever you are implementing a protocol, so you can remember where your delegate methods are defined.

> **Note**   You will get a compiler warning for every required method you do not define. Methods with the optional flag add useful but nonessential behavior, and thus will not throw compiler warnings.

To complete the cycle of using a delegate, you need to give the originating class a way of sending protocol messages. See Listing 2-6.

Listing 2-6. Modified Header File for Class Sending Protocol Messages

```
#import <UIKit/UIKit.h>

@protocol CameraViewControllerDelegate <NSObject>

-(void)cameraViewController:(UIViewController *)controller hasImage:(UIImage *)image;

@optional
-(void)cameraViewController:(UIViewController *)controller didCancel:(BOOL)state;

@end

@interface CameraViewController : UIViewController

@property (nonatomic, strong) UIImage *capturedImage;

@property (nonatomic, weak) id <CameraViewControllerDelegate> delegate;

@end
```

As you can see, you need to add a generic delegate object (of class id) to the source class. After defining this object, you can safely make calls to the delegate object through the defined protocol messages, as shown in Listing 2-7.

Listing 2-7. Modified Implementation File for Originating Class

```
#import "CameraViewController.h"

@implementation CameraViewController

- (id)initWithNibName:(NSString *)nibNameOrNil bundle:(NSBundle *)nibBundleOrNil
{
    self = [super initWithNibName:nibNameOrNil bundle:nibBundleOrNil];
    if (self) {
        // Custom initialization
    }
    return self;
}
```

```objc
- (void)viewDidLoad
{
    [super viewDidLoad];
    // Do any additional setup after loading the view.
}

#pragma mark - action handlers

-(IBAction)takePictureButtonPressed:(id)sender
{
    [self.delegate cameraViewController:self hasImage:self.capturedImage];
}

-(IBAction)cancelButtonPressed:(id)sender
{
    [self.delegate cameraViewController:self didCancel:YES];
}

@end
```

In summary, the core concepts for protocols are as follows:

1. Define a protocol by specifying its methods and their priorities.

2. Implement a protocol in your target class by defining all its required methods.

3. Define an instance of a generic delegate object in the source class, and use it to send protocol messages.

Using the Image Picker to Access Saved Pictures

Referring back to the example in Figure 2-3, you want to present the image picker when the user clicks the Take Picture button from the main view controller. In order to accomplish this functionality, you will need to learn how to configure the image picker, how to present it, and how to handle the image data that is sent back via its protocol methods.

Configuring and Presenting the Image Picker

To make things simple, you'll start by configuring the image picker to select saved pictures. Listing 2-8 provides an example of a button handler that presents the image picker.

Listing 2-8. Configuring and Presenting an Image Picker

```objc
-(IBAction)showPicker:(id)sender
{
    UIImagePickerController *imagePicker = [[UIImagePickerController alloc] init];
    imagePicker.sourceType = UIImagePickerControllerSourceTypeSavedPhotosAlbum;

    [self presentViewController:imagePicker animated:YES completion:^{
        NSLog(@"Image picker presented!");
    }];
}
```

> **Note**   The caret syntax in the preceding code specifies a *completion handler*, a code block that executes when the method has completed. If you do not want to implement the block, replace the ^{ ... } parameter with `nil`.

This example uses the completion handler to generate a log message indicating that the animation which presents the image picker has completed. If you don't want to do anything after the animation completes, you can set the block parameter to nil.

To present the image picker, you need to perform three steps: initialize the object, specify the source type, and present the view controller. This example uses the [UIViewController presentViewController:] method to present the image picker modally, as this is the user interface that most apps implement. *Modal* presentation means showing a view on top of another view, like a pop-up window.

> **Note**   You do not need to include any external header files or frameworks to use UIImagePicker; it is part of UIkit!

To select the image picker as the data source, set the [UIImagePickerController sourceType] parameter to UIImagePickerControllerSourceTypePhotoLibrary. Table 2-2 lists the possible options for UIImagePickerControllerSourceType.

Table 2-2. UIImagePickerControllerSourceType Constant Values

Constant Name	Specified Behavior
UIImagePickerControllerSourceTypePhotoLibrary	Presents an image thumbnail browser, initialized with all of the photo albums on a user's phone (for example, Saved Photos, Camera Roll, Photo Stream)
UIImagePickerControllerSourceTypeSavedPhotosAlbum	Presents an image thumbnail browser, initialized with only the Camera Roll album
UIImagePickerControllerSourceTypeCamera	Presents the iOS system-wide camera controller. Built-in, device-dependent controls include: Cancel, Take Picture, Flash On/Off, Switch Camera

> **Note**   The default source type is UIImagePickerControllerSourceTypePhotoLibrary. This setting is automatically applied if you do not specify a source type.

Handling Data from the Image Picker

Listing 2-8 showed how to present the image picker and configure it to use the thumbnail browser, but it did not specify what should happen when the user selects the image or presses the Cancel button within the image picker. To do this, you need to implement the UIImagePickerControllerDelegate protocol.

As explained in the "Working with Protocols and Delegates" section, the first step to using a protocol is to declare your receiver as a receiver in your header file:

```
@interface FirstViewController : UIViewController < UIImagePickerControllerDelegate>
```

Similarly, you need to let the image picker know that your class is the delegate object, so you set the delegate property on the UIImagePicker object you created earlier.

To present the image picker, implement a button handler similar to the one in Listing 2-9. Remember, to make this work, you need to create a button in Interface Builder, and tie to the IBAction for the handler.

Listing 2-9. Button Handler to Present Image Picker

```
-(IBAction)showPicker:(id)sender
{
    UIImagePickerController *imagePicker = [[UIImagePickerController alloc] init];
    imagePicker.sourceType = UIImagePickerControllerSourceTypeSavedPhotosAlbum;
    imagePicker.delegate = self;

    [self presentViewController:imagePicker animated:YES completion:^{
        NSLog(@"Image picker presented!");
    }];
}
```

Now that you have indicated that the main view controller will implement the protocol's methods, you need to implement them. The delegate method that indicates an image has been chosen is as follows:

```
- (void)imagePickerController:(UIImagePickerController *)picker
                  didFinishPickingMediaWithInfo:(NSDictionary *)info
```

The returned values for this method are the image picker that sent the message, and a dictionary object containing information about the selected asset. You can find a table containing all of the relevant key/value pairs provided by the info dictionary in Table 2-3.

Table 2-3. UIImagePickerController Media Information Dictionary Key/Value Pairs for Photos

Key Name	Stored Value
UIImagePickerControllerMediaType	NSString object identifying the media type (image or movie)
UIImagePickerControllerOriginalImage	UIImage object containing the original image data for the selected asset
UIImagePickerControllerEditedImage	UIImage object containing the original image data for the selected asset (if editing was turned on)
UIImagePickerControllerCropRect	CGRect containing the coordinates for the cropping rectangle the user selected (if editing was turned on)
UIImagePickerControllerMediaMetadata	NSDictionary containing metadata for images saved with the system camera

In this case, you are most interested in the value at the UIImagePickerControllerOriginalImage key, so in the delegate method, you want to extract the UIImage object. After setting the UIImage object as the contents of the image view, you can call the dismiss message on the picker to close it, as shown in Listing 2-10.

Listing 2-10. Receiving the Image Picker didFinishPickingMedia Method

```
-(void)imagePickerController:(UIImagePickerController *)picker
                    didFinishPickingMediaWithInfo:(NSDictionary *)info
{
    UIImage *selectedImage = [info objectForKey:UIImagePickerControllerOriginalImage];
    [self.imageView setImage:selectedImage];

    [picker
        dismissViewControllerAnimated:YES completion:^{
        NSLog(@"Image selected!");
    }];
}
```

Similarly, when the user presses the Cancel button in the image picker, you want to close the picker, so you need to implement the cancel delegate method and then call the [UIViewController dismiss ViewControllerAnimated:completion:] message on the image picker. See Listing 2-11.

Listing 2-11. Receiving the Image Picker Cancel Message

```
-(void)imagePickerControllerDidCancel:(UIImagePickerController *)picker
{
    [picker dismissViewControllerAnimated:YES completion:^{
        NSLog(@"Picker cancelled without doing anything");
    }];
}
```

Voila! You can now present an image picker and use the selected image in your app!

> **Note**   UIPickerController is limited because it is intended to select only one picture at a time. In Chapter 3, you will explore how to build a custom view controller that allows users to select multiple pictures.

Using the Image Picker to Take Pictures

At first glance, you might think configuring the image picker to use the hardware camera would be as easy as setting the sourceType to UIImagePickerControllerSourceTypeCamera. Unfortunately, this one-liner can be quite deceptive. While it is a valid and crucial part of the configuration, there are other steps involved. First, you need to make sure the device on which your app is running has a camera, and that your app has permission to access it. Apple calls this design pattern *dynamic configuration*, and you need to follow it closely to make sure your app works on the widest possible variety of devices.

Conveniently, as a means to implement dynamic configuration, UIImagePickerController comes with a series of public methods you can use to determine the state of a device or feature you would like to use. Table 2-4 lists these methods and the features to which they correspond.

Table 2-4. UIImagePickerController Device Detection Methods

Method Signature	Intended Purpose
+ (BOOL)isSourceTypeAvailable: UIImagePickerControllerSourceType)sourceType	Indicates whether the specified source type (album or camera) is available on the device
+ (BOOL)isCameraDeviceAvailable: (UIImagePickerControllerCameraDevice) cameraDevice	Indicates whether the desired camera is available on the device
+ (BOOL)isFlashAvailableForCameraDevice: (UIImagePickerControllerCameraDevice) cameraDevice	Indicates whether flash is available for the selected camera (front or rear)
+ (NSArray *) availableMediaTypesForSourceType: (UIImagePickerControllerSourceType) sourceType	Indicates the media types that are supported by the selected source type (album or hardware)
+ (NSArray *) availableCaptureModesForCameraDevice: (UIImagePickerControllerCameraDevice) cameraDevice	Indicates the capture modes that are available for the selected camera (images, movies, both.)

> **Note**   Many of these device detection options are intended for configuring the image picker to use video. You will revisit them in more detail in later chapters.

In the interest of simplicity, Listing 2-12 modifies the [MainViewController showPicker:] method shown earlier, adding the ability to detect that a hardware camera exists on the device, and how to set the source type accordingly. If a camera does not exist, the code simply displays the photo album, as in the previous example.

Listing 2-12. Button Handler for Displaying the Camera Controller

```
-(IBAction)showPicker:(id)sender
{
    UIImagePickerController *imagePicker = [[UIImagePickerController alloc] init];
    imagePicker.delegate = self;

    imagePicker.sourceType = UIImagePickerControllerSourceTypeSavedPhotosAlbum;

    if ([UIImagePickerController isSourceTypeAvailable:
        UIImagePickerControllerSourceTypeCamera]) {
        imagePicker.sourceType = UIImagePickerControllerSourceTypeCamera;
    }

    [self presentViewController:imagePicker animated:YES completion:^{
        NSLog(@"Image picker presented!");
    }];
}
```

EXERCISE: LETTING THE USER SELECT THE IMAGE PICKER TYPE

By combining device detection logic with an action sheet, you can give the user the option to select the image picker type at runtime. Instead of configuring the image picker right away, let's use the detection logic to configure an action sheet:

```
-(IBAction)showPickerActionSheet:(id)sender
{
    UIActionSheet *pickerActionSheet = nil;

    if ([UIImagePickerController isSourceTypeAvailable:UIImagePickerControllerSourceTypeCamera]) {
        pickerActionSheet = [[UIActionSheet alloc] initWithTitle:@"Select a source type"
                                        delegate:self cancelButtonTitle:@"Cancel"
destructiveButtonTitle:nil
                                        otherButtonTitles:@"Use Photo Albums", @"Take Photo", nil];
    } else {
        pickerActionSheet = [[UIActionSheet alloc] initWithTitle:@"Select a source type"
                                        delegate:self cancelButtonTitle:@"Cancel"
destructiveButtonTitle:nil
                                        otherButtonTitles:@"Use Photo Albums", nil];
    }

    [pickerActionSheet showInView:self.view];
}
```

Next, you need to indicate that your class implements the UIActionSheetDelegate protocol, so modify the class definition, as shown in bold in the following code:

```
@interface FirstViewController : UIViewController <UIActionSheetDelegate,
                   UIImagePickerControllerDelegate, UINavigationControllerDelegate>
```

By implementing the didDIsmissWithButtonIndex: delegate method, the app will now present the image picker, and configure the source type based on the button the user clicked:

```
-(void)actionSheet:(UIActionSheet *)actionSheet didDismissWithButtonIndex:(NSInteger)buttonIndex
{
    UIImagePickerController *imagePicker = [[UIImagePickerController alloc] init];
    imagePicker.delegate = self;

    switch (buttonIndex) {
        case 0:
            imagePicker.sourceType = UIImagePickerControllerSourceTypePhotoLibrary;
            break;
        case 1:
            imagePicker.sourceType = UIImagePickerControllerSourceTypeCamera;
            break;
        default:
            break;
    }

    [self presentViewController:imagePicker animated:YES completion:^{
        NSLog(@"Image picker presented!");
    }];

}
```

This code snippet uses a switch statement instead of an if-else, because there are three possible options in the action sheet: "Use Gallery", "Use Camera", and "Cancel". The Cancel button is always the last one in the list. The system destroys action sheets when you select "Cancel," which is why there is no extra logic to handle it here.

> **Note**   The default behavior of the Cancel button is to destroy the action sheet without performing an action, which is exactly what the example should do.

Understanding User Interface Limitations of the Image Picker

As you have seen, UIImagePicker is a convenient way to access Apple's system-wide camera controller and saved images thumbnail browser. Unfortunately, because it encapsulates system-wide resources, it also places restrictions on how you can present the view controller. Table 2-5 shows the default states of the image picker on both iPhone and iPad devices.

Table 2-5. *UIImagePickerController User Interface States*

	iPhone	iPad
Camera	Always a full-screen modal	Always a full-screen modal
Photo albums	Always a full-screen modal, in portrait orientation	Can be presented as a full-screen modal or within a popover controller

The previous examples were primarily designed for the iPhone. Next, you'll learn about the modifications you need to make to account for the iPad.

Presenting the Photo Album on an iPad

To improve the user experience of this app, you could present the photo gallery interface on an iPad by using a popover view controller. Most apps choose to launch popovers from a UIToolbarBarButtonItem, as shown in Figure 2-4.

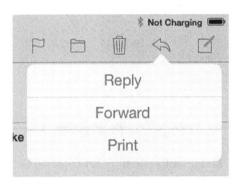

Figure 2-4. *Example of a popover launched from a UIToolBarButtonItem*

A popover has several unique properties that require it to be initialized differently from a normal view controller.

The first requirement for a popover is that it must not be destroyed when you present it, so you need to store it as an instance variable of the class:

```
@property (nonatomic, strong) UIPopoverController *popover;
```

Next, UIPopoverController conforms to the UIAppearanceContainer protocol, meaning it is intended to be a container for another view controller and must be initialized with a content view controller. Listing 2-13 modifies the button handler to present the image picker as the contentViewController for a popover view controller.

Listing 2-13. Button Handler for Showing the Image Picker in a Popover

```
-(IBAction)showPicker:(id)sender
{
    UIImagePickerController *imagePicker = [[UIImagePickerController alloc] init];
    imagePicker.delegate = self;

    imagePicker.sourceType = UIImagePickerControllerSourceTypeSavedPhotosAlbum;

    if ([UIImagePickerController isSourceTypeAvailable:UIImagePickerControllerSourceTypeCamera]) {

        imagePicker.sourceType = UIImagePickerControllerSourceTypeCamera;

    }

    self.popover = [[UIPopoverController alloc] initWithContentViewController:imagePicker];

}
```

You may see popover controllers with buttons at the top or bottom. To do this, embed your target view controller in a navigation controller and add buttons to its toolbars. We won't show that in this example, though.

Finally, a popover requires an *origin*—some place for it to "pop out" of. This example doesn't use a navigation controller; instead it presents the popover from the frame of the Take Picture button: .

```
[self.popover presentPopoverFromRect:self.actionButton.frame inView:self.view
            permittedArrowDirections:UIPopoverArrowDirectionDown animated:YES];
```

As further proof of how much Apple wants you to use a UIBarButtonItem to present the popover, they provide a presentPopoverFromBarButtonItem API.

> **Note**   The preceding code specifies a permittedArrowDirection of
> UIPopoverArrowDirectionDown forces the popover to pop out of the Take Picture button in a
> downward direction, meaning the popover content will appear beneath the button. The default value is
> UIPopoverArrowDirectionAny, which is a better choice for handling multiple device orientations.

To programmatically dismiss the popover, call the [UIViewController dismissPopoverAnimated:] method, just as you would to dimiss any other view controller. The pivotal actions in this case are choosing an image or dismissing the controller, so add this code to the UIImagePickerController delegate methods, as shown in Listing 2-14.

Listing 2-14. Adding Popovers as Part of the Camera Delegate Workflow

```
-(void)imagePickerController:(UIImagePickerController *)picker
                           didFinishPickingMediaWithInfo:(NSDictionary *)info
{
    UIImage *selectedImage = [info objectForKey:UIImagePickerControllerOriginalImage];
    [self.imageView setImage:selectedImage];

    [picker dismissViewControllerAnimated:YES completion:^{
        NSLog(@"Image selected!");
    }];

    if (self.popover != nil) {
        [self.popover dismissPopoverAnimated:YES];
        self.popover = nil;
    }

}

-(void)imagePickerControllerDidCancel:(UIImagePickerController *)picker
{
    [picker dismissViewControllerAnimated:YES completion:^{
        NSLog(@"Picker cancelled without doing anything");
    }];

    if (self.popover != nil) {
        [self.popover dismissPopoverAnimated:YES];
        self.popover = nil;
    }
}
```

You can control state persistence (whether or not you want the popover to remember where users were the last time they used the popover) by choosing to reload the content view only when an image is selected, or every time the popover is presented. The best user experience generally comes from reloading the content view each time the popover is presented. This example does this by always reinitializing the popover when the Take Picture button is pressed; see Listing 2-15.

Listing 2-15. Persisting Popover State

```
-(IBAction)showPicker:(id)sender
{
    UIImagePickerController *imagePicker = [[UIImagePickerController alloc] init];
                                        imagePicker.delegate = self;

    imagePicker.sourceType = UIImagePickerControllerSourceTypeSavedPhotosAlbum;

    if ([UIImagePickerController isSourceTypeAvailable:
        UIImagePickerControllerSourceTypeCamera]) {

        imagePicker.sourceType = UIImagePickerControllerSourceTypeCamera;

    }
```

```
if (UI_USER_INTERFACE_IDIOM() == UIUserInterfaceIdiomPad &&
    imagePicker.sourceType != UIImagePickerControllerSourceTypeCamera) {
    //iPad

    self.popover = [[UIPopoverController alloc]
                    initWithContentViewController:imagePicker];

    [self.popover presentPopoverFromRect:self.actionButton.frame
                  inView:self.view
                  permittedArrowDirections:UIPopoverArrowDirectionDown animated:YES];

} else {
    //iPhone

    [self presentViewController:imagePicker animated:YES completion:^{
        NSLog(@"Image picker presented!");
    }];
}
}
```

> **Note** You can also control the size of a popover by using the [UIPopoverController popoverContentSize] property. This is useful when you do not want to use the default size of 320×600 pixels.

Summary

This chapter introduced you to the UIImage, UIImageView, and UIImagePIckerController classes. You have seen the basics of using the UIImage class to load data and a little bit about what it provides under the hood. You saw how to use UIImageView to put a UIImage on the screen and how to use it to dynamically handle unexpected file sizes. Finally, you saw how to use the UIImagePicker to import pictures from the camera, learned about how device capabilities and protocols can help you implement this class safely, and ported the simple camera app over to the iPad.

Chapter 3

Doing Useful Things with Your Images

In this chapter, you will see how to improve your image-based applications by adding special effects, transforming images, and exporting apps from your apps. Additionally, you will be exposed to new user interfaces for working with images that can help you handle more-advanced use cases and build compelling user experiences.

This chapter assumes that you have a basic level of understanding about using the UIImage class to represent image data and using the UIImageView class to display image data. If you already have a firm grasp of these subjects, feel free to dive straight into this chapter and concentrate on the topics you are most interested in. If you still need a refresher, I recommend reviewing Chapter 2.

Manipulating Images

Two common tasks you will encounter when dealing with images in iOS are adjusting their size and orientation. While the UIImage class allows you to scale images at runtime depending on the frame size, this is not a permanent solution and can slow down your apps. Similarly, UIImage provides very limited (and inconsistent) control over cropping.

For a more permanent solution, you should implement what Apple calls a *graphics context*. A graphics context is a data type provided by Apple's Quartz framework that represents a drawing area to which you can save information. Quartz is Apple's drawing engine. It sits at a lower level than UIkit, allowing you more-direct control over drawing operations. You can use a graphics context to draw 2D graphics, display bitmap image data, and even display PDFs.

For all image manipulation operations, you need to do the following:

1. Create a context that meets your target dimensions.

2. Use CGRect and CGContext helper methods to create a frame for cropping, resizing, or rotation.

3. Draw the manipulated image by placing it on the context.

4. Export a snapshot of the context to a file or UIImage object.

5. Close the context to indicate that your image manipulation operation has completed, and that the view is ready for another operation.

You will notice that many of the steps are related to setup and teardown. Graphics contexts are unique to each view, but shared within views. A graphics context is nil until you call the UIGraphicsGetCurrentContext helper method, which will try to retrieve the current context for the view or create a new one. To preserve your changes, you need to close the context you are working on before attempting any other operations.

You can think of a context like a physical canvas. You can add items to a canvas, rotate them within the canvas without affecting the overall size, and even cut them to fit. Drawing an object is like gluing it down and cutting away the edges. Exporting is equivalent to calling the work of art ready and sending it to a framer.

Resizing an Image

To resize an image, the main operations you need to focus on are calculating your target image size and then drawing the image within that frame. As highlighted earlier, once you are satisfied with your changes, you need to export the resulting image from the context to *save* it.

The most frequent reason for resizing an image is to create a *thumbnail*, a smaller version of an image that is appropriate for displaying in a collection of multiple items. When displaying a large number of items, you should optimize for speed by loading files that are small in both their file size and dimensions.

After you have determined the bounding size (or limits) for your thumbnail (for example, 50 pixels by 50 pixels), you scale the image down to fit this frame. To preserve the aspect ratio of the image, you pick one dimension that will remain fixed and use that to calculate a scaling factor. Figure 3-1 illustrates the process of resizing an image.

Step 1: Determine target
frame size

Original Image

Desired Size

Step 2: Pick a dimension
that you want to match

Match Height

Desired Size

Step 3: Scaling factor = target dimension / original
Ex) 30 pixels / 50 pixels = 0.6

Step 4: Multiply both dimensions of target
image by scaling factor to resize

Resized Image

Figure 3-1. Process of resizing an image

> **Note** Using a fixed dimension lets you create a better user experience, by making the thumbnail images all the same width or height.

You find the scaling factor by dividing your target (fixed) dimension by the matching dimension from the source image: For example, if you were matching heights, you would use the height of the image.

```
CGSize originalImageSize = self.originalImage.size;
float targetHeight = 150.0f;
float scaleFactor = targetHeight / originalImageSize.height;
```

You calculate your target frame by multiplying the remaining dimension by the scaling factor:

```
float targetWidth = originalImageSize.width * scaleFactor;
CGRect targetFrame = CGRectMake(0, 0, targetWidth, targetHeight);
```

For the final step, you create your scaled-down image by creating a context based on the target frame size and calling the [UIImage drawInRect:] instance method to draw it on the context. When you are finished, save a snapshot of the context to a UIImage object and close the context:

```
UIGraphicsBeginImageContext(targetFrame.size);
[self.originalImage drawInRect:targetFrame];
resizedImage = UIGraphicsGetImageFromCurrentImageContext();
UIGraphicsEndImageContext();
[self.imageView setImage:resizedImage];
```

Listing 3-1 provides an example of the completed method, which puts together all of these steps.

Listing 3-1. Resizing an Image

```
-(IBAction)shrink:(id)sender
{
    UIImage *resizedImage = nil;

    CGSize originalImageSize = self.originalImage.size;
    float targetHeight = 150.0f;
    float scaleFactor = targetHeight / originalImageSize.height;
    float targetWidth = originalImageSize.width * scaleFactor;

    CGRect targetFrame = CGRectMake(0, 0, targetWidth, targetHeight);

    UIGraphicsBeginImageContext(targetFrame.size);

    [self.originalImage drawInRect:targetFrame];

    resizedImage = UIGraphicsGetImageFromCurrentImageContext();

    UIGraphicsEndImageContext();

    [self.imageView setImage:resizedImage];
}
```

Remember, when resizing an image, most of your code will be dedicated to calculating the new frame size and placing it correctly within your graphics context.

Cropping an Image

Cropping an image employs a very similar process to resizing an image, except that rather than shrinking the entire image down to the target frame's size, you need to resize it and reposition it to fit within the cropping frame. A common reason for cropping an image is to make a consistent image thumbnail (for example, a square), regardless of the source image's dimensions.

Similar to resizing, your first step is to find a scaling factor for your image. Since you want to preserve the natural aspect ratio of your images (that is, make sure they are not distorted), you should use the smaller dimension as the baseline. From there, you can center the image in the bounding frame and crop away the excess. You can find an updated graphic illustrating the crop process in Figure 3-2.

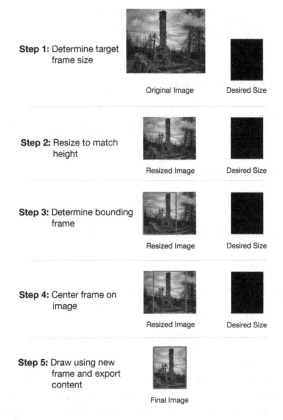

Figure 3-2. *Process of cropping an image*

Listing 3-2 provides an implementation of the cropping process.

Listing 3-2. Cropping an Image

```
-(IBAction)crop:(id)sender
{
    UIImage *resizedImage = nil;
    CGSize originalImageSize = self.originalImage.size;
    CGSize targetImageSize = CGSizeMake(150.0f, 150.0f);
    float scaleFactor, tempImageHeight, tempImageWidth;
    CGRect croppingRect;

    BOOL favorsX = NO;

    if (originalImageSize.width > originalImageSize.height) {
        scaleFactor = targetImageSize.height / originalImageSize.height;
        favorsX = YES;
    } else {
        scaleFactor = targetImageSize.width / originalImageSize.width;
        favorsX = NO;
    }
```

```
    tempImageHeight = originalImageSize.height * scaleFactor;
    tempImageWidth = originalImageSize.width * scaleFactor;

    if (favorsX) {
        float delta = (tempImageWidth - targetImageSize.width) / 2;
        croppingRect = CGRectMake(-1.0f * delta, 0, tempImageWidth, tempImageHeight);
    } else {
        float delta = (tempImageHeight - targetImageSize.height) / 2;
        croppingRect = CGRectMake(0, -1.0f * delta, tempImageWidth, tempImageHeight);
    }

    UIGraphicsBeginImageContext(targetImageSize);

    [self.originalImage drawInRect:croppingRect];

    resizedImage = UIGraphicsGetImageFromCurrentImageContext();

    UIGraphicsEndImageContext();

    [self.imageView setImage:resizedImage];

    self.statusLabel.text = @"Effect: Crop";

}
```

You will notice that the key logic in this method centers around finding the smaller dimension, repositioning the image, and saving the changes by removing everything outside the bounding frame. You shift the image to fit in the center of frame, depending on whether it needs more cropping in the x or y dimension (as indicated by the `favorsX` variable). This example multiplies one of the origin values by -1.0 to indicate that the image needs to be shifted in the negative direction (left for x, up for y). Just as when resizing images, you must export a snapshot of your graphics context when you are finished, to preserve your changes.

If you do not want to scale down the image and just want to crop out a portion of it at a specified (x,y) position, you can ignore the scale step. In this case, the most important operation is positioning the bounding frame by calling [`UIView drawRect:`] with the correct target coordinates. An example of a crop operation that ignores scaling is provided in Listing 3-3.

Listing 3-3. Cropping Without Scaling at a Specified (x,y) Position

```
-(IBAction)crop:(id)sender
{
    UIImage *resizedImage = nil;
    CGSize originalImageSize = self.originalImage.size;
    CGSize targetImageSize = CGSizeMake(150.0f, 150.0f);

    float originX = 10.0f;
    float originY = 20.0f;
    float scaleFactor, tempImageHeight, tempImageWidth;
    CGRect croppingRect = CGRectMake(originX, originY, originalImageSize.width,
        originalImageSize.height);
    UIGraphicsBeginImageContext(targetImageSize);
```

```
[self.originalImage drawInRect:croppingRect];

resizedImage = UIGraphicsGetImageFromCurrentImageContext();

UIGraphicsEndImageContext();

[self.imageView setImage:resizedImage];

self.statusLabel.text = @"Effect: Crop";

}
```

You can find a sample project illustrating cropping and resizing in the source code bundle for this book (see the Source Code/Download area of the Apress web site, www.apress.com). The project is named ImageTransformations and can be found in the Chapter 3 folder. As shown in Figure 3-3, the project provides an image view to preview the image, and buttons to crop it, resize it, and restore it to its original size.

Figure 3-3. ImageTransformations project

Saving Images

To get the most use out of your photos, including those you manipulated in your app, you often need the ability to save them to disk or back to the photo album. Unless they are using an app that declares it deletes all images after a certain period of time (such as Snapchat), most users expect to be able to retrieve images they created with your app, the next time they open it. The ability to save images is important because it will satisfy this expectation, and it will allow users to export images they create to e-mail or other apps.

Saving Images to Files

The process of saving images to disk is quite simple. Much like any other data operation, you need to extract the binary data for the image, and write this data to a file.

To extract the binary data for an image, you can use the UIkit convenience methods, `UIImagePNRepresentation()` and `UIImageJPEGRepresentation()`. Both of these methods return `NSData` objects, as shown here:

```
NSData *imageData = UIImagePNGRepresentation(self.originalImage);
```

You would use `UIImagePNGRepresentation()` when you are trying to preserve alpha (transparency) information in your image. Its only parameter is your input `UIImage`. If your image does not contain any alpha information, and you are looking for compression options, you should use `UIImageJPEGRepresentation()`. Its parameters are your input `UIImage` and a `float` between 0.0 and 1.0 representing your compression quality. Lower values represent higher compression values, with lower quality; 0.6 or 0.7 is a good trade-off between file size and image quality for most applications:

```
NSData *imageData = UIImageJPEGRepresentation(self.originalImage, 0.7f);
```

After the binary data for the image is ready, you write it to a file. You can use the `NSData` instance method `[NSData writeToFile:]` to write the data to disk. This method requires a target location for the file. Just as when reading a file from within your app bundle, you can use your app's document directory as an interface to your device's file system. An example of saving an image to the documents folder is provided in Listing 3-4.

Listing 3-4. Saving an Image to the Documents Folder

```
-(IBAction)saveToDisk:(id)sender
{
    NSArray *paths = NSSearchPathForDirectoriesInDomains(NSDocumentDirectory, NSUserDomainMask,
                     YES);
    NSString *documentsDirectory = [paths objectAtIndex:0];
    NSString *filePath = [documentsDirectory stringByAppendingPathComponent:@"image.jpg"];

    NSData *imageData = UIImageJPEGRepresentation(self.originalImage, 0.7f);
    NSError *error = nil;
    NSString *alertMessage = nil;
```

```
//check if the file exists before trying to write it
if ([[NSFileManager defaultManager] fileExistsAtPath:filePath]) {

    NSDateFormatter *dateFormat = [[NSDateFormatter alloc] init];
    [dateFormat setDateFormat:@"yyyyMMddHHmm"];

    NSString *dateString = [dateFormat stringFromDate:[NSDate date]];

    NSString *fileName = [NSString stringWithFormat:@"image-%@.jpg", dateString];

    filePath = [documentsDirectory stringByAppendingPathComponent:fileName];
}

[imageData writeToFile:filePath options:NSDataWritingAtomic error:&error];

if (error == nil) {
    alertMessage = @"Saved to 'Documents' folder successfully!";
} else {
    alertMessage = @"Could not save image :(";
}

UIAlertView *alertView = [[UIAlertView alloc] initWithTitle:@"Status"
                               message:alertMessage delegate:nil cancelButtonTitle:@"OK"
                               otherButtonTitles:nil];
[alertView show];
}
```

> **Caution**   Apple's APIs do not provide automatic file naming, so remember to check for existing file names before attempting to write your file.

In Listing 3-4, the object representing the image takes the format self.originalImage. This indicates that the image is an instance variable that belongs to the class, rather than a specific method. Instance variables are important when you need to manipulate the same object multiple times within a class, without passing it as a parameter. You create an instance variable by declaring it in your header file:

```
@property (nonatomic, strong) UIImage *originalImage;
```

Now that the files are saved in the documents folder, you can access them the next time you load the app.

If you want users to be able to download the output from your app to their computers, you need to perform one last step: enabling iTunes File Sharing for your app. You can do this by navigating over to the Info tab of Project Settings, and then adding the key Application Supports iTunes File Sharing, as shown in Figure 3-4.

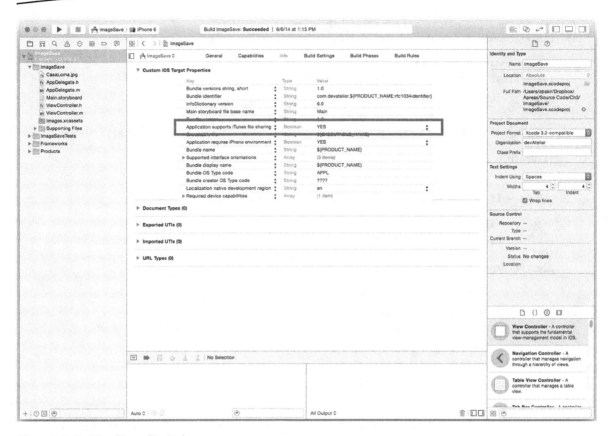

Figure 3-4. Enabling iTunes file sharing

Users can now view their files by selecting their device in iTunes and scrolling down to the File Sharing section of the Apps tab. By clicking your app's name in the installed apps list, they will see the contents of your app's documents folder, as shown in Figure 3-5.

Figure 3-5. Viewing files in iTunes

Saving Images to the Photo Library

For many photo-based apps, you will want to be able to give other apps access to images that were created or manipulated within your app. In this case, it would be more appropriate to save the images directly to the system's photo library. To facilitate this, Apple provides a convenience method, `UIImageWriteToSavedPhotosAlbum()`, which allows you to save a `UIImage` object directly to the Camera Roll photo album.

To use the `UIImageWriteToSavedPhotosAlbum()` method, you need pass the `UIImage` object you want to save and, optionally, a completion handler that will execute when the operation has finished. You can use your completion handler to determine whether the save was successful and to perform a subsequent action, such as displaying a `UIAlertView`:

```
UIImageWriteToSavedPhotosAlbum(self.originalImage, self,
                        @selector(image:didFinishSavingWithError:contextInfo:), nil);
```

If you are using a completion handler, be careful to pass both the `completionTarget` parameter (in this case, `self`) and the selector for your handler method. Otherwise, your code will not know what method to use at runtime or where to look for it. Listing 3-5 provides an example of a completion handler that shows an alert view.

Listing 3-5. Completion Handler That Shows an Alert View

```
- (void)image:(UIImage *)image didFinishSavingWithError:(NSError *)
                                               error contextInfo:(void *)contextInfo
{
    NSString *alertMessage = nil;
    if (error == nil) {
        alertMessage = @"Saved to Camera Roll successfully!";
    } else {
        alertMessage = @"Could not save image :(";
    }

    UIAlertView *alertView = [[UIAlertView alloc] initWithTitle:@"Status"
                                message:alertMessage delegate:nil cancelButtonTitle:@"OK"
                                otherButtonTitles:nil];
    [alertView show];
}
```

In the source code bundle, I provide a sample project called ImageSave, which illustrates both ways of saving an image. As shown in Figure 3-6, this app provides an image view and two buttons to trigger the save actions.

Figure 3-6. ImageSave project

Loading Images from the Internet

You can never predict how long it will take to load an image from the Internet. Although you can use the [NSData initWithContentsOfUrl:] method to load the image data, it will not provide you with error handling, and will it be a blocking operation, meaning your app will not be able to respond to other events until the download has completed. A better approach is to download an image in the background, and to refresh the UIImageView with the downloaded result when the data is ready.

To download image data in the background of your app, you use the NSURLConnection class. This class gives you the ability to control a download (start/stop) and options to control where it will execute (in the foreground or background) and whether the response will be handled via a delegate or completion block.

You start by initializing your UIImageView with a placeholder image, or a nil value:

```
[self.imageView setImage:nil];
```

Next, you initialize an NSURLRequest object containing the target URL:

```
NSURL *imageUrl = [NSURL URLWithString:@"http://www.devatelier.com/images/flower.png"];
NSURLRequest *urlRequest = [NSURLRequest requestWithURL:imageUrl];
```

The NSURLRequest object wraps the URL in an HTTP GET command, which is how browsers and other apps send download requests to a web server.

To streamline this implementation, I suggest using the NSURLConnection method that allows you to specify a completion block: [NSURLConnection sendAsynchronousRequest:]. Using a completion handler enables you to execute a block of code as soon as a method finishes, without needing to persist variables or create extra methods. It is a class method, so you do not need to instantiate an object to use it:

```
[NSURLConnection sendAsynchronousRequest:urlRequest queue:[NSOperationQueue mainQueue]
              completionHandler:^(NSURLResponse *response, NSData *data,
              NSError *connectionError) { ... }];
```

You see that the completion handler for this method returns an NSData object and an NSError object. If the download fails, the error object will be nil; otherwise, it will contain a non-nil value. Listing 3-6 presents a method that initiates a download and creates a UIImage object from the resulting data if the download is successful. If the download fails, the application will display an alert view indicating the failure to the user.

Listing 3-6. Loading an Image from the Internet

```
-(IBAction)start:(id)sender
{
    NSURL *imageUrl = [NSURL URLWithString:@"http://www.devatelier.com/images/flower.png"];
    NSURLRequest *urlRequest = [NSURLRequest requestWithURL:imageUrl];

    [self.imageView setImage:nil];
```

```
[NSURLConnection sendAsynchronousRequest:urlRequest queue:[NSOperationQueue mainQueue]
            completionHandler:^(NSURLResponse *response, NSData *data,
            NSError *connectionError) {

    if (connectionError == nil) {

        UIImage *newImage = [UIImage imageWithData:data];
        [self.imageView setImage:newImage];

    } else {
        UIAlertView *alertView = [[UIAlertView alloc] initWithTitle:@"Error"

            message:@"Could not load image :(" delegate:nil cancelButtonTitle:@"OK"
            otherButtonTitles:nil];
        [alertView show];
    }
}];
}
```

Adding an Activity Indicator

In many apps, you will notice a spinning animation that indicates an operation is in progress (such as downloading an image), as shown in Figure 3-7. You can add a spinner (or *activity indicator*) to any view via the UIActivityIndicatorView class.

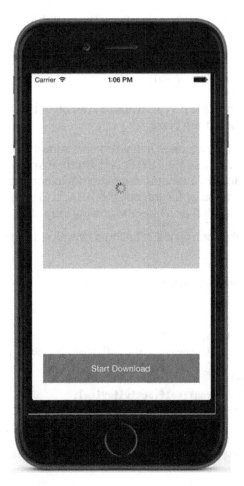

Figure 3-7. View with activity indicator superimposed

To add a UIActivityIndicatorView to a UIImageView, you follow many of the same initialization steps you would use with any other UIView, including setting up the container frame and adding the UIActivityIndicatorView as a subview on top of the UIImageView.

By reviewing Figure 3-7, you will notice that the UIActivityIndicatorView is very small in comparison to the UIImageView. To accommodate for the size difference, you could find the center of the UIImageView and use this as the origin for the UIActivityIndicatorView. An example of adding an activity indictor to an image view is provided in Listing 3-7.

Listing 3-7. Adding an Activity Indicator to an Image View

```
//calculate the mid-way point of the image view
CGFloat indicatorWidth, indicatorHeight;
indicatorWidth = indicatorHeight = 100.0f;

CGFloat originX = (self.imageView.frame.size.width - indicatorWidth) / 2;
CGFloat originY = (self.imageView.frame.size.height - indicatorHeight) / 2;
```

```
CGRect activityFrame = CGRectMake(originX, originY, indicatorWidth, indicatorHeight);

self.activityView = [[UIActivityIndicatorView alloc] initWithFrame:activityFrame];
self.activityView.color = [UIColor blackColor];
[self.imageView addSubview:self.activityView];
```

You declare the UIImageView and UIActivityIndidatorView objects as instance variables, since you will need to access them throughout the class.

After the UIActivityIndicatorView has been initialized and added to the UIImageView, you are ready to make magic happen. You should use the [UIActivityIndicatorView startAnimating] instance method to start animating the activity indicator when the download operation begins. When the operation completes, due to success or failure, call the [UIActivityIndicatorView stopAnimating] instance method to stop the animation and hide the activity indicator.

Listing 3-8 shows an example that combines initiating a download with starting and stopping the activity indicator.

Listing 3-8. Loading an Image and Mirroring Status with an Activity Indicator

```
-(IBAction)start:(id)sender
{
    NSURL *imageUrl = [NSURL URLWithString:@" @"http://images.devatelier.com/castle.jpg "];
    NSURLRequest *urlRequest = [NSURLRequest requestWithURL:imageUrl];

    [self.imageView setImage:nil];
    [self.imageView bringSubviewToFront:self.activityView];
    [self.activityView startAnimating];

    [NSURLConnection sendAsynchronousRequest:urlRequest queue:[NSOperationQueue mainQueue]
                   completionHandler:^(NSURLResponse *response, NSData *data,
                   NSError *connectionError) {

        [self.activityView stopAnimating];

        if (connectionError == nil) {

            UIImage *newImage = [UIImage imageWithData:data];
            [self.imageView setImage:newImage];

        } else {
            UIAlertView *alertView = [[UIAlertView alloc] initWithTitle:@"Error"
message:@"Could not load image :(" delegate:nil cancelButtonTitle:@"OK" otherButtonTitles:nil];
            [alertView show];
        }
    }];
}
```

> **Note**   Views are displayed in the order they were added. I am using the [UIView bringSubviewToFront:] instance method in this example to force the activity indicator to appear at the top of the view stack.

The ImageDownload project in the source code bundle for this chapter implements the user interface that was illustrated in Figure 3-7. When the user presses the Start Download button, the image will start downloading in the background and display the activity indicator. When the download has completed, the indicator will disappear and the image view will be reloaded with the downloaded image.

Adding Effects to Your Images

Arguably, the most striking change that Apple introduced with iOS 7 was its new visual design language and the tools it provided developers to implement this language. iOS 7 marked Apple's shift from its traditional skeumorphic user interface approach (taking cues from the real world) to flat, clean, digital-first design.

In this section, you will see how to begin using this design language. You will leverage traditional methods, such as gradients, to give depth to images, and you will see how blurring and motion effects can give your app access to many of the compelling visual effects Apple uses in its apps.

Adding Gradients

To add depth and accentuate overlays on top of your images (such as text), you can use gradients. Luckily for us, there's an API for that!

The Quartz class you can use to draw a gradient over a view is called CAGradientLayer. It is a subclass of CALayer, the view drawing class, intended for drawing gradients based on input colors and color stop points. A *stop point* determines where regions should stop and begin to intersect with each other. There is no limit on the number of colors or stop points you can have, but you should try to practice good design and implement a nondistracting gradient. As shown in Figure 3-8, different numbers of stop points can create drastically different effects based on how you place them and use your color areas.

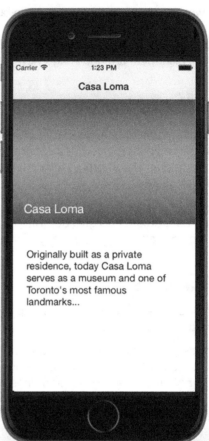

Figure 3-8. A gradient with two stop points vs. a gradient with three stop points

Listing 3-9 shows an example of adding a gradient to a UIImageView.

Listing 3-9. Adding a Gradient to a UIImageView

```
UIColor *darkestColor = [UIColor colorWithWhite:0.1f alpha:0.7f];
UIColor *lightestColor = [UIColor colorWithWhite:0.7f alpha:0.1f];

CAGradientLayer *headerGradient = [CAGradientLayer layer];
headerGradient.colors = [NSArray arrayWithObjects:(id)darkestColor.CGColor,
                         (id)lightestColor.CGColor, (id)darkestColor.CGColor,  nil];

headerGradient.frame = self.headerImageView.bounds;
[self.headerImageView.layer insertSublayer:headerGradient atIndex:0];
```

Note   If you do not define any stop points, the default values will be evenly distributed.

To create a gradient, you start by creating a `CAGradientLayer` object. From there, specify the colors to use. For this example, I wanted the image to display a rounded effect, so I used three stop points and colors that shift from darker to lighter, and then back to darker.

> **Note** When placing a gradient over an image, I strongly suggest using a `UIColor` method that allows you to specify an alpha value. Alpha values determine the transparency of a layer. An alpha value of `0.0` means the layer is completely transparent, while an alpha value of `1.0` means the layer is completely opaque. Alternate your alpha values to make the gradient effect stronger or weaker in different positions, all the while not completing masking your image.

Figure 3-9 shows an example of the output of the gradient.

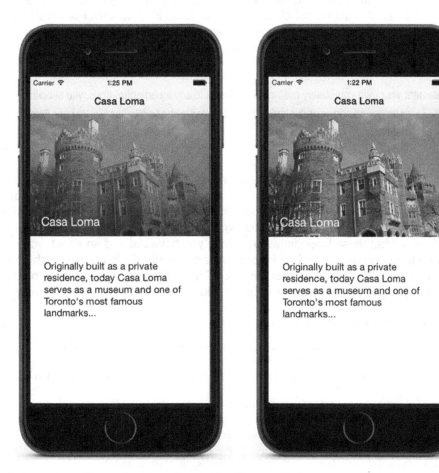

Figure 3-9. An image view with a gradient vs. an image view with no gradient

Using gradients, you can create powerful visual effects with only a few simple lines of code, helping your images achieve a more realistic sense of lighting. Gradients can also accentuate overlays better than drop shadows alone. The effect used in this example is the same as the one Facebook uses on its profile pages.

The sample project that employs gradients is named ImageGradient.

Making Your Images Move with Your Device

One of the most visually exciting user interface features that came with iOS 7 was the ability to add motion effects to any view. *Motion effects* allow you to move the view in response to accelerator events, causing an app to feel more immersive and accentuate the most important parts of your UI. Apple uses motion effects to animate the iOS 7+ home screen, lock screen, alert views, and Safari tab browser on the iPhone.

Apple exposes the ability to access and create motion effects through the UIMotionEffect abstract class. As an abstract class, it must be subclassed in order to be instantiated. Fortunately, however, Apple provides a very simple subclass that moves a view horizontally or vertically based on accelerometer changes, called UIInterpolatingMotionEffect.

> **Note**   To implement your own completely custom behaviors and advanced animations, you subclass UIMotionEffect directly, and add your custom logic in the keyPathsAndRelativeValuesFor ViewerOffsets: method.

To use UIInterpolatingMotionEffect, you must instantiate an object with a keyPath representing the view property you want to modify based on the motion event (for example, the center x position) and the type of motion you want to react to (for example, horizontal movement). For many motion effects, you will be exposing areas of the view that are hidden, so you must also define relative limits that let the motion effect know what these boundaries are. Once you have defined an effect, you can add it to a view by using the [UIView addMotionEffect:] instance method. You can pass this method one UIMotionEffect object directly, or a UIMotionEffectGroup object if you are trying to add multiple effects at one time. Listing 3-10 shows an example of adding motion effects to a UIImageView.

Listing 3-10. Adding Motion Effects to a UIImageView

```
UIInterpolatingMotionEffect *horizontalEffect = [[UIInterpolatingMotionEffect alloc]
                        initWithKeyPath:@"center.x"
                        type:UIInterpolatingMotionEffectTypeTiltAlongHorizontalAxis];

UIInterpolatingMotionEffect *verticalEffect = [[UIInterpolatingMotionEffect alloc]
                        initWithKeyPath:@"center.y"
                        type:UIInterpolatingMotionEffectTypeTiltAlongVerticalAxis];

horizontalEffect.minimumRelativeValue  = [NSNumber numberWithInteger:-50];
horizontalEffect.maximumRelativeValue  = [NSNumber numberWithInteger:50];

verticalEffect.minimumRelativeValue  = [NSNumber numberWithInteger:-50];
verticalEffect.maximumRelativeValue  = [NSNumber numberWithInteger:50];
```

```
//set bg image effects
[self.backgroundImageView addMotionEffect:horizontalEffect];
[self.backgroundImageView addMotionEffect:verticalEffect];
```

In Listing 3-10, I set the motion effect on the background view. As the intent of a motion effect is to highlight or diminish a view in the view hierarchy, it is often appropriate to apply the effect to a view that is in the background or an action view in the foreground (for example, a UIAlertView).

> **Note**   The Reduce Motion switch in iOS's accessibility screen allows a user to disable motion effects across the entire system (including your app). This cannot be overridden, so remember to design for this limitation.

The sample project in the source code bundle that employs motion effects is named ImageTilt. As shown in Figure 3-10, there are no buttons. The input comes from tilting the device. You will notice that the image moves, but the label does not.

Figure 3-10. The ImageTilt project's motion effects

Adding Blurring to Your Images

Another exciting visual effect Apple brought with the design language of iOS 7 was an emphasis on blurring background images to highlight important parts of your user interface. You can see this effect quite frequently when you open Siri, as shown in Figure 3-11.

Figure 3-11. Blur effect in Siri

Many of the core concepts required to create a blurred background take advantage of creating a graphics context to manipulate an image, and then using `CGAffineTransform` to modify the source image. Apple prefers to use *Gaussian blur* effects, which reduce details in images through a mathematical effect that creates smoothing. Fortunately, Apple created a category class for `UIImage` at the Apple Worldwide Developers Conference (WWDC) 2013 called `UIImage+ImageEffects.h` that manages the graphics context for the calculation, performs the blur function, and returns the results. I have included the `ImageEffects` category in the sample code for this chapter. You can also find it on the iOS Dev Center by searching for the WWDC session "Implementing Engaging UI on iOS."

Categories in iOS allow you to extend a class without subclassing it. Categories allow you to write very small files that can add several methods to existing classes, for the purpose of adding functionality.

To use the `ImageEffects` category, you include `UIImage+ImageEffects.h` in your class. From there, you can use the additional methods it provides as you would with any other `UIImage` method. Figure 3-12 compares the results provided by each blur effect.

Figure 3-12. Extra Light Effect blur, Light Effect blur, and Dark Effect blur on the same image

The blur effect you should use depends on your user interface and the color of your image. For a light image, it is better to use `[UIImage applyLightEffect:]`, whereas `[UIImage applyDarkEffect:]` is more appropriate for dark images. As you can see here, selecting an effect is a one-liner:

```
UIImage *blurredImage = [self.originalImage applyLightEffect];
```

The sample project that adds blurring to an image is named ImageBlur. As you can see in Figure 3-13, the project has three buttons, which toggle between blur types. I highly recommend testing the project with some of your own images to see how blurring affects them.

Figure 3-13. *ImageBlur project*

Summary

In this chapter, you saw how to use the canvas-like abilities of graphics contexts to manipulate images. From there, you saw how to export images to files and the photo album, to be able to reuse them later or share them with other apps. To make your apps faster, you saw how to load images from the Internet without blocking the user interface. Finally, you began to see how to use many of Apple's visual effects methods to add an extra sense of depth to your images.

Chapter 4

Advanced Photo Interfaces

In this chapter, you will explore lower-level camera programming topics by building your own image-capture and photo-picker classes, similar to the defaults provided by UIImagePickerController. Along the way, you will see how to configure the hardware camera for image capture, how to access photos directly from the Photos app, and what you need to do to present this raw data in a user interface.

You will use the UIImagePickerController as your reference for functionality, so if you are unsure how to present the class or handle its output, it would be a good idea to review Chapter 2.

Although it may seem like a lot of work to replicate functionality iOS already offers, having a camera interface that looks radically different from the rest of your app, or that does not allow users to make modifications to improve the quality of their pictures, will greatly impact your functionality and drive users away.

Building a Custom Camera Interface

The first exercise is to replicate the basic image-capture interface provided by UIImagePickerController. As shown in Figure 4-1, the project uses a nonstandard interface and exposes an expanded set of hardware controls.

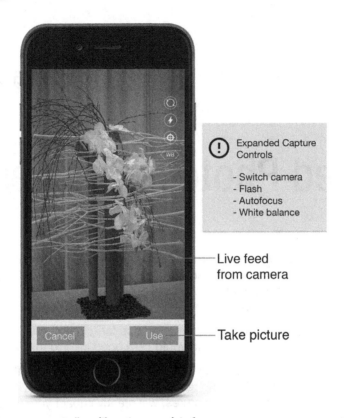

Figure 4-1. Mock-up of the camera controller with custom user interface

To make this happen, the application must be able to do the following:

- Discover and configure the camera hardware

- Display a live feed of the data from the camera

- Modify the capture settings from the UI

- Capture a picture when the user clicks the Take Picture button

Ideally, you should use a class that lets you configure a camera "object" and access the data stream that it generates. At the same time, you don't want to have to write the hardware drivers yourself, so it's better to use something that abstracts this layer. Luckily, that functionality exists in the AVFoundation framework, which is included as part of Cocoa Touch.

As its name implies, AVFoundation is one of Apple's media frameworks for capturing, manipulating, and storing audio and video assets. The video-capture APIs in AVFoundation let you access the raw video stream coming from the camera, and provide high-level configuration capabilities for hardware controls, such as the flash or autofocus.

You can build an image-capture interface from a video stream by remembering that a video stream is nothing but a series of images called *frames*. To capture an image, you just need to extract a frame from the video. To make sure the result is accurate, you want to extract a frame when the image is in focus.

In this section, you will see how to use AVFoundation to set up the camera, display a live feed, and capture frames or change settings based on user interface events. To speed up the workflow, this section uses storyboards and Interface Builder to build the user interface.

As with previous exercises in this book, you can find the source code for this project in the Source Code/Download area of the Apress web site (www.apress.com), under the Chapter 4 folder. The project for this application is called MyCamera.

Initializing the Hardware Interface

In situations where your application attempts to access a shared resource (such as hardware) or perform an operation with a high potential for failure, Apple suggests using a *session* design pattern. This pattern pipes all your operations through the session object, which provides error reduction and traffic control features, such as semaphores. Sessions also reduce errors by streamlining the process for setting up and tearing down complicated interfaces. You will see this design pattern in use when accessing audio hardware or performing network operations.

To begin using AVFoundation classes in your project, you need to add the framework to your project, and also include it in any classes that use it. The easiest way to add a framework to your project is by adding it to the Linked Frameworks and Libraries array for your application. You can modify this array by clicking your project name in the Xcode Project Navigator, and scrolling to the bottom of the General tab, as shown in Figure 4-2.

Figure 4-2. Finding the Linked Frameworks and Libraries array

You can choose which framework to add by clicking the Plus button at the bottom of the Linked Frameworks and Libraries pane. Doing this displays a navigator showing the frameworks that are installed on your development computer. You can filter the list further by typing the name of your desired framework. Select a framework and click the Add button to add it to your project (see Figure 4-3).

Figure 4-3. Xcode's framework picker

After adding the AVFoundation framework to your project, you include it in your file by adding it to the top of the header file for each class that uses it. The header file for the MyCamera application is ViewController.h:

```
#include <AVFoundation/AVFoundation.h>
```

The AVFoundation class you need to manage hardware sessions is called AVCaptureSession. This class manages the hardware interfaces and provides high-level start and stop operations. Instantiating a session object is very easy; just call the init method on the AVCaptureSession object:

```
AVCaptureSession *session = [[AVCaptureSession alloc] init];
```

> **Note**   You will need to share your session object with all classes trying to access it in the app, so remember to declare it as an instance variable or singleton.

When you are ready to use hardware devices through the session, you add them as *inputs*. This is a two-step process: first you identify the hardware device you want to use, and then you configure it to send its data to your session. Hardware devices are represented by the AVCaptureDevice class, through which you can query for device permissions and hardware availability, and configure capture settings for the device.

Before you can start sending commands to a device, you need to discover it. You use the [AVCaptureDevice defaultDeviceWithMediaType:] class method to discover the default hardware device for a specific media type. Use the AVMediaTypeVideo constant to specify video devices:

```
AVCaptureDevice *camera = [AVCaptureDevice defaultDeviceWithMediaType:AVMediaTypeVideo];
```

> **Note**   To discover all devices that match a type, use the [AVCaptureDevice devicesWithMediaType:] class method. In order to match a specific property (such as camera positions), you will need to iterate through the results. You can use the position property to determine if a camera is on the front or rear of the device.

After finding a device, you need to add it to your session. To configure a device for use with AVCaptureSession, you need to instantiate it as an AVDeviceCaptureInput object. AVDeviceCaptureInput attempts to initialize the hardware device and returns an object if it succeeds, or an NSError if it fails. After the object is ready, use the [AVCaptureSession canAddInput:] method to make sure the device is available for use by your application, and then call the [AVCaptureSession addInput:] instance method to add it to your session. You can find an example that illustrates this process in Listing 4-1.

Listing 4-1. Adding a Camera Input

```
NSError *error = nil;
AVCaptureDeviceInput *cameraInput = [AVCaptureDeviceInput
                                deviceInputWithDevice:camera
                                error:&error];

if (error == nil && [self.session canAddInput:cameraInput]) {
    [self.session addInput:cameraInput];
}
```

> **Caution**   To reduce errors, you should always make sure an input is available before trying to add it. Remember, the camera is a shared resource, and you need to play nice with others!

Accessing the Live Camera Feed

After establishing an interface to the camera hardware, you need some way of displaying the output on the screen. To display the live video feed, you need to perform three steps:

1. Access the data source containing the live video stream.

2. Place the video stream on a view.

3. Start the stream.

The AVFoundation class responsible for mirroring the video output from a session is AVCaptureVideoPreviewLayer. This class is a subclass of CALayer, more commonly known as a Core Animation Layer. Core Animation Layers are the backing class to which you send image data before painting it on the screen. Layers represent content, while views represent where the content will be displayed.

Much like cels in traditional animation, you can combine layers to represent more-complicated data, or you can move them around independently. Because video streams are inherently a quickly changing series of images, it makes more sense from a performance standpoint to write the content directly to a layer, rather than tearing down views for every frame change.

You instantiate the AVCapturePreviewLayer object by calling the [AVCapturePreviewLayer initWithSession:] constructor method, passing in your session object as the input parameter:

```
AVCaptureVideoPreviewLayer *previewLayer =
    [[AVCaptureVideoPreviewLayer alloc] initWithSession:self.session];
```

To correctly display a layer, you need to specify its dimensions and position. For the MyCamera project, you will use a UIView property called previewView to display the camera live feed. To center the video layer on this view and give it the same bounds, you can use the following snippet:

```
CGRect layerRect = self.previewView.bounds;
CGPoint layerCenter = CGPointMake(CGRectGetMidX(layerRect),
    CGRectGetMidY(layerRect));
[previewLayer setBounds:layerRect];
[previewLayer setPosition:layerCenter];
```

To display the video layer, however, you need to give the layer a drawing target. You want to draw the video on the view, so add the preview layer as a sublayer on top of the view:

```
[self.previewView.layer addSublayer:previewLayer];
```

By default, the preview layer resizes the camera output to fit within its container frame, while preserving aspect ratio. By setting the videoGravity property to AVLayerVideoGravityResize, you can change the scaling to aspect fill:

```
[previewLayer setVideoGravity:AVLayerVideoGravityResize];
```

The final step is to start the stream, which you do by calling the [AVCaptureSession startRunning] method on the session object:

```
[self.session startRunning];
```

The complete camera setup code for the ViewController class is in Listing 4-2. It is wrapped in the [self viewDidLoad:] method because you need to initialize the camera when the view is initialized.

Listing 4-2. Initializing the Camera Input

```objc
- (void)viewDidLoad
{
    [super viewDidLoad];
        // Do any additional setup after loading the view.
    self.session = [[AVCaptureSession alloc] init];
    AVCaptureDevice *camera = [AVCaptureDevice
        defaultDeviceWithMediaType:AVMediaTypeVideo];
    NSError *error = nil;

    AVCaptureDeviceInput *cameraInput = [AVCaptureDeviceInput
        deviceInputWithDevice:camera error:&error];

    if (error == nil && [self.session canAddInput:cameraInput]) {
        [self.session addInput:cameraInput];

        AVCaptureVideoPreviewLayer *previewLayer =
            [[AVCaptureVideoPreviewLayer alloc]
                initWithSession:self.session];

        CGRect layerRect = self.previewView.bounds;
        CGPoint layerCenter = CGPointMake(CGRectGetMidX(layerRect),
                                CGRectGetMidY(layerRect));

        [previewLayer setBounds:layerRect];
        [previewLayer setPosition:layerCenter];

        [previewLayer setVideoGravity:AVLayerVideoGravityResize];

        [self.previewView.layer addSublayer:previewLayer];

        [self.session startRunning];
    }
}
```

Capturing a Still Image

Similarly to the way you added an *input* to the AVCaptureSession to determine the input device, you need to add an *output* to determine how to export data. For this example, you want to export a photo—represented as a single frame of video—when the user is ready.

The base class for AVCaptureSession output objects is AVCaptureOutput, however, as an abstract class that specifies only what information is required for a capture object. Luckily, though, AVFoundation comes with a number of AVCaptureObject subclasses you can use for desired export formats. Several of the most popular subclasses are enumerated in Table 4-1.

Table 4-1. Popular AVCaptureOutput Subclasses

Subclass	Capture Output
AVCaptureMovieFileOutput	QuickTime movie file
AVCaptureVideoDataOutput	Video frames—intended for processing
AVCaptureAudioFileOutput	Audio files supported by Core Audio (.MP3, .AIFF, .WAV, .AAC)
AVCaptureAudioDataOutput	Audio buffer— intended for processing
AVCaptureMetadataOutput	Media file metadata properties (for example, GPS location, exposure level)
AVCaptureStillImageOutput	Still images and metadata

To capture a still image, use the AVCaptureStillImageOutput subclass. The method to capture images using this class is defined as an instance method, so declare an AVCaptureStillImageOutput object as an instance variable:

```
self.stillImageOutput = [[AVCaptureStillImageOutput alloc] init];
```

Although you do not have to configure the output object to capture raw data, it is a good idea to compress the data by saving it as a JPEG file (.JPG). To do this, you need to specify the codec type in a configuration dictionary. You specify JPEG format using the kCMVideoCodecType_JPEG constant for the value at the AVVideoCodecKey key. After the dictionary is ready, save your settings using the [AVStillImageOutput setOutputSettings:] method, as shown in Listing 4-3.

Listing 4-3. Configuring an Output Object

```
NSMutableDictionary *configDict = [NSMutableDictionary new];
[configDict setObject:AVVideoCodecJPEG forKey:AVVideoCodecKey];
[self.stillImageOutput setOutputSettings:configDict];
```

Again, just as when adding an input object, you should check to make sure the output object is available before adding it to your session, as shown in Listing 4-4.

Listing 4-4. Adding an Output Object

```
if ([self.session canAddOutput:self.stillImageOutput]) {
    [self.session addOutput:self.stillImageOutput];
}
```

Now that you have set up an output object, you can use it to capture still images. The API reference for the AVCaptureStillImageOutput class shows that you can use the [AVCaptureStillImageAsynchro nouslyFromConnection:completionHandler] instance method. Unfortunately, though, you need to set up a *connection* to use this method. A connection, represented by the AVCaptureConnection class, is an interface that links the input and output objects. Luckily, connections are created automatically when you add outputs to a session. You can query for a connection by specifying the output object and media type you are looking for (for example, audio or video), as shown in Listing 4-5.

Listing 4-5. Querying for a Connection Object

```
AVCaptureConnection *connection = [self.stillImageOutput
    connectionWithMediaType:AVMediaTypeVideo];
```

Having created a connection object, you can now call a block to capture still images. The completion handler returns a low-level media buffer (CMSampleBufferRef) that points to the still image, or an NSError object if the operation failed. You can save the image by calling the [AVCaptureStillImageOutput jpegStillImageNSDataRespresentation:] class method, which returns the NSData representation for the still image as a JPEG file with valid EXIF metadata. After retrieving the NSData for the image, you can save it to disk or convert it to a UIImage object.

In Listing 4-6, a button handler encapsulates the entire process of capturing an image. In the MyCamera project, this would be triggered by the Shoot button. If this method is able to capture an image successfully, it will send a didFinishWithImage message to its camera delegate. If the capture fails, it logs the error by sending the cancel message and logging the error as a string using [NSLog description].

Listing 4-6. Capturing a Still Image

```
-(IBAction)finish:(id)sender
{
    AVCaptureConnection *connection = [self.stillImageOutput
        connectionWithMediaType:AVMediaTypeVideo];

    //[[self.stillImageOutput connectionWithMediaType:AVMediaTypeVideo]
        setVideoOrientation:[connection videoOrientation]];

    [self.stillImageOutput
        captureStillImageAsynchronouslyFromConnection:connection
        completionHandler:^(CMSampleBufferRef imageDataSampleBuffer,
        NSError *error) {

        if (imageDataSampleBuffer != nil) {

            NSData *imageData = [AVCaptureStillImageOutput
             jpegStillImageNSDataRepresentation:imageDataSampleBuffer];

            UIImage *image = [UIImage imageWithData:imageData];

            [self.delegate didFinishWithImage:image];
        } else {

            NSLog(@"error description: %@", [error description]);

            [self.delegate cancel];
        }

    }];
```

> **Note**   EXIF (Exchangeable Image File Format) metadata is an industry standard for capturing information about a picture that was taken. Your iOS capture device produces values that include exposure, orientation, date taken, and flash setting. You can find a complete listing of all valid key/value pairs in Apple's "CGImageProperties Reference" (available in Apple's online iOS Developer Library).

Because the goal is to implement a workflow much like `UIImagePickerController`, you want to dismiss the camera interface as soon as the user has taken a picture. To speed up the process, and free up the camera for other processes, call the `[AVCaptureSession stopRunning]` method on the session in the `[UIViewController viewWillDisappear]` method for the camera controller class, as shown in Listing 4-7.

Listing 4-7. Stopping the Capture Session

```
- (void)viewWillDisappear:(BOOL)animated
{
    [super viewWillDisappear:animated];
    [self.session stopRunning];
}
```

> **Caution**   The old method for cleaning up view controllers, `[UIViewController viewDidUnload]`, has been deprecated starting with iOS 6.0. Do not attempt to define this function, as your code will never be called.

Accessing Hardware Controls

The final component to complete the custom camera controller is an interface to configure the camera's capture settings. This sample application focuses on switching cameras (for example, front/rear) and configuring the flash, autofocus, and exposure settings. These examples demonstrate two important patterns with camera development:

- You must always lock your device configuration before changing it.
- You should use touch events to drive area-specific settings (for example, autofocus, exposure).

Switching Cameras

The first hardware control you will build is a button that allows users to switch between the front and rear cameras on the device. Much like the default camera in iOS, the example will retain the ability to see a live preview of the camera output and take pictures, and allow users to toggle the cameras as often as they like. Remembering what you learned earlier about AVFoundation's capture stack, you can implement camera switching by switching the active input on the session.

To switch cameras at runtime, you need to maintain pointers to each hardware device. Whereas in the earlier example, you found the default camera device using the [AVCaptureDevice defaultDeviceWithMediaType] instance method, this time you need to maintain an array of devices. The method that returns an array of AVCaptureDevice objects is [AVCaptureDevice devicesWithMediaType:]:

```
self.cameraArray = [AVCaptureDevice
                    devicesWithMediaType:AVMediaTypeVideo];
```

Initialize the NSArray as an instance variable of the target class, because you need to be able to query it again before switching cameras (in other words, you should not allow the user to switch cameras if they're using a device with only one camera).

You can use the _position_ property of the AVCaptureDevice to determine the front and rear cameras. As with the earlier example, you need to create an AVCaptureDeviceInput object to tie the AVCaptureDevice to the capture session. This example initializes device objects as instance variables to make it easy to modify their capture settings later. Similarly, you should initialize input objects as instance variables so you can toggle devices later. You toggle devices by switching the active input object on the session. You can find an example which illustrates this process in Listing 4-8.

Listing 4-8. Initializing the Camera Inputs

```
-(void)initializeCameras
{
    NSArray *cameraArray = [AVCaptureDevice
                            devicesWithMediaType:AVMediaTypeVideo];

    NSError *error = nil;

    self.rearCamera = nil;
    self.frontCamera = nil;

    if ([self.cameraArray count] > 1) {

        for (AVCaptureDevice *camera in self.cameraArray) {
            if (camera.position == AVCaptureDevicePositionBack) {
                self.rearCamera = camera;
            } else if (camera.position == AVCaptureDevicePositionFront)
            {
                self.frontCamera = camera;
            }
        }
```

```
        self.rearCameraInput = [AVCaptureDeviceInput
                                deviceInputWithDevice:self.rearCamera
                                error:&error];
        self.frontCameraInput = [AVCaptureDeviceInput
                                deviceInputWithDevice:self.frontCamera
                                error:&error];

    } else {
        self.rearCamera = [AVCaptureDevice
            defaultDeviceWithMediaType:AVMediaTypeVideo];
        self.rearCameraInput = [AVCaptureDeviceInput
            deviceInputWithDevice:self.rearCamera
            error:&error];
    }

    self.currentDevice = self.rearCamera;
}
```

You can see that the code in Listing 4-8 falls back to the default capture device if the camera array contains only one object. Because the capture setting changes affect only the device the user has set to active, the code also keeps a pointer to the current device.

Now that you have pointers for each capture device, you need to implement the code to switch the active camera when the user presses the Camera button in the preview view. In this example, we have implemented the method with a return type of IBAction, because it is an event handler tied to an object in Interface Builder (in this case, the Camera button). If the device has two cameras, the app displays a multiple-choice action sheet to allow users to save their selection. If there is a failure, it displays an error alert. You can find a handler method that performs all of the initialization code in Listing 4-9.

Listing 4-9. Action Sheet for Selecting a Camera

```
-(IBAction)switchCamera:(id)sender {

    if ([self.cameraArray count] > 1) {

        //present an action sheet

        UIActionSheet *cameraSheet = [[UIActionSheet alloc]
            initWithTitle:@"Choose Camera"
            delegate:self cancelButtonTitle:@"Cancel"
            destructiveButtonTitle:nil
            otherButtonTitles:@"Front Camera", @"Rear Camera", nil];
        cameraSheet.tag = 100;
        [cameraSheet showInView:self.view];

    } else {
        //we only have one camera, show an error message

        UIAlertView *alert = [[UIAlertView alloc]
                            initWithTitle:@"Error"
```

```
            message:@"You only have one camera" delegate:nil
                cancelButtonTitle:@"OK"
                otherButtonTitles:nil];
        [alert show];
    }

}
```

To support the action sheet, you need to declare the view controller as a delegate. To do that, modify the class signature as shown here:

```
@interface CameraViewController : UIViewController
        <UIActionSheetDelegate>
```

In the action sheet button handler, [UIActionSheetDelegate actionSheet:didDismissWithButton Index:], the main logic checks the tag of the incoming action sheet, and passes the button index to the target method. In this case, you want to pass it to the switchToCameraWithIndex: method, as shown in Listing 4-10.

Listing 4-10. Action Sheet Button Handler

```
-(void) actionSheet:(UIActionSheet *)actionSheet
        didDismissWithButtonIndex:(NSInteger)buttonIndex
{
    switch (actionSheet.tag) {
        case 100:
            [self switchToCameraWithIndex:buttonIndex];
            break;
    }
}
```

You are now ready to implement the code to switch the active camera. The ultimate target of the change operation will be the capture session, because you add or remove input devices to or from a session. To prevent conflicts, you need to "take a lock" on the target object to indicate you will be changing the capture settings, before committing any changes. The lock for AVCaptureSession is [AVCaptureSession beginConfiguration]:

```
[self.session beginConfiguration];
```

Next, you need to line the button selections up to the target devices. Action sheet button indexes progress in a top-down manner, meaning the topmost item will have an index of 0. In this example, Front Camera is the top item. You switch to the front camera by removing the rear camera as an input on the capture session, and then adding the front camera input. To mirror the selection, you also need to update the currentDevice pointer in the class, and the label for the Switch Camera button:

```
if (buttonIndex == 0) { //front camera

        [self.session removeInput:self.rearCameraInput];

        if ([self.session canAddInput:self.frontCameraInput]) {
            [self.session addInput:self.frontCameraInput];
        }
```

```
    self.cameraButton.titleLabel.text = @"Camera: Front";
    self.currentDevice = self.frontCamera;


}
```

For the final product, add an `else` `if` statement for the Rear Camera option in the action sheet, and release the configuration lock for the session object, as shown in Listing 4-11.

Listing 4-11. Complete Implementation for Switching Between Two Cameras

```
-(void)switchToCameraWithIndex:(NSInteger)buttonIndex
{
    [self.session beginConfiguration];

    if (buttonIndex == 0) {

        [self.session removeInput:self.rearCameraInput];

        if ([self.session canAddInput:self.frontCameraInput]) {
            [self.session addInput:self.frontCameraInput];
        }

        self.cameraButton.titleLabel.text = @"Camera: Front";
        self.currentDevice = self.frontCamera;

    } else if (buttonIndex == 1) {

        [self.session removeInput:self.frontCameraInput];

        if ([self.session canAddInput:self.rearCameraInput]) {
            [self.session addInput:self.rearCameraInput];
        }

        self.cameraButton.titleLabel.text = @"Camera: Rear";
        self.currentDevice = self.frontCamera;
    }

    [self.session commitConfiguration];
}
```

Changing Flash Modes

Changing flash modes in the app follows a process very similar to changing cameras; the key exception is that you are operating on the AVCaptureDevice level, rather than the AVCaptureSession level. Much like the Change Camera example, this example uses a button to change flash modes, and presents users with an action sheet to make their selection. The flash modes supported by iOS are Automatic, On, and Off.

The code in Listing 4-12 checks whether the current input device supports flash mode before presenting the picker. This error-checking step is critical, because it allows the app to support older iPhones and circumvents the assumption that all the system's built-in cameras support the flash feature. On many devices, the front camera does not have a flash.

Listing 4-12. Change Flash Mode Event Handler

```
-(IBAction)flashMode:(id)sender {
    if ([self.currentDevice isFlashAvailable]) {
        UIActionSheet *cameraSheet = [[UIActionSheet alloc]
                                      initWithTitle:@"Flash Mode"
                                      delegate:self
                                      cancelButtonTitle:@"Cancel"
                                      destructiveButtonTitle:nil
                                      otherButtonTitles:@"Auto",
                                      @"On" , @"Off", nil];
        cameraSheet.tag = 101;
        [cameraSheet showInView:self.view];
    } else {
        //
        UIAlertView *alert = [[UIAlertView alloc]
                              initWithTitle:@"Error"
                              message:@"Flash not supported"
                              delegate:nil
                              cancelButtonTitle:@"OK"
                              otherButtonTitles:nil];
        [alert show];
    }
}
```

The next step is to expand the action sheet button handler to support this new action sheet, as shown in Listing 4-13. Give the action sheet a unique tag so you can identify it.

Listing 4-13. Modified Action Sheet Button Handler

```
-(void) actionSheet:(UIActionSheet *)actionSheet
      didDismissWithButtonIndex:(NSInteger)buttonIndex
{
    switch (actionSheet.tag) {
        case 100:
            [self switchToCameraWithIndex:buttonIndex];
            break;
        case 101:
            [self switchToFlashWithIndex:buttonIndex];
            break;
        default:
            break;
    }
}
```

You switch a device's flash mode by setting its flashMode property. Listing 4-14 uses a switch statement at the beginning of the [switchToFlashWithIndex:] method to correlate button selections with valid flashMode constants. To commit the configuration change, try to take the lock for the device, and then release it when you are done. As additional error checking, the example makes sure the device supports the selected flash mode before trying to set it.

Listing 4-14. Changing the Flash Mode for a Device

```
-(void)switchToFlashWithIndex:(NSInteger)buttonIndex
{
    NSError *error = nil;

    AVCaptureFlashMode flashMode = 0;

    switch (buttonIndex) {
        case 0: {
            flashMode = AVCaptureFlashModeAuto;
            self.flashButton.titleLabel.text = @"Flash: Auto";
            break;
        }
        case 1: {
            flashMode = AVCaptureFlashModeOn;
            self.flashButton.titleLabel.text = @"Flash: On";
            break;
        }
        case 2: {
            flashMode = AVCaptureFlashModeOff;
            self.flashButton.titleLabel.text = @"Flash: Off";
            break;
        }
        default:
            break;
    }

    if ([self.currentDevice lockForConfiguration:&error]) {

        self.currentDevice.flashMode = flashMode;

        [self.currentDevice unlockForConfiguration];
    } else {
        NSLog(@"could not set flash mode");
    }

}
```

Changing Autofocus Modes

Setting the autofocus modes on the camera follows the exact same process as setting the flash (presenting an action sheet, choosing a mode, and querying for compatibility before committing). But there is one major addition: you need to define a focal point for the camera.

As with previous examples, this example uses a button handler to present an action sheet if the current camera device supports autofocus, as shown in Listing 4-15.

Listing 4-15. Change Focus Mode Button Handler

```
-(IBAction)focusMode:(id)sender {
    if ([self.currentDevice isFocusPointOfInterestSupported]) {
        UIActionSheet *focusSheet = [[UIActionSheet alloc]
                                     initWithTitle:@"Focus Mode"
                                     delegate:self
                                     cancelButtonTitle:@"Cancel"
                                     destructiveButtonTitle:nil
                                     otherButtonTitles:@"Auto",
                                         @"Continuous Auto" ,
                                         @"Fixed", nil];
        focusSheet.tag = 102;
        [focusSheet showInView:self.view];
    } else {
        //
        UIAlertView *alert = [[UIAlertView alloc]
                              initWithTitle:@"Error"
                              message:@"Autofocus not supported"
                              delegate:nil
                              cancelButtonTitle:@"OK"
                              otherButtonTitles:nil];
        [alert show];
    }
}
```

As with the previous examples, expand the action sheet handler to support the new sheet, as shown in Listing 4-16.

Listing 4-16. Modified Action Sheet Handler

```
-(void) actionSheet:(UIActionSheet *)actionSheet
        didDismissWithButtonIndex:(NSInteger)buttonIndex
{
    switch (actionSheet.tag) {
        case 100:
            [self switchToCameraWithIndex:buttonIndex];
            break;
        case 101:
            [self switchToFlashWithIndex:buttonIndex];
            break;
        case 102:
            [self switchToFocusWithIndex:buttonIndex];
            break;
        default:
            break;
    }
}
```

Just as when changing flash mode, the code converts the button options to valid constants, takes a configuration lock, and commits the changes if they are supported by the device. You can find a method that encapsulates the autofocus mode switching logic in Listing 4-17.

Listing 4-17.   Switching Autofocus Modes

```
-(void)switchToFocusWithIndex:(NSInteger)buttonIndex
{
    NSError *error = nil;

    AVCaptureFocusMode focusMode = 0;

    switch (buttonIndex) {
        case 0: {
            focusMode = AVCaptureFocusModeAutoFocus;
            self.focusButton.titleLabel.text = @"Focus: Auto";
            break;
        }
        case 1: {
            focusMode = AVCaptureFocusModeContinuousAutoFocus;
            self.focusButton.titleLabel.text = @"Focus: Cont";
            break;
        }
        case 2: {
            focusMode = AVCaptureFocusModeLocked;
            self.focusButton.titleLabel.text = @"Focus: Fixed";
            break;
        }
        default:
            break;
    }

    if ([self.currentDevice lockForConfiguration:&error] &&
        [self.currentDevice
        isFocusModeSupported:focusMode]) {

        self.currentDevice.focusMode = focusMode;

        [self.currentDevice unlockForConfiguration];
    } else {
        NSLog(@"could not set focus mode");
    }

}
```

By default, the focal point is at the center of the screen, but often a user will have a subject in the left or right third of the frame. To fully take advantage of autofocus, you want to let the user refocus the camera to some new focal point. When using the default camera in iOS, you may remember that a rectangle appears when you press the screen. This happens through the use of a UITapGestureRecognizer object.

Gesture recognizers allow you to call a method when a touch gesture from the user (such as tapping the screen or pinching your fingers in/out) occurs, and provides you with properties such as where the touch event happened on the screen. The signature for a gesture recognizer handler method looks similar to that of a normal event handler, except the parameter type is UIGestureRecognizer:

```
-(IBAction)didTapPreview:(UIGestureRecognizer *)gestureRecognizer;
```

You use the method [UIGestureRecognizer locationInView:] to determine the x and y coordinates of the touch event, relative to the origin of the view you pass in as an input parameter.

To configure the camera to focus to a specific point, use the instance method [AVCaptureDevice setFocusPointOfInterest:focusPoint]. The input parameter is a CGPoint object with x and y values between 0.0 and 1.0 that correspond to the relative position of the focal point within the frame. For example, a value of (0.5, 0.75) would center the focal point horizontally, and place it one-fourth of the way above the bottom of the frame, vertically.

You convert gesture recognizer touch coordinates from absolute to relative positions by dividing the touch event's x position by the frame's width, and dividing the touch event's y position by the frame's height, as shown in Listing 4-18.

Listing 4-18. Converting Absolute Positions to Relative Positions

```
CGPoint tapPoint = [gestureRecognizer
                    locationInView:gestureRecognizer.view];
CGFloat relativeX = tapPoint.x / self.previewView.frame.size.width;
CGFloat relativeY = tapPoint.y / self.previewView.frame.size.height;
CGPoint focusPoint = CGPointMake(relativeX, relativeY);
```

Finally, tie everything together by adding the position code and capture setting configuration code into the gesture recognizer handler, as shown in Listing 4-19.

Listing 4-19. Setting Focal Point from a Tap Gesture Handler

```
-(void)didTapPreview:(UIGestureRecognizer *)gestureRecognizer
{
    CGPoint tapPoint = [gestureRecognizer
        locationInView:gestureRecognizer.view];
    CGFloat relativeX = tapPoint.x / self.previewView.frame.size.width;
    CGFloat relativeY = tapPoint.y /
        self.previewView.frame.size.height;
    CGPoint focusPoint = CGPointMake(relativeX, relativeY);

    AVCaptureFocusMode focusMode = self.currentDevice.focusMode;

    NSError *error = nil;

    if ([self.currentDevice isFocusPointOfInterestSupported] &&
        [self.currentDevice isFocusModeSupported:focusMode])
    {
        if ([self.currentDevice lockForConfiguration:&error])
        {
            [self.currentDevice setFocusMode:focusMode];
```

```
        [self.currentDevice setFocusPointOfInterest:focusPoint];
        [self.currentDevice unlockForConfiguration];
    }
}

    self.tapPosition.text = [NSString stringWithFormat:
                            @"Tap Position: (%0.f, %0.f)",
                            tapPoint.x, tapPoint.y];
}
```

Changing Exposure Modes

Modifying exposure settings has all of the same properties and background knowledge requirements as changing autofocus settings:

- Use a button and action sheet to select exposure mode.

- Query for compatibility before setting desired exposure mode.

- Set the focal point for exposure settings based on a touch event.

Therefore, the button handler should look very familiar. The major difference is that this functionality will allow the user to select only Continuous Auto-Exposure or Fixed Exposure. You can find a button handler that presents the exposure mode action sheet in Listing 4-20.

Listing 4-20. Action Sheet Button Handler, Including Exposure

```
-(IBAction)exposureMode:(id)sender {
    if ([self.currentDevice isExposurePointOfInterestSupported]) {
        //
        UIActionSheet *exposureSheet =
            [[UIActionSheet alloc]
                initWithTitle:@"Exposure Mode"
                delegate:self
                cancelButtonTitle:@"Cancel"
                destructiveButtonTitle:nil
                otherButtonTitles:@"Continuous Auto" , @"Fixed", nil];
        exposureSheet.tag = 103;
        [exposureSheet showInView:self.view];
    } else {
        //
        UIAlertView *alert = [[UIAlertView alloc]
                                initWithTitle:@"Error"
                                message:@"Flash not supported"
                                delegate:nil
                                cancelButtonTitle:@"OK"
                                otherButtonTitles:nil];
        [alert show];
    }
}
```

The final action sheet handler adds the tag for the exposure sheet, as shown in Listing 4-21.

Listing 4-21. Exposure Mode Button Handler

```
-(void) actionSheet:(UIActionSheet *)actionSheet didDismissWithButtonIndex:(NSInteger)buttonIndex
{
    switch (actionSheet.tag) {
        case 100:
            [self switchToCameraWithIndex:buttonIndex];
            break;
        case 101:
            [self switchToFlashWithIndex:buttonIndex];
            break;
        case 102:
            [self switchToFocusWithIndex:buttonIndex];
            break;
        case 103:
            [self switchToExposureWithIndex:buttonIndex];
            break;
        default:
            break;
    }
}
```

You set exposure settings in the manner that should now be extremely familiar—converting indices to constants, and taking a lock, as shown in Listing 4-22.

Listing 4-22. Setting Exposure Mode

```
-(void)switchToExposureWithIndex:(NSInteger)buttonIndex
{
    NSError *error = nil;

    AVCaptureExposureMode exposureMode = 0;

    switch (buttonIndex) {
        case 0: {
            exposureMode = AVCaptureExposureModeContinuousAutoExposure;
            self.exposureButton.titleLabel.text = @"Exposure: Cont";
            break;
        }
        case 1: {
            exposureMode = AVCaptureExposureModeLocked;
            self.exposureButton.titleLabel.text = @"Exposure: Fixed";
            break;
        }
    }

    if ([self.currentDevice isExposureModeSupported:exposureMode] &&
        [self.currentDevice lockForConfiguration:&error]) {
```

```
    self.currentDevice.exposureMode = exposureMode;

    [self.currentDevice unlockForConfiguration];
} else {
    NSLog(@"could not set exposure mode");
}

}
```

The final gesture recognizer duplicates the autofocus logic, except for exposure, as shown in Listing 4-23.

Listing 4-23. Tap Gesture Recognizer, Including Exposure Settings

```
-(void)didTapPreview:(UIGestureRecognizer *)gestureRecognizer
{
    CGPoint tapPoint = [gestureRecognizer
                        locationInView:gestureRecognizer.view];
    CGFloat relativeX = tapPoint.x / self.previewView.frame.size.width;
    CGFloat relativeY = tapPoint.y /
                        self.previewView.frame.size.height;
    CGPoint focusPoint = CGPointMake(relativeX, relativeY);

    AVCaptureExposureMode exposureMode =
                        self.currentDevice.exposureMode;
    AVCaptureFocusMode focusMode = self.currentDevice.focusMode;

    NSError *error = nil;

    if ([self.currentDevice lockForConfiguration:&error])
    {
        if ([self.currentDevice isFocusPointOfInterestSupported] &&
            [self.currentDevice isFocusModeSupported:focusMode])
        {
            [self.currentDevice setFocusMode:focusMode];
            [self.currentDevice setFocusPointOfInterest:focusPoint];
        }
        if ([self.currentDevice isExposurePointOfInterestSupported] &&
            [self.currentDevice isExposureModeSupported:exposureMode])
        {
            [self.currentDevice setExposureMode:exposureMode];
            [self.currentDevice setExposurePointOfInterest:focusPoint];
        }
        [self.currentDevice unlockForConfiguration];
    }

    self.tapPosition.text =
        [NSString stringWithFormat:@"Tap Position: (%0.f, %0.f)",
                                tapPoint.x, tapPoint.y];
}
```

Handling Different Screen Sizes

While you do not need to add any extra configuration options to your AVCaptureSession to handle different screen sizes (for example, the iPad, iPhone 4S, or iPhone 5), you will want to make sure you are following the best practices for universal (multi-device) user interface development.

If you are using one storyboard for both your tablet and phone user interfaces, make sure you have enabled auto-layout for your camera controller interface so that it will grow (or shrink) with your screen size. It is a good idea to assign fixed dimensions to your controls while letting the preview area adjust to fill your screen size.

In contrast, if you are using separate storyboards for your tablet and phone user interfaces, remember to lay out your camera controller on both storyboards. Make sure all your outlets and actions are set correctly on both storyboards, and try to optimize your user interface for each device. You may find that short captions or a limited set of exposed configuration options are appropriate for a phone interface, while expanded captions and a comprehensive set of configuration options are perfect for a tablet interface. Once again, try to let your preview area expand with the screen, as it is your user's primary feedback interface.

Caution   Remember, auto-layout is not available for NIB-based user interfaces, so be careful to duplicate your changes across all screen-size versions of an interface, or begin transitioning over to storyboards.

Building a Custom Image Picker

In this section, you will build a custom image picker, using the same logic as with the custom camera controller—to implement use cases. Apple does not provide a UIImagePickerController out of the box. For this app, you want to be able to theme the image picker, and be able to select multiple images before returning to the original view. Figure 4-4 shows a flow diagram and mock-up of the image picker.

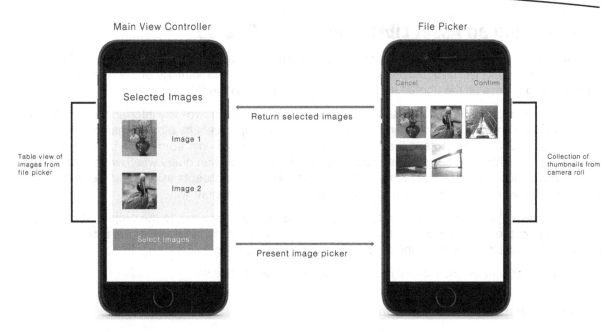

Figure 4-4. Flow diagram and mock-up of the custom image picker

Much like a UIImagePickerController, you want to present the image picker modally, dismissing it after users confirm their selection(s). Because this example adds functionality to a familiar user interface, it presents the thumbnail images in a grid implemented via the UICollectionView class. The app represents a selection by highlighting the selected item and displaying a filled-in check box over it. Deselecting an item will undo both those state changes. The app destroys the modal view after users have confirmed their changes or decided to cancel the view. The selected images will appear in a scrollable table view on the parent view controller.

To accomplish this workflow, you need to perform the following steps, which are covered in this section:

1. Initialize a data source containing images from the camera roll.

2. Present these images in a UICollectionView.

3. Configure the UICollectionView to allow multiple selections.

4. Create a programmatic interface for returning selected images.

You'll be using the Assets Library framework as the data source. Because this framework and the UICollectionView class may be unfamiliar to most readers, you'll also see background information on both.

You can find the source code for this application in the Chapter 4 folder of the source code bundle. This project is called MyPicker.

Instantiating an Asset Library as a Data Source

The first step in building the photo browser is to instantiate a data source. While there is no API that will allow you to just "get all UIImages on the device," you can take advantage of the Assets Library framework to access all the photos and videos available through the Photos app.

Asset libraries, represented by the ALAssetsLibrary class, provide a two-way interface to the Photos app for reading and writing photos and videos. You can look up assets by album, unique URL, or media type, and save assets to the Photos app or create new albums from within your apps. Additionally, as with other apps that access shared resources, you can query whether your app has permission to access the photos. While iOS does not have such concepts as a global file system, limited interfaces like this allow apps to share data in a safe, consistent way.

To instantiate an Asset Library, you first add the AssetsLibrary.framework to the project. As with the MyCamera project, you can add the framework to your project by adding it to the Linked Frameworks and Libraries array under your project's general settings.

After adding the framework, include its header file in the target class:

```
#import <AssetsLibrary/AssetsLibrary.h>
```

> **Note**   The import keyword allows you to reduce code size by checking for duplicates before adding a file, unlike the include keyword.

Now that the groundwork is in place, you can instantiate an Assets Library:

```
ALAssetsLibrary *assetsLibrary = [[ALAssetsLibrary alloc] init];
```

Just as you need to select an album or timeline to view photos from the Photos app, you need to specify a *group* to discover assets through an Asset Library. Represented by the ALAssetGroup class, asset groups allow you to access a subset of assets from the Photos app based on one or more filters. While asset groups allow you to replicate some of the functionality of an NSSet, such as providing the number of items in the set, they also allow for more-advanced functionality and can provide information such as a thumbnail image for a group or permission status.

To retrieve an asset group, use the Asset Library API [ALAssetsLibrary enumerateGroupsWithTypes: usingBlock:failureBlock]. You pass this API an NSInteger that represents the filters to include in the search, a block that will be called each time an ALAssetGroup is found, and a block that will be called if a failure occurs. Because there is no way of guaranteeing how processor- or time-intensive group lookup will be (a user could have hundreds of albums, many of which are hidden), block syntax is appropriate for this API. Blocks make apps faster by giving developers a way to run snippets of code in the background, freeing up the main thread for time-sensitive operations, such as feedback from user-interface elements (for example, catching button presses).

Listing 4-24 returns groups that represent photos in the Saved Photos and Photo Stream galleries. The example prints log messages upon success or failure.

Listing 4-24. Enumerating Asset Groups

```
NSInteger photoFilters = ALAssetsGroupPhotoStream |
                         ALAssetsGroupSavedPhotos;

[assetsLibrary enumerateGroupsWithTypes:photoFilters
    usingBlock:^(ALAssetsGroup *group, BOOL *stop) {
        [group enumerateAssetsUsingBlock:^(ALAsset *result,
        NSUInteger index, BOOL *stop) {
            NSLog(@"success! asset found");
        }];

    } failureBlock:^(NSError *error) {
        NSLog(@"error! %@", [error description]);
    }
];
```

The filter values represent bits in a mask, so by ORing them together, you can combine filters. Table 4-2 shows a list of filter values and what they represent.

Table 4-2. Frequently Used Asset Group Filters

Constant	Asset Group
ALAssetsGroupLibrary	Library—all assets on the device, originating from iTunes
ALAssetsGroupAlbum	All albums on the device, except for Photo Stream or Shared Streams
ALAssetsGroupEvent	All Event albums
ALAssetsGroupFace	All Face albums
ALAssetsGroupSavedPhotos	Camera Roll album
ALAssetsGroupPhotoStream	Photo Stream album (iCloud)
ALAssetsGroupAll	All albums except for those coming from iTunes

Now that you have a set of asset groups ready, you can implement the logic to iterate through each individual asset. The ALAsset class represents assets. Much like ALAssetGroups, they are more intelligent than the base classes you might expect to represent such binary data. ALAssets maintain unique internal URLs corresponding to every version of an asset that exists, such as the original version and multiple edited versions. They also provide access to derived properties, such as thumbnails, for an asset, and even support saving new versions of assets.

To access the ALAssets represented by an ALAssetGroup, you use an API similar to the group discovery API: [ALAssetGroup enumerateAssetsUsingBlock:]. As with the group discovery API, the block you define will be called every time the API finds an asset and is ready to access. To keep things simple, this example appends every valid (non-nil), photo result to an NSMutableArray of assets. You'll use this data structure to populate the collection view later.

Listing 4-25. Enumerating Image Assets

```
self.assetsLibrary = [[ALAssetsLibrary alloc] init];
self.images = [NSMutableArray new];

NSInteger photoFilters = ALAssetsGroupPhotoStream |
                         ALAssetsGroupSavedPhotos;

[self.assetsLibrary enumerateGroupsWithTypes:photoFilters
    usingBlock:^(ALAssetsGroup *group, BOOL *stop) {
        [group enumerateAssetsUsingBlock:^(ALAsset *result, NSUInteger
                                            index, BOOL *stop) {
            if (result != nil) {
                    [self.images addObject:result];
            }
        }];
    } failureBlock:^(NSError *error) {
        NSLog(@"error! %@", [error description]);
    }
];
```

QUICK GUIDE TO BLOCKS

In Objective-C, blocks are a language feature that allow you to specify *anonymous methods*—pieces of code that act like a method but do not need to be declared with a signature. Blocks are a great way of creating a "disposable" method that is called from only one specific code path. Additionally, you can define blocks as a parameter for a method. Throughout this book, you will see mention of *completion blocks*; these are blocks defined in the method call that get called immediately when a method completes.

Block signatures have a jarring syntax compared to methods. The signature for a block is as follows:

```
void (^myBlock)(NSString* string1, NSString *string2, int count);
```

The first keyword, void, is the return type for the block. myBlock is the block name; it is always preceded by a caret symbol. The contents of the final set of parentheses are the parameter types. Blocks are closer to C in syntax style and do not require labels for parameters.

A block's signature specifies its return type, name, and parameters, just like a method's. To define a block, append the code for the block in curly braces, just as you would a method. Blocks are treated as *inline* functions by the compiler, meaning they do not break a line of code, so make sure you add a semicolon to the end of the line:

```
int finalPhotoCount = ^(int count1, int count2) {
    return count1+count2;};
```

You use the same syntax to call a block with parameters as you do a method, by specifying the parameter types and code for the block. For example, blocks were used to enumerate the assets and groups in Listing 4-25.

```
[group enumerateAssetsUsingBlock:^(ALAsset *result, NSUInteger index,
    BOOL *stop) {
        if (result != nil) {
            [self.images addObject:result];
        }
}];
```

One of the more perilous aspects of a block is that its variable scoping is different from that of a normal method. You can create local variables within a block, and you can access instance variables from outside the block. However, by default, all outside variables in a block are passed *by copy*, meaning you can see their contents, but you cannot modify them. To declare a local or instance variable so that it can be modified by a block, you need to add the __block keyword in front of its type:

```
__block NSInteger photoCount;
```

You use a similar pattern for instance variables, adding the __block keyword after the attributes and before the type:

```
@property (nonatomic, assign) __block NSInteger photoCount;
```

Using a block is like driving a Ferrari without brakes. You can go incredibly fast, but you need to be aware of your limitations and how to work around them.

Using the UICollectionView Class to Enumerate Assets

If you built the examples in the previous section, you now have an array containing a set of assets that correspond to photos from the Saved Photos and Photo Stream galleries. At this point, you can build a collection view user interface to represent these items.

Introduced with iOS 6, *collection views* refer to the graphics-based navigation interface that you may be familiar with from the iBooks app, and from older versions of the Photos app (see Figure 4-5). In a collection view, items are generally represented by a graphical representation (such as album art or book covers), and flow from left to right, top to bottom. Much like with a table view, you define a data source for the view, specify what each item (called a *cell*) should look like, and define the behaviors that should occur when the user interacts with an item. Unlike a table view, you do not need to specify how many items will be in each column or row; the UICollectionView class will automatically fit items into the grid based on the cell size and the container view size. That makes it easy to pass in linear data sets. Similarly, you can group data in sections, as you would with a table view.

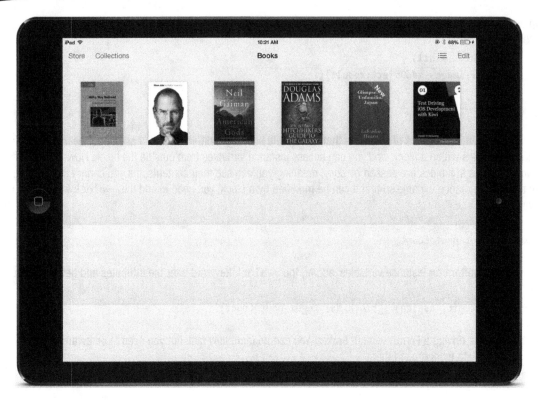

Figure 4-5. Screenshot of the collection view in iBooks

To add a collection view to the application, drag a Collection View Controller from Interface Builder's object library. Make sure you instantiate your own subclass of UICollectionViewController so that you can tie the data source to the view, and implement your own action handlers. If you are implementing an iPad interface, remember to duplicate these settings in the iPad storyboard as well. You can find a screenshot of the storyboard in Figure 4-6.

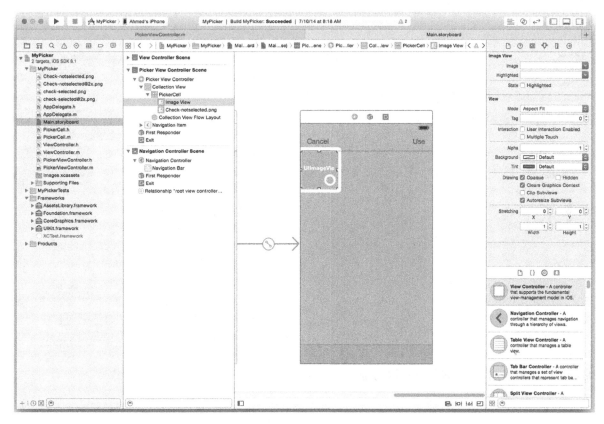

Figure 4-6. Adding a collection view in Interface Builder

The easiest way to think of a `UICollectionView` is as a more advanced `UITableView`. Like a table view, a collection view needs to be initialized with an array of data, and each item is represented by a cell. For the MyPicker project, you will want each cell to contain an image and a check box representing its state.

The default Interface Builder template for a `UICollectionView` comes with an empty `UICollectionViewCell`. In order to make it display two images (one for the contents and one for the check box), you need to follow these steps:

1. Create a new subclass of `UICollectionViewCell`. Set this as the parent class for your cell (use the Interface Builder attributes inspector for this).

2. Give the cell a new reuse identifier (use the Interface Builder attributes inspector for this).

3. Add two `UIImage` properties to the cell to represent the image and check box. Tie these to your class by using Xcode.

When working with a `UICollectionViewCell`, make sure you have the cell selected in Interface Builder; otherwise, you will have trouble modifying it. As shown in Figure 4-7, you can easily select items by using the Scene Navigator in Interface Builder (the left pane).

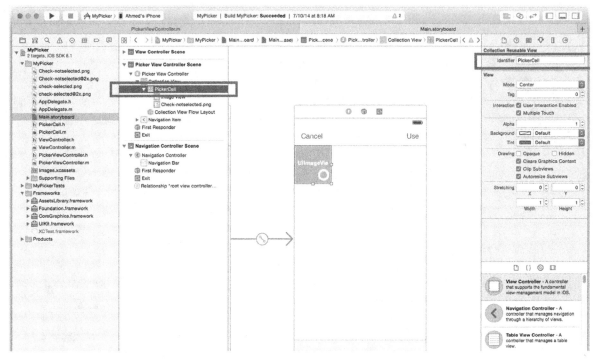

Figure 4-7. Setting a reuse identifier in Interface Builder

> **Note**   If you are having trouble setting your reuse identifier, make sure you have selected the
> UICollectionViewCell, not one of its subviews.

Much as with a UITableView, you need to implement a series of delegate methods to fully realize
the collection view. The first step is to let the collection view know how many sections the data
source has, and how many rows you want in each section. You define the number of sections by
implementing the [UICollectionViewDataSource numberOfSectionsInCollectionView] protocol
method. In this method, the return type is an integer that specifies the number of sections. This
simple example loads assets from a one-dimensional array, so you can return 1 as the number of
sections, as shown in Listing 4-26.

Listing 4-26. Initializing Collection View Section Count

```
- (NSInteger)numberOfSectionsInCollectionView:(UICollectionView *)collectionView
{
    return 1;
}
```

The real configuration work happens in defining the number of rows for each section. For this example, the number of rows is equal to the number of items in the array, so you can simply return the count property. You implement this in the delegate method, [UICollectionView numberOfItemsInSection:], which takes the section number as input and returns the row count, as shown in Listing 4-27.

Listing 4-27. Initializing Collection View Row Count

```
- (NSInteger)collectionView:(UICollectionView *)view numberOfItemsInSection:(NSInteger)section;
{
    return [self.images count];
}
```

You may run into timing issues, depending on where you initialize your input array. For example, if you make your Asset Library calls from the [UIViewController viewDidLoad] method, you will notice that the [UICollectionView numberOfItemsInSection:] method initializes the collection view with a count of 0, even if you have found several items. This is due to the asynchronous nature of block programming. Because the lookup code runs in the background, there is nothing preventing the system from executing the collection view initialization code immediately against the still-empty array.

While this may seem like a pretty big bug, it's nothing to worry about, because there's an API that lets you refresh the collection view's data source at any time. This API is [UICollectionView reloadData]. It immediately calls the [UICollectionView numberOfSections] and [UICollectionView numberOfItemsInSection:] methods again, which then return accurate initialization values. All you need to do is call that method when you are confident the array has been fully populated. The sample application calls it when it has finished iterating through all the groups. The refresh code block is illustrated in Listing 4-28.

Listing 4-28. Refreshing the Collection View

```
[self.assetsLibrary enumerateGroupsWithTypes:photoFilters
    usingBlock:^(ALAssetsGroup *group, BOOL *stop) {
    [group enumerateAssetsUsingBlock:^(ALAsset *result, NSUInteger
                                        index, BOOL *stop) {
    if (result != nil) {
        [self.images addObject:result];
    }
}];

    [self.collectionView reloadData];
} failureBlock:^(NSError *error) {
    NSLog(@"error! %@", [error description]);
}];
```

Now that you can be confident about the data source, you need to make sure each UICollectionViewCell is initialized with information from the assets. You initialize the cells using the [UICollectionView cellForItemAtIndexPath:] method, where the inputs are the collection view and the NSIndexPath value for each item. Following the pattern of initializing table view cells, the first step is to retrieve a cell to work on, which you do with the [UICollectionView dequeueReusableCellWith ReuseIdentifier:forIndexPath:] method. Pass in the indexPath and the reuse identifier you defined in Interface Builder. To access the image view for the custom cells, make sure to cast the object after retrieving it. You can find the basic initialization code in Listing 4-29.

Listing 4-29. Initializing a Collection View Cell

```
- (UICollectionViewCell *)collectionView:(
        UICollectionView *)collectionView
            cellForItemAtIndexPath:(NSIndexPath *)indexPath
{
    PickerCell *cell = (PickerCell *)[collectionView
        dequeueReusableCellWithReuseIdentifier:@"PickerCell"
            forIndexPath:indexPath];

    return cell;
}
```

Having retrieved the cell, you now need to retrieve the asset that goes with it. Because the data source is a one-dimensional array, you know that the row numbers will line up exactly with the index of each item in the array. Therefore, to retrieve each asset, all you need to do is call [NSArray objectAtIndex:] with the row property of the indexPath. If the data source were a multidimensional array, you could pass in the section number as well.

```
ALAsset *asset = [self.images objectAtIndex:indexPath.row];
```

An indexPath in Cocoa Touch is a two-dimensional array that contains sections (the first dimension) and rows (the second dimension). You need to translate an indexPath to a single-dimensional array by accessing its row contents for the current section, which is why you will often see indexPath.row used in a lot of code.

The goal for this sample application is to build a thumbnail browser, similar to the default one provided by the UIImagePickerController class. Although you could create your own thumbnail from the full image data stored in the ALAsset, in the interests of speed and memory, you should use the one available through the derived properties in the class. ALAsset exposes two properties: [ALAsset thumbnail] and [ALAsset aspectRatioThumbnail], which both return CGImageRefs, or pointers to image data, for each asset. The difference is that thumbnail returns a thumbnail cropped to a square aspect ratio, while aspectRatioThumbnail returns a thumbnail that preserves the original aspect ratio of the asset.

You can create a UIImage from the CGImageRef value using the initialization method [UIImage imageWithCGImage:], passing in the pointer directly. From there, you simply set the image property on the cell's image view, and you are good to go. You can find the completed initialization method for a cell in Listing 4-30.

Listing 4-30. Initializing a Collection View Cell with a Thumbnail

```
- (UICollectionViewCell *)collectionView:(
        UICollectionView *)collectionView
        cellForItemAtIndexPath:(NSIndexPath *)indexPath
{
    PickerCell *cell = (PickerCell *)[collectionView
    dequeueReusableCellWithReuseIdentifier:@"PickerCell"
        forIndexPath:indexPath];
```

```
ALAsset *asset = [self.images objectAtIndex:indexPath.row];
cell.imageView.image = [UIImage imageWithCGImage:asset.aspectRatioThumbnail];

    return cell;
}
```

Enabling Multiple Selection

As stated at the beginning of the chapter, one of the most compelling reasons for building your own image picker is to cover use cases that are not supported by Apple through the UIImagePickerController class, such as selecting multiple images at once. By taking advantage of UICollectionView's multiple selection APIs, you can fill this gap without too much extra work.

To enable multiple image selection, you need to perform three high-level tasks:

- Enable multiple-selection on the collection view
- Add or remove items to or from a data structure based on their selection status
- Update each item's user interface based on its selection status

To enable multiple-selection, all you need to do is enable the allowMultipleSelection flag on the collection view:

```
[self.collectionView setAllowsMultipleSelection:YES];
```

To return multiple images when users dismiss the custom image picker, you need to store the images to a data structure that grows or shrinks based on the user's selections. You could store the items in an NSMutableArray, but you would need to write your own wrapper code to make sure items do not already exist in the structure before adding them, which could slow down the app or increase its memory footprint. A more elegant solution is to use an NSMutableDictionary, keyed by asset index number. By keying assets directly to the index number, you are not dependent on what order items are added to the dictionary, and you can employ very fast, direct lookups. When users select an asset, you do not need to worry about duplicates, because you can tie only one object to the key. And when users deselect an asset, you can instantly find and remove the asset from the dictionary based on the index number.

The final step is to update the user interface to mirror changes in selection state. The two delegate methods needed to implement this behavior are [UICollectionView didDeselectItemAtIndexPath:] and [UICollectionView didSelectItemAtIndexPath:]. Much as when you were building the items, the core operations for these functions are to first look up the appropriate cell objects and then modify specific values. This application indicates that an item is selected by changing its background color and the state of an overlay image placed over the thumbnail. Since the app respects the original aspect ratio of the images, and the collection cells are square, there's some space to play with in the background. By adding an overlay image, you can also create an interface that users are familiar with from other apps that allow multiple item selection, such as the iOS mail app. The logic for selecting and deselecting cells is illustrated in Listing 4-31.

Listing 4-31. Logic for Selecting and Deselecting Collection View Cells

```
-(void)collectionView:(UICollectionView *)collectionView
        didSelectItemAtIndexPath:(NSIndexPath *)indexPath
{
    PickerCell *cell = (PickerCell *)[collectionView
        cellForItemAtIndexPath:indexPath];

    cell.overlayView.image = [UIImage imageNamed:@"Check-selected"];
    cell.imageView.backgroundColor = [UIColor whiteColor];

    [self.selectedImages setObject:[self.images
                                    objectAtIndex:indexPath.row]
                                    forKey:[NSNumber
                                    numberWithInteger:indexPath.row]];
}

- (void)collectionView:(UICollectionView *)collectionView
        didDeselectItemAtIndexPath:(NSIndexPath *)indexPath
{
    PickerCell *cell = (PickerCell *)[collectionView
        cellForItemAtIndexPath:indexPath];

    cell.overlayView.image = [UIImage imageNamed:@"Check-notselected"];
    cell.imageView.backgroundColor = [UIColor purpleColor];

    if ([self.selectedImages objectForKey:[NSNumber
                    numberWithInteger:indexPath.row]] != nil) {
        [self.selectedImages removeObjectForKey:[NSNumber
                    numberWithInteger:indexPath.row]];
    }

}
```

Creating an Interface for Returning Image Data

The final step for the custom image picker is to build a programmatic interface for returning the user's image selections back to the calling class. You also need a way of passing back a cancel message, indicating that the user did not select any images.

Harkening back to the earlier discussion of message passing, you may remember that there are several ways of building an interface between two classes, ranging from loose implementations such as notification and key/value observing, to very strict ones including protocols and delegation. While a notification-based system could work here, these systems are often more appropriate for background tasks or classes that want to subscribe to a service, meaning they could easily remove themselves as an observer and still operate fine. Because you are trying to build an experience that is similar to the native UIImagePickerController, you should try to use a design pattern similar to the native functionality, which includes defining specific messages and having a pointer back to the calling class. In this case, the most appropriate message-passing system would be delegation.

To specify which messages to pass, you must first define the protocol. In this case, you are going to pass either a didSelectImages message, along with a list of assets the user selected, or a cancel message, which indicates that the user selected nothing and wants to dismiss the image picker. To make life easier for the users of this interface, this implementation passes back an array of images with the didSelectImages message, and nothing with the cancel message. You can find an example of the protocol definition in Listing 4-32.

Listing 4-32. Defining a Protocol for the Image Picker

```
#import <UIKit/UIKit.h>
#import <AssetsLibrary/AssetsLibrary.h>

@protocol PickerDelegate <NSObject>

-(void)didSelectImages:(NSArray *)images;
-(void)cancel;

@end

@interface PickerViewController : UICollectionViewController

@property (nonatomic, strong) NSMutableArray *images;
@property (nonatomic, strong) ALAssetsLibrary *assetsLibrary;
@property (nonatomic, strong) NSMutableDictionary *selectedImages;
@property (nonatomic, weak) id <PickerDelegate> delegate;

-(IBAction)cancel:(id)sender;
-(IBAction)done:(id)sender;

@end
```

From within the image picker class, call the protocol methods in the action button handlers. The didSelectImages handler builds an array of assets to pass back by iterating through the selection dictionary and returning the image representations of the non-nil assets indicated by each index. For the cancel handler, you can simply send a cancel message to the delegate object. You can find these calls in Listing 4-33.

Listing 4-33. Calling Protocol Methods from the Image Picker

```
-(IBAction)done:(id)sender
{
    NSMutableArray *imageArray = [NSMutableArray new];
    for (id key in self.selectedImages.allKeys) {
        if ([self.selectedImages objectForKey:key] != nil) {
            [imageArray addObject:[self.selectedImages
                               objectForKey:key]];
        }
    }

    [self.delegate didSelectImages:imageArray];
}
```

```
-(IBAction)cancel:(id)sender
{

    [self.delegate cancel];
}
```

In the parent view controller, which calls the image picker, declare that you'll be using a delegate for the image picker class within the class signature when you instantiate the image picker, as shown in Listing 4-34.

Listing 4-34. Specifying That the Target Class Implements the Picker Protocol

```
@interface ViewController : UIViewController <PickerDelegate,
                            UITableViewDelegate, UITableViewDataSource>
```

Although that code declares the class as a delegate of the picker protocol, you still need to initialize it.

The delegate method implementations tell the table view to load the thumbnails from the asset array upon receiving a didSelectImages message, and then dismiss the image picker controller. Or, for a cancel message, it simply needs to dismiss the image picker controller to get back to the normal user interface. You can find examples of the picker delegate methods in Listing 4-35.

Listing 4-35. Implementing the Picker Delegate Methods

```
#pragma mark - Picker Delegate methods

-(void)cancel
{
    [self dismissViewControllerAnimated:YES completion:nil];
}

-(void)didSelectImages:(NSArray *)images
{
    [self dismissViewControllerAnimated:YES completion:nil];

    self.imageArray = [images copy];

    [self.tableView reloadData];
}
```

Creating Image Data from Asset Representations

Now that you have created an interface to pass back selected assets, there's one more step required to make it work more like the native image picker: it needs to return some UIImage objects. To extract the original image data from an ALAsset, you need to perform the following steps:

- Extract the desired version, or *representation*, of the asset to an ALAssetRepresentation object.

- Save a pointer to the image data for the asset by using the [ALAssetRepresentation fullResolutionImage] instance method.

- Query the ALAsset's metadata to determine the correct orientation for the image.

- Create a UIImage object based on the orientation and the extracted CGImageRef.

As mentioned earlier in the chapter, one of the strengths of the ALAsset class is its ability to store not only raw image data, but also metadata and multiple versions of an image (called *representations*). A representation can cover such changes as different compression formats or resolutions. The ALAssetRepresentation class stores representation information and has instance methods that let you query for image pointers, metadata, raw data, and storage URLs/UTIs (universal type identifiers).

You create an ALAssetRepresentation object from an ALAsset object either by passing in the UTI for the desired representation or by calling [ALAsset defaultRepresentation], which returns the first available, saved representation of an image:

```
ALAssetRepresentation *defaultRepresentation = [asset defaultRepresentation];
```

Similarly, you can get a pointer to the image data for a representation by calling the [ALAssetRepresentation fullResolutionImage] instance method on the representation object. The return type is CGImageRef, a pointer to image data, which reduces object size and increases speed (similar to ALAsset thumbnails).

```
CGImageRef imagePtr = [defaultRepresentation fullResolutionImage];
```

To create a UIImage object from a CGImageRef, use the [UIImage imageFromCGImage:] or [UIImage imageFromCGImage:scale:orientation:] instance methods. As it is an extremely common use case for people to take pictures in landscape or portrait mode, you should initialize the image with orientation data to make sure it displays correctly. The instance method takes a UIImageOrientation scalar as its input, so you need to query the ALAsset object for the orientation information. Set the default value to UIImageOrientationUp—just in case no orientation information is available. You can find an This process is illustrated in Listing 4-36.

Listing 4-36. Querying for Asset Orientation

```
UIImageOrientation imageOrientation = UIImageOrientationUp;
NSNumber *orientation =
    [asset valueForProperty:@"ALAssetPropertyOrientation"];
if (orientation != nil) {
    imageOrientation = [orientation integerValue];
}
```

Note   Querying the ALAssetRepresentation for orientation returns an ALAssetOrientation scalar, which does not accurately represent how the image was taken.

Having collected all of the necessary puzzle pieces, you can now create an image object:

```
UIImage *image = [UIImage imageWithCGImage:imagePtr scale:1.0f orientation:imageOrientation];
```

Summary

This chapter presented detailed exercises for building your own camera and image picker controllers with the goal of learning how you can gain more control over photo-related APIs and build your own user interfaces to supply missing functionality. By using lower-level frameworks, you should have a firm sense of how the UIImagePickerController class works. I hope you also gained a deeper understanding of how images are captured and stored at the system level.

In the camera controller exercise, you explored the AVFoundation framework and how you can use its video capture capabilities to build a live preview of a camera feed, as well as how to export frames as images. You also saw one way to perform faster view operations using CALayer objects and how to manipulate the capture settings of the camera using AVCaptureDevice.

The image picker exercise showed how the AssetsLibrary framework gives you a convenient, lower-level API for querying media items on the device. You saw how to filter assets by groups and asset type, and how to add the results to a list. You also saw how to display such results in a UICollectionView, and how to manipulate the settings of the collection view to allow users to select multiple images.

Part 2

Audio

Chapter 5

Playing and Recording Audio Files

In this chapter, you will explore how to use audio resources in your app by building applications to play and record audio using iOS's AVFoundation framework for audio-visual tasks. Much like image files, audio is stored as binary data, and must be decoded before your application can use it. A huge difference, however, is that audio files are stored as a stream of data, indexed by time, rather than a stream that represents one static image. As is so often the case, "there's an API for that," and you will take advantage of iOS's built-in audio player and recorder classes to build your apps. Just as you dealt with images, you will see how AVFoundation takes care of the details, allowing you to focus on building great user experiences rather than on implementing low-level audio codecs.

Playing Audio Files

The AVAudioPlayer class in iOS provides a *headless* interface for playing audio files within your app. This class allows you to control playback for single or multiple files (for example, play, pause, and seek), loop audio files, and monitor audio levels for currently playing items. You can use this class for both local files, such as those in your app's documents directory, or for network resources, such as network audio streams. This chapter covers local audio playback; however, you will learn about network stream playback in Chapter 6.

To practice using the AVAudioPlayer class, you will build the music player app shown in Figure 5-1.

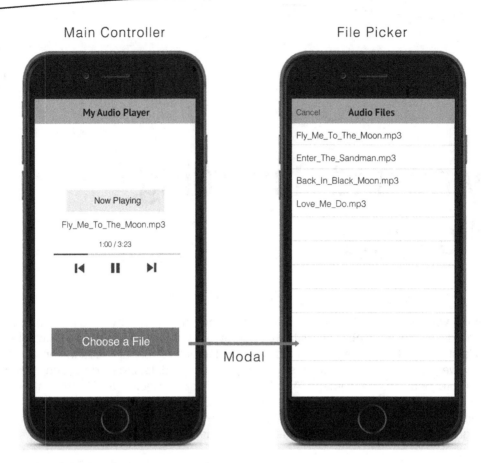

Main Controller   File Picker

Figure 5-1. *Mock-up of simple audio player*

This app allows a user to select an audio file stored in the app's project bundle and control its playback. The playback controls are Play/Pause (depending on state), Fast-Forward, and Rewind (15 seconds). To indicate status, the app shows playback progress and the name of the currently playing file.

File selection is handled through a `UITableViewController`. The user can select a file by clicking its name, which dismisses the file picker. Clicking the Cancel button also dismisses the file picker.

To enable this functionality, you need to do the following:

1. Request audio playback permission from iOS.

2. Build a user interface to select an audio file for playback.

3. Initialize the audio player with the selected file.

4. Build a user interface to control playback.

You can find all the source code for this application in Source Code/Download area of the Apress web site (www.apress.com), in the MyPlayer project, in the Chapter 5 folder.

Getting Started

As shown in Figure 5-1, the primary controls for the MyPlayer application are on the main view controller.

You start out in a familiar manner by creating a project using the Single-View Application template in Xcode. By default, Xcode will use the `ViewController` class to represent your main view controller; in the MyPlayer project, this file has been renamed `MainViewController`. You can rename a class in Xcode by right-clicking it and selecting Rename from the Refactor menu, as shown in Figure 5-2.

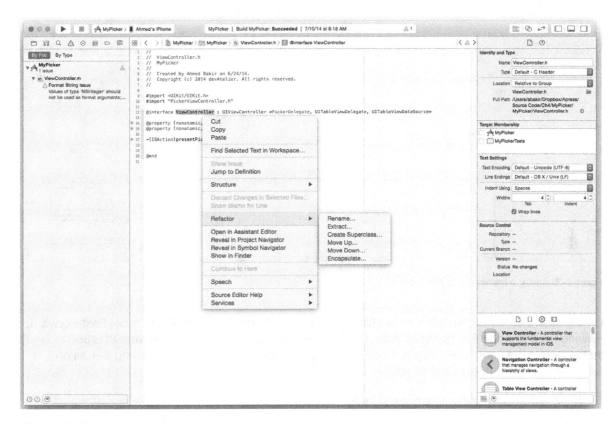

Figure 5-2. How to rename a class

To instantiate the audio player, you will need to include the `AVAudioPlayer` class in `MainViewController.h`, which will require you to include the `AVFoundation` framework in the project. As with the examples in Chapter 4, you can add a framework to a project by selecting your project file in Xcode and scrolling to the Linked Frameworks and Libraries pane at the bottom of the General tab, as shown in Figure 5-3.

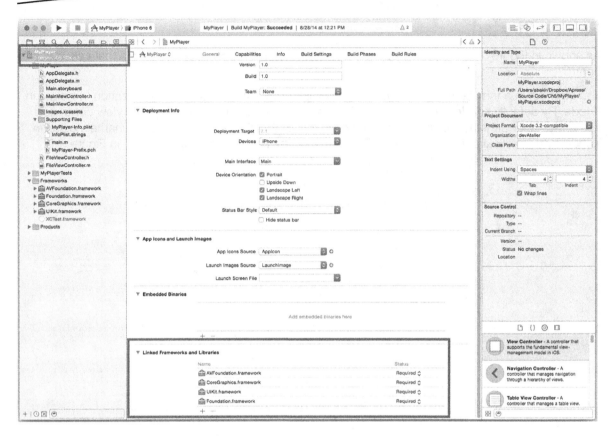

Figure 5-3. Adding a framework to your project

On the main view controller, use several UIButton instances to represent the Play/Pause, Fast-Forward, Rewind, and Choose File controls. Add a UIProgressView for the progress bar, and UILabel instances for the song title and playback time. You can use the header file in Listing 5-1 as an example of outlets to connect to your storyboard file.

Listing 5-1. Header File for MyPlayer main view controller

```objc
#import <UIKit/UIKit.h>
#import <AVFoundation/AVFoundation.h>
#import "FileViewController.h"

@interface MainViewController : UIViewController
    <FileControllerDelegate,AVAudioPlayerDelegate>
@property (nonatomic, strong) IBOutlet UILabel *timeLabel;
@property (nonatomic, strong) IBOutlet UILabel *titleLabel;
@property (nonatomic, strong) IBOutlet UIButton *chooseButton;
@property (nonatomic, strong) IBOutlet UIButton *playButton;
@property (nonatomic, strong) IBOutlet UIButton *skipForwardButton;
@property (nonatomic, strong) IBOutlet UIButton *skipBackwardButton;
@property (nonatomic, strong) IBOutlet UIProgressView *progressBar;
@property (nonatomic, strong) NSString *selectedFilePath;
```

```
@property (nonatomic, strong) AVAudioPlayer *audioPlayer;
@property (nonatomic, strong) NSTimer *timer;

-(IBAction)play:(id)sender;
-(IBAction)skipForward:(id)sender;
-(IBAction)skipBackward:(id)sender;

@end
```

Using the New File command in Xcode, create a second view controller for the file picker, which is a subclass of UITableViewController. In the MyPlayer project, this class is named FileViewController. Make the appropriate connections in Interface Builder to tie this class to your storyboard.

In order to add a Cancel button to the file picker, you will need to embed the file picker in a UINavigationController. This gives you a toolbar at the top of the view that you can add bar button items to. You can easily add a navigation controller to a view controller by selecting the Embed In option from the Editor menu in Xcode, as shown in Figure 5-4.

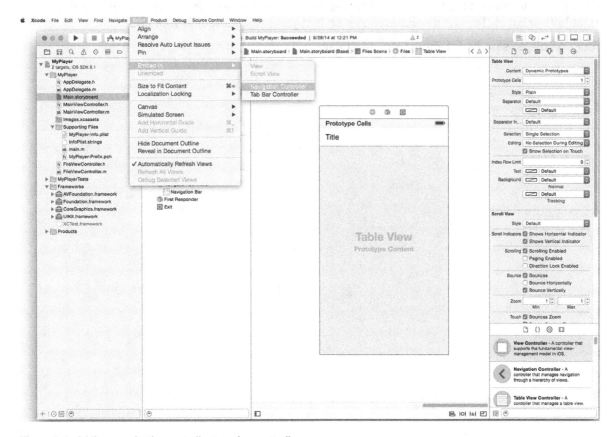

Figure 5-4. Adding a navigation controller to a view controller

You can find a header for the FileViewController class in Listing 5-2. In your header file, make sure you define a protocol for passing back messages and the appropriate properties for your storyboard.

Listing 5-2. Header File for FileViewController Class

```
#import <UIKit/UIKit.h>

@protocol FileControllerDelegate <NSObject>
-(void)cancel;
-(void)didFinishWithFile:(NSString *)filePath;
@end

@interface FileViewController : UITableViewController
@property (nonatomic, strong) NSMutableArray *fileArray;
@property (nonatomic, strong) id <FileControllerDelegate> delegate;

-(IBAction)closeView:(id)sender;

@end
```

To complete your storyboard, connect all of the actions and properties. Make sure the Choose File button is set to present the FileViewController modally, and make sure the default cell for the UITableViewController has a *reuse identifier* so that you can access it in your code.

Your completed storyboard should look like Figure 5-5.

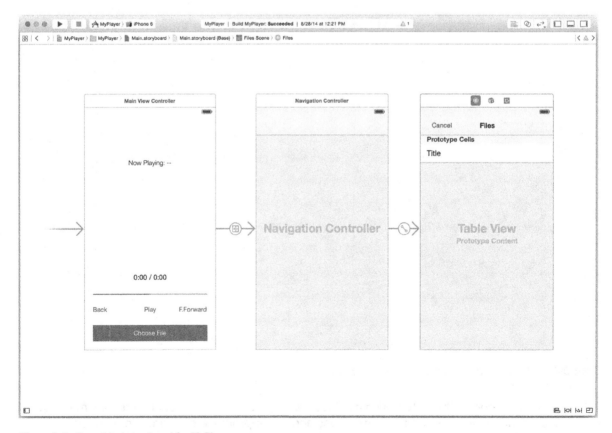

Figure 5-5. Completed storyboard for MyPlayer app

My implementation of the MyPlayer application includes only an iPhone user interface. If you are creating a universal application, make sure you apply the same settings to your iPad-specific storyboard.

Configuring an Audio Session

Much like the camera, your iOS device's audio capabilities are a shared resource. Apple provides access to the system's audio controller via the concept of an *audio session*, represented by AVAudioSession. All iOS apps come with a default audio session, but your app will not be able to take advantage of the full range of audio features until you configure it.

Configuring an audio session allows you to specify the type of audio activities your app will be performing (such as recording and playback), your preferences for how your app should interact with other apps competing for audio resources (for example, mixing tracks, ignoring all other audio sources), and ways to handle hardware events (such as a user unplugging the headphones).

While this may seem like a lot of effort to implement audio playback, AVFoundation provides several shortcuts to make configuring a session easy, as illustrated in Listing 5-3.

Listing 5-3. Configuring Your Audio Session for Playback

```
- (void)viewDidLoad
{
    [super viewDidLoad];
        // Do any additional setup after loading the view,
        // typically from a nib.

    NSError *error = nil;
    [[AVAudioSession sharedInstance]
        setCategory:AVAudioSessionCategoryPlayback
                                    error:&error];
    if (error == nil) {
        NSLog(@"audio session initialized successfully");
    } else {
        NSLog(@"error initializing Playing audio files:audio session: %@",
            [error description]);
    }
}
```

In this example, you can access your app's audio session via the singleton object, [AVAudioSession sharedInstance], which as previously mentioned is auto-generated with the app. Our app is automatically configured to be the delegate object for all audio session messages. To specify that your app plays audio, use the system macro AVAudioSessionCategoryPlayback, which indicates the app needs to take control of the system's audio resources to play sounds. Add this block of code to the [UIViewController viewDidLoad:] method of the main view controller to specify that your app wants control of the audio session when the view loads.

USING SINGLETONS

A *singleton* is an object that is instantiated once in an application. All operations are performed on a shared object. Unlike a global variable, a singleton is *lazy loaded*, meaning it is instantiated the first time it is called.

A singleton is convenient when you are accessing a shared resource because it allows you to make a manager through which you can pass all your operations. By using a single manager object that is shared across the entire application, you do not need to duplicate setup/teardown code (it is called only when your object is initialized or destroyed) and can be sure that your operations will be performed on a valid object.

To declare a singleton, you define a public method in your header file, with the name of the shared object. If you wanted your app delegate to be accessible as a singleton, your header file would look like this:

```
#import <UIKit/UIKit.h>

@interface AppDelegate : UIResponder <UIApplicationDelegate>

@property (strong, nonatomic) UIWindow *window;
+(AppDelegate*)sharedInstance;

@end
```

To implement your lazy-loading logic, define a global variable (`static` object) to store your shared object, and pass all messages through the `sharedInstance` method. If the global variable has already been initialized, it will return the pointer; otherwise, it will initialize the object and return the pointer.

```
static AppDelegate *shared;
+(AppDelegate*)sharedInstance{
    if (!shared || shared==nil) {
        shared = [[AppDelegate alloc] init];
    }
    return shared;
}
```

You can use your singleton object in any class by including its header file and passing messages to it, as you would any other object:

```
#include "AppDelegate.h"

@implementation myClass

-(void)viewDidLoad {
    [[appDelegate sharedInstance] refreshSession];
}
```

Although this example uses the AVAudioSessionCategoryPlayback macro, you can take advantage of a wide variety of preconfigured macros. Table 5-1 lists the most common macros and their uses.

Table 5-1. Popular AVAudioSessionCategoryPlayback Macros

Macro (Constant) Name	Intended Use
AVAudioSessionCategorySoloAmbient	The default audio session configuration for all apps. Playback continues until the user silences the device or locks the screen. Your app takes complete control of audio playback, and refuses audio events from other apps.
AVAudioSessionCategoryAmbient	Apps where audio playback is optional, but not required. Playback continues until the user silences the device. Other apps can still send audio events.
AVAudioSessionCategoryPlayback	Apps that require audio playback to function properly. Playback continues if the user silences the device. Can be configured to allow audio events from other apps.
AVAudioSessionCategoryRecord	Apps that require audio recording capabilities. Can be configured to allow background audio recording.
AVAudioSessionCategoryPlayAndRecord	Apps that require both audio recording and playback capabilities. Can be configured to continue in the background, and to accept audio events from other apps.

Selecting an Audio File

To populate the FileViewController, you need to scan the app's documents folder for MP3 and M4A files. You can use the resulting array as the data source for the table view.

You can find and retrieve an NSArray of all of the files in a directory by using the [NSFileManager contentsOfDirectoryAtPath:] method on an instance of the system file manager. You determine the type of each file by comparing its pathExtension component with the extension for the type of file you are looking for. The pathExtension property is a derived property available on all NSString objects. When called, it will attempt to return the part of the string that follows the period (.). Listing 5-4 shows a method that implements this behavior. Make a call to this method at the bottom of [self viewDidLoad] in your FileViewController class.

Listing 5-4. Building a List of Audio Files

```
-(void)initializeFileArray
{
    NSArray *paths = NSSearchPathForDirectoriesInDomains(
                    NSDocumentDirectory,
                    NSUserDomainMask, YES);
    NSString *documentsDirectory = [paths objectAtIndex:0];
    NSError *error = nil;
```

```
        NSArray *allFiles = [[NSFileManager defaultManager]
                             contentsOfDirectoryAtPath:documentsDirectory
                             error:&error];

    if (error == nil) {

        self.fileArray = [NSMutableArray new];

        for (NSString *file in allFiles) {
            if ([[file pathExtension] isEqualToString:@"mp3"] ||
                [[file pathExtension] isEqualToString:@"m4a"]) {
                [self.fileArray addObject:file];
            }
        }

    } else {
        NSLog(@"error looking up files: %@", [error description]);
    }
}
```

You will use the fileArray property throughout this class as the data source, so remember to declare it as an instance variable in the header file for your file view controller.

Now that you have populated your file array, implement the required UITableViewDelegate methods to start using it as a data source for the table. Listing 5-5 shows how to use the fileArray property to populate the section and row counts for the table view data source delegate methods.

Listing 5-5. Using an Array to Populate a Table

```
- (NSInteger)numberOfSectionsInTableView:(UITableView *)tableView
{
    // Return the number of sections.
    return 1;
}

- (NSInteger)tableView:(UITableView *)tableView
        numberOfRowsInSection:(NSInteger)section
{
    // Return the number of rows in the section.
    return [self.fileArray count];
}
```

To display the file name in each table view cell, you can use the [NSString lastPathComponent] derived property, as shown in Listing 5-6. This property works like [NSString pathExtension], except it extracts the characters after the final forward-slash character (/) in a string. Remember to use the reuse identifier you defined for your cell in Interface Builder.

Listing 5-6. Displaying the File Name in a Table View Cell

```
- (UITableViewCell *)tableView:(UITableView *)tableView
    cellForRowAtIndexPath:(NSIndexPath *)indexPath
{
    UITableViewCell *cell = [tableView
        dequeueReusableCellWithIdentifier:@"fileCell"
        forIndexPath:indexPath];

    // Configure the cell...

    NSString *filePath = [self.fileArray objectAtIndex:indexPath.row];

    cell.textLabel.text = [filePath lastPathComponent];

    return cell;
}
```

When a user selects a table view cell, you should return the entire file path of the selected item from your file array. This will allow your music player to play the file directly. As with the previous camera examples, this app passes back selections via a custom-defined protocol. The protocol definition from the header file is shown in Listing 5-7.

Listing 5-7. Protocol Definition for FileControllerView

```
@protocol FileControllerDelegate <NSObject>

-(void)cancel;
-(void)didFinishWithFile:(NSString *)filePath;

@end
```

You can use the protocol shown in Listing 5-8 to pass back the file path.

Listing 5-8. Passing Back the File Path When Selecting a Table View Cell

```
-(void)tableView:(UITableView *)tableView
    didSelectRowAtIndexPath:(NSIndexPath *)indexPath
{
    NSString *filePath = [self.fileArray objectAtIndex:indexPath.row];

    [self.delegate didFinishWithFile:filePath];

}
```

After defining the protocol, modify your main view controller's header file to indicate you will implement it, as shown in Listing 5-9.

Listing 5-9. Modified Header File for Main View Controller

```
#import <UIKit/UIKit.h>
#import <AVFoundation/AVFoundation.h>
#import "FileViewController.h"
```

```
@interface MainViewController : UIViewController
    <FileControllerDelegate>

@property (nonatomic, strong) IBOutlet UILabel *timeLabel;
@property (nonatomic, strong) IBOutlet UILabel *titleLabel;

@property (nonatomic, strong) IBOutlet UIButton *chooseButton;
@property (nonatomic, strong) IBOutlet UIButton *playButton;
@property (nonatomic, strong) IBOutlet UIButton *skipForwardButton;
@property (nonatomic, strong) IBOutlet UIButton *skipBackwardButton;

@property (nonatomic, strong) IBOutlet UIProgressView *progressBar;

@property (nonatomic, strong) NSString *selectedFilePath;

@end
```

Listing 5-10 shows how to implement the delegate methods by dismissing the file picker when the cancel message is received, and saving the selected file path when the didFinishWithFile: message is received.

Listing 5-10. File Picker Delegate Method Implementations

```
-(void)cancel
{
    [self dismissViewControllerAnimated:YES completion:nil];
}

-(void)didFinishWithFile:(NSString *)filePath
{
    self.selectedFilePath = filePath;
    [self dismissViewControllerAnimated:YES completion:nil];
}
```

Remember to declare your main view controller as a delegate for the protocol when the Present File Picker segue is selected, in the [UIViewController prepareForSegue:] method, as shown in Listing 5-11. Use the segue name you created in Interface Builder to select the button.

Listing 5-11. Declaring the Main View Controller as a Delegate

```
- (void)prepareForSegue:(UIStoryboardSegue *)segue sender:(id)sender
{
    if ([[segue identifier] isEqualToString:@"showFilePicker"]) {
        FileViewController *fileViewController =
          (FileViewController *)segue.destinationViewController;
        fileViewController.delegate = self;
    }
}
```

You may be thinking, "This is cool and all, but how do I get music into my app?" You can actually use iTunes to manage data on apps that enable iTunes File Sharing. You can navigate to the file manager interface in iTunes by selecting your device and navigating over to the Apps tab. As shown in Figure 5-6, scrolling to the bottom of the page shows a list of apps that enable file sharing. Selecting them lets you manage files in their documents directories.

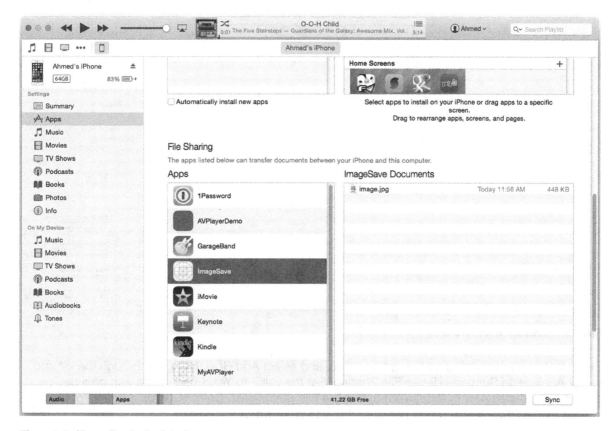

Figure 5-6. *iTunes file-sharing interface*

To configure your application to support file sharing, single-click your project file to modify its settings, and click the Info tab, as shown in Figure 5-7.

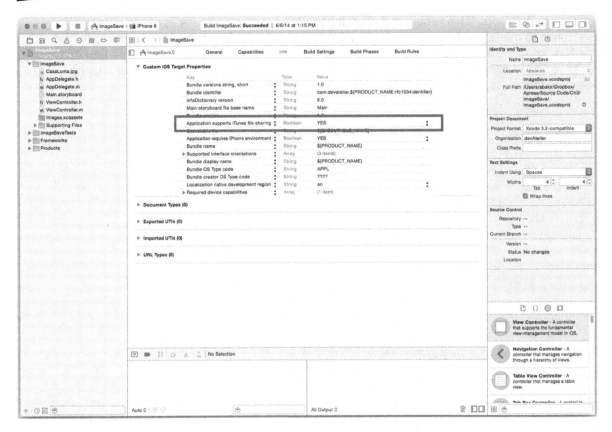

Figure 5-7. Enabling iTunes file sharing

Right-click any row to bring up the option menu, and select Add Row. Navigate through the list and select Application Supports iTunes File Sharing. Set the value to Yes. Loading the app on a device and opening iTunes now includes your app in the File Sharing list. Drag and drop a couple of files into the app so that the file picker has something to work with.

Setting Up the Audio Player

Now that your app can load audio files, you are ready to start using the AVAudioPlayer class to play the files. You integrate an audio player into your class by adding it as a property and implementing its protocol methods.

Because this app plays only one music file at a time, you want to implement your AVAudioPlayer object as an instance variable of your main view controller (the one that contains the player). The audio player sends back messages via a protocol, so, similarly, you should also indicate that your class will implement that protocol. Listing 5-12 shows a modified version of the header file that includes these changes.

Listing 5-12. Adding the Audio Player and Its Protocol to Your Header File

```
#import <UIKit/UIKit.h>
#import <AVFoundation/AVFoundation.h>
#import "FileViewController.h"

@interface MainViewController : UIViewController <FileControllerDelegate,
AVAudioPlayerDelegate>

@property (nonatomic, strong) IBOutlet UILabel *timeLabel;
@property (nonatomic, strong) IBOutlet UILabel *titleLabel;

@property (nonatomic, strong) IBOutlet UIButton *chooseButton;
@property (nonatomic, strong) IBOutlet UIButton *playButton;
@property (nonatomic, strong) IBOutlet UIButton *skipForwardButton;
@property (nonatomic, strong) IBOutlet UIButton *skipBackwardButton;

@property (nonatomic, strong) IBOutlet UIProgressView *progressBar;

@property (nonatomic, strong) NSString *selectedFilePath;

@property (nonatomic, strong) AVAudioPlayer *audioPlayer;

@end
```

> **Note**   If you want to write an app whose audio playback can be controlled by multiple views, it is best to encapsulate your audio player instance in a singleton class, and to have all classes access it through that.

Now that you have added the audio player object to your class, you need to initialize it. The AVAudioPlayer class comes with two primary init methods, [AVAudioPlayer initWithContentsOfURL:error:] and [AVAudioPlayer initWithData:error:]. Remember, you're passing back the file path for the target audio file when the file view controller completes, meaning you can use the URL-based init method. The player cannot be initialized without a source file, so put the initialization functionality in the delegate method that receives a file from the file view controller, as shown in Listing 5-13.

Listing 5-13. Initializing the Audio Player When a File Is Selected

```
-(void)didFinishWithFile:(NSString *)filePath

    self.selectedFilePath = filePath;

    NSError *error = nil;
    NSURL *fileURL = [NSURL fileURLWithPath:self.selectedFilePath];

    self.audioPlayer = [[AVAudioPlayer alloc]
                        initWithContentsOfURL:fileURL error:&error];
    self.audioPlayer.delegate = self;
```

```
    if (error == nil) {
        NSLog(@"audio player initialized successfully");
    } else {
        NSLog(@"error initializing Playing audio files:audio player: %@",
            [error description]);
    }

    //dismiss the file picker
    [self dismissViewControllerAnimated:YES completion:nil];
}
```

Note that the preceding code converts the file path to a URL before sending it to the audio player. While both a file path and a URL are valid references to a file location, you need to convert the file path to the NSURL data type to comply with the API. You may be wondering why we did not use the NSData-based init method. To use this method, you need to load the file into memory. While that's appropriate for a file downloaded from a network source (where you don't want to save the file to disk), it adds extra overhead that you don't need for this app.

Building a Playback Interface

Now that the audio player is initialized, you might think the app would be ready to start playing files. Unfortunately, AVAudioPlayer is a *headless* class, meaning it provides no user interface. To start and control audio playback, you need to trigger them via user actions.

Starting or Pausing Playback

The primary control for your audio player is the Play button. As its name indicates, users will use this to initiate playback. It serves a dual purpose: if a music file is already playing, you want to let the user pause playback by clicking this button.

The method that starts playback using the audio player is [AVAudioPlayer play], which tells the audio player to start processing the input file and automatically begins playback as soon as the player is ready. You should make this call from the button handler for the Play button, as shown in Listing 5-14. Make sure to tie this function to your storyboard in Interface Builder.

Listing 5-14. Initiating Audio Playback

```
-(IBAction)play:(id)sender
{
    [self.audioPlayer play];
}
```

Unlike images, audio and video files are treated as streams of data by the system and require additional time to build up a memory buffer where they can preload data. The buffer allows the player to have enough data so it can play back the file at the default speed (1x). Unfortunately, you cannot predict how long it will take to fill the buffer, so the [AVAudioPlayer play] method is *asynchronous* (meaning it will not block other events in your app).

> **Note**   You can force the audio player to buffer a file with the [AVAudioPlayer prepareToPlay]
> method. This method is automatically called as part of [AVAudioPlayer play], but calling it separately
> speeds up your user experience, especially if you do not expect to automatically start playing a file as soon as
> the user selects it.

At this point, your app can play the file, but cannot yet pause it. The [AVAudioPlayer pause:] pauses
the player. However, before calling the pause method, you should check to see if the audio player
is currently playing a file. You query the playback status of the audio player via the [AVAudioPlayer
isPlaying] property, as shown in the example in Listing 5-15.

Listing 5-15. Using Playback Status to Determine Button Action

```
-(IBAction)play:(id)sender
{
    if ([self.audioPlayer isPlaying]) {
        [self.audioPlayer pause];
        self.playButton.titleLabel.text = @"Play";
    } else {
        [self.audioPlayer play];
        self.playButton.titleLabel.text = @"Pause";
    }

}
```

In addition to changing the action, the code also changes the title of the button. This is a critical
step, because you want to reflect the state change to the user.

To complete the playback cycle, you need to reset the user interface when playback has completed.
You may remember that one of the first steps in setting up the audio player was to declare that the
main view controller would implement the AVAudioPlayerDelegate protocol. The delegate method that
the player sends when it has completed playing a file is audioPlayerDidFinishPlaying:Successfully:.
As shown in Listing 5-16, all you need to do is reset the Play button's text when this message is
received. Because the app uses runtime logic to determine the action, you do not need to rewire the
button.

Listing 5-16. Resetting the User Interface Using the Delegate

```
-(void)audioPlayerDidFinishPlaying:(AVAudioPlayer *)player
                                successfully:(BOOL)flag
{
    if (flag) {
        self.playButton.titleLabel.text = @"Play";
    }
}
```

Skipping Forward or Backward

Now that you can play or pause a file, you can move onto another common playback function: the ability to skip forward or backward. As with the Play button, the app controls these functions via button handlers. Unlike the Play button, however, the functionality is discrete enough so that each function should have a separate UI element.

You can force the audio player to seek to a specific time in a file by setting the value of the [AVAudioPlayer currentTime] property to a desired time. For this app, you want to be able to skip forward or backward by 15 seconds.

For the skip-forward functionality, you can get the desired time by adding 15 to the current time value from the audio player. The NSTimeInterval data type counts in seconds. To prevent the user from skipping beyond the end of the file (which is an invalid action), you compare the new calculated target time to the duration of the file, before setting the new time value for the player. You can get the duration of the current file from the audio player by using the [AVAudioPlayer duration] property.

Listing 5-17 shows the skip-forward implementation.

Listing 5-17. Button Handler for Skipping Forward

```
-(IBAction)skipForward:(id)sender
{
    if ([self.audioPlayer isPlaying]) {

        NSTimeInterval desiredTime =
            self.audioPlayer.currentTime + 15.0f;
        if (desiredTime < self.audioPlayer.duration) {
            self.audioPlayer.currentTime = desiredTime;
        }
    }
}
```

You follow similar logic to implement skipping backward. However, instead of checking the duration of the file, compare the calculated time to 0 (the start of the file). If the user attempts to skip backward when the player is less than 15 seconds into playback, you send the user to the beginning of the file. Otherwise, send the user to the position 15 seconds before the current position. Listing 5-18 shows an example.

Listing 5-18. Button Handler for Skipping Backward

```
-(IBAction)skipBackward:(id)sender
{
    if ([self.audioPlayer isPlaying]) {
        NSTimeInterval desiredTime =
            self.audioPlayer.currentTime - 15.0f;
        if (desiredTime < 0) {
            self.audioPlayer.currentTime = 0.0f;
        } else {
            self.audioPlayer.currentTime = desiredTime;
        }
    }
}
```

> **Caution**   While you might think you could use the AVAudioPlayer method [AVAudioPlayer playAtTime:] to seek to a certain point in a file's timeline, this is not a use case the API supports. Instead, this method is intended to delay the start time of the player, which would be useful if, for example, you wanted to display a countdown timer or perform another action before an audio file starts playing.

Displaying Playback Progress

As the final piece of your music player app, you want to be able to display the progress for the currently playing track. Unfortunately, there is no delegate method or notification that will automatically give you this value. However, you can accomplish the desired result by using an NSTimer that fires every second.

The NSTimer class triggers a method after a specified time delay or on a recurring basis. You initialize timers by using a time interval that specifies the delay between calls, the method selector that needs to be called when the timer fires, and whether or not the timer should repeat. A caveat with repeating timers is that they will fire until specifically *invalidated* (stopped), so you need to maintain a pointer to the timer. You can do this by declaring your timer as an instance variable in the main view controller:

```
@property (nonatomic, strong) NSTimer *timer;
```

You want to start the timer when the user hits the Play button, so place your initialization code in the Play button handler, as shown in Listing 5-19. The Play button is managed by your storyboard, so it does not need to be initialized when changing state, only updated.

Listing 5-19. Initializing a Timer When the User Starts Playing a File

```
-(IBAction)play:(id)sender
{
    if ([self.audioPlayer isPlaying]) {
        [self.audioPlayer pause];
        self.playButton.titleLabel.text = @"Play";
        self.timer = [NSTimer timerWithTimeInterval:1.0f target:self
            selector:@selector(updateProgress) userInfo:nil
            repeats:YES];

    } else {
        [self.audioPlayer play];
        self.playButton.titleLabel.text = @"Pause";
        [self.timer invalidate];
    }

}
```

You may be wondering why the timer object is reinitialized when playback is started, and destroyed when playback stops. There is no way to pause a timer, except by destroying it using the [NSTimer invalidate] method. For this reason, you need to re-create the timer to restart it. The audioPlayer object does not need to be reinitialized because it is an instance variable, and is reset only when you change files.

This example specifies [self updateProgress] as the method to call whenever the timer fires. Therefore, you will want to update the progress bar and progress label with the player's current time and song duration in that method. As with the skip forward/backward examples, you can use the [AVAudioPlayer currentTime] and [AVAudioPlayer duration] properties to retrieve these values. Listing 5-20 shows an implementation of the [self updateProgress] method for the main view controller.

Listing 5-20. Method to Update Progress Bar and Label

```
-(void)updateProgress
{
    NSInteger durationMinutes = [self.audioPlayer duration] / 60;
    NSInteger durationSeconds = [self.audioPlayer duration] -
                                  durationMinutes * 60;

    NSInteger currentTimeMinutes = [self.audioPlayer currentTime] / 60;
    NSInteger currentTimeSeconds = [self.audioPlayer currentTime] -
                                  currentTimeMinutes * 60;
    NSString *progressString =
        [NSString stringWithFormat:@"%d:%02d / %d:%02d",
        currentTimeMinutes, currentTimeSeconds, durationMinutes,
        durationSeconds];
    self.timeLabel.text = progressString;

    self.progressBar.progress = [self.audioPlayer currentTime] /
                                  [self.audioPlayer duration];

}
```

There are two interesting things about the preceding code. First, to display the time in a human-readable format, it extracts the minutes and seconds from the raw seconds output of the current time and progress values. While displaying total seconds is a perfectly valid way of representing progress, it is not one that your users will be able to make much use of. Second, the method simply passes a division result to the progress bar. The UIProgressView represents the *full* status of the progress bar based on the [UIProgressView progress] property, which is a value between 0.0 and 1.0. By dividing the current time by the duration, you get an accurate progress value to pass along.

While it is great that everything is working now, you must take a final step to make sure the progress is updated correctly the *next* time you try to play a file: you need to invalidate the timer. You already saw how to invalidate the timer when the user presses the Pause button; now you also need to invalidate the timer when the file has finished playing. Listing 5-21 shows an example of the modified audioPlayerDidFinishPlaying:successfully delegate method.

Listing 5-21. Invalidating the Timer in the Audio Player Delegate Method

```
-(void)audioPlayerDidFinishPlaying:(AVAudioPlayer *)player
                      successfully:(BOOL)flag
{
    if (flag) {
        self.playButton.titleLabel.text = @"Play";
        [self.timer invalidate];
    }
}
```

Recording Audio Files

You can apply many of the lessons you learned from playing back audio to the process of recording audio. As with playing audio, you need to request permission for the audio session before you can use the audio hardware, and some delay may occur. Similarly, you can use an event-driven class to start/stop the recording, AVAudioRecorder, which is also headless.

The additional requirements that come from using the audio recorder are as follows:

- You need an audio session capable of recording.

- You need to configure the microphone before using it.

- You need to build a playback interface to preview your recordings.

To learn how to use the AVAudioRecorder class, you will build the audio recorder player app shown in Figure 5-8.

Figure 5-8. Mock-up of simple audio recorder

The only input in this app is the audio recorder, so you can implement it as a single-view application. The user triggers recording via the microphone button. Like the Play button from the audio player app, the state of this button changes to stop when recording is active. To allow the user to preview the recording, you can reuse the playback interface from the audio player app. This app also provides a Reset button so users can delete the recording if they are not satisfied with it.

You can find all the source code for this application in the MyRecorder project, in the Chapter 6 folder of the source code bundle.

Getting Started

For this project, you can reuse most of your work from the audio player app as a base. The main additions are as follows:

- Adding an audio recorder object to your main view controller
- Adding controls for recording
- Adding extra logic to enable playback from the audio recorder.

Using the header file for the audio player as a reference, you can add your audio recorder and new buttons to the main view controller. Listing 5-22 shows an example.

Listing 5-22. Header File for Audio Recorder App

```
#import <UIKit/UIKit.h>
#import <AVFoundation/AVFoundation.h>

@interface MainViewController : UIViewController
    <AVAudioPlayerDelegate>

@property (nonatomic, strong) IBOutlet UILabel *timeLabel;

@property (nonatomic, strong) IBOutlet UIButton *recordButton;
@property (nonatomic, strong) IBOutlet UIButton *playButton;
@property (nonatomic, strong) IBOutlet UIButton *resetButton;

@property (nonatomic, strong) IBOutlet UIProgressView *progressBar;

@property (nonatomic, strong) AVAudioPlayer *audioPlayer;
@property (nonatomic, strong) AVAudioRecorder *audioRecorder;

@property (nonatomic, strong) NSTimer *timer;

-(IBAction)record:(id)sender;
-(IBAction)play:(id)sender;
-(IBAction)reset:(id)sender;

@end
```

As with the AVAudioPlayer class, AVAudioRecorder requires the AVFoundation framework to compile. Follow the same process you used with the audio player app to add the framework to your project.

Having defined your properties and methods, lay out your storyboard and connect your actions using Interface Builder. The result should look the screenshot in Figure 5-9.

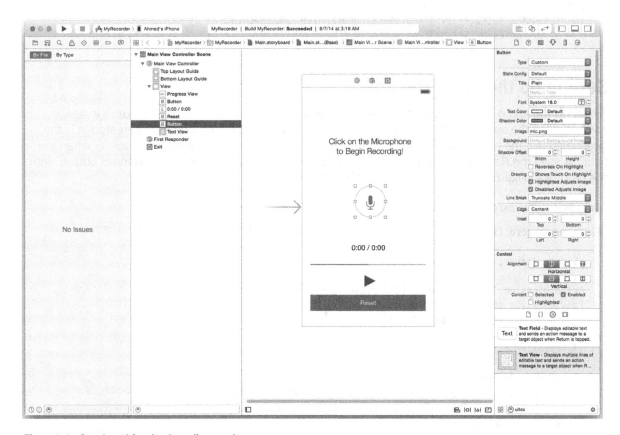

Figure 5-9. Storyboard for simple audio recorder

Configuring the Audio Session

Just as you did with the audio player, you need to initialize the audio session before using the audio recorder. Because your app will need both playback and recording abilities, use the AVAudioSessionCategoryPlayAndRecord macro to configure the audio session.

You will want to prepare the audio session as soon as the user presses the Record button, so configure the session in the button handler, as shown in Listing 5-23.

Listing 5-23. Initializing the Audio Session for Recording

```
-(IBAction)record:(id)sender
{
    NSError *error;

    AVAudioSession *audioSession = [AVAudioSession sharedInstance];
    [audioSession setCategory:AVAudioSessionCategoryPlayAndRecord
                error:&error];
}
```

Setting Up the Audio Recorder

To set up the audio recorder, use the [AVAudioRecorder initWithURL:settings:error:] instance method. Like the audio player, it takes a URL. However, the URL the recorder is interested in is the *destination* for the recording. As with the audio session, you want to initialize the recorder when the user presses the Record button. A modified version of the button handler for the Record button, with the recorder initialization logic, is provided in Listing 5-24.

Listing 5-24. Initializing the Audio Recorder

```
-(IBAction)record:(id)sender
{
    NSError *error;

    AVAudioSession *audioSession = [AVAudioSession sharedInstance];
    [audioSession setCategory:AVAudioSessionCategoryPlayAndRecord
                error:&error];

    if (error == nil) {

        NSArray *paths =
            NSSearchPathForDirectoriesInDomains(NSDocumentDirectory,
            NSUserDomainMask, YES);
        NSString *documentsDirectory = [paths objectAtIndex:0];

        NSString *filePath = [documentsDirectory
            stringByAppendingPathComponent:@"recording.m4a"];
        NSURL *fileURL = [NSURL fileURLWithPath:filePath];

        NSMutableDictionary *settingsDict = [NSMutableDictionary new];
        [settingsDict setObject:[NSNumber numberWithInt:44100.0]
                            forKey:AVSampleRateKey];
        [settingsDict setObject:[NSNumber numberWithInt:2]
                            forKey:AVNumberOfChannelsKey];
        [settingsDict setObject:[NSNumber
                            numberWithInt:AVAudioQualityMedium]
            forKey:AVEncoderAudioQualityKey];
        [settingsDict setObject:[NSNumber numberWithInt:16]
                            forKey:AVEncoderBitRateKey];
```

```
        self.audioRecorder = [[AVAudioRecorder alloc]
                              initWithURL:fileURL

                              settings:settingsDict error:&error];

    if (error == nil) {

        NSLog(@"audio recorder initialized successfully!");

    } else {
        NSLog(@"error initializing audio recorder: %@",
            [error description]);
    }

} else {
    NSLog(@"error initializing Playing audio files:audio session: %@",
        [error description]);
}
}
```

As with the audio player, for this app, you will use the documents directory as the destination for the user's recording. You can create the full path for your file by appending the file name to the documents directory. The audio recorder will create a new file if the file specified by the URL does not exist, or it will overwrite the existing file if it does.

You may also be wondering about the settings parameter. This is a dictionary of key/value pairs that configure the hardware's capture settings. The preceding example configures the microphone to capture 16-bit stereo audio at moderate quality. This is a good, middle-of-the-road configuration, in which the recording will sound better than a phone call, but without the data overhead of a full, uncompressed audio recording.

Building the Recording Interface

As with the AVAudioPlayer class, the AVAudioRecorder class is headless, so you have to implement your own user interface to control the recording process. For this application, you want to add controls for recording-specific functionality: starting and stopping the recording, saving the file, and deleting the recording. With a few exceptions, you can reuse the playback interface from the audio player app to preview the recording.

Starting or Stopping the Recording

You use the [AVAudioRecorder record] method to begin recording an audio file. Similarly, the [AVAudioRecorder stop] method stops recording. As with the audio player app, you use a single button to toggle the recording state. Following the same pattern you used with audio APIs, you query the recording status of the recorder object by using the [AVAudioRecorder isRecording] property. Listing 5-25 shows a modified version of the Record button handler that implements this flow.

Listing 5-25. Starting or Stopping the Audio Recorder

```
-(IBAction)record:(id)sender
{
    NSError *error;

    AVAudioSession *audioSession = [AVAudioSession sharedInstance];
    [audioSession setCategory:AVAudioSessionCategoryPlayAndRecord
                    error:&error];

    if (error == nil) {

        NSArray *paths =
            NSSearchPathForDirectoriesInDomains(NSDocumentDirectory,
            NSUserDomainMask, YES);
        NSString *documentsDirectory = [paths objectAtIndex:0];

        NSString *filePath = [documentsDirectory
                            stringByAppendingPathComponent:@"recording.m4a"];

        NSURL *fileURL = [NSURL fileURLWithPath:filePath];

        NSMutableDictionary *settingsDict = [NSMutableDictionary new];
        [settingsDict setObject:[NSNumber numberWithInt:44100.0]
                            forKey:AVSampleRateKey];
        [settingsDict setObject:[NSNumber numberWithInt:2]
                            forKey:AVNumberOfChannelsKey];
        [settingsDict setObject:[NSNumber
                            numberWithInt:AVAudioQualityMedium]
                            forKey:AVEncoderAudioQualityKey];
        [settingsDict setObject:[NSNumber numberWithInt:16]
                            forKey:AVEncoderBitRateKey];

        self.audioRecorder = [[AVAudioRecorder alloc]
                            initWithURL:fileURL
                            settings:settingsDict
                            error:&error];

        if (error == nil) {

            if ([self.audioRecorder isRecording]) {

                [self.audioRecorder record];
                self.recordButton.titleLabel.text = @"Stop";

            } else {
                [self.audioRecorder stop];
                self.recordButton.titleLabel.text = @"Record";

            }
```

```
        } else {
            NSLog(@"error initializing audio recorder: %@",
                    [error description]);
        }

    } else {
        NSLog(@"error initializing Playing audio files:audio session: %@",
                [error description]);
    }
}
```

As with the audio player, remember to update your button label based on the recording state.

Playing Back the Recording

One of the initialization parameters for the audio recorder object was the destination URL for the recorded file. One of the initialization parameters for the audio player was the URL for the file to use as the audio source. Through this lucky coincidence, previewing the audio file is as simple as passing the recording file's URL to the audio player, which you want to do in the Play button handler, as shown in Listing 5-26.

Listing 5-26. Previewing the Audio Recording

```
-(IBAction)play:(id)sender
{
    NSError *error = nil;

    if ([self.audioRecorder isRecording]) {
        [self.audioRecorder stop];
    }

    if ([self.audioPlayer isPlaying]) {

        [self.audioPlayer stop];
        self.playButton.titleLabel.text = @"Play";

    } else {

        self.audioPlayer = [[AVAudioPlayer alloc]
            initWithContentsOfURL:[self.audioRecorder url]
            error:&error];

        if (error == nil) {

            [self.audioPlayer play];
            self.playButton.titleLabel.text = @"Stop";
```

```
        } else {
            NSLog(@"error initializing Playing audio files:audio player: %@",
                [error description]);
        }

    }
}
```

Note that rather than storing the recording file's URL in a variable, you can grab it directly from the recording object via the [AVAudioRecorder url] property. One more caveat in this example is that it checks the recording status before playing back the file. You need to stop the recording before attempting to play back the file; otherwise, you will create a feedback loop (an endless echo) that will render your recording useless.

Saving the Recording

You do not need to do any extra work to save the recording. The AVAudioRecorder automatically closes the file buffer and saves the recording to disk as soon as the user chooses to stop recording.

One major use case you need to cover is a user who expects to record multiple audio files. You can resolve this by using the NSFileManager class. To prevent a recorded file from being overwritten each time the user stops recording, call the [NSFileManager fileExistsAtPath:] instance method. To create unique file names, check to make sure the desired file does not exist before recording. If the file exists, add a unique identifier to the end of the file name, such as a count. Listing 5-27 shows a modified version of the Record button handler that adds this logic before initializing the recorder object.

Listing 5-27. Creating Unique File Names

```
-(IBAction)record:(id)sender
{
    NSError *error;

    AVAudioSession *audioSession = [AVAudioSession sharedInstance];
    [audioSession setCategory:AVAudioSessionCategoryPlayAndRecord
                    error:&error];

    if (error == nil) {

        NSArray *paths =
            NSSearchPathForDirectoriesInDomains(NSDocumentDirectory,

            NSUserDomainMask, YES);
        NSString *documentsDirectory = [paths objectAtIndex:0];

        NSString *filePath = [documentsDirectory
            stringByAppendingPathComponent:@"recording.m4a"];
        NSInteger count = 0;
```

```objc
    while ([[NSFileManager defaultManager]
            fileExistsAtPath:filePath]) {
        NSString *fileName = [NSString
            stringWithFormat:@"recording-%d", count];
        filePath = [documentsDirectory
                    stringByAppendingPathComponent:fileName];
        count++;
    }

    NSURL *fileURL = [NSURL fileURLWithPath:filePath];

    NSMutableDictionary *settingsDict = [NSMutableDictionary new];
    [settingsDict setObject:[NSNumber numberWithInt:44100.0]
                            forKey:AVSampleRateKey];
    [settingsDict setObject:[NSNumber numberWithInt:2]
                            forKey:AVNumberOfChannelsKey];
    [settingsDict setObject:[NSNumber
                            numberWithInt:AVAudioQualityMedium]
                            forKey:AVEncoderAudioQualityKey];
    [settingsDict setObject:[NSNumber numberWithInt:16]
                    forKey:AVEncoderBitRateKey];


    self.audioRecorder = [[AVAudioRecorder alloc]
                            initWithURL:fileURL
                            settings:settingsDict
                            error:&error];

    if (error == nil) {

        if ([self.audioRecorder isRecording]) {

            [self.audioRecorder record];
            self.recordButton.titleLabel.text = @"Stop";

        } else {
            [self.audioRecorder stop];
            self.recordButton.titleLabel.text = @"Record";

        }

    } else {
        NSLog(@"error initializing audio recorder: %@",
            [error description]);
    }

} else {
    NSLog(@"error initializing Playing audio files:audio session: %@",
        [error description]);
}
}
}
```

> **Caution**   The only way to change the recording file path is by creating a new recorder object. Remember to notify the user of this in your app, either through an alert or by indicating that the old recording has completed.

Deleting the Recording

Sometimes, a user will be so unhappy with a recording and will want to delete it outright. To delete an active recording, use the [AVAudioRecorder deleteRecording] instance method, as shown in Listing 5-28. This method deletes the file that you initialized the recorder object with. As with other recording events, make sure you stop the recorder before attempting to delete the file.

Listing 5-28. Deleting an Audio Recording

```
-(IBAction)delete:(id)sender
{
    if ([self.audioRecorder isRecording]) {
        [self.audioRecorder stop];
    }

    [self.audioRecorder deleteRecording];
}
```

Summary

In this chapter, you saw how to use the AVAudioPlayer and AVAudioRecorder classes to play and record audio within your app. You learned that, as when accessing the camera, both classes require you to use the AVAudioSession class as a gatekeeper to the system's shared resources. Because of the indeterminate nature of starting a session, you saw how to implement an event-based flow for handling messages from the player and recorder. Remember that both classes are headless, so you have to implement the user interface—but doing so is straightforward. Finally, note that after having configured the session correctly for recording, there is a huge overlap in the concepts that drive the audio player and recorder.

Chapter 6

Using External Audio Sources

In this chapter, you will see how to use external sources to play more types of audio in your app. By expanding on the audio basics you saw in Chapter 5, this chapter describes how to play music from iTunes and from streaming audio sources, and to play event sounds (short sound effects that are triggered when an event happens, such as pressing a button) in your apps. While implementing these new audio sources, you will see how to reuse the same design patterns you first encountered while playing simple audio files (such as requesting a shared resource, event-driven message handling, and implementing a custom user interface) in other classes, and how to hook extra logic into them to enable your app to play multiple source types.

The major sections in this chapter (about iTunes, streaming audio, and event sounds) are backed by sample projects you can find in the Chapter 6 folder of the source code bundle provided with the book. (See the Source Code/Download area of the Apress web site, www.apress.com).

Importing Music from iTunes

In Chapter 5, you learned how to use audio files within your app. However, you had to import all the audio files you wanted to use, either by including them with your app, or through iTunes file sharing. Fortunately, Apple provides access to the iPod music library on a user's device via the MPMusicPlayerController class. This is useful when you want to let users play their own music within your app, or when you want your app to provide controls for the user's currently loaded playlist.

The *MP* in MPMediaPlayerController derives from the framework it is built upon: the MediaPlayer framework. The MediaPlayer framework is built specifically for media playback, allowing it to tackle more-complicated tasks, such as playing back video, decoding bookmark information from podcasts and audiobooks, and accessing the iPod app. The MediaPlayer framework will play a key role in later chapters, where you will use it to play back video.

Similar to the AVAudioPlayer class you used earlier to play sound files, the MPMusicPlayerController class lets you build a custom media player within your app, complete with playback controls and methods to query playback status. Some of these controls are already familiar, such as playing, pausing, and seeking, as well as new controls that mimic the behavior of the iPod app, such as toggling the shuffle behavior of a playlist. Unfortunately, MPMusicPlayerController is also a headless class, which means you must implement your own user interface. Additionally, as a class designed to interface with the iPod music library, you can use it to play back only iTunes media. You can get around this limitation by continuing to maintain an AVAudioPlayer object for playback of other audio files.

In this section, you will learn how to use the MPMediaPlayerController class to play iPod media library music in your apps by building the music player application shown in Figure 6-1. You can find this app in the source code bundle for the book, under the Chapter 6 folder. The project is called MyPod.

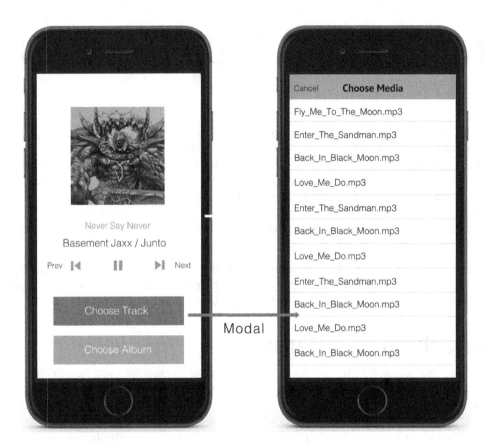

Figure 6-1. *Mock-up of MyPod project*

The MyPod application allows a user to select a song or album to play by clicking one of the buttons at the bottom of the main view controller. Users can navigate between items by using the table view controller. After a user has selected a song or album, the app provides playback controls for the currently playing song and controls for navigating through the current playlist.

The goal of the MyPod application is to show you the key concepts of implementing an MPMusicPlayerController-based music player, which are as follows:

- Initializing the music player

- Specifying a media query (you can think of this as a playlist)

- Building a playback interface

- Displaying track information (metadata)

Getting Started

As with the other projects in this book, you start by creating a project based on the Single-View Application template. Use the mock-up shown in Figure 6-1 to help you select the user interface elements to add to your storyboard. Be sure to add a table view controller so users can select music. You do not need to link the two view controllers via a segue, as you will be using a button handler to manage the transitions. Your completed storyboard should look similar to the screenshot in Figure 6-2.

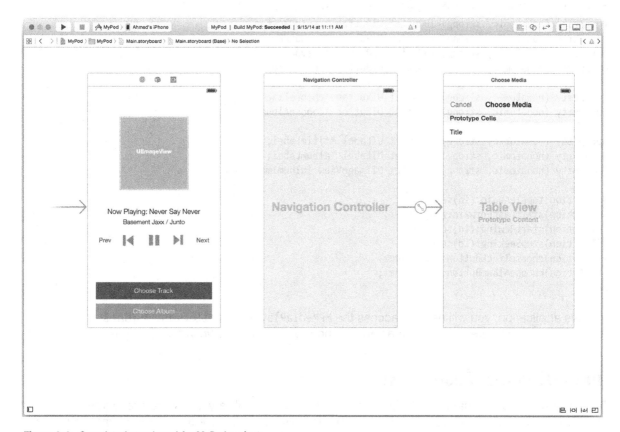

Figure 6-2. Completed storyboard for MyPod project

The MainViewController class represents the main view for this application. Before implementing the class, make sure you add the MediaPlayer framework to the project. At the top of the header file (MainViewController.h), include the framework:

```
#import <MediaPlayer/MediaPlayer.h>
```

Listing 6-1 shows a header file you can use when implementing the MainViewController class. As always, use these properties to link your storyboard to the class.

Listing 6-1. Header File for MainViewController Class

```
#import <UIKit/UIKit.h>
#import <MediaPlayer/MediaPlayer.h>
#import "MediaTableViewController.h"

@interface MainViewController : UIViewController

@property (nonatomic, strong) MPMusicPlayerController *musicPlayer;

@property (nonatomic, strong) IBOutlet UIButton *playButton;
@property (nonatomic, strong) IBOutlet UIButton *rewindButton;
@property (nonatomic, strong) IBOutlet UIButton *forwardButton;
@property (nonatomic, strong) IBOutlet UIButton *prevButton;
@property (nonatomic, strong) IBOutlet UIButton *nextButton;

@property (nonatomic, strong) IBOutlet UIButton *chooseTrackButton;
@property (nonatomic, strong) IBOutlet UIButton *chooseAlbumButton;

@property (nonatomic, strong) IBOutlet UILabel *titleLabel;
@property (nonatomic, strong) IBOutlet UILabel *albumLabel;
@property (nonatomic, strong) IBOutlet UIImageView *albumImageView;

-(IBAction)toggleAudio:(id)sender;
-(IBAction)startFastForward:(id)sender;
-(IBAction)startRewind:(id)sender;
-(IBAction)stopSeeking:(id)sender;
-(IBAction)chooseTrackButton:(id)sender;
-(IBAction)chooseAlbumButton:(id)sender;
@end
```

For this application, you will need to access the MPMediaPlayerController object from several functions, so make sure you define it as an instance variable, as shown in the example.

Initializing the Music Player

Much like the hardware camera or microphone, the iPod music library is a shared resource. The MPMusicPlayerController class works with this limitation by allowing you to implement a music player as an application music player or an iPod music player. An *application music player* is one that can pull in media items from the iPod music player, but does not have any effect on the status of the iPod app. An *iPod music player* is a media player within your app that acts more like a remote to the iPod app than an independent music player. All your playback setting changes and media selections will affect the iPod app. This is appropriate for an app where you want to let users control or change their *Now Playing* playlist from within your app.

You instantiate your music player by calling the appropriate class method for the type of music player you want to implement:

```
self.musicPlayer = [MPMusicPlayerController applicationMusicPlayer];
```

The MyPod application implements its music player as an application music player. To implement an iPod music player, call the [MPMusicPlayerController iPodMusicPlayer] class method. In order to initialize the object correctly, place this call in the [self viewDidLoad] method for your class, as shown in Listing 6-2.

Listing 6-2. Initializing the Music Player

```
- (void)viewDidLoad
{
    [super viewDidLoad];
        // Do any additional setup after loading the view,
        // typically from a nib.

    self.musicPlayer = [MPMusicPlayerController applicationMusicPlayer];
}
```

Specifying a Media Queue (Playlist)

Before you can start playing music using the MPMusicPlayerController class, you need to specify a queue of media items that the music player should play. You can think of a media queue as a playlist; it is a list of items that play in First In, First Out order (the first item that is added to the queue will be the first to play).

By default, initializing a new MPMediaQuery item ([[MPMediaQuery alloc] init]) will return an unsorted list of all items in the iPod media library. To make your media queue useful, you should try to specify the following:

- The type of items to filter the results by (for example, songs, playlists, albums, or podcasts)

- How to group the results (for example, by song title, album name, or artist)

- Additional filters to match specific requirements (for example, match only a certain artist)

Using these criteria, you could build a query such as this: Find all songs where the artist is Pink Floyd, sorted by song title.

You can quickly specify a media type and grouping order for your media query by initializing your query object with one of the MPMediaQuery class methods. For the Pink Floyd example, you could use the [MPMediaQuery songsQuery] class method instead of the default constructor.

```
MPMediaQuery *pinkFloydQuery = [MPMediaQuery songsQuery];
```

You can find a table of some of the most popular MPMediaQuery class methods and their resulting queries in Table 6-1.

Table 6-1. Popular MPMediaQuery Class Methods

Method Name	Resulting Query
[MPMediaQuery albumsQuery]	Returns a list of music items (songs), sorted by album title
[MPMediaQuery artistsQuery]	Returns a list of music items (songs), sorted by artist name
[MPMediaQuery compilationsQuery]	Returns a list of compilation items (albums), sorted by album title
[MPMediaQuery playlistsQuery]	Returns a list of playlist items, sorted by playlist title
[MPMediaQuery songsQuery]	Returns a list of music items (songs), sorted by song title

You can manually change the grouping type for the media query by specifying a value for the groupingType property. You can find a table of popular grouping types in Table 6-2.

Table 6-2. Popular MPMediaGrouping Types

Key	Behavior
MPMediaGroupingTitle	Groups and sorts music items by album title
MPMediaGroupingArtist	Groups and sorts music items by artist name
MPMediaGroupingAlbum	Groups and sorts music item by album title and track number
MPMediaGroupingGenre	Groups and sorts items by genre
MPMediaGroupingPlaylist	Groups and sorts collections by playlist title

To filter the results to match a specific requirement (for example, Artist = Pink Floyd), you will need to use an MPMediaPropertyPredicate. To build a media property predicate, you need to specify three parameters:

- The property you are trying to match (for example, artist)
- The match value (for example, Pink Floyd)
- The type of comparison (contains or equalTo)

For the Pink Floyd example, the predicate would look like this:

```
MPMediaPropertyPredicate *artistPredicate = [MPMediaPropertyPredicate
    predicateWithValue:@"PinkFloyd"
    forProperty:MPMediaItemPropertyArtist
    comparisonType:MPMediaPredicateComparisonEqualTo];
```

After building the predicate, add it to the query by using the [MPMediaQuery addFilterPredicate:] instance method:

```
[pinkFloydQuery addFilterPredicate:artistPredicate];
```

> **Note** A query can have multiple predicates—but make sure they don't conflict with each other.

Load your query into the media player by using the [`MPMusicPlayerController setQueueWithQuery:`] method. Listing 6-3 shows a function that generates the Pink Floyd query and sets the media queue for a shared music player object.

Listing 6-3. Setting a Media Queue

```
MPMediaQuery *pinkFloydQuery = [MPMediaQuery songsQuery];
MPMediaPropertyPredicate *artistPredicate =
    [MPMediaPropertyPredicate predicateWithValue:@"Pink Floyd"
    forProperty:MPMediaItemPropertyArtist
    comparisonType:MPMediaPredicateComparisonEqualTo];
[pinkFloydQuery addFilterPredicate:artistPredicate];
[self.musicPlayer setQueueWithQuery:pinkFloydQuery];
```

For the MyPod project, you will need to set the query after the picker table view has returned, via delegate methods.

Creating an Item Selection Interface

You will now use media queries to build the item selection interface for the MyPod app. The goal is to build a class that you can reuse to select songs, albums, or other media types. To put this in the context of media queries, you will use this class to determine the predicate filter for your query (for example, song title.) You will use two media queries for this task: one to generate the list of all songs (or albums), and another to pass the final result back to the music player.

Because the goal is to build a reusable class, you will want to make your interfaces as generic as possible, including both the input and the output. Listing 6-4 shows a sample header file for the selection interface, represented by the `MediaTableViewController` class in the sample project.

Listing 6-4. Header File for MediaTableViewController Class

```
#import <UIKit/UIKit.h>

@protocol MediaTableDelegate <NSObject>

-(void)didFinishWithItem:(NSString *)item andType:(NSString *)type;
-(void)didCancel;

@end

@interface MediaTableViewController : UITableViewController

@property (nonatomic, strong) NSArray *itemsArray;
@property (nonatomic, strong) NSString *mediaType;

-(id)initWithArray:(NSArray *)array withType:(NString *)type;

@end
```

Note that the initialization method takes an NSArray as the input. This is convenient, because media queries return an array of results, and you can easily initialize table views from an array. Also note the protocol for returning the result, which uses NSString to represent the selected item. Again, this is an appropriate choice, because you want to build a class that returns the comparison string for a predicate. Because you want to be able to reuse this class, note that the media type is one of the parameters. Writing the code this way lets you to handle the result in the class that implements the protocol.

Start by creating the button handler to present the MediaTableViewController when the user presses the Choose Track button. The key tasks are to create a media query that you can use as a data source, and to present the table view controller. Because you are looking for songs, use the [MPMediaQuery songsQuery] class method to create your query. Listing 6-5 shows an implementation of this method. You put this button handler in your main view controller.

Listing 6-5. Button Handler for the Choose Track button

```
-(IBAction)chooseTrackButton:(id)sender
{
    NSMutableArray *items = [NSMutableArray new];

    MPMediaQuery *query = [MPMediaQuery songsQuery];

    for (MPMediaItem *item in query.items) {
        NSString *trackName =
            [item valueForProperty:MPMediaItemPropertyTitle];
        [items addObject:trackName];
    }

    MediaTableViewController *mediaTableVC =
        [[MediaTableViewControlleralloc] initWithItems:items];
    [self presentViewController:mediaTableVC animated:YES
        completion:nil];

}
```

You may be wondering why I chose to extract the song titles from the media query item rather than passing the results array (the items property) directly. The answer is that to make your classes more reusable, you want to reduce dependencies. By processing the media items before sending them to the MediaTableViewController, you don't need to include the header for the MediaPlayer in your class.

Follow the same pattern for the Choose Album button, except use the [MPMediaQuery compilationsQuery] class method and specify *albums* as your return type. Listing 6-6 contains the implementation for the Choose Album button handler.

Listing 6-6. Button Handler for Choose Album Button

```
-(IBAction)chooseAlbumButton:(id)sender
{
    NSMutableArray *items = [NSMutableArray new];

    MPMediaQuery *query = [MPMediaQuery compilationsQuery];
```

```
    for (MPMediaItem *item in query.items) {
        NSString *albumName = [item
            valueForProperty:MPMediaItemPropertyTitle];
        [items addObject:albumName];
    }

    MediaTableViewController *mediaTableVC =
        [[MediaTableViewController alloc] initWithItems:items];
    [self presentViewController:mediaTableVC animated:YES
        completion:nil];
}
```

To populate the table view for the `MediaTableViewController`, use the `itemsArray` property to populate the cell count and set the label for each cell. The methods to populate the table view for the `MediaTableViewController` are in Listing 6-7. Remember, these would go in your `MediaTableViewController.m` file. The `[MediaTableViewController initWithItems]` method uses the default Cocoa Touch init method as a design pattern.

Listing 6-7. Populating the MediaTableViewController Table View

```
- (id)initWithItems:(NSArray *)array withType:(NSString *)type
{
    self = [super init];
    if (self) {
        // Custom initialization
        self.itemsArray = array;
        self.mediaType = type;
    }
    return self;
}


- (NSInteger)numberOfSectionsInTableView:(UITableView *)tableView
{
    // Return the number of sections.
    return 1;
}


- (NSInteger)tableView:(UITableView *)tableView
    numberOfRowsInSection:(NSInteger)section
{
    // Return the number of rows in the section.
    return [self.itemsArray count];
}

- (UITableViewCell *)tableView:(UITableView *)tableView
    cellForRowAtIndexPath:(NSIndexPath *)indexPath
{
    UITableViewCell *cell =
        [tableView dequeueReusableCellWithIdentifier:@"itemCell"
        forIndexPath:indexPath];
```

```
    // Configure the cell...
    cell.textLabel.text = [self.itemsArray
        objectAtIndex:indexPath.row];
    return cell;
}
```

You handle the item selection in a pattern similar to the other item projects in this book: send a message from the table view controller via the protocol, and handle it in the main view controller. The selection action needs to occur first. When a cell has been selected, send a message via the protocol in the [self tableView:didSelectRowAtIndexPath:] method for the MediaTableViewController class, as shown in Listing 6-8.

Listing 6-8. Sending a Protocol Message for Selecting a Media Item

```
-(void)tableView:(UITableView *)tableView
    didSelectRowAtIndexPath:(NSIndexPath *)indexPath
{
    NSString *selectedItem = [self.itemsArray
        objectAtIndex:indexPath.row];
    [self.delegate didFinishWithItem:selectedItem
        andType:self.mediaType];
}
```

Handle the protocol messages in your main view controller. Based on the returned media type, you set a predicate by using the filterName string as the match text. In the handler method, use an if() statement to compare the media type, so that you can use different code blocks to handle albums and songs. You will use this predicate to initialize the active queue for the music player via the [MPMusicPlayerController setQueueWithQuery:] method. Listing 6-9 shows example delegate methods that implement this logic for the MediaTableDelegate protocol.

Listing 6-9. Setting a Media Queue after Receiving a Protocol Message

```
-(void)didFinishWithItem:(NSString *)item andType:(NSString *)type
{

    if ([type isEqualToString:@"songs"]) {
        MPMediaQuery *query = [MPMediaQuery songsQuery];
        MPMediaPropertyPredicate *predicate =
            [MPMediaPropertyPredicate predicateWithValue:item
            forProperty:MPMediaItemPropertyArtist
            comparisonType:MPMediaPredicateComparisonEqualTo];

        [query addFilterPredicate:predicate];
        [self.musicPlayer setQueueWithQuery:query];

    } else if ([type isEqualToString:@"albums"]) {
        MPMediaQuery *query = [MPMediaQuery albumsQuery];
        MPMediaPropertyPredicate *predicate =
                [MPMediaPropertyPredicate predicateWithValue:item
                forProperty:MPMediaItemPropertyAlbumTitle
                comparisonType:MPMediaPredicateComparisonEqualTo];
```

```
    [query addFilterPredicate:predicate];
    [self.musicPlayer setQueueWithQuery:query];

}

    [self dismissViewControllerAnimated:YES completion:nil];
}
```

Building a Playback Interface

Having created your media query, you can now start building the playback interface.
The MPMediaPlayerController class implements the MPMediaPlayback protocol, which allows you to
reuse many of the playback messages you used to play sound files.

To start playback by using the MPMediaPlayerController class, use the [MPMediaPlayerController
play] method, which works exactly like its AVAudioPlayer counterpart, by starting (or resuming)
playback of the item at the front of the media queue. To pause playback, use the
[MPMediaPlayerController pause] method, which pauses the currently playing item. Playing the
item after pausing resumes play from the position where the media was paused. In the MyPod
project, playback is controlled by one button, just as in the simple audio file player from the last
chapter. The handler for this button is in Listing 6-10.

Listing 6-10. Toggling Playback for the MyPod Project

```
-(IBAction)toggleAudio:(id)sender
{
    if ([self.musicPlayer playbackState] ==
        MPMusicPlaybackStatePlaying) {
        [self.musicPlayer pause];
        self.playButton.titleLabel.text = @"Play";
    } else {
        [self.musicPlayer play];
        self.playButton.titleLabel.text = @"Pause";
    }
}
```

As with the simple audio player, to toggle playback state with one button, you should poll the media
player for its playback state by using the [MPMusicPlayerController playbackState] property. If
you want to completely stop playback of an item, implement a separate Stop button, using the
[MPMediaPlayerController stop] method. Stop works exactly like Pause, except it resets the
playback position to the beginning of the track the next time the user resumes playback.

In the simple audio player application, you implemented Fast Forward and Rewind buttons by
skipping 15 seconds forward or backward in the track. This functionality is also available in the
MPMusicPlayerController class, and you can implement it in the same manner—by changing the
currentPlaybackTime property of your MPMusicPlayerController object. Listing 6-11 shows an
example of seeking forward. For a more complete implementation, refer to Chapter 5; you can reuse
the same logic.

Listing 6-11. Seeking Forward 15 Seconds in a Track

```
-(IBAction)seekForward:(id)sender
{
    if ([self.musicPlayer playbackState] ==
        MPMusicPlaybackStatePlaying) {

        NSTimeInterval desiredTime =
            self.musicPlayer.currentPlaybackTime + 15.0f;
        if (desiredTime <
            self.musicPlayer.nowPlayingItem.playbackDuration) {
            self.musicPlayer.currentPlaybackTime = desiredTime;
        }
    }
}
```

To start taking advantage of the MediaPlayer framework, you implement Fast Forward in a slightly different manner. The MediaPlayer framework lets you speed up playback of an item during a seek operation, producing a sound effect similar to one you would hear when fast-forwarding a cassette tape (that's my obligatory 1980s reference). However, this new implementation is completely user-interface driven, meaning that seeking begins when the user presses the button, and stops when the user releases the button. You no longer need to modify the currentPlaybackTime property using this technique.

To begin fast-forwarding, call the [MPMediaPlayerController beginSeekingForward] method on your media player object. Similarly, you would call the [MPMediaPlayerController beginSeekingBackward] method to begin rewinding. When you have finished seeking, for both events, you need to call the [MPMediaPlayerController endSeeking] method. Listing 6-12 shows these calls, wrapped in event handlers, as they appear in the MyPod project.

Listing 6-12. Event Handlers for Fast-Forwarding and Rewinding

```
-(IBAction)startFastForward:(id)sender
{
    [self.musicPlayer beginSeekingForward];
}

-(IBAction)startRewind:(id)sender
{
    [self.musicPlayer beginSeekingBackward];
}

-(IBAction)stopSeeking:(id)sender
{
    [self.musicPlayer endSeeking];
}
```

To tie these event handlers to your storyboard, you need to change the events that you are using in Interface Builder. To handle the event that gets triggered when a user presses down a button, tie the [MainViewController startFastForward:] method to the Touch Down event for your Fast Forward button in Interface Builder. To handle the event that gets triggered when you release the button, tie the [MainViewController stopSeeking:] method to the Touch Up Inside event in Interface Builder. Figure 6-3 is a screenshot of how the completed connections for the Fast Forward button should look in Interface Builder. You would follow the same process to connect the events for the Rewind button.

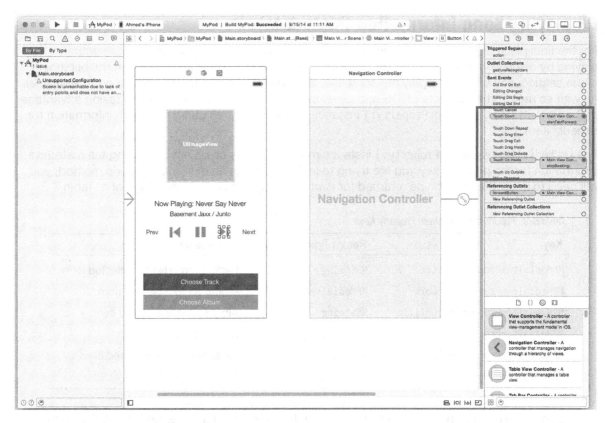

Figure 6-3. Interface Builder connections for Fast Forward button

To complete the playback interface for the MyPod project, you need to implement the Previous and Next buttons that support navigating through the currently loaded media queue (the playlist). You navigate through a media queue by using the [MPMediaPlayerController skipToNextItem] and [MPMediaPlayerController skipToPreviousItem] methods on your media player object. If the queue has only one item, or if you are at the beginning or end, these methods will stop playback of the currently playing item. Listing 6-13 shows the event handlers that wrap these methods.

Listing 6-13. Event Handlers for Playlist Navigation

```
-(IBAction)nextTrack:(id)sender
{
    [self.musicPlayer skipToNextItem];
}
```

```
-(IBAction)prevTrack:(id)sender
{
    [self.musicPlayer skipToPreviousItem];
}
```

Displaying Song Information (Metadata)

For the final piece of the MyPod project, you need to let the user know which song is currently playing by displaying its information (or metadata). Referring back to the mock-up at the beginning of the section, you want to display the song title, artist name, album title, and album art (if available). As with so many other aspects of iOS app development, there's an API for that! By taking advantage of the [MPMediaItem valueForProperty:] instance method, you can query metadata information for a media item.

The [MPMediaItem valueForProperty:] instance method returns an object containing the metadata information for the property key you are trying to look up. As it is an extremely generic method, you will need to know the object type returned for each property to take full advantage of it. Table 6-3

Table 6-3. Popular MPMediaItem Property Keys

Key	Return Type	Represents
MPMediaItemPropertyArtist	NSString	Performing artist for selected item
MPMediaItemPropertyArtwork	MPMediaItemArtwork	Album art for selected item
MPMediaItemPropertyAlbumTitle	NSString	Album title for selected item
MPMediaItemPropertyGenre	NSString	Genre for selected item
MPMediaItemPropertyReleaseDate	NSString	Release date for selected item
MPMediaItemPropertyTyle	NSString	Title for selected item

lists some of the most popular properties, including the information they represent and their return types. The property keys are constant values defined in the MPMediaItem class.

For properties returned as NSString objects, such as MPMediaItemPropertyTitle, you can just save the output to a string, or use it to initialize a label. For example, to initialize the titleLabel of the main view controller, set the text property of the label to the returned value:

```
self.titleLabel.text = [currentMediaItem valueForProperty:MPMediaItemPropertyTitle];
```

Referring back to Table 6-3, note that the MPMediaItemPropertyArtwork key, which represents the album art, returns an MPMediaItemArtwork object. To use this output with a UIImageView, you need to use the [MPMediaItemArtwork imageWithSize:] instance method to generate a UIImage object, as shown in Listing 6-14.

Listing 6-14. Generating a UIImage from a MPMediaItemArtwork Object

```
MPMediaItem *currentItem = self.musicPlayer.nowPlayingItem;
MPMediaItemArtwork *albumArt = [currentItem
    valueForProperty:MPMediaItemPropertyArtwork];
CGSize imageFrameSize = self.albumImageView.frame.size;
self.albumImageView.image = [albumArt imageWithSize:imageFrameSize];
```

The [MPMediaItemArtwork imageWithSize:] method uses a CGSize parameter to determine the width and height of the generated image. As shown in the example, you can pass in the size property from the UIImageView's frame.

The last question you may have is, "Where should I make the call to get all this metadata?" Because you will need to update the displayed metadata each time the playlist advances, you should retrieve metadata and set your labels whenever the MPMusicPlayerControllerNowPlayingItemDidChangeNotification notification occurs. Listing 6-15 shows an example that catches the notification via a block method.

Listing 6-15. Catching the Notification for "Now Playing" Changes

```
[[NSNotificationCenter defaultCenter] addObserverForName:
    @"MPMusicPlayerControllerVolumeDidChangeNotification"
    object:self queue:nil
    usingBlock:^(NSNotification *note) {

        MPMediaItem *currentItem = self.musicPlayer.nowPlayingItem;
        MPMediaItemArtwork *albumArt =
            [currentItem valueForProperty:MPMediaItemPropertyArtwork];
        CGSize imageFrameSize = self.albumImageView.frame.size;
        self.albumImageView.image =
            [albumArt imageWithSize:imageFrameSize];

        NSString *artistName =
            [currentItem valueForProperty:MPMediaItemPropertyTitle];
        NSString *albumName =
            [currentItem valueForProperty:MPMediaItemPropertyAlbumTitle];

        self.titleLabel.text =
            [currentItem valueForProperty:MPMediaItemPropertyTitle];
        self.albumLabel.text = [NSString stringWithFormat:@"%@ / %@",
                                artistName, albumName];

}];
```

To start receiving notifications, you need to let the music player know that it should generate them. You can do this by calling the [MPMusicPlayerController beginGeneratingPlaybackNotifications] instance method. Listing 6-16 contains a complete version of the [self viewDidLoad] method for the main view controller, which includes this step.

Listing 6-16. Complete Implementation for Creating a Media Player and Catching Notifications

```
- (void)viewDidLoad
{
    [super viewDidLoad];
        // Do any additional setup after loading the view,
        // typically from a nib.

    self.musicPlayer = [MPMusicPlayerController
                        applicationMusicPlayer];

    [self.musicPlayer beginGeneratingPlaybackNotifications];

    [[NSNotificationCenter defaultCenter] addObserverForName:
        @"MPMusicPlayerControllerNowPlayingItemDidChangeNotification"
        object:self
        queue:nil usingBlock:^(NSNotification *note) {

        MPMediaItem *currentItem = self.musicPlayer.nowPlayingItem;
        MPMediaItemArtwork *albumArt = [currentItem
            valueForProperty:MPMediaItemPropertyArtwork];
        CGSize imageFrameSize = self.albumImageView.frame.size;

        self.albumImageView.image =
            [albumArt imageWithSize:imageFrameSize];

        NSString *artistName =
            [currentItem valueForProperty:MPMediaItemPropertyTitle];
        NSString *albumName =
            [currentItem valueForProperty:MPMediaItemPropertyAlbumTitle];

        self.titleLabel.text =
            [currentItem valueForProperty:MPMediaItemPropertyTitle];
        self.albumLabel.text = [NSString stringWithFormat:@"%@ / %@",
                                artistName, albumName];

    }];
}
```

Notifications are a core concept for many MediaPlayer classes, especially those for video playback. For a more detailed explanation of the concept, skip to the beginning of Chapter 10, "Playing and Recording Video".

Streaming Music

Now that you know how to play audio files and iPod media in your apps, it is time to explore another major audio source: streaming audio services. Many radio stations offer online versions of their broadcasts, and a great number of radio stations operate online only. The technology is called *streaming audio* because, instead of downloading a file, you connect to a server that broadcasts a continuous *stream* of audio data to anyone who connects (also known as *multicasting*). The stream is generally encoded in one of the same compression formats (codecs) that audio files use (for example, MP3, OGG, or others), but unlike a file, it does not have a beginning or terminating header. On the player side, when an application connects to a stream, it saves the data to a bucket in memory called a *buffer*. Playback begins when the buffer has collected enough data to play back audio (or video) continuously.

Using the `AVPlayer` class, you can access the `AVFoundation` framework's streaming audio player. The `AVAudioPlayer` class you used previously for audio file playback does not support buffer management, making it a poor choice for streaming audio. Conveniently, the `AVPlayer` class follows many of the same design patterns of the `AVAudioPlayer` and `MPMusicPlayerController` classes, meaning you can reuse the same general logic for playback.

To integrate streaming radio services in your app, you can modify the MyPlayer app from Chapter 5, converting it to use streaming audio instead of audio files. You will simplify the user interface to look like the mock-up in Figure 6-4, reducing the controls to a Play button, and an alert box where users can enter a stream URL. This project is included in the Chapter 6 folder of the source code bundle as the MyStreamingPlayer project.

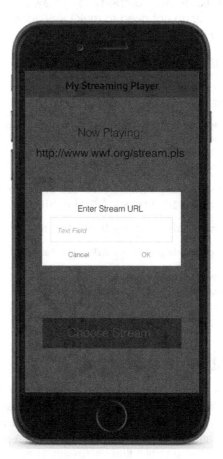

Figure 6-4. Mock-up for MyStreamingPlayer app

Getting Started

To start implementing the MyStreamingPlayer project, make a copy of the MyPlayer project, renaming it appropriately.

Tip   You can quickly rename a project by double-clicking its name in the Source Code Navigator (the left pane of Xcode).

In Interface Builder, remove all the buttons from the main view controller except for the Play button and the Choose File button. Rename the Choose File button to *Choose Stream*. In your code, delete the now-extraneous code for the buttons you removed. Because you want to use the AVPlayer class (which can play streaming files) instead of the AVAudioPlayer class (which cannot), change the object type of the audioPlayer property to AVPlayer. Because both classes are part of the AVFoundation framework, you do not need to make any additional changes. Your final header file should look like the example in Listing 6-17.

Listing 6-17. Header File for MainViewController Class

```
#import <UIKit/UIKit.h>
#import <AVFoundation/AVFoundation.h>

@interface MainViewController : UIViewController <UIAlertViewDelegate>

@property (nonatomic, strong) IBOutlet UILabel *timeLabel;
@property (nonatomic, strong) IBOutlet UILabel *titleLabel;

@property (nonatomic, strong) IBOutlet UIButton *chooseButton;
@property (nonatomic, strong) IBOutlet UIButton *playButton;

@property (nonatomic, strong) NSURL *selectedURL;

@property (nonatomic, strong) AVPlayer *audioPlayer;

-(IBAction)play:(id)sender;
-(IBAction)chooseStream:(id)sender;

@end
```

Connecting to a Stream

You will use a UIAlertView to allow the user to enter a stream URL. You can find valid stream URLs on most radio stations' sites by looking for a link that ends in .pls. A .pls file is a playlist that contains the URLs for several streaming radio channels. Multicast streams often have restrictions on the number of users who can connect simultaneously. Using a playlist helps with congestion, because the player will traverse the playlist until it finds a stream it can connect to. You want to present the UIAlertView when the user presses the Choose Stream button. Listing 6-18 contains an example of the event handler for this action. Make sure you tie this action handler to your button in Interface Builder.

Listing 6-18. Presenting a UIAlertView to Choose a Stream

```
-(IBAction)chooseStream:(id)sender
{
    UIAlertView *alertView = [[UIAlertView alloc]
        initWithTitle:@"Enter Stream URL" message:@""
        delegate:self cancelButtonTitle:@"Cancel"
            otherButtonTitles:@"OK", nil];
    [alertView setAlertViewStyle:UIAlertViewStylePlainTextInput];
    [alertView show];
}
```

Set the UIAlertView to present a text box by using the [UIAlertView setAlertViewStyle:] instance method. In the next section, you will see how to handle the result.

Playing Streaming Audio

After a user has entered a stream URL, you use that information to initialize the AVPlayer object for the main view controller. Much like the AVAudioPlayer class, you can load items into an AVPlayer item during the initialization path. Listing 6-19 shows the delegate method for the UIAlertView, which initializes the AVPlayer and changes the title of the Now Playing label.

Listing 6-19. Initializing the AVPlayer

```
-(void)alertView:(UIAlertView *)alertView didDismissWithButtonIndex:(NSInteger)buttonIndex
{
    if (buttonIndex == 1) {
        NSString *selectedUrlString =
            [alertView textFieldAtIndex:0].text;
        self.selectedURL = [NSURL URLWithString:selectedUrlString];
        self.titleLabel.text = [NSString stringWithFormat:
                            @"Now Playing: %@", selectedUrlString];
        self.audioPlayer = [[AVPlayer alloc] initWithURL:
                        self.selectedURL];
    }
}
```

To play audio, reuse the same basic logic from the other two media player apps—start or stop based on the playback status. For the AVPlayer class, you query status through the status property. If the value is AVPlayerStatusReadyToPlay, the player is ready to start playing back audio; otherwise, it is already playing, or an error occurred while connecting to the stream. You can find out if an error occurred by checking whether the error status is non-nil. Listing 6-20 shows the action handler for the Play button that attempts to start playback or displays an error.

Listing 6-20. Action Handler for Play Button

```objc
-(IBAction)play:(id)sender
{
    if (self.audioPlayer.error != nil) {
        UIAlertView *alert = [[UIAlertView alloc]
                              initWithTitle:@"Error"
            message:[self.audioPlayer.error description] delegate:self
                      cancelButtonTitle:@"OK" otherButtonTitles:nil];
        [alert show];
    } else {
        if ([self.audioPlayer status] != AVPlayerStatusReadyToPlay) {
            [self.audioPlayer pause];
            self.playButton.titleLabel.text = @"Play";

        } else {
            [self.audioPlayer play];
            self.playButton.titleLabel.text = @"Pause";
        }
    }
}
```

Playing Event Sounds (Including Vibration)

Often, you will want to play a short sound effect in response to a user-interface event, such as a snap sound when a user takes a picture with the camera, or a typing sound when the user enters text. As you may remember from Chapter 5, the process for playing sounds by using the AVAudioPlayer class requires a lot of setup, and may take a few seconds to initialize. Therefore, to play very short sound files (of less than 30 seconds), Apple recommends using the System Sound Services APIs, which are bundled with the AudioToolbox framework.

The idea behind System Sound Services is to create a programmatic interface that re-creates the functionality of the Sound Effects panel in OS X, shown in Figure 6-5. This panel, accessible from the Sound system preference pane, lets you specify the named sound effect that should play when an alert view or other action happens on the computer.

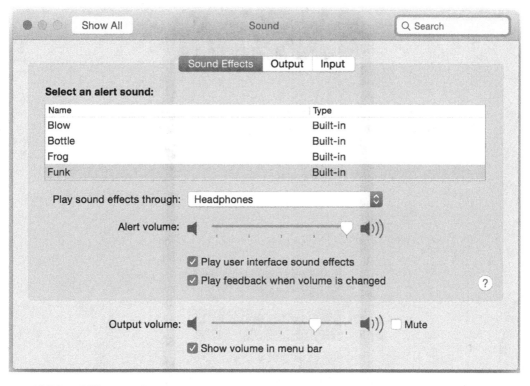

Figure 6-5. OS X Sound Effects panel

While iOS has its own system sounds panel, as of this writing, Apple does not allow you to access it within your app. However, by defining your own system sounds, you can take advantage of the same functionality.

To play a system sound, implement the following steps:

1. Create a URL reference to the sound file you want to play.

2. Create a `SystemSoundID` object using this URL reference.

3. Play your desired sound by referencing its `SystemSoundID` object.

Getting Started

To help you learn how to use system sounds, you will implement the SystemSounds project in the in the `Chapter 6` folder of the source code bundle. SystemSounds is a simple, single-view application that plays a sound effect or causes your device to vibrate, depending on which button is pressed. Figure 6-6 shows a mock-up of the application.

Figure 6-6. Mock-up of SystemSounds project

Before getting started with system sounds, you need to include the AudioToolbox framework in your project. You can find this framework in the usual manner by navigating to your project settings and using the framework browser that appears in the Link Binary with Libraries section under the Build Phases tab.

Next, you need to include the AudioToolbox.h header file for the framework in the class that will be implementing it. For the SampleSounds project, this class is the MainViewController:

```
#import <AudioToolbox/AudioToolbox.h>
```

> **Note**   The AudioToolbox framework is separate from AVFoundation, so remember to include both if you want to use them in the same project.

Creating a System Sound

The `AudioToolbox` framework derives part of its speed advantage over `AVFoundation` because it's a C-based framework. At a compiler level, Objective-C is implemented on top of C, so working directly in C allows the framework to reduce overhead and represent data in a way that is closer to what the hardware expects.

As a result, to initialize your system sounds, you need to provide the system with a URL reference (`CFURLRef`), rather than a `NSURL` object. The `CFBundleCopyResourceURL()` method allows you to create a URL reference in a similar manner to retrieving a file url; by specifying the path of the main bundle and the name and type of your desired file. Listing 6-21 shows an example method that creates URL references.

Listing 6-21. Creating a URL Reference to a Sound File

```
- (void)initializeSystemSound
{
    CFBundleRef mainBundle = CFBundleGetMainBundle();
    CFURLRef clickUrlRef = CFBundleCopyResourceURL(mainBundle,
        CFSTR("click"), CFSTR("wav"), nil);

}
```

To reduce overhead, the `AudioToolbox` classes accept only uncompressed audio files (also known as *Linear PCM files*). To meet this requirement, you should always use AIF and WAV files for your system sounds.

To operate at a low level, your sound files will need to be loaded in memory, so make sure you include them in your main bundle by adding them to your project (refer to Chapter 2 for a more detailed explanation of bundles). To access the main bundle, you need to use a bundle reference (`CFBundleRef`), which you can easily find by using the `CFGetMainBundle()` function. Because you are operating at the C level, you cannot use the `NSString` class; instead, you need to use string references (`CFStringRef`). A quick shortcut for creating a one-time-use `CFStringRef` is the macro function `CFStr()`.

> **Note** You may be wondering why I keep using parentheses for method calls in this example. This is C-style syntax! Always use the correct syntax for the framework you are referencing. Try to avoid C-style calls to Objective-C frameworks; doing so will make debugging more difficult.

Now that you have a valid reference to your sound file, you need to create a system sound ID object (`SystemSoundID`) to play it, using the `AudioToolbox` framework. You'll reuse this object throughout the calling class, so make sure you declare it as an instance variable. Because you need to use C syntax for the `AudioToolbox` classes, you need to declare the variable within your class's `@implementation` block:

```
SystemSoundID clickSoundId;
```

In the sample project, you can find this declaration in the `MainViewController.m` file.

You can initialize your `SystemSoundID` object by calling the `AudioServicesCreateSystemSoundID()` function with the URL reference you generated earlier and a pointer to the system sound ID object. Listing 6-22 shows a modified version of the `[self initializeSystemSounds]` method, which creates a pointer for a system sound ID at runtime.

Listing 6-22. Creating a SystemSoundID Object

```
- (void)initializeSystemSound
{
    CFBundleRef mainBundle = CFBundleGetMainBundle();
    CFURLRef clickUrlRef = CFBundleCopyResourceURL(mainBundle,
        CFSTR("click"), CFSTR("wav"), nil);

    AudioServicesCreateSystemSoundID (clickUrlRef, &clickSoundId);
}
```

In a manner similar to the way you needed to pass `NSError` objects *by reference* when you initialized an audio session in the preceding chapter, you also need to pass your `systemSoundId` object by reference to initialize them. As a refresher, when passing by reference, you can change the contents of the object you pass in, rather than modifying a copy of it in memory.

If you need to create multiple system sounds, follow the process to create a URL reference and `SystemSoundID` object for each sound.

As a final note, you need to initialize all your system sound ID objects before you can call them, so call the `[self initializeSystemSounds]` method from a method that is part of your initialization process. The sample project makes this call from `[self viewDidLoad]` in the `MainViewController` class.

Playing a System Sound

Now that you have initialized your system sounds, you can play them by calling the `AudioServicesPlaySystemSound()` method with your `SystemSoundID` object. After system sounds are initialized, you can call them at any time during the lifetime of a class. Listing 6-23 shows an example of a button handler that plays a system sound.

Listing 6-23. Playing a System Sound

```
-(IBAction)playSound:(id)sender
{
    AudioServicesPlaySystemSound(clickSoundId);
}
```

> **Caution**   System Sound Services is intended for very simple audio files only. It is able to play back only 30-second files, using the user's current audio settings (volume, mute, and so forth), one at a time. If you require more-advanced playback, continue to use the `AVAudioPlayer` class.

Making the Device Vibrate

System Sound Services offers two options for making a user's device vibrate: either when a system sound is played, or in place of a system sound.

> **Note**   Vibration is available only on iPhone devices; however, there's no harm in calling these APIs on incompatible devices; the `vibrate` command will simply be ignored.

To make a device vibrate when a system sound is played, instead of calling the `AudioServicesPlaySystemSound()` method, use the `AudioServicesPlayAlertSound()` method, as shown in Listing 6-24.

Listing 6-24. Playing a System Sound with Vibration

```
-(IBAction)playSoundAndVibrate:(id)sender
{
    AudioServicesPlayAlertSound(clickSoundId);
}
```

Apple makes one exception to their rule of "no globally accessible system sounds": when you want the device to vibrate without playing a sound. To do that, call the `AudioServicesPlaySystemSound()` method with the AudioToolbox constant for vibration, kSystemSoundID_Vibrate. Listing 6-25 shows an example.

Listing 6-25. Making the Device Vibrate Without Playing a Sound

```
-(IBAction)vibrate:(id)sender
{
    AudioServicesPlaySystemSound(kSystemSoundID_Vibrate);
}
```

> **Note**   As when playing regular system sounds, you can have only one vibration effect active at a time. At the time of this writing, there are no public APIs to control vibration intensity or playback length.

Summary

In this chapter, you saw how to integrate three new audio sources into your apps: iPod music files, streaming audio, and system sounds. In implementing the MyPod app, you saw how the `MediaPlayer` framework gives you deep access into the iPod app, yet follows many of the same design patterns as the `AVFoundation` playback classes. With the MyStreamingPlayer app, you learned how to modify your audio file player to play streaming audio—which consisted primarily of using the `AVPlayer` class instead of the `AVAudioPlayer` class. With the SystemSounds app, you learned how to use the `SystemsSounds` classes to integrate C-based code into your apps to play short sound files quickly, or to vibrate the phone.

As a final takeaway, remember, none of these classes are mutually exclusive; you can use any or all of the them in the same app, as long as you maintain an object for each audio source you are trying to play.

Chapter 7

Advanced Audio Topics

In Chapters 5 and 6, you learned how to build audio player applications that accept a wide variety of input sources, including local files, a user's iPod music library, and streaming radio. You also learned how to use media players based on the `AVFoundation` and `MediaPlayer` frameworks and saw some of their similarities.

In this chapter, you will learn ways to make your audio apps even more powerful by adding features that free your audio from interference by other device tasks. These features will allow your apps to keep operating when users initiate an external event, such as backgrounding your app or unplugging the headphones. Along the way, you will also explore some additional, cool features such as AirPlay and "remote controls," which allow users to interact with your app outside its built-in user interface.

Backgrounding Audio

In the MyPlayer project in Chapter 5, you built an application that would play sound files in the application's documents directory. Unfortunately, you may have noticed that sending the application to the background (either by setting the device to "sleep" or opening another application) paused playback. However, with a few tweaks to your project settings and audio session, you can make your `AVFoundation`-based audio applications continue playback even when they are backgrounded. Here are the major changes you need to make:

- Adding background modes to your application
- Selecting a background-compatible session type

In this section, you will modify the MyPlayer project from Chapter 5 to allow it to play audio in the background. You'll find a copy of the project with the background audio modifications in the Chapter 7 folder of the source code bundle (see the Source Code/Download area of the Apress web site at www.apress.com). The project retains the MyPlayer name. While building the initial version of the MyPlayer project in Chapter 5, you saw how to do the following:

- Initialize the music player
- Specify a media query (you can think of this as a playlist)
- Build a playback interface
- Display song information (metadata)

Setting Background Modes

The first step in enabling background audio is to change your project settings to reflect the fact that your app will use the Audio *background service*. Background services are iOS's mechanism for allowing you to keep a small subset of processes from your application alive when it is backgrounded. Unlike modern desktop computers, which are designed to run multiple applications simultaneously, iOS devices are designed to keep one application active at a time. Because of the limited resources on these devices, it does not make sense to allow all processes to stay active all the time. Instead, when the user launches or selects a different application, the previous application is *backgrounded*, meaning it's suspended until it's either closed or becomes the active application again.

Apple realizes that some applications, such as music players or navigation applications, need to continue operating when they have been backgrounded, so iOS uses background services to define a white list of the processes that are allowed to continue in the background.

To use background services, you need to add values to the UIBackgroundModes key in your project settings. In Xcode 6, you can do this by selecting your project file (MyPlayer.xcodeproj) from the Project Navigator and then selecting the Capabilities tab, as shown in Figure 7-1.

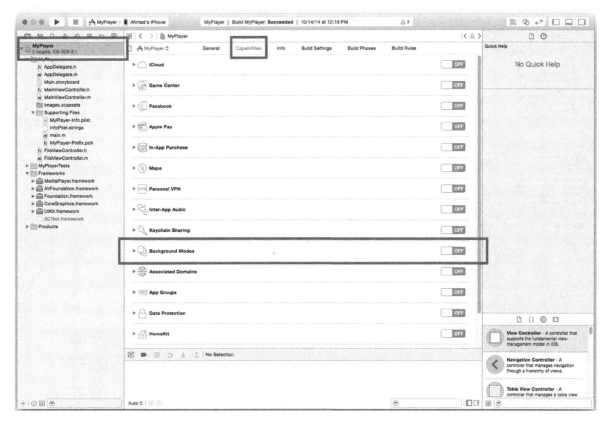

Figure 7-1. *The Capabilities tab in Xcode*

After toggling the switch in the Background Modes section to On, you will see a series of check boxes that allow you to select background modes. For the MyPlayer app, you want to enable Audio and AirPlay. After toggling the check box, your screen should look like Figure 7-2.

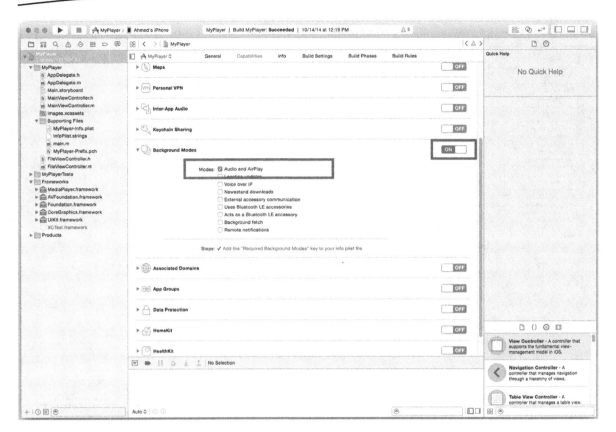

Figure 7-2. *Completed background mode settings*

The Capabilities tab in Xcode provides a user-friendly interface for modifying common project settings. If you are using Xcode 5, or prefer the traditional way of changing application settings, you can use the Info tab. The key you need to add is called Required Background Modes (or UIBackgroundModes). Figure 7-3 shows an example of how the settings look in the Info tab.

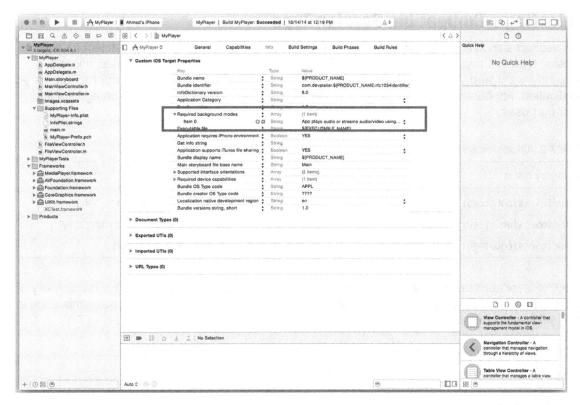

Figure 7-3. *Using the Info tab to specify background modes*

The UIBackgroundModes key can take an array of values as its input, so you can add multiple values to specify multiple background services.

Table 7-1 lists the most popular UIBackgroundModes keys and what they represent. Remember, these are the only kinds of tasks you can keep alive when your app is backgrounded.

Table 7-1. *Major Background Modes Supported by iOS*

Name	Key	Purpose
Audio and AirPlay	audio	Allows app to play back audio in the background
Location updates	location	Allows app to use location services in the background (to provide location-based information)
External accessory communication	external-accessory	Allows app to communicate in the background with a connected hardware accessory
Uses Bluetooth LE accessory	bluetooth-peripheral	Allows app to communicate in the background with a Bluetooth accessory
Background fetch	fetch	Allows app to periodically fetch information in the background
Remote notification	remote-notification	Allows app to update information in the background, based on notifications

Selecting a Compatible Session Type

The second step in enabling background audio for the MyPlayer application is to select an audio session type that supports backgrounding. Compared to setting background modes, this is a straightforward step. All you need to do is choose the audio session that is most appropriate for your application. For convenience, Table 7-2 lists the background-compatible session categories and their purposes.

Table 7-2. AVAudioSession Categories Compatible with Backgrounding

Category Name	Purpose
AVAudioSessionCategoryPlayback	Playing sound files (single-duplex playback only)
AVAudioSessionCategoryRecord	Recording sound files (single-duplex recording only)
AVAudioSessionCategoryPlayAndRecord	Full-duplex audio playback and recording

The MyPlayer application only needs to play audio, so the AVAudioSessionCategoryPlayback key is most appropriate. Because you need to initialize the session along with the view, place this code in the [self viewDidLoad] method for the MainViewController class, as shown in Listing 7-1.

Listing 7-1. Initializing Your Audio Session

```
- (void)viewDidLoad
{
    [super viewDidLoad];
        // Do any additional setup after loading the view, typically
        // from a nib.

    NSError *error = nil;
    [[AVAudioSession sharedInstance]
        setCategory:AVAudioSessionCategoryPlayback error:&error];
    if (error == nil) {
        NSLog(@"audio session initialized successfully");
    } else {
        NSLog(@"error initializing audio session: %@",
            [error description]);
    }
}
```

To test that you have configured background audio correctly, select a music file within your app and wait for it to begin playing. Then press the Home button. The music should continue playing even though your app is backgrounded.

Using the Now Playing Center

Another cool feature that many developers like to use to enhance the user experience of their audio-driven application is the Now Playing center. The Now Playing center is a global resource in iOS that appears in the lock screen, the multitasking menu, and any Made for iPod–compatible connected devices (such as radios or car dashboards), as well as any app that specifically requests the information.

As shown in Figure 7-4, within the lock screen and multitasking modal, the Now Playing center shows the song title, album or artist information (depending on the application), playback progress, and album art (on the lock screen). These screens also expose a limited set of playback controls, including Play/Pause and Back/Forward.

Figure 7-4. Now Playing information on lock screen and multitasking menu

In this section, you will see how to make your audio apps compatible with the system's Now Playing center by implementing the `MPNowPlayingInfoCenter` class and remote-control events.

You might be scratching your head at the term *remote control*, because everyone knows the iPhone isn't a remote control for TVs (on its own, at least). But in the context of media apps, *remote control* refers to the hardware controls included on Made for iPhone (MFi) headsets, such as those that come packaged with iPhones. These same controls are piped through the Now Playing center and, as a bonus, you can take advantage of them to make your applications compatible with MFi headsets.

Just as you did in the previous section with backgrounding audio, you will add Now Playing support by continuing to extend the MyPlayer application.

> **Note**   The MPNowPlayingInfoCenter class is meant for one-way communication to the Now Playing center. The only way to get information on currently playing tracks is by implementing an iPod music library application, as described in Chapter 6.

Displaying Metadata

As stated earlier, the Now Playing center on iOS devices is a shared system resource. As the name implies, the MPNowPlayingInfoCenter class is part of the MediaPlayer framework, but this does not prevent it from working with AVFoundation media players. Any type of application can send messages to the MPNowPlayingInfoCenter class—as long as they are properly formatted.

To enable Now Playing support in the MyPlayer application, you need to include the MediaPlayer framework in your project and add it to the header file for the MainViewController class (MainViewController.h):

```
#import <MediaPlayer/MediaPlayer.h>
```

As a shared resource (just like the camera), you access the Now Playing center via a singleton, which you can retrieve via the [MPNowPlayingInfoCenter defaultCenter] public method:

```
MPNowPlayingInfoCenter *infoCenter = [MPNowPlayingInfoCenter defaultCenter];
```

To set values for the Now Playing center, you need to initialize the nowPlayingInfo property with an NSDictionary object containing your new metadata values:

```
[infoCenter setNowPlayingInfo:myMetaDataDict];
```

Table 7-3 shows the valid keys for the nowPlayingInfo dictionary, as well as their types and what they represent. These keys are used in the MPMediaItem class. You must pass them exactly as specified, or your app may crash at runtime.

Table 7-3. Valid Keys for nowPlayingInfo Dictionary

Key	Type	Purpose
MPMediaItemPropertyArtist	NSString	Performing artist for selected item
MPMediaItemPropertyArtwork	MPMediaItemArtwork	Album art for selected item
MPMediaItemPropertyAlbumTitle	NSString	Album title for selected item
MPMediaItemPropertyGenre	NSString	Genre for selected item
MPNowPlayingInfoElapsedPlaybackTime	NSNumber	Playback progress for selected item (in seconds)
MPMediaItemPropertyPlaybackDuration	NSNumber	Length of selected item (in seconds)
MPMediaItemPropertyTitle	NSString	Title for selected item

Looking back at Figure 7-4, you will see that the Now Playing values common to both the lock screen and multitasking screens include Song Title, Album Name, and Playback Duration. For an MPMusicPlayerController-based application, where you are using iPod music items, you can get this information directly from the MPMediaItem that is currently playing, as shown in Listing 7-2.

Listing 7-2. Setting Metadata Information from an MPMediaItem

```
-(void)viewDidLoad {
...
[[NSNotificationCenter defaultCenter]
       addObserverForName:
           @"MPMusicPlayerControllerNowPlayingItemDidChangeNotification"
        selector:@selector(updateNPCenter:)  object:nil];
}

-(void)updateNPCenter:(NSNotification *)note {

       MPMediaItem *currentItem = self.musicPlayer.nowPlayingItem;
       MPMediaItemArtwork *albumArt =
           [currentItem valueForProperty:MPMediaItemPropertyArtwork];
       CGSize imageFrameSize = self.albumImageView.frame.size;
       self.albumImageView.image =
       [albumArt imageWithSize:imageFrameSize];

       NSString *artistName =
           [currentItem valueForProperty:MPMediaItemPropertyTitle];
       NSString *albumName =
           [currentItem
           valueForProperty:MPMediaItemPropertyAlbumTitle];
       NSString *songTitle =
           [currentItem valueForProperty:MPMediaItemPropertyTitle];

       self.titleLabel.text =
           [currentItem valueForProperty:songTitle];
       self.albumLabel.text = [NSString stringWithFormat:@"%@ / %@",
                              artistName, albumName];
```

```
        MPNowPlayingInfoCenter *infoCenter =
            [MPNowPlayingInfoCenter defaultCenter];
        NSDictionary *infoDict = [NSDictionary
            dictionaryWithObjects:@[songTitle, artistName,
            albumName, albumArt] forKeys:@[MPMediaItemPropertyTitle,
            MPMediaItemPropertyAlbumArtist,
            MPMediaItemPropertyAlbumTitle,
            MPMediaItemPropertyArtwork]];
        [infoCenter setNowPlayingInfo:infoDict];
        ;

}
```

In the MyPlayer application, the primary key for music files was the file name. For applications for which you don't have all the metadata information, you can insert placeholder items for missing information. For the MyPlayer application, use the file name for the Song Title, the application's name as the Album Title, the file duration as the Playback Duration, and a placeholder image as the Album Art, as shown in Listing 7-3.

Listing 7-3. Setting Metadata Information for the MyPlayer Application

```
NSString *songTitle = [filePath lastPathComponent];
NSString *artistName = @"MyPlayer";
MPMediaItemArtwork *albumArt = [[MPMediaItemArtwork alloc]
    initWithImage:[UIImage imageNamed:@"Placeholder"]];
```

You may be wondering, "When do I call this code?" The answer: you should update the Now Playing center whenever your playlist changes—for example, when the user selects a new song or when you load a new item into the playlist. The MyPlayer application updates it whenever the File Picker controller completes. Listing 7-4 shows code for the entire process of setting Now Playing information in the File Picker delegate.

Listing 7-4. Setting Now Playing Information in the File Picker Delegate

```
-(void)didFinishWithFile:(NSString *)filePath
{
    self.selectedFilePath = filePath;

    NSError *error = nil;
    NSURL *fileURL = [NSURL fileURLWithPath:self.selectedFilePath];

    self.audioPlayer = [[AVAudioPlayer alloc]
                        initWithContentsOfURL:fileURL error:&error];
    self.audioPlayer.delegate = self;

    if (error == nil) {
        NSLog(@"audio player initialized successfully");

        self.timer = [NSTimer timerWithTimeInterval:1.0f target:self
                      selector:@selector(updateProgress) userInfo:nil
                      repeats:YES];
```

```
        NSString *songTitle = [filePath lastPathComponent];
        NSString *artistName = @"MyPlayer";
        MPMediaItemArtwork *albumArt = [[MPMediaItemArtwork alloc]
            initWithImage:[UIImage imageNamed:@"Placeholder"]];

        MPNowPlayingInfoCenter *infoCenter = [MPNowPlayingInfoCenter defaultCenter];
        NSDictionary *infoDict =
            [NSDictionary dictionaryWithObjects:@[songTitle, artistName, albumArt]
            forKeys:@[MPMediaItemPropertyTitle, MPMediaItemPropertyAlbumArtist,
            MPMediaItemPropertyArtwork]];
        [infoCenter setNowPlayingInfo:infoDict];


    } else {
        NSLog(@"error initializing audio player: %@",
            [error description]);
    }


    //dismiss the file picker
    [self dismissViewControllerAnimated:YES completion:nil];
}
```

As a final step, for the best user experience, you should update the Elapsed Playback Time for items every second, so that the user can see progress. In the MyPlayer app, you added timers to update the user interface within the app every second; you can piggyback off this logic by adding a call to update the Now Playing information, as shown in Listing 7-5.

Listing 7-5. Updated Timer Delegate That Adds Now Playing Updates

```
-(void)updateProgress
{
    NSInteger durationMinutes = [self.audioPlayer duration] / 60;
    NSInteger durationSeconds = [self.audioPlayer duration]
                                - durationMinutes * 60;

    NSInteger currentTimeMinutes = [self.audioPlayer currentTime] / 60;
    NSInteger currentTimeSeconds = [self.audioPlayer currentTime]
                                   - currentTimeMinutes * 60;
    NSString *progressString =
        [NSString stringWithFormat:@"%d:%02d / %d:%02d",
        currentTimeMinutes, currentTimeSeconds, durationMinutes,
        durationSeconds];
    self.timeLabel.text = progressString;

    self.progressBar.progress = [self.audioPlayer currentTime] /
                                [self.audioPlayer duration];

    NSNumber *numCurrentTimeSeconds = [NSNumber numberWithInt:currentTimeSeconds];
    NSNumber *numDurationSeconds = [NSNumber numberWithInt:durationSeconds];
```

```
    NSString *songTitle = [self.selectedFilePath lastPathComponent];
    NSString *artistName = @"MyPlayer";
    MPMediaItemArtwork *albumArt = [[MPMediaItemArtwork alloc]
        initWithImage:[UIImage imageNamed:@"Placeholder"]];


    MPNowPlayingInfoCenter *infoCenter = [MPNowPlayingInfoCenter defaultCenter];
    NSDictionary *infoDict = [NSDictionary
        dictionaryWithObjects:@[songTitle, artistName, albumArt,
            numDurationSeconds, numCurrentTimeSeconds]
            forKeys:@[MPMediaItemPropertyTitle,
            MPMediaItemPropertyAlbumArtist,
            MPMediaItemPropertyArtwork,
            MPMediaItemPropertyPlaybackDuration,
            MPNowPlayingInfoPropertyElapsedPlaybackTime]];
    [infoCenter setNowPlayingInfo:infoDict];

}
```

You would use this same logic to update playback progress in an `MPMusicPlayerController`-based application.

Enabling Playback Controls (Remote Controls)

To build a robust user experience for the Now Playing center, you need to add remote-control support to your application. As mentioned at the beginning of the section, this is the mechanism that drives both Made for iPhone headsets and the Now Playing center controls.

To enable remote-control support for your application, you need to register it as being capable of receiving remote-control events and then implement the delegate method for those events.

Events in iOS are messages fired when hardware interaction events occur, such as a user touching the screen, rotating the device, or using a headset. They are represented by the `UIEvent` class, which is part of the `UIKit` framework, meaning you do not need to include any additional frameworks or classes in your code to use them.

You have not had to worry about `UIEvent`s thus far in your code because Apple includes support for basic touch events in `UIKit`. However, to take advantage of more-advanced events, such as the remote-control events, you need to register your application as being capable of handling those events. The API call for adding remote-control support to your application is `[[UIApplication sharedApplication] beginReceivingRemoteControlEvents]`.

Note   The `[UIApplication sharedApplication]` object specifies the singleton for your application.

An application may have many views that respond to the same event, so as an additional step, you need to specify that your playback interface should be the primary receiver for remote-control events by declaring it as the "first responder" for events. You specify that a view is a first responder by first indicating that your class *can become* a first responder and then specifying that your view *is* one (by default, first responder support is turned off for new views).

To specify that a view can become a first responder, implement the [UIResponder canBecomeFirstResponder] method in your view. Listing 7-6 shows how to do this for the MainViewController class.

Listing 7-6. Adding First Responder Support to the MainViewController Class

```
- (void)viewDidLoad
{
    [super viewDidLoad];
        // Do any additional setup after loading the view, typically
        //from a nib.

    NSError *error = nil;
    [[AVAudioSession sharedInstance]
        setCategory:AVAudioSessionCategoryPlayback error:&error];
    if (error == nil) {
        NSLog(@"audio session initialized successfully");
                    [self becomeFirstResponder];
    } else {
        NSLog(@"error initializing audio session: %@",
            [error description]);
    }

)
}


-(BOOL)canBecomeFirstResponder
{
    return YES;
}
```

To answer the "when" question again, you need to specify that your application is ready to become a first responder and receive remote-control events when the view with the playback interface loads. For the MyPlayer application, this should happen in the)MainViewController's [self viewDidLoad] method, as shown in Listing 7-7.

Listing 7-7. Adding Remote-Control Event Support to the MainViewController Class

```
- (void)viewDidLoad
{
    [super viewDidLoad];
        // Do any additional setup after loading the view, typically
        // from a nib.

    NSError *error = nil;
    [[AVAudioSession sharedInstance]
        setCategory:AVAudioSessionCategoryPlayback error:&error];
```

```
    if (error == nil) {
        NSLog(@"audio session initialized successfully");

        [[UIApplication sharedApplication] beginReceivingRemoteControlEvents]
        [self becomeFirstResponder];
    } else {
        NSLog(@"error initializing audio session: %@",
            [error description]);
    }
    )
}
```

Now that the `MainViewController` class is ready to receive events, you need to handle them. The delegate method for handling remote-control events is `[UIResponder remoteControlReceivedWithEvent:]`. The parameter used by this method is a `UIEvent`. The type property on the input determines the kind of event received. You typically use a `switch` statement to handle different kinds of remote-control events. Table 7-4 lists all the possible remote-control events.

Table 7-4. Remote-Control Event Subtypes

Subtype Name	Purpose
UIEventSubtypeMotionShake	Device was shaken
UIEventSubtypeRemoteControlPlay	Play button
UIEventSubtypeRemoteControlPause	Pause button
UIEventSubtypeRemoteControlStop	Stop button
UIEventSubtypeRemoteControlTogglePlayPause	Toggle Play/Pause button
UIEventSubtypeRemoteControlNextTrack	Skip to next track
UIEventSubtypeRemoteControlPreviousTrack	Skip to previous track
UIEventSubtypeRemoteControlBeginSeekingBackward	Begin seeking backward (button pressed down)
UIEventSubtypeRemoteControlEndSeekingBackward	End seeking backward (button released)
UIEventSubtypeRemoteControlBeginSeekingForward	Begin seeking forward (button pressed down)
UIEventSubtypeRemoteControlEndSeekingForward	End seeking forward (button released)

Note   You do not need to handle all of the event types in your application, only the ones that are relevant to your application.

Listing 7-8 shows an example implementation for the `MainViewController` class.

Listing 7-8. Remote-Control Event Handler for the MainViewController Class

```
-(void)remoteControlReceivedWithEvent:(UIEvent *)event
{
    switch (event.subtype) {
        case UIEventSubtypeRemoteControlPlay:
        case UIEventSubtypeRemoteControlPause:
        case UIEventSubtypeRemoteControlTogglePlayPause:
            [self play:nil];
            break;
        case UIEventSubtypeRemoteControlNextTrack:
            [self skipForward:nil];
            break;
        case UIEventSubtypeRemoteControlPreviousTrack:
            [self skipBackward:nil];
            break;
        default:
            break;
    }
}
```

The MyPlayer application includes controls for toggling feedback and seeking forward/backward. Thus, in Listing 7-8, I implemented support only for those two actions. To further simplify things, the listing shows that it is possible to handle multiple events by using the same logic.

For the final step of this process, you need to clean up when your playback interface is released from memory. Specifically, the `MainViewController` class needs to specify that it is no longer a first responder and that it should stop receiving remote-control events. This happens in the view's [self dealloc] method, as shown in Listing 7-9.

Listing 7-9. Cleaning Up Remote-Control Events

```
-(void)dealloc
{
    [self resignFirstResponder];
}
```

Building a More Robust Audio Session

By adding background audio and Now Playing support, you have significantly expanded the functionality of the MyPlayer application. It now operates more like an iPod application. However, to get full parity, you need to expand the MyPlayer application to handle unexpected external events, such as audio interruptions from the Phone application, or route changes originating from the user plugging in headphones.

When listening to music with the iPod application, you may have noticed that playback stops when you bring up Siri and resumes when you dismiss her, and that playback pauses when you unplug your headphones (so you can avoid impressing any bystanders with your unique musical preferences). These actions are not the default in iOS; however, Cocoa Touch provides delegates and notifications that allow you to implement them in your apps.

In this section, you will see how to build a more robust audio session for your audio applications by implementing the AVAudioSessionDelegate to handle audio interruptions, and by responding to AVAudioSessionRouteChangeNotification notifications to handle output device (route) changes. As with the previous sections in this chapter, you will continue to use the MyPlayer application as a sandbox for these new features.

Handling Audio Interruptions

An *audio interruption* in iOS is any event that interrupts your application's audio session. Such events might be an incoming phone call, alarm, notification sounds, or Siri. The default behavior for audio interruptions in iOS is to follow the settings prescribed by the audio session you have chosen for your application. However, by responding to the AVAudioSessionInterruptionNotification notification, you can catch interruptions and insert your own playback handling code.

> **Note** The AVAudioSessionInterruptionNotification notification is not exclusive to AVFoundation-based media players. Any class, including those that use the MediaPlayer framework for playback, can implement the AVAudioSessionInterruptionNotification notification.

Table 7-5 lists the default interruption behaviors for each kind of AVAudioSession.

Table 7-5. Default Interruption Behaviors for AVAudioSession Types

Subtype Name	Purpose
[MPMediaQuery albumsQuery]	Returns a list of music items (songs), sorted by album title
[MPMediaQuery artistsQuery]	Returns a list of music items (songs), sorted by artist name
[MPMediaQuery compilationsQuery]	Returns a list of compilation items (albums), sorted by album title
[MPMediaQuery playlistsQuery]	Returns a list of playlist items, sorted by playlist title
[MPMediaQuery songsQuery]	Returns a list of music items (songs), sorted by song title

Because the AVAudioSessionInterruptionNotification notification is defined in AVAudioSession.h, you do not need to include any extra classes in your header file. As with all projects that implement notifications, your next step is to declare an *observer* method for the notification (a method that gets called every time the notification is caught). As shown in Listing 7-10, you add this declaration in your class's [self viewDidLoad] method, because the class needs to be ready to catch notifications as soon as it is initialized. The selector for the observer method is [self caughtInterruption:], which you will implement in the next step.

Listing 7-10. Adding a Notification Observer for the MainViewController Class

```
- (void)viewDidLoad
{
    [super viewDidLoad];
        // Do any additional setup after loading the view, typically
        // from a nib.

    NSError *error = nil;
    [[AVAudioSession sharedInstance]
        setCategory:AVAudioSessionCategoryPlayback error:&error];
    if (error == nil) {
        NSLog(@"audio session initialized successfully");
            [[NSNotificationCenter defaultCenter] addObserver:self
                selector:@selector(caughtInterruption:)
                name:AVAudioSessionInterruptionNotification object:nil];
    } else {
        NSLog(@"error initializing audio session: %@",
                [error description]);
    }

}
```

To fully support audio interruptions, you need to add custom code to handle two unique events: when the interruption begins and when it ends. To create the best user experience, when an interruption begins, you should pause playback immediately. It is generally a good practice to create an instance variable for your class that indicates the session was interrupted. For the MainViewController class, I've defined it as playbackInterrupted:

```
@property (nonatomic, retain) BOOL playbackInterrupted;
```

When an interruption ends, you should try to resume playback when applicable. You can determine applicability by checking the playbackInterrupted variable and the playback state of the media player.

Notifications send relevant information back to their observers via an NSDictionary object that is set as the userInfo property. Notifications specify unique names and userInfo keys for their information. The key that represents the type of audio interruption that was caught is AVAudioSessionInterruptionType, which maps to an integer-based enum. Its values are AVAudioSessionInterruptionTypeBegan and AVAudioSessionInterruptionTypeEnded.

Based on this information, the observer method, ([self caughtInterruption:]), checks the AVAudioSessionInterruptionType key in the notification. Pause or resume the player and set the playbackInterrupted instance variable to the correct value, as shown in Listing 7-11.

Listing 7-11. Audio Interruption Notification Observer Method

```
-(void)caughtInterruption:(NSNotification *)notification
{
    NSDictionary *userInfo = notification.userInfo;

    NSNumber *type =[userInfo
                     objectForKey:AVAudioSessionInterruptionTypeKey];
    if ([type integerValue] == AVAudioSessionInterruptionTypeBegan) {
        if (self.audioPlayer.playing) {
            [self.audioPlayer pause];
            self.playbackInterrupted = YES;
        }
    } else {
        if (self.audioPlayer.playing || self.playbackInterrupted) {
            [self.audioPlayer play];
            self.playbackInterrupted = NO;
        }
    }
}
```

To add an extra layer of safety around the playbackInterrupted flag, make sure you set its value to NO whenever the user manually selects a control in the user interface. Listing 7-12 shows an example for the Play button.

Listing 7-12. Updated Play Button Handler for the MainViewController Class

```
-(IBAction)play:(id)sender
{
    if ([self.audioPlayer isPlaying]) {
        [self.audioPlayer pause];
        self.playButton.titleLabel.text = @"Play";
        self.timer = [NSTimer timerWithTimeInterval:1.0f
                      target:self
                      selector:@selector(updateProgress)
                      userInfo:nil repeats:YES];

    } else {
        [self.audioPlayer play];
        self.playButton.titleLabel.text = @"Pause";
        [self.timer invalidate];
    }
    self.playbackInterrupted = NO;
}
```

Handling Hardware (Route) Changes

When creating audio apps, you should know about yet another obscure notification: AVAudioSessionRouteChangeNotification. This notification fires whenever the user changes the hardware output for audio on the device. Actions that trigger this notification include plugging in (or removing) headphones, connecting to an iPod dock, or connecting to an AirPlay-enabled device.

Like the AVAudioSessionInterruptionNotification notification, you start out by adding an observer to your class (MainViewController), as shown in Listing 7-13.

Listing 7-13. Adding an Observer for the Route Change Notification

```
- (void)viewDidLoad
{
    [super viewDidLoad];
        // Do any additional setup after loading the view, typically
        // from a nib.

    NSError *error = nil;
    [[AVAudioSession sharedInstance]
        setCategory:AVAudioSessionCategoryPlayback error:&error];
    if (error == nil) {
        NSLog(@"audio session initialized successfully");
        [[NSNotificationCenter defaultCenter]
          addObserver:self selector:@selector(caughtInterruption:)
          name:AVAudioSessionInterruptionNotification object:nil];

        [[NSNotificationCenter defaultCenter]
            addObserver:self selector:@selector(routeChanged:)
            name:AVAudioSessionRouteChangeNotification object:nil];
    } else {
        NSLog(@"error initializing audio session: %@",
            [error description]);
    }
}
```

In general, a user who plugs in a pair of headphones wants to listen to music privately. Similarly, a user who switches to AirPlay probably wants to do a sound check before the music starts playing. Taking this into consideration, when the user changes the input device (*route*), you should pause playback.

> **Note**   These are not hard and fast rules, just suggestions. Some apps, such as streaming video players, may be expected to continue to operate normally regardless of output device changes.

For the best user experience, when an AVAudioSessionRouteChangeNotification notification is received, you should check the AVAudioSessionRouteChangeReason key to get information on why the route changed. The relevant values are listed in Table 7-6.

Table 7-6. *Route Change Types*

Type	Purpose
AVAudioSessionRouteChangeReasonNewDeviceAvailable	User connected new output device
AVAudioSessionRouteChangeReasonOldDeviceUnavailable	Output device disconnected or failed
AVAudioSessionRouteChangeReasonWakeFromSleep	iOS device woke from sleep
AVAudioSessionRouteChangeReasonNoSuitableRouteForCategory	No output available for selected audio session type

As you can see from Table 7-6, there are several reasons that a route could change, ranging from user-initiated changes to device failures. For the MyPlayer app, as per the earlier discussion, you should pause playback whenever a user initiates a route change. In the case of device failure (AVAudioSessionRouteChangeReasonNoSuitableRouteForCategory), you should stop playback. The observer method for the MainViewController class ([self routeChanged:]) is shown in Listing 7-14.

Listing 7-14. *Observer Method for Route Changes*

```
-(void)routeChanged:(NSNotification *)notification
{
    NSDictionary *userInfo = notification.userInfo;

    NSNumber *reason =[userInfo
                       objectForKey:AVAudioSessionRouteChangeReasonKey];
    switch ([reason integerValue]) {
        case AVAudioSessionRouteChangeReasonNoSuitableRouteForCategory:
            [self.audioPlayer stop];
            break;
        case AVAudioSessionRouteChangeReasonNewDeviceAvailable:
        case AVAudioSessionRouteChangeReasonOldDeviceUnavailable:
        case AVAudioSessionRouteChangeReasonWakeFromSleep:
            [self.audioPlayer pause];
            break;
        default:
            break;
    }

}
```

Using AirPlay

Although the list of possibilities for creating our audio-based applications is endless, this chapter covers only one more topic: AirPlay. AirPlay is Apple's proprietary technology for streaming media over WiFi networks. AirPlay lets users stream media from iOS or OS X devices directly to AirPlay-compatible devices such as Apple TVs, Apple AirPort routers, or compatible third-party stereos. AirPlay is a discovery-based protocol; when an open AirPlay device is detected on a network, it will show up in the available devices list for the system. You can view the output device list available to your iOS device by selecting the AirPlay button in the multitasking menu, as shown in Figure 7-5.

Figure 7-5. AirPlay device list

> **Note**   AirPlay does not work over Bluetooth. Users must be connected to a WiFi network to use AirPlay.

AirPlay can operate in either of two major modes: piping app output only, or mirroring the entire device. Mirroring pipes a copy of the user's OS X or iOS screen directly to AirPlay—system screens and all. This is often convenient for learning environments where an instructor is trying to demonstrate a feature, or for low-vision accessibility applications. AirPlay mirroring is overkill for simple cases, such as piping video or audio from an app to an Apple TV. To pipe content, you need to implement AirPlay support in your apps.

Fortunately, Apple builds AirPlay support into the MediaPlayer and AVFoundation frameworks, allowing you to use AirPlay without a significant amount of additional work. As you will see in the discussion of video applications in Chapter 8, the MPMoviePlayerController adds an AirPlay button directly to your playback control set when an AirPlay device has been discovered on your network, as shown in Figure 7-6.

Figure 7-6. AirPlay control for MPMoviePlayerController

For audio applications that use the AVAudioPlayer or MPMusicPlayerController classes, you can add a similar AirPlay control to your application via the MPVolumeView class. This class exposes a volume slider and an AirPlay selector, just like the one in the MPMoviePlayerController class.

Note   You can opt out of the volume slider by setting the showsVolumeSlider property to NO.

As the name implies, the MPVolumeView class is a view, so you need to designate an area on your storyboard to contain it. There is no MPVolumeView control in the Interface Builder drag-and-drop component library; therefore, you need to use the same method you used in the camera-based applications you've already seen—you need to add the MPVolumeView as a subview of a generic UIView.

For the MyPlayer application, I added a new UIView property called airPlayView to the MainViewController.h header file:

```
@property (nonatomic, strong) UIView *airPlayView;
```

After adding this property to your class, modify your storyboard to add and link the view, as shown in Figure 7-7.

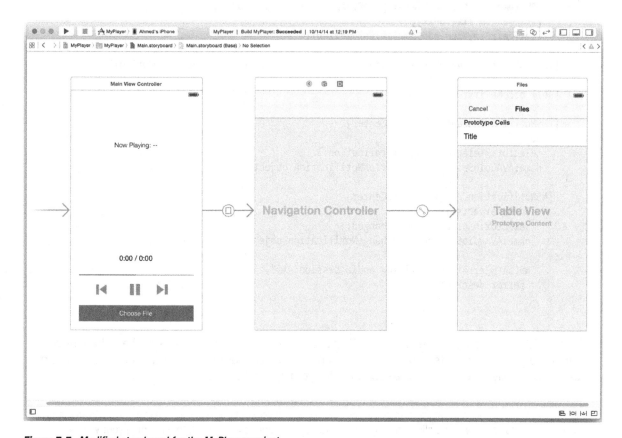

Figure 7-7. Modified storyboard for the MyPlayer project

Next, you need to initialize the MPVolumeView. Luckily, the MPVolumeView is very straightforward to initialize; all you need to do is initialize the object and add it as a subview, properly. As shown in Listing 7-15, this needs to happen in your [self viewDidLoad] method.

Listing 7-15. Initializing an MPVolumeView

```
- (void)viewDidLoad
{
    [super viewDidLoad];
        // Do any additional setup after loading the view, typically
        // from a nib.

    NSError *error = nil;
    [[AVAudioSession sharedInstance]
        setCategory:AVAudioSessionCategoryPlayback error:&error];
    if (error == nil) {
        NSLog(@"audio session initialized successfully");

            MPVolumeView *volumeView = [ [MPVolumeView alloc] init] ;
            [volumeView sizeToFit];
            [self.airPlayView addSubview:volumeView];

        [[UIApplication sharedApplication]                     beginReceivingRemoteControlEvents];

        [self becomeFirstResponder];

        [[NSNotificationCenter defaultCenter]
            addObserver:self
            selector:@selector(caughtInterruption:)
            name:AVAudioSessionInterruptionNotification object:nil];

        [[NSNotificationCenter defaultCenter]
            addObserver:self
            selector:@selector(routeChanged:)
            name:AVAudioSessionRouteChangeNotification object:nil];
    } else {
            NSLog(@"error initializing audio session: %@",
             [error description]);
    }
}
```

If that looks simple, the good news is, it is. That's all the work you need to do! AirPlay plugs directly into the remote-control events and the Now Playing center. By adding these handlers to your code, you can build a fully functional user experience for your AirPlay application.

Note   By default, the volume slider is white. If you do not see your volume slider, try changing your view's background color.

Summary

In this chapter, you saw how to expand the performance of your audio-based applications significantly by adding support for backgrounded audio, the Now Playing center, and notifications for route changes and audio interruptions. By adding these features, you also saw that implementing AirPlay involved only adding an `MPVolumeView` to your class. While it is impossible to predict everything the user will do with your app, you can take advantage of the limited background audio features Apple provides to help make your apps more enjoyable to use.

Part 3

Video

Chapter 8

Playing and Recording Video

In this chapter, you will dive into using video in your apps, discovering how to play and record video files. As a format, video is more complex than still images or photos, and requires significant low-level support. Fortunately, there are APIs to provide that low-level support for you.

The chapter illustrates how to use the `MPMoviePlayerController` class to play back video files. You will also revisit using the `UIImagePickerController` class to record video files. Fortunately, you will find that you can apply a significant portion of the techniques you saw in the earlier image and audio chapters to the video topics here. In fact, both the projects in this chapter borrow code directly from earlier projects.

Along the way, you will get a brief lesson on notifications, because understanding notifications is essential when using the `MediaPlayer` framework. The video player doesn't even define a delegate—that's how important notifications are!

Playing Video Files

As with photos and audio, Apple provides an "easy" way and a "hard" way to do everything with video. The easy way usually means using a built-in user interface to accomplish your task—but you have to design around the limitations Apple has put in place. The hard way means using a lower-level framework to achieve the same functionality—but you have to create the user interface and session-handling code yourself.

First, you will see how to play video the easy way, using Apple's built-in video playback interface: the `MPMoviePlayerController` class. You can use the `MPMoviePlayerController` class to play video from files or network streams, as shown in Figure 8-1. Additionally, the class exposes a basic set of playback controls (including Play/Pause, Seek, and AirPlay), and gives you the option to play audio files through the same interface. If you have ever watched a movie via the web browser, you are already familiar with the `MPMoviePlayerController` class from a user's perspective.

Figure 8-1. Browser-based video displayed using the MPMoviePlayerController class

From a developer's perspective, the MPMoviePlayerController class is limited, because you are stuck both with Apple's size limitations (full-screen or windowed) and its controls (all or none).

> **Note**   In Chapter 9 you will see how to use AVFoundation to get around the user-interface limitations of the MPMoviePlayerController class by building your own video-player class.

In this section, you will explore how to use the MPMoviePlayerController class by implementing the MyVideoPlayer application shown in Figure 8-2. This application is included in the Chapter 8 folder of the source code bundle. (See the Source Code/Download area of the Apress web site, www.apress.com.)

Figure 8-2. Mock-up for MyVideoPlayer project

The MyVideoPlayer application has a simple user interface, consisting mainly of a file picker that lets users select a video file to play, and a video player embedded in a `UIView` that lets users watch a selected video. The playback controls for this embedded player come from the `MPMoviePlayerController` class itself. Note that they resemble the controls on browser-embedded videos—that is because Safari and this app use the same class to display video!

You may recognize the file picker from the MyPlayer music player application in Chapter 5. You built a generic, reusable class for picking files in that project. Here, you will reuse it directly, allowing you to focus on video-specific features.

Compared to audio playback, video requires a more complicated setup process and more asynchronous handling of state changes (video files are usually very large). You will cover these core competencies for video playback while building the MyVideoPlayer project:

- ▪ Initialize the video player with valid content
- ▪ Configure the video player for different playback modes
- ▪ Use notifications to detect errors in playback state changes

Getting Started

As mentioned earlier, the MyVideoPlayer project relies heavily on the MyPlayer application for its design and user-interface components, including the file picker interface. Throughout this section, you will see code samples taken directly from the MyPod project. For a more detailed explanation of how they work, refer to Chapter 6.

Similar to the MyPod application, start out by creating a new project using the Single-View Application template in Xcode. Because the MPMoviePlayerController class is a part of the MediaPlayer framework, make sure one of your first steps is to include it in the project.

As with previous applications, the main view controller is the primary driver of the user interface. You can use the header file in Listing 8-1 as a guide for adding the required user interface elements. Note that the MediaPlayer framework is included at the top of the file, because the MainViewController class instantiates the media player.

Listing 8-1. Header File for MainViewController Class

```
#import <UIKit/UIKit.h>
#import <MediaPlayer/MediaPlayer.h>
#import "FileViewController.h"

@interface MainViewController : UIViewController <FileControllerDelegate>

@property (nonatomic, strong) IBOutlet UIView *playerView;
@property (nonatomic, strong) MPMoviePlayerController *moviePlayer;

@end
```

You may have noticed that the code declares the playerView property as a UIView, instead of a more specific class. When you need to implement a video player as a subview, the design pattern is to set the video layer subview of another element—similar to the custom camera interface you built in Chapter 4. Remember to connect every property to its matching element in your storyboard.

You can use the FileViewController class without modifications directly from the MyPod project for this application. The header and implementation files for the class are shown in Listings 8-2 and 8-3.

Listing 8-2. Header File for FileViewController Class

```
#import <UIKit/UIKit.h>

@protocol FileControllerDelegate <NSObject>

-(void)cancel;
-(void)didFinishWithFile:(NSString *)filePath;

@end

@interface FileViewController : UITableViewController

-(id)initWithFileArray:(NSArray *)fileArray;
```

```
@property (nonatomic, strong) NSMutableArray *fileArray;

@property (nonatomic, strong) id <FileControllerDelegate> delegate;

-(IBAction)closeView:(id)sender;

@end
```

Listing 8-3. Implementation File for FileViewController Class

```
#import "FileViewController.h"

@implementation FileViewController

-(id)initWithFileArray:(NSArray *)fileArray
{
    self = [super init];
    if (self) {
        self.fileArray = fileArray;
    }
    return self;
}

- (void)viewDidLoad
{
    [super viewDidLoad];

    // Uncomment the following line to preserve selection
    // between presentations.
    // self.clearsSelectionOnViewWillAppear = NO;

    // Uncomment the following line to display an Edit button in
    // the navigation bar for this view controller.
    // self.navigationItem.rightBarButtonItem = self.editButtonItem;
}

- (void)didReceiveMemoryWarning
{
    [super didReceiveMemoryWarning];
    // Dispose of any resources that can be re-created.
}

#pragma mark - Table view data source

- (NSInteger)numberOfSectionsInTableView:(UITableView *)tableView
{
    // Return the number of sections.
    return 1;
}
```

```objc
- (NSInteger)tableView:(UITableView *)tableView
    numberOfRowsInSection:(NSInteger)section
{
    // Return the number of rows in the section.
    return [self.fileArray count];
}

- (UITableViewCell *)tableView:(UITableView *)tableView
    cellForRowAtIndexPath:(NSIndexPath *)indexPath
{
    UITableViewCell *cell =
        [tableView dequeueReusableCellWithIdentifier:@"fileCell"
         forIndexPath:indexPath];

    // Configure the cell...

    NSString *filePath = [self.fileArray objectAtIndex:indexPath.row];

    cell.textLabel.text = [filePath lastPathComponent];

    return cell;
}

-(void)tableView:(UITableView *)tableView
    didSelectRowAtIndexPath:(NSIndexPath *)indexPath
{
    NSString *filePath = [self.fileArray objectAtIndex:indexPath.row];

    [self.delegate didFinishWithFile:filePath];

}

-(IBAction)closeView:(id)sender
{
    [self.delegate cancel];
}

@end
```

As with the MyPod project, you will need to use a table view controller and a navigation controller to represent the file picker on the storyboard. Refer to Chapter 5 for a more detailed explanation of this process (remember that the table view controller is "embedded" in the navigation controller). Your completed storyboard should look like the example in Figure 8-3.

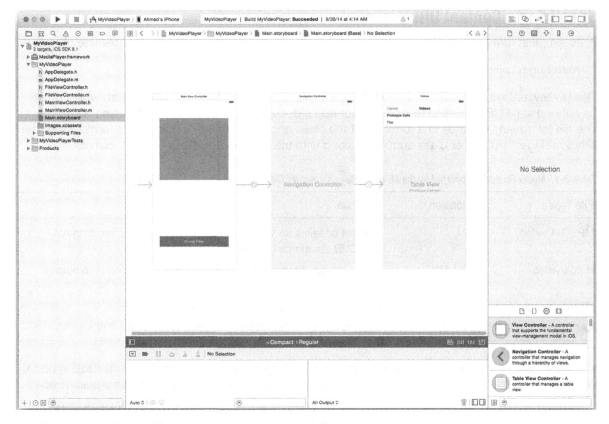

Figure 8-3. Storyboard for the MyVideoPlayer application

Initializing the Video Player

To use the MPMoviePlayerController class to play video files, you must first initialize the class. Because you're using the "easy" approach, the MPMoviePlayerController class will abstract tasks such as grabbing the audio and video playback sessions for you. Your primary objectives in initializing the class are to do the following:

- Specify the contentURL property for the movie player
- Set the parent view for your movie player
- Register your class to handle MPMoviePlayerPlaybackStateChanged notifications

When integrating the MPMoviePlayerController class, the majority of your work is related to presentation and message handling. Unlike the media APIs you covered for photos and audio, the MPMovieplayerController class uses notifications as its primary mechanism for message passing. The class does not even define a delegate property, meaning you must use notifications to handle all events from the media player. Notifications can be a jarring topic for developers coming from other ecosystems, but you will find a detailed explanation of how they work in the "Getting Started with Notifications" sidebar later in this chapter.

Specifying a Content URL

In its simplest form, you initialize an MPMoviePlayerController object by using a single line of code:

```
[MPMoviePlayerController alloc] initWithContentURL:];
```

The [MPMoviePlayerController initWithContentURL:] method takes an NSURL object, which must be either a valid URL pointing to a file in your app's document directory or a video stream. The file (or stream) must be in a format that the class accepts. Table 8-1 lists the file formats that the MPMoviePlayerController class supports, along with the intended purpose of each format.

Table 8-1. Media Formats Supported by the MPMoviePlayerController Class

File Type	Extension	Purpose
MPEG-4 video	MP4	Current baseline for video compression, more efficient than AVI and DVD standards (MPEG-2)
H.264 video	MOV, MP4	Apple-driven standard for HD video, more advanced than normal MPEG-4
MPEG-3 audio	MP3	Industry standard for lossy audio compression
AAC audio	M4A	Apple's format for MPEG-4 compressed audio

When the user plays a video file, the output displays in the view indicated by your initialization code. When the user plays an audio file, the QuickTime logo appears in the view, acting as a placeholder.

Note that this method only initializes the object; errors do not occur until you try to play the file. Errors are passed back via an MPMoviePlayerPlaybackState notification, which you will handle along with other notification handlers later in this chapter.

Using the File Picker as a Data Source

To use the file picker with the MyVideoPlayer project, you need to modify the segue handler, [self prepareForSegueWithIdentifier:]. Rather than initializing the file picker with iPod media as before, this time you want to populate it with files supported by the MediaPlayer framework. As with the MyPlayer application from Chapter 5, you can generate this list by searching for files in your app's documents directory whose file extensions match the supported file formats. After the input array is ready, you can present the file picker. This logic would go in the segue handler for the main view controller, as shown in Listing 8-4.

Listing 8-4. Segue Handler for Populating and Presenting the File Picker

```
-(void)prepareForSegue:(UIStoryboardSegue *)segue sender:(id)sender
{
    if ([segue.identifier isEqualToString:@"showFilePicker"]) {
        NSMutableArray *videoArray = [NSMutableArray new];

        NSArray *paths =
            NSSearchPathForDirectoriesInDomains(NSDocumentDirectory,
            NSUserDomainMask, YES);
```

```
        NSString *documentsDirectory = [paths objectAtIndex:0];
        NSError *error = nil;

        NSArray *allFiles = [[NSFileManager defaultManager]
            contentsOfDirectoryAtPath:documentsDirectory error:&error];

        if (error == nil) {

            for (NSString *file in allFiles) {
                if ([[file pathExtension] isEqualToString:@"m4v"] ||
                    [[file pathExtension] isEqualToString:@"mov"]) {
                    [videoArray addObject:file];
                }
            }

        } else {
            NSLog(@"error looking up files: %@", [error description]);
        }

        UINavigationController *navigationController =
            (UINavigationController *)segue.destinationViewController;
        FileViewController *fileVC =
            (FileViewController *)navigationController.topViewController;
        fileVC.delegate = self;
        fileVC.fileArray = videoArray;
    }
}
```

You should display the file name for each cell, so use that to populate the input array.

Likewise, remember to specify that you will be implementing the FileControllerDelegate protocol in your main view controller's header file:

```
@interface MainViewController : UIViewController
    <FileControllerDelegate>
```

The FileControllerDelegate protocol specifies a method that returns a file path when the user has picked a file. You can use this to initialize the MPMoviePlayerController object in the MainViewController class. In your main view controller's [FileControllerDelegate didFinishWithItem:] delegate method, convert the filePath string to an NSURL object and use it to initialize your class's mediaPlayer object. As with previous applications, your media player should be an instance variable, because many methods will access it. You can find an example in Listing 8-5.

Listing 8-5. Initializing the Video Player after the User Has Selected an Item

```
-(void)didFinishWithFile:(NSString *)filePath
{
    NSURL *fileURL = [NSURL URLWithString:filePath];
    self.moviePlayer = [[MPMoviePlayerController alloc]
        initWithContentURL:fileURL];

    //Dismisses the file picker
    [self dismissViewControllerAnimated:YES completion:nil];
}
```

Specifying a Parent View for the Media Player

Although your video player object has been allocated in memory, you still need to specify a parent view to display it on your app. This process is similar to the way you added a video layer to a view when you created the custom camera app in Chapter 4—give your player the same bounding frame as its parent view and then add it as a subview.

As with all UIView objects, you need to specify the view dimensions and its position. The frame attribute is a CGRect data structure that contains the dimensions of a view and its (x,y) position relative to the top left of the screen. With all views, a second attribute, bounds, specifies the visible area of a view (its *bounding* frame). The bounds attribute's (x,y) position is relative to the origin of the *frame*, not to the origin of the screen. By default, the bounds attribute is set to the top-left position of the target view, but you can change it if you are trying to reposition or clip a subview.

The goal for this app is to make the movie player fill the visible area of the playerView. Therefore, the frame for the MPMoviePlayerController's view needs to match the dimensions of the playerView and have a relative position. The bounds attribute is the perfect solution for this problem:

```
self.moviePlayer.view.frame = self.playerView.bounds;
```

After setting the frame for the MPMoviePlayerController object, add its view as a subview on top of the playerView, which will make it a visible property:

```
[self.playerView addSubview:self.moviePlayer.view];
```

Now you will be at your final solution, as shown in Listing 8-6.

Listing 8-6. Adding View Positioning to Your Initialization Code

```
-(void)didFinishWithFile:(NSString *)filePath
{
    NSURL *fileURL = [NSURL URLWithString:filePath];
    self.moviePlayer = [[MPMoviePlayerController alloc]
        initWithContentURL:fileURL];

    self.moviePlayer.view.frame = self.playerView.bounds;
    [self.playerView addSubview:self.moviePlayer.view];

    //Dismisses the file picker
    [self dismissViewControllerAnimated:YES completion:nil];
}
```

> **Note**   If you want a movie player that operates only in full-screen mode, use the MPMediaPlayerViewController class. The initialization path and notifications are the same as for the MPMediaPlayerController; the major operational difference is that the object is released when the view is dismissed.

Adding Notification Handling to Your Class

As the final step in initializing the media player, you need to register the MainViewController as a receiver of MPMoviePlaybackStateDidChangeNotification notifications. The MPMoviePlayerController class is completely dependent on notifications for its message passing, unlike the audio player and camera classes you used earlier, which use delegates. You can find a more detailed explanation of how to use notifications in the following sidebar, but here's the quick summary: to handle notifications, you need to explicitly state which notifications your class will handle, and tie those to handler methods.

GETTING STARTED WITH NOTIFICATIONS

In any programming language, *message passing* is how you send information between processes. Calling a method on an instance of a class is one of the simplest forms of message passing: you are letting the receiver (the object) know what message (method) to perform, and with what data (parameters).

It is not always convenient or wise to send a message to another class directly. For a very generic class, you do not want to include the header files of every other class that could call one of its methods. Similarly, you do not want to include everything required to call a message on a fairly complicated class.

To solve this problem, Cocoa Touch provides three specialized ways of performing generic message passing between classes:

- Protocols
- Notifications
- Key-value observing

You should already be familiar with protocols from previous chapters. Protocols are ideal when you want to define limited interfaces for passing data between two classes (for instance, the camera and the class that needs an image from a camera). However, protocols can also be very strict. Every method in a protocol's definition is implicitly defined as being required, meaning the delegate class needs to implement all the methods to be fully compliant.

The MPMediaPlayerController class can issue many kinds of messages, including playback state, stream errors, and presentation mode changes (for example, full-screen). Using a delegate to implement all of these could get unwieldy. For the media player, you want a message-passing scheme that allows a receiving class to handle only the messages it wants, without a huge overhead.

Notifications are ideal when you want to use a loose message-passing scheme. A notification is a name-based message-passing system in which anyone can *post* a notification by sending a properly formed message using that name, and anyone can handle (*observe*) a notification by declaring they can receive properly formatted messages using that name. This magic is enabled by a *notification center* object, which acts as an intermediary for all the notifications.

The third generic message-passing scheme, key-value observing (KVO), works similarly to notifications, except that instead of being a name-based system, KVO is based on an instance of an object changing. For instance, "when the count variable changes, call the increaseCount method." While useful in some cases, this is not appropriate for the media player, because you will not be monitoring changes on a property.

There are two major APIs for declaring your class as an *observer* of a notification: [NSNotificationCenter addObserver:selector:name:object] and [NSNotificationCenter addObserverForName:object:queue: usingBlock]. Both require you to specify the name of the notification you want to observe and how it should be handled. The main difference between these two is that the first calls a method at runtime (via the @selector parameter) whenever the notification is caught, whereas the second executes a block. As an example, if you were trying catch a MPMoviePlayerLoadStateDidChangeNotification notification with a handler method declared as [self stateChanged:], your code would look like this:

```
[[NSNotificationCenter defaultCenter] addObserver:self
    selector:@selector(stateChanged:)
    name:MPMoviePlayerPlaybackStateDidChangeNotification
    object:nil];
```

You may have questions about the [NSNotificationCenter defaultCenter] code snippet. This is a singleton that provides a notification center object your application can use—without any specialized setup. Until your code becomes sophisticated enough to require filtering notifications by which notification center they are sent to, this should be fine for most apps.

To send a notification, you *post* an NSNotification object by using the method [NSNotificationCenter postNotification:object:userInfo]. With this method, you need to specify the name of the notification you are posting and any information you are passing along, by adding it to an NSDictionary object via the userInfo parameter. If you were posting a custom notification, named MyCustomNotification, the code would look like this:

```
NSDictionary *myDict = [NSDictionary dictionaryWithObject:@"ahmed"
                                        forKey:@"userName"];
[[NSNotificationCenter defaultCenter]
     postNotificationName:@"MyCustomNotification" object:self
     userInfo:myDict];
```

One last thing about notifications: always remember to remove observers for a class when it is being deallocated. Unless you explicitly remove observers, the notification center will try to keep using your class to handle incoming notifications, which could cause your application to crash. To remove observers, use the method [NSNotificationCenter removeObserver:name:object]. For the MyCustomNotification example, the call would look like this:

```
[[NSNotificationCenter defaultCenter] removeObserver:self
    name:MPMoviePlayerPlaybackStateDidChangeNotification
    object:nil];
```

As you can see, notifications are a quick way of setting up message passing. For classes that need to enforce a specific message-passing scheme, delegates are ideal, but if you are just trying to make a simple scheme that anyone can choose to respond to, notifications are the perfect solution.

As covered in the preceding sidebar, the first step in handling notifications is to declare your class as an observer. Because this is a class-level operation, you can set the observers in the [self viewDidLoad] method for the MainViewController class. By making this a class-level operation, you are ready if the media player is initialized several times or if it is never initialized at all (the messages will never be sent if the media player is never initialized). Listing 8-7 shows the modified [self viewDidLoad] method for the MainViewController class.

Listing 8-7. Adding Notification Observers to Your Class

```
- (void)viewDidLoad {
    [super viewDidLoad];
    // Do any additional setup after loading the view,
    // typically from a nib.

    [[NSNotificationCenter defaultCenter] addObserver:self
        selector:@selector(playbackFinished:)
        name:MPMoviePlayerPlaybackDidFinishNotification object:nil];

    [[NSNotificationCenter defaultCenter] addObserver:self
        selector:@selector(loadStateChanged:)
        name:MPMoviePlayerLoadStateDidChangeNotification object:nil];
}
```

In this example, I used the [NSNotificationCenter addObserver:selector:name:object] API to set the observers so that I could specify a method to use as the notification handler instead of a block — mostly to make the code easier for you to read when it is split up.

The MPMoviePlayerPlaybackDidFinishNotification notification returns an MPMovieFinishReason constant via the MPMoviePlayerPlaybackDidFinishReasonUserInfoKey key and an error via the error key. If the finish reason is MPMovieFinishReasonPlaybackError, you should extract the error object and notify the user via an error message or UIAlertView. You can find the [self playbackFinished:] method for the MainViewController class in Listing 8-8.

Listing 8-8. Displaying the Playback Error

```
-(void)playbackFinished:(NSNotification *) notification
{
    NSDictionary *userInfo = notification.userInfo;
    NSNumber *finishReason = [userInfo
        objectForKey:MPMoviePlayerPlaybackDidFinishReasonUserInfoKey];

    if ([finishReason integerValue] ==
        MPMovieFinishReasonPlaybackError) {
        NSError *error = [userInfo objectForKey:@"error"];
        NSString *errorString = [error description];

        UIAlertView *alert = [[UIAlertView alloc]
            initWithTitle:@"Error!"
            message:errorString delegate:nil
            cancelButtonTitle:@"OK" otherButtonTitles:nil];
        [alert show];
    }
}
```

The MPMoviePlayerLoadStateDidChangeNotification notification does not set any keys in the userInfo dictionary, but you know that when it fires, the player has transitioned between load states (the major states are Unknown, Playable, Playthrough OK/Loaded, and Stalled). As with the audio player, loading a video file is an indeterminate operation, meaning you cannot predict how long it will take for the file to load. For this reason, you should use the [MPMediaPlayerController prepareToPlay] method to start loading the video file, and trigger the [MPMediaPlayerController play] method after the file has loaded. You can find out if the media player is ready to play a file by comparing the loadState property to the value MPMovieLoadStatePlayable, as shown in Listing 8-9.

Listing 8-9. Automatically Starting the Media Player

```
-(void)loadStateChanged:(NSNotification *) notification
{
    if (self.moviePlayer.loadState == MPMovieLoadStatePlayable) {

        [self.moviePlayer play];
    }
}
```

For the final step, remember that you need to remove your notifications to clean up after the class fully. Exactly as in the sidebar, you would place your calls to [NSNotificationCenter removeObserver:name:object] in the MainViewController's [self dealloc] method, as shown in Listing 8-10.

Listing 8-10. Removing Your Notification Observers

```
- (void)dealloc
{
    [[NSNotificationCenter defaultCenter] removeObserver:self
        name:MPMoviePlayerPlaybackDidFinishNotification
    object:nil];
    [[NSNotificationCenter defaultCenter] removeObserver:self
        name:MPMoviePlayerLoadStateDidChangeNotification
        object:nil];
}
```

Configuring the Video Player

Now that you have finished all the steps required to initialize your media player, you can start playing video files. However, to get the best performance out of the MPMediaPlayerController class, you need to configure it by specifying values for a couple of additional video-specific properties: the source type and AirPlay.

Specifying a Source Type (Local File or Network Stream)

The default source type configuration for the MPMoviePlayerController class is *unknown*. This makes the class take a wait-and-see approach to loading the video. It tries to load data from the source and then—based on what it finds out about the source—it will configure the movie player to play from a file or network stream. By specifying a value for the movieSourceType property, you can remove this intermediary step and speed up load times considerably.

The movieSourceType property takes MPMovieSourceType constant values as its input. The value for local files is MPMovieSourceTypeFile, while the value for network streams is MPMovieSourceTypeStreaming. The MyVideoPlayer application lets users pick only local files, so I used the MPMovieSourceTypeFile value:

```
self.videoPlayer.movieSourceType = MPMovieSourceTypeFile;
```

Specifying AirPlay Support

In both windowed and full-screen modes, the video player supports AirPlay as a playback control. As covered in Chapter 7, AirPlay is Apple's proprietary technology that allows users to stream audio and video content from their iOS devices to an Apple TV. For a video file to work with AirPlay, it needs to be encoded in the H.264 video codec (one of the formats supported by the `MPMoviePlayerController` class); for a video stream to be compatible with AirPlay, it needs to be transmitted using the Apple HTTP Live Streaming (HLS) protocol. Note that the `MPMoviePlayerController` can play many file types and streams that are not AirPlay-compatible, and will show the AirPlay control only if it is playing an AirPlay-compatible item.

When a video file is played in AirPlay, your movie player view will be replaced with a placeholder image, as shown in Figure 8-4. All the playback controls will still be available in the movie player on the device, but the video will play only on the Apple TV.

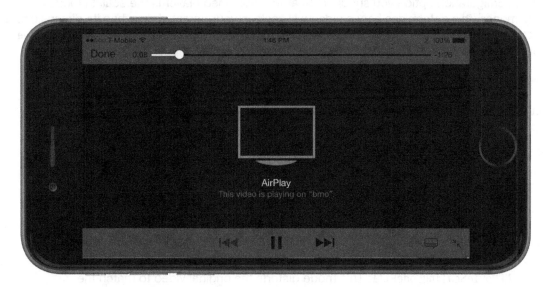

Figure 8-4. Placeholder image for AirPlay video playback

By default, the AirPlay icon pops up automatically for all AirPlay-compatible video files and streams played through the `MPMoviePlayerController`. If you are building an application that needs to disable this feature, you can do so via the `allowsAirPlay` property. Setting this value to `NO` prevents the AirPlay control from appearing in the movie player.

```
self.videoPlayer.allowsAirPlay = NO;
```

> **Note**   Disabling AirPlay support in your movie player will not prevent it from showing up if the user has AirPlay Mirroring turned on for their device. To disable this feature, you need to implement Secondary Display support in your app. A tutorial for this feature is available on Apple's Developer Library site.

Specifying Control Types

By default, the MPMediaPlayerController class provides built-in playback controls on top of the video layer. For many applications, you will want to change the control style or completely hide the controls. You can toggle this via the controlStyle property, which accepts a constant of the type MPMovieControlStyle. On iOS 7 and later, there are two styles you can use: MPMovieControlStyleNone, which completely hides the controls, and MPMovieControlStyleFullscreen, which shows a full set of controls, including fast-forward, rewind, and audio control. The default control style is MPMovieControlStyleFullscreen:

```
self.moviePlayer.controlStyle = MPMovieControlStyleFullscreen;
```

Specifying a Scaling Mode

One final configuration option you should look at for your video player is the scaling mode. As with images, this determines how a video will scale in your parent view, when its dimensions do not match exactly. You can set the content scaling mode for a movie player via the scalingMode property, which takes an MPMovieScalingModeFill constant as its input:

```
self.moviePlayer.scalingMode = MPMovieScalingModeAspectFit;
```

Similar to the images, the available scaling modes are as follows:

> MPMovieScalingModeNone: This mode provides no scaling and places the source video in the target view (cropped or letterboxed, depending on size).

> MPMovieScalingModeAspectFit: This mode scales the video up or down to the dimensions of the target view as far as possible without distorting the original video.

> MPMovieScalingModeAspectFill: This mode scales the video to match the dimensions of the target view, without distorting the video (the excess will be cropped).

> MPMovieScalingModeFill: This mode distorts the original video to match the dimensions of the target view.

The default value is MPMovieScalingModeAspectFit.

Starting Playback

As you may remember from the audio player examples in Chapters 6 and 6, you cannot predict how long it will take to load a media file. It takes longer to load a larger file (which a video most certainly is!). For this reason, you should make a call to [MPMoviePlayerController prepareToPlay] as soon as you have finished initializing and configuring the video player. Because the initialization code adds a handler for MPMoviePlayerLoadStateDidChangeNotification notifications, you can automatically start playing the file when the file has loaded.

Listing 8-11 shows the complete initialization method for the video player, including the pre-loading step just described.

Listing 8-11. Full Initialization Method for Video Player

```
-(void)didFinishWithFile:(NSString *)filePath
{
    NSURL *fileURL = [NSURL URLWithString:filePath];
    self.moviePlayer = [[MPMoviePlayerController alloc]
        initWithContentURL:fileURL];
    self.moviePlayer.movieSourceType = MPMovieSourceTypeFile;
    self.moviePlayer.allowsAirPlay = YES;
    self.moviePlayer.scalingMode = MPMovieScalingModeAspectFit;
    self.moviePlayer.controlStyle = MPMovieControlStyleEmbedded;

    self.moviePlayer.view.frame = self.playerView.bounds;
    [self.playerView addSubview:self.moviePlayer.view];

    [self.moviePlayer prepareToPlay];

    //Dismisses the file picker
    [self dismissViewControllerAnimated:YES completion:nil];
}
```

To test that your video player application is working, use the Choose Video button to select a video, and then make sure it plays in the embedded video player. Because you are using embedded controls, you will be able to control playback via the built-in scrubber.

Recording Video Files

The easiest way to record video in Cocoa Touch is to use the UIImagePickerController class. You may remember this class from Chapter 2, where you used it to take pictures via iOS's built-in camera interface. If you have ever used the native Camera app to capture video, you already familiar with this interface, shown in Figure 8-5.

Figure 8-5. *UIImagePickerController video-capture interface*

However, unlike the Camera app, the UIImagePickerController class presents your user with a confirmation screen after they have completed recording, as shown in Figure 8-6. This allows your users to review and even edit their captured video by trimming them before moving on.

Figure 8-6. *UIImagePickerController video preview interface*

By modifying your configuration options and `UIImagePickerDelegate` handler methods, you can repurpose your photo-capture code to add video-capture functionality.

In this section, you will modify the MyVideoPlayer app by adding a button for capturing video. Captured video is saved in the app's documents directory and picked up by the file picker, so that users can watch them just like any other video. The new project is included in the `Chapter 8` folder of the source code bundle as MyVideoRecorder.

If you are still uncomfortable with using the `UIImagePickerController` class, you should review the projects in Chapter 2 before moving on with this topic. The CameraApp project includes an in-depth explanation of the `UIImagePickerController` class and delegates. The goal of the MyVideoRecorder project is to highlight how you need to make only a few modifications to allow a photo app to handle video.

Getting Started

You will use the MyVideoPlayer project as a base for the MyVideoRecorder project. Start by making a copy of the project and renaming the root folder MyVideoRecorder. To make this change reflect across the rest of the project, double-click the project file (MyVideoPlayer.xcodeproj) to open it in Xcode. Then, carefully click the project's name in the Project Navigator and rename it as shown in the upper-left corner of Figure 8-7.

Figure 8-7. Renaming a project

If you are having trouble selecting the file's name, keep trying. You need to be careful to make sure your click is registered on top of the text for the name, not just in the cell.

Next, add a button to the user interface to allow the user to bring up the video-capture interface. This process requires you to declare that the MainViewController class implements the UIImagePickerDelegate protocol and add the new button to the Interface Builder. Remember the UIImagePickerDelegate protocol is how the UIImagePickerController class sends back messages indicating the camera controller has captured media or wants to be dismissed. Listing 8-12 shows the modified header file for the MainViewController.

Listing 8-12. Header Files Changes for MyVideoRecorder Project

```
#import <UIKit/UIKit.h>
#import <MediaPlayer/MediaPlayer.h>
#import "FileViewController.h"

@interface MainViewController : UIViewController
    <FileControllerDelegate, UIImagePickerControllerDelegate,
    UINavigationControllerDelegate>

@property (nonatomic, strong) IBOutlet UIView *playerView;
@property (nonatomic, strong) MPMoviePlayerController *moviePlayer;
@property (nonatomic, strong) UIImagePickerController *videoRecorder;

-(IBAction)showPicker:(id)sender;
@end
```

Figure 8-8 shows the storyboard for the new user interface. Because the process of dismissing the camera controller is handled by the image picker delegate methods, you do not need to add any additional segues or connections in Interface Builder for the `MainViewController` class, beyond the ones for the Record Video button (tying it to the class and to a handler method).

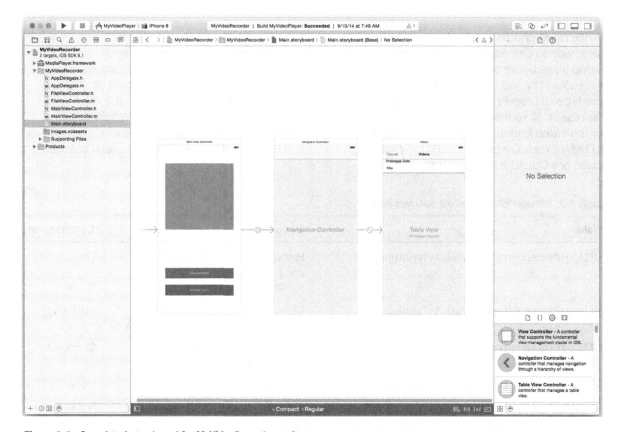

Figure 8-8. Completed storyboard for MyVideoRecorder project

Configuring the Image Picker for Video

Just as when taking pictures, you need to initialize and configure an instance of the UIImagePickerController class when the user presses the Record Video button in the app. You may recall from Chapter 2 that, at minimum, to configure an image picker, you need to specify a source type (the camera or a photo album) and a delegate for the image data:

```
UIImagePickerController *moviePicker = [[UIImagePickerController alloc] init];
moviePicker.delegate = self;
```

To configure your UIImagePickerController object to capture video, specify video as the only accepted media type. You can set media types via the mediaTypes parameter, which takes an array of media type constants. The constant for video is kUTTypeMovie; by default, the parameter is initialized with the constant for images, kUTTypeImage:

```
self.videoPlayer.mediaTypes = [NSArray arrayWithObjects:kUTTypeMovie];
```

> **Note**   If you add both constants to the mediaTypes array, the user will be presented with the option to toggle capture interfaces, like in the iOS Camera app.

While most photos captured on an iOS device grow to only a couple of megabytes in size, videos can easily grow to be hundreds (or thousands) of megabytes large. To keep video sizes under control, you set values for two additional properties on the image picker: videoQuality and videoMaximumDuration. The videoQuality property takes a constant of the type UIImagePickerControllerQualityType. Table 8-2 lists these values and what they represent. Note that the values you choose affect video quality by determining the resolution of the video frame and the strength of the compression algorithm. The default value is UIImagePickerControllerQualityTypeMedium. All videos generated by the UIImagePickerController class are QuickTime movie files (.MOV).

Table 8-2. UIImagePickerControllerQualityType Values

Value	Resolution	Compression
UIImagePickerControllerQualityTypeHigh	Highest available on device (for example, 3264×2248 for iPhone 6)	Low
UIImagePickerControllerQualityTypeMedium	Mid-range for device (for example, 1280×720 for iPhone 6)	Medium
UIImagePickerControllerQualityTypeLow	Low enough to be transmitted via cell signal (144×192)	Strongest
UIImagePickerControllerQualityType640x480	640×480	None
UIImagePickerControllerQualityTypeIFrame1280x720	1280×720	None
UIImagePickerControllerQualityTypeIFrame960x540	960×540	None

The videoMaximumDuration property takes a CGFloat value that corresponds to the maximum length for videos that users can capture using the image picker. When the user has reached the maximum capture length, the image picker will automatically stop and bring up the preview interface for the user. The default value for this property is set to 600 seconds (10 minutes), but your final value should depend on your application's intended purpose and any external requirements you may have (such as uploading to a video-sharing service or a custom web service).

```
self.videoRecorder.maximumVideoDuration = 30.0f;
```

Finally, to allow users to edit their videos before returning to the main user interface, enable the allowsEditing property on your image picker object. This property takes a Boolean value as its input and returns an entry value in the results dictionary for the image picker, which represents the URL for the edited video. The video-editing interface appears after the user has finished recording, and does not require any additional work on your part.

```
self.videoRecorder.allowsEditing = YES;
```

The complete implementation for initializing the image picker for the MyVideoRecorder project is in Listing 8-13. This code is encapsulated in the handler for the Record Video button.

Listing 8-13. Initializing the Image Picker for Recording Video

```
-(IBAction)showPicker:(id)sender
{
    self.videoRecorder = [[UIImagePickerController alloc] init];
    self.videoRecorder.sourceType =
        UIImagePickerControllerSourceTypeCamera;
    self.videoRecorder.mediaTypes =
        [NSArray arrayWithObject:(NSString *)kUTTypeMovie];
    self.videoRecorder.delegate = self;
    self.videoRecorder.videoMaximumDuration = 30.0f;
    self.videoRecorder.videoQuality =
        UIImagePickerControllerQualityTypeMedium;
    self.videoRecorder.allowsEditing = YES;

    [self presentViewController:self.videoRecorder
                       animated:YES
                     completion:nil];
}
```

Saving Video Recordings

The delegate method that fires when the image picker completes with captured media is [UIImagePickerController imagePickerController:didFinishPickingMediaWithInfo:]. To properly handle video from the image picker, you need to learn how to use additional keys in the results dictionary. For your reference, Table 8-3 lists all the keys in the userInfo results dictionary.

Table 8-3. Keys Returned by the Image Picker Results Dictionary

Key	Return Type	Value
UIImagePickerControllerMediaType	NSString	Type of media (image or video)
UIImagePickerControllerOriginalImage	UIImage	Unedited image data
UIImagePickerControllerEditedImage	UIImage	Edited image data
UIImagePickerControllerCropRect	NSValue (Cast to NSRect)	Cropping rectangle
UIImagePickerControllerMediaURL	NSURL	URL for unedited movie
UIImagePickerControllerReferenceURL	NSURL	URL for final movie (edited or not)

The first assumption you need to change from the MyCamera app is that all results from the image picker are images. To check the return type of a file, retrieve the value represented by the UIImagePickerControllerMediaType key. This will be an NSString, which you should compare against kUTTypeMovie for movies:

```
if ([[info objectForKey:UIImagePickerControllerMediaType]
    isEqualToString:(NSString *)kUTTypeMovie]) {
        //custom code goes here
}
```

Next, you want to determine whether the user edited the video. The results dictionary provides two keys representing the user's recorded video: UIImagePickerControllerMediaURL, which returns the URL for the final, edited version of the media item, and UIImagePickerControllerReferenceURL, which returns the URL for the original media item. The general practice for most apps is to use the edited version of the video. If you want to give the user a choice of what version to use, compare the two values; if the values represented by the keys differ, you know the user edited the video:

```
if ([[info objectForKey:UIImagePickerControllerMediaURL]
    isEqualToString:[info
      objectForKey:UIImagePickerControllerReferenceURL]]) {
      movieURL = [info objectForKey:UIImagePickerControllerMediaURL];
} else {
    movieURL = [info
        objectForKey:UIImagePickerControllerReferenceURL];
}
```

Finally, to save your users a lot of headaches, you need to save your videos to the documents directory with human-readable names. In my apps, I like to append a timestamp to a string, such as Movie or my app's name. This way, users can easily retrieve videos based on the time that they were created. You can create a timestamp easily with the NSDateFormatter class.

```
NSDateFormatter *dateFormat = [[NSDateFormatter alloc] init];
[dateFormat setDateFormat:@"yyyyMMddHHmm"];
```

To get the contents of the file, use the [NSData dataWithContentsOfURL:] method:

```
NSData *movieData = [NSData dataWithContentsOfURL:movieURL];
```

Listing 8-14 shows an implementation for the [UIImagePickerController imagePickerController :didFinishPickingMediaWithInfo:] delegate method that puts together all of these steps. In the MyVideoRecorder project, this method is defined in the MainViewController class. You will also find the delegate method to cancel the image picker, which simply dismisses the image picker.

Listing 8-14. Image Picker Delegate Methods for MyVideoRecorder Project

```
-(void)imagePickerController:(UIImagePickerController *)picker
    didFinishPickingMediaWithInfo:(NSDictionary *)info
{

    NSArray *paths =
        NSSearchPathForDirectoriesInDomains(NSDocumentDirectory,
        NSUserDomainMask, YES);
    NSString *documentsDirectory = [paths objectAtIndex:0];
    NSString *filePath = [documentsDirectory
        stringByAppendingPathComponent:@"movie.mov"];

    if ([[info objectForKey:UIImagePickerControllerMediaType]
        isEqualToString:(NSString *)kUTTypeMovie]) {

        NSURL *movieURL = nil;

        if ([[info objectForKey:UIImagePickerControllerMediaURL]
            isEqualToString:[info
                    objectForKey:UIImagePickerControllerReferenceURL]]) {
            movieURL = [info
                    objectForKey:UIImagePickerControllerMediaURL];
        } else {
            movieURL = [info
                    objectForKey:UIImagePickerControllerReferenceURL];
        }

        NSData *movieData = [NSData dataWithContentsOfURL:movieURL];
        NSError *error = nil;
        NSString *alertMessage = nil;

        //check if the file exists before trying to write it
        if ([[NSFileManager defaultManager]
            fileExistsAtPath:filePath]) {
          NSDateFormatter *dateFormat =
                [[NSDateFormatter alloc] init];
        [dateFormat setDateFormat:@"yyyyMMddHHmm"];

            NSString *dateString =
                [dateFormat stringFromDate:[NSDate date]];

            NSString *fileName =
                [NSString stringWithFormat:@"movie-%@.mov",
                    dateString];
```

```
            filePath = [documentsDirectory
                stringByAppendingPathComponent:fileName];
        }

        [movieData writeToFile:filePath options:NSDataWritingAtomic
            error:&error];

        if (error == nil) {
            alertMessage =
                @"Saved to 'Documents' folder successfully!";
        } else {

            alertMessage = @"Could not save movie :(";
        }
    }
}

-(void)imagePickerControllerDidCancel:(UIImagePickerController *)picker
{
    [self dismissViewControllerAnimated:YES completion:nil];
}
```

You can verify that your recorded videos are playable by selecting them with the Choose Video button in the application. They should play just like any other video file in the documents folder.

Summary

In this chapter, you saw how to use the MPMoviePlayerController class to play video and how to use the UIImagePickerController class to record video. In the MyVideoPlayer application, you saw that most of the differences between using the MediaPlayer framework to play audio and video lie in configuring the player's playback settings and parent view. To help catch errors and auto-play content, you saw how to implement notification observers.

In the MyVideoRecorder application, you learned how to add video recording to the MyVideoPlayer application by integrating the UIImagePickerController. You saw, once again, that by switching this class to handle only video and adding some extra configuration options, you could create a user experience that enables easy video capture.

Chapter 9

Building a Custom Video-Playback Interface

Following the trend of the image and audio units in the book, now that you have learned how to use Apple's built-in interfaces for video playback and recording, you are ready to start learning how to "take control" of their core functionality. In this chapter, you will learn how to customize a video-playback interface, allowing you to expose your branding and the controls that are most appropriate for your app.

To accomplish this, you will need to build your own user interface on top of AVFoundation's media-playback features, just as you did with the audio applications you developed in Chapters 6–8. While this may seem daunting, the good news is that the media-playback layer is relatively easy to set up; most of the work is in building your user experience.

The fundamental steps to implement an AVFoundation -based video player are as follows:

1. Set up a media player using the AVPlayer class.

2. Use the AVPlayerLayer class to display video.

3. Create custom playback controls using Interface Builder.

4. Create handlers for playback controls and state changes.

In this chapter, you will learn how to implement these steps by swapping the video player from the MyVideoPlayer project with a custom subclass that you develop. This project is included in the Chapter 9 folder of the source code bundle as MyCustomVideoPlayer. To help ease the transition, you will design a notification-based messaging system that mimics the MPMoviePlayerController class very closely.

Most video applications need to expose a full set of controls during full-screen mode, so the project focuses on building controls for a full-screen video-playback interface. You can find the updated mock-up for the video-playback interface in Figure 9-1.

Figure 9-1. *Mock-up for MyCustomVideoPlayer video-playback interface*

Comparing the new video-playback interface to the default iOS video interface, shown in Figure 9-2, you can see that this project places greater emphasis on phone operation. Rather than having to squint to find the Play button or to seek a couple of seconds, the larger buttons in the center reduce users' chances of making mistakes. During playback, the slider at the bottom of the screen updates to show current progress, displayed by advancing the slider to the right. Users can also use this control to *scrub* (skip) to any point in the video. Users can toggle playback or skip forward or backward by a few seconds by using the controls in the center of the screen. After a few seconds of inactivity, the controls disappear, making them available without being a distraction or taking up screen real estate.

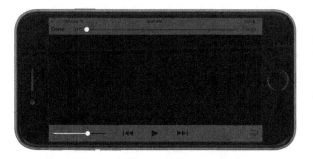 

Figure 9-2. Default iOS video-playback interface (left) vs. custom playback interface (right)

Getting Started

To get started with the MyCustomVideoPlayer project, make a copy of the MyVideoPlayer project from Chapter 10 and rename it **MyCustomVideoPlayer**. If you are unsure of how to clone a project, refer to the "Recording Video Files" section of Chapter 8, where you cloned the MyVideoPlayer project to create the MyVideoRecorder project.

Because this project uses the AVFoundation framework for media playback instead of the MediaPlayer framework, make the appropriate change in the Linked Libraries and Frameworks section under your project settings. As shown in Figure 9-3, your final list of frameworks should include only the AVFoundation framework.

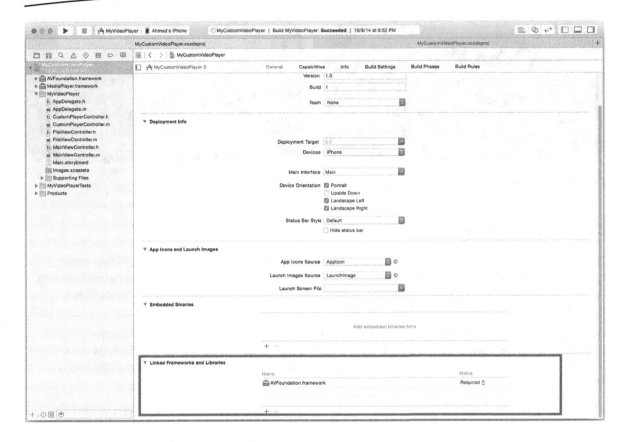

Figure 9-3. *List of frameworks for MyCustomVideoPlayer project*

For the new video-playback interface, add a subclass of UIViewController to your project. As with previous projects, you can create a subclass by choosing New ä File from the File menu in Xcode. As shown in Figure 9-4, when you are asked to select a parent class, enter UIViewController. In the MyCustomVideoPlayer project, this class is named CustomPlayerController.

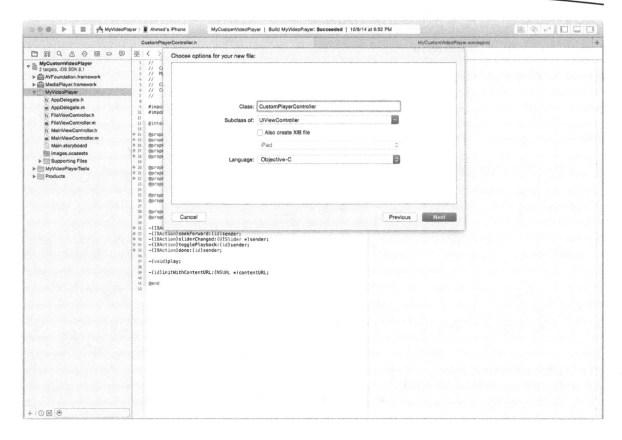

Figure 9-4. Creating a subclass

Add a constructor named [CustomPlayerController initWithContentURL:] to the
CustomPlayerController class. This will help you mimic the MPMoviePlayerController class, which uses
[MPMoviePlayerController initWIthContentURL:] as its constructor. You can find the initial header file (.h)
and implementation file (.m) for the CustomPlayerController class in Listings 9-1 and 9-2, respectively.

Listing 9-1. Header File for CustomPlayerController Class

```objc
#import <UIKit/UIKit.h>
#import <AVFoundation/AVFoundation.h>

@interface CustomPlayerController : UIViewController

-(id)initWithContentURL:(NSURL *)contentURL;

@end
```

Listing 9-2. Implementation File for CustomPlayerController Class

```
#import "CustomPlayerController.h"

@interface CustomPlayerController ()

@end

@implementation CustomPlayerController

-(id)initWithContentURL:(NSURL *)contentURL
{
    self = [super init];
    if (self) {
        ....
    }
    return self;
}

- (void)viewDidLoad {
    [super viewDidLoad];
    // Do any additional setup after loading the view.
}

- (void)didReceiveMemoryWarning {
    [super didReceiveMemoryWarning];
    // Dispose of any resources that can be re-created.
}

- (BOOL)shouldAutorotate
{
    return NO;
}

@end
```

To link this class to your MainViewController, include it in your header file, and change the type
of the moviePlayer from MPMoviePlayerController to CustomPlayerController. Although nothing
is defined in this class yet, you will build a set of controls and notifications that closely mimic the
design of the MPMoviePlayerController class. The completed header file for the MainViewController
class is included in Listing 9-3.

Listing 9-3. Header File for MainViewController Class

```
#import <UIKit/UIKit.h>
#import "CustomPlayerController.h"
#import "FileViewController.h"

@interface MainViewController : UIViewController
    <FileControllerDelegate>
```

```
@property (nonatomic, strong) IBOutlet UIView *playerView;
@property (nonatomic, strong) CustomPlayerController *moviePlayer;

@end
```

For this project, the goal is to focus on the fundamentals of building a custom playback interface. Most users expect to see a full set of controls during full-screen mode; these examples will help you build a full-screen playback controller.

To present the new playback controller in full-screen mode, change the presenting code in the file picker delegate, [FileControllerDelegate didFinishWithFile:]. After a user picks a file, you should attempt to initialize the CustomPlayerController with the selected content URL. As shown in Listing 9-4, replace all the MPMoviePlayerController initialization code with a call to [CustomPlayerController initWithContentURL:]. To streamline the message-passing process, you will encapsulate the setup code from the MPMoviePlayerController into the initialization method for the CustomPlayerController class.

Listing 9-4. Presenting Your CustomPlayerController

```
-(void)didFinishWithFile:(NSString *)filePath
{
    NSArray *paths =
        NSSearchPathForDirectoriesInDomains(NSDocumentDirectory,
    NSUserDomainMask, YES);
    NSString *documentsDirectory = [paths objectAtIndex:0];
    NSString *relativePath = [documentsDirectory
        stringByAppendingPathComponent:filePath];

    NSURL *fileURL = [NSURL fileURLWithPath:relativePath];
    self.moviePlayer = [[CustomPlayerController alloc]
        initWithContentURL:fileURL];

}
```

Building the User Interface

One advantage of building your own video-playback interface with the AVFoundation framework is that you can lay out your own user interface by using Interface Builder. Another popular method for customizing the playback interface is by subclassing the MPPlayerViewController class and overriding the control bar. Unfortunately, you cannot build a storyboard element by using a subclass of MPPlayerViewController, as it will not register as an Interface Builder–compatible object.

When using the AVFoundation framework, you can avoid this hassle by creating a new subclass of UIViewController and placing items directly on a storyboard. Additionally, you can take advantage of auto-layout, which will allow your user interface to scale across multiple screen sizes.

To begin, drag a view controller from the Interface Builder Object Library onto your storyboard. In the Attributes Inspector, enter **CustomPlayerController** as the name for both the Class and Storyboard ID, as shown in Figure 9-5.

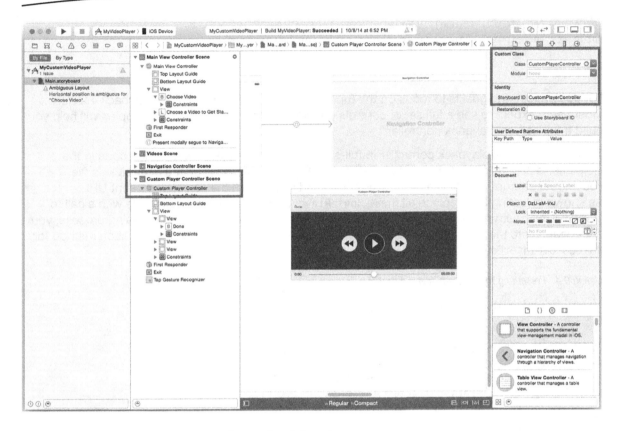

Figure 9-5. Attributes for CustomPlayerController storyboard element

Because you will present the CustomPlayerController programmatically, you do not need to define a segue. However, to pick up your custom user interface, you will need to initialize your CustomPlayerController object by using the storyboard, instead of using the default constructor. As shown in Listing 9-5, you can perform this operation by getting a reference to the UIStoryboard object for your project and then pulling the CustomPlayerController's storyboard by using its storyboard ID. This code replaces the generic [super init] call in your [self initWithContentUrl:] method.

Listing 9-5. Initializing the CustomPlayerController from a Storyboard

```
-(id)initWithContentURL:(NSURL *)contentURL
{
    UIStoryboard *storyboard = [UIStoryboard
        storyboardWithName:@"Main" bundle:nil];
    CustomPlayerController *myViewController = [storyboard
    instantiateViewControllerWithIdentifier:@"CustomPlayerController"];

    self = myViewController;
    if (self) {
        ....
    }
    return self;
}
```

In Figure 9-6, I have extracted the playback interface from the application's Mock-up. Note that there are three main areas to the user interface: a control bar at the top, a control bar at the bottom, and a control area at the center of the screen.

Figure 9-6. *Mock-up of video-playback interface*

To build the control areas, drag and drop three UView objects from the Object Library onto your storyboard, as shown in Figure 9-7. The top and bottom views will act as informal navigation bars, and the center view will be used to place the controls.

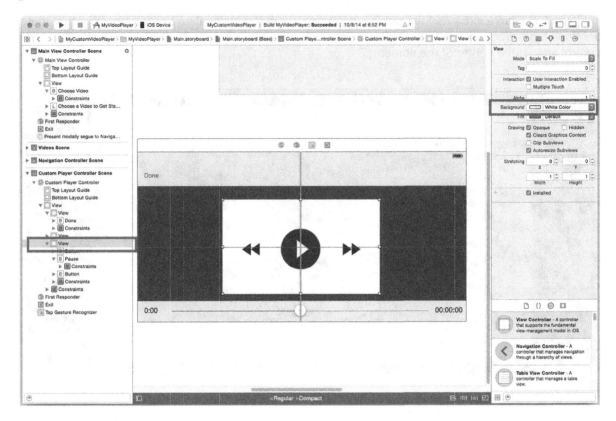

Figure 9-7. Adding container views

To support multiple screen sizes, you need to enable *auto-layout* for your elements. With auto-layout, you specify which positioning elements need to be constrained (fixed), and allow the rest to grow to fit the screen. As shown in Figure 9-8, you set constraints by selecting an item in Interface Builder, navigating to the Pin button at the bottom of the window (circled below), and then clicking on the dotted lines or check boxes representing the elements you want to "pin."

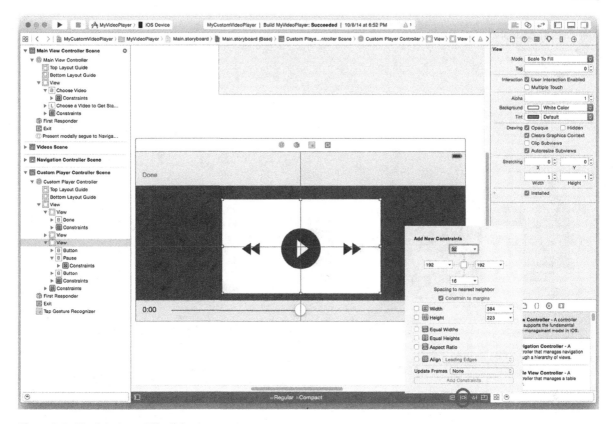

Figure 9-8. The Auto-Layout Pin dialog box

For the navigation bars, pin the views to the left and right of the screen, and to the top or bottom. You can find an example for the bottom navigation bar in Figure 9-9. Follow the same process for the top bar.

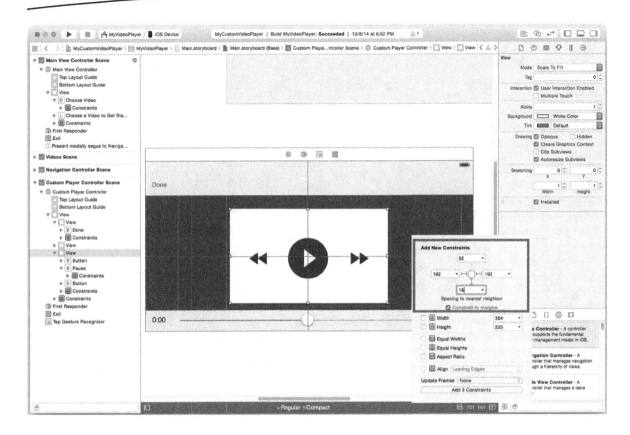

Figure 9-9. Pinning the bottom navigation bar

For the center control panel, you do not need to worry about the screen size; instead, you need to worry about maintaining its position in the center of the screen. To center this panel, pin its width and height, then use the Align button to align the element in the center of its container, as shown in Figure 9-10.

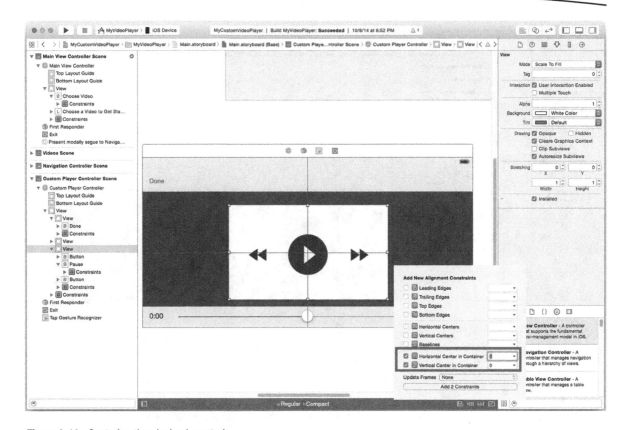

Figure 9-10. *Centering the playback controls*

Next, you are ready to begin adding the controls to the playback interface. Use Figure 9-6 as your guide, but pay careful attention to make sure that when you place the elements, you drop them directly on top of a view. This mimics adding an element as a subview and allows you to show or hide an entire panel by modifying the container. For example, to hide all the playback controls, all you need to do is hide the center control panel. You can verify that elements have been added as subviews by confirming their hierarchical position in the *Document Outline* (Interface Builder's left pane). Using Figure 9-11 as a reference, you can confirm that the Current Time label has been added to the control bar at the bottom of the screen because the label appears underneath the view in the element hierarchy.

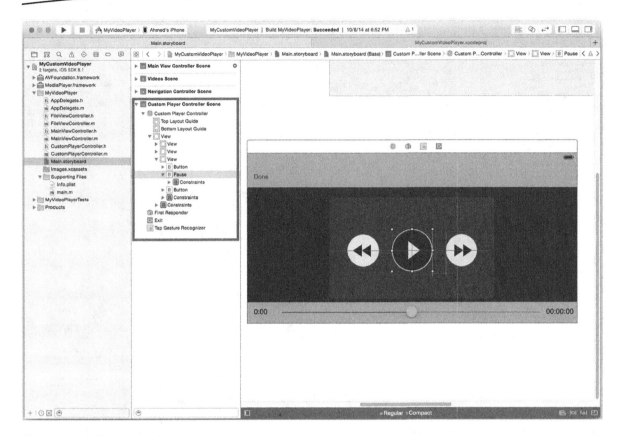

Figure 9-11. Verifying view hierarchy

To help you connect the rest of your user interface, Listing 9-6 shows the header file for the
CustomPlayerController class. Connect the button actions to the *touch up inside* events of the
buttons, and connect the slider events to the Value Changed events of the sliders.

Listing 9-6. Header File for CustomPlayerController Class

```
#import <UIKit/UIKit.h>
#import <AVFoundation/AVFoundation.h>

@interface CustomPlayerController : UIViewController

@property (nonatomic, strong) IBOutlet UIView *controlView;
@property (nonatomic, strong) IBOutlet UIButton *playbackButton;
@property (nonatomic, strong) IBOutlet UIButton *seekFwdButton;
@property (nonatomic, strong) IBOutlet UIButton *seekBackButton;
@property (nonatomic, strong) IBOutlet UIButton *doneButton;

@property (nonatomic, strong) IBOutlet UISlider *timeSlider;
@property (nonatomic, strong) IBOutlet UILabel *progressLabel;
@property (nonatomic, strong) IBOutlet UILabel *totalTimeLabel;
```

```
-(IBAction)seekBackward:(id)sender;
-(IBAction)seekForward:(id)sender;
-(IBAction)sliderChanged:(UISlider *)sender;
-(IBAction)togglePlayback:(id)sender;
-(IBAction)done:(id)sender;

-(void)play;

-(id)initWithContentURL:(NSURL *)contentURL;

@end
```

To hide the center control panel, remember to link the `controlView` property of the class. Once this is done, you can set the background color of the element to *clear* in order to make the playback controls look like they are floating.

Using the AVPlayer Class for Media Playback

The `AVFoundation` framework allows you to play back video files via the `AVPlayer` class. Although it does not provide a user interface, this class provides playback controls (including scrubbing and toggling playback), events (including *loading state* or *playback complete*), and limited hardware controls (including AirPlay and Volume). The class is designed to take `AVPlayerItem` objects as its input, and can pass its output directly to the `AVPlayerLayer` class, which you can display on top of a `UIView`. To control playback, you will need to add instance variables for the `AVPlayerItem` and `AVPlayer` to the `CustomPlayerController` header file:

```
@property (nonatomic, strong) AVPlayerItem *playerItem;
@property (nonatomic, strong) AVPlayer *player;
```

To check the validity of your input with the `AVPlayer` class, you need to attempt to load the file. When the `AVPlayer` object has a `status` of `AVStatusReadyToPlay`, the file is ready to play. To catch this change, you need to use key-value observing (KVO), a message-passing mechanism that works on a subscription basis, like notifications. For KVO, you specify a property (*key*) that you want to *observe* on an object. For `AVPlayer` status changes, you want to observe the `status` property. You can find a detailed explanation of key-value observing in Chapter 12, where you will develop a more sophisticated `AVPlayer`-based media player using the new `AVKit` framework.

Listing 9-7 shows how I begin the `AVPlayer` initialization process—by creating an `AVPlayerItem` with the input URL, initializing an `AVPlayer` object, and setting an observer.

Listing 9-7. Initializing the AVPlayer

```
-(id)initWithContentURL:(NSURL *)contentURL
{
    UIStoryboard *storyboard = [UIStoryboard
        storyboardWithName:@"Main" bundle:nil];
    CustomPlayerController *myViewController = [storyboard
    instantiateViewControllerWithIdentifier:@"CustomPlayerController"];
```

```
        self = myViewController;
        if (self) {

            self.playerItem = [[AVPlayerItem alloc]
                initWithURL:contentURL];
            self.player = [AVPlayer playerWithPlayerItem:self.playerItem];
            [self.player addObserver:self forKeyPath:@"status"
                options:0 context:nil];
}

        return self;
}
```

All KVO messages are handled by the [UIViewController observeValueForKeyPath:ofObject:
change:context:] method for a class. Changes in the status property will indicate that the
AVPlayer was able to load the file successfully (AVPlayerStatusReadyToPlay) or that it failed
(AVPlayerStatusFailed). To identify KVO messages, before performing any logic, compare the
incoming object and keyPath. As shown in Listing 9-8, you can use the self.player instance
variable and status for these parameters in the CustomPlayerController class.

Listing 9-8. Handling AVPlayer KVO Messages

```
-(void)observeValueForKeyPath:(NSString *)keyPath
    ofObject:(id)object change:(NSDictionary *)change
    context:(void *)context
{
    if (object == self.player && [keyPath isEqualToString:@"status"]) {

        if (self.player.status == AVPlayerStatusReadyToPlay) {
            ...
        } else {
            ...
        }

        [self.player removeObserver:self forKeyPath:@"status"];
    }
}
```

If the file loaded successfully, you are ready to initialize the AVPlayerLayer, which displays the
output of the AVPlayer. The AVPlayerLayer works like the AVCaptureVideoPreviewLayer you used in
Chapter 4 to mirror a live feed from the camera. It outputs video data directly to a layer, the lower-
level object that provides content for a UIView. As shown in Listing 9-9, to display the video layer,
match its dimensions to the *bounding frame* of the target view (in this case, the main area of the
CustomViewController), and add it as a sublayer.

Listing 9-9. Adding an AVPlayerLayer to the CustomViewController

```
-(void)observeValueForKeyPath:(NSString *)keyPath ofObject:(id)object
    change:(NSDictionary *)change context:(void *)context
{
    if (object == self.player && [keyPath isEqualToString:@"status"]) {
```

```objc
    if (self.player.status == AVPlayerStatusReadyToPlay) {

        AVPlayerLayer *playerLayer = [AVPlayerLayer
            playerLayerWithPlayer:self.player];
        playerLayer.frame = self.view.bounds;
        playerLayer.videoGravity = AVLayerVideoGravityResizeAspect;
        [self.view.layer addSublayer:playerLayer];

        playerLayer.needsDisplayOnBoundsChange = YES;
        self.view.layer.needsDisplayOnBoundsChange = YES;

    } else {
        NSDictionary *userDict = [NSDictionary
            dictionaryWithObjects:@[@"error",
                @"Unable to load file"]
            forKeys:@[ @"status", @"reason"]];
        [[NSNotificationCenter defaultCenter]
            postNotificationName:@"customPlayerLoadStateChanged"
            object:self userInfo:userDict];
    }

    [self.player removeObserver:self forKeyPath:@"status"];
    }
}
```

To make the video scale to fit in the container, remember to set the videoGravity property of the AVPlayerLayer to AVLayerVideoGravityResizeAspect.

Creating MediaPlayer-like Notifications

To maintain parity with the MPMoviePlayerController class, you should post a notification to indicate that the load state of the player has changed. In my example, I call this notification customPlayerLoadStateChanged. As shown in Listing 9-10, I added the status and error keys to the userDict (a notification's preferred mechanism for passing variables), to make the messages more descriptive. I use ready as the status value for *success* and error as the value for *failure*.

Listing 9-10. Posting Notifications for AVPlayer State Changes

```objc
-(void)observeValueForKeyPath:(NSString *)keyPath ofObject:(id)object
    change:(NSDictionary *)change context:(void *)context
{
    if (object == self.player && [keyPath isEqualToString:@"status"]) {

        if (self.player.status == AVPlayerStatusReadyToPlay) {

            AVPlayerLayer *playerLayer = [AVPlayerLayer
                playerLayerWithPlayer:self.player];
            playerLayer.frame = self.view.bounds;
            playerLayer.videoGravity = AVLayerVideoGravityResizeAspect;
            [self.view.layer addSublayer:playerLayer];
```

```
        playerLayer.needsDisplayOnBoundsChange = YES;
        self.view.layer.needsDisplayOnBoundsChange = YES;

        [self showControls:nil];
        self.controlTimer = [NSTimer
            scheduledTimerWithTimeInterval:2.0f target:self
            selector:@selector(hideControls:) userInfo:nil
            repeats:NO];

        NSDictionary *userDict = [NSDictionary
            dictionaryWithObject:@"ready" forKey:@"status"];

        [[NSNotificationCenter defaultCenter]
            postNotificationName:@"customPlayerLoadStateChanged"
            object:self userInfo:userDict];

    } else {
        NSDictionary *userDict = [NSDictionary
            dictionaryWithObjects:@[@"error", @"Unable to load file"]
            forKeys:@[ @"status", @"reason"]];
        [[NSNotificationCenter defaultCenter]
            postNotificationName:@"customPlayerLoadStateChanged"
            object:self userInfo:userDict];
    }

    [self.player removeObserver:self forKeyPath:@"status"];
    }
}
```

To handle this notification, you need to add an observer in the `MainViewController` class. You can find the modified `[self viewDidLoad]` method for the `MainViewController` class in Listing 9-11. In this example, I use `[self loadStateChanged:]` as the handler for the notification, just as in the MyVideoPlayer project.

Listing 9-11. Adding an Observer for AVPlayer State Changes

```
-(id)initWithContentURL:(NSURL *)contentURL
{
    UIStoryboard *storyboard = [UIStoryboard storyboardWithName:@"Main"
        bundle:nil];
    CustomPlayerController *myViewController = [storyboard
    instantiateViewControllerWithIdentifier:@"CustomPlayerController"];

    self = myViewController;
    if (self) {

        self.playerItem = [[AVPlayerItem alloc]
            initWithURL:contentURL];
        self.player = [AVPlayer playerWithPlayerItem:self.playerItem];
```

```
        [self.player addObserver:self forKeyPath:@"status" options:0
            context:nil];

        self.isPlaying = NO;
    }
    return self;
}
```

In the [self loadStateChanged] method, you should decode the notification, by checking for ready or error. By handling the state-change message in the MainViewController class instead of the CustomPlayerController class, you can avoid presenting the playback interface if the file failed to load. As shown in Listing 9-12, extract the status and error keys from userDict. If the status is ready, present the CustomPlayerController modally and call the play message to start playback; otherwise, display an alert view containing the error string.

Listing 9-12. Handling AVPlayer State Changes

```
-(void)loadStateChanged:(NSNotification *) notification
{
    NSDictionary *userInfo = notification.userInfo;
    NSString *status = [userInfo objectForKey:@"status"];

    if ([status isEqualToString:@"ready"]) {
        //dismiss the picker
        [self dismissViewControllerAnimated:YES completion:^{

            [self presentViewController:self.moviePlayer animated:NO
                        completion:^{
                            [self.moviePlayer play];
                        }];

        }];

    } else {
        NSString *errorString = [userInfo objectForKey:@"error"];

        UIAlertView *alert = [[UIAlertView alloc]
            initWithTitle:@"Error!" message:errorString
            delegate:nil cancelButtonTitle:@"OK"
            otherButtonTitles:nil];
        [alert show];
    }

}
```

Building Playback Controls

Having created the user interface, initialized an AVPlayer object, and set up MediaPlayer-like notifications, you are ready to start implementing the playback controls and user-interface updates. The main controls for the CustomPlayerController include skipping forward or backward, toggling playback, and scrubbing to a specific time in the player. The user can dismiss the playback interface via the Done button in the top control view.

Toggling Playback

In the header file for the CustomPlayerController class, I declared [CustomPlayerController togglePlayback:] as the method to toggle playback state. To build a familiar user interface, use one button to start or stop playback. In order to determine which action should execute, add a BOOL instance variable to the CustomPlayerController class:

```
@property (nonatomic, assign) BOOL isPlaying;
```

You can control the playback, using the [AVPlayer play] and [AVPlayer pause] methods on your AVPlayer object. As shown in Listing 9-13, to maintain state, update the isPlaying property and your user interface after starting or stopping playback.

Listing 9-13. Toggling Playback

```
-(IBAction)togglePlayback:(id)sender
{
    if (self.isPlaying) {
        [self.player pause];

        [self.playbackButton setTitle:@"Play"
            forState:UIControlStateNormal];

    } else {
        [self.player play];

        [self.playbackButton setTitle:@"Pause"
            forState:UIControlStateNormal];

    }
    self.isPlaying = !self.isPlaying;
}
```

Skipping Forward/Backward

Similar to how you can use the AVPlayer object to start or stop media playback, you can also use it to seek backward or forward a few seconds in playback. This is a convenient feature when users want to rewind to catch a shot they have missed, or skip a shot they are not interested in.

To implement skipping, you will use a method similar to the one employed in Chapter 6. Query the currently playing item for its playback position, and then check whether the desired time (+/- 5 seconds) is valid. If the user tries to skip backward less than 5 seconds into a video, skip to the beginning. If they try to skip forward with less than 5 seconds remaining, ignore the event. As with code for updating the user interface, you can determine the playback position of a file by querying the currentTime property on the AVPlayerItem object.

You can find the [self skipForward] and [self skipBackward] methods for the CustomPlayerController class in Listings 9-14 and 9-15. After seeking to your new playback position, update the user interface immediately so that the user knows about the change.

Listing 9-14. Seeking Forward

```
-(IBAction)seekForward:(id)sender
{
    NSInteger duration = CMTimeGetSeconds([self.playerItem duration]);
    NSInteger currentTime = CMTimeGetSeconds(
        [self.playerItem currentTime]);

    float desiredTime = currentTime + 5;
    if (desiredTime < duration) {
        CMTime seekTime = CMTimeMakeWithSeconds(desiredTime, 1);
        [self.player seekToTime:seekTime];

        [self updateProgress];
    }
}
```

Listing 9-15. Seeking Backward

```
-(IBAction)seekBackward:(id)sender
{
    NSInteger currentTime = CMTimeGetSeconds([self.playerItem
        currentTime]);

    float desiredTime = currentTime - 5;

    if (desiredTime < 0) {
        CMTime seekTime = CMTimeMakeWithSeconds(0.0f, 1);
        [self.player seekToTime:seekTime];
    } else {
        CMTime seekTime = CMTimeMakeWithSeconds(desiredTime, 1);
        [self.player seekToTime:seekTime];
    }

    [self updateProgress];
}
```

Using the Playback Scrubber

To enable seeking via the slider in the bottom bar, you need to implement the value changed event for the element. The *value changed* event fires when the user has finished moving the indicator element inside of the slider. While *touch up inside* was appropriate for the buttons (because the final event was releasing the button), for sliders, you need to catch when the user has completely finished changing the value, not just when the user's finger has left the element (which could be triggered by touching any part of the slider).

For the event's handler method, add an IBAction handler method called sliderChanged: to your CustomViewController header file:

```
-(IBAction)sliderChanged:(id)sender;
```

To catch the *value changed* event, tie the event to the timeSlider in your storyboard. As shown in Figure 9-12, as with other user-interface events, hold down the Value Changed radio button in the Connections Inspector and drag your cursor over to the CustomViewController in your storyboard. When you release your cursor, a list of valid IBAction methods will show up. Select the sliderChanged: method.

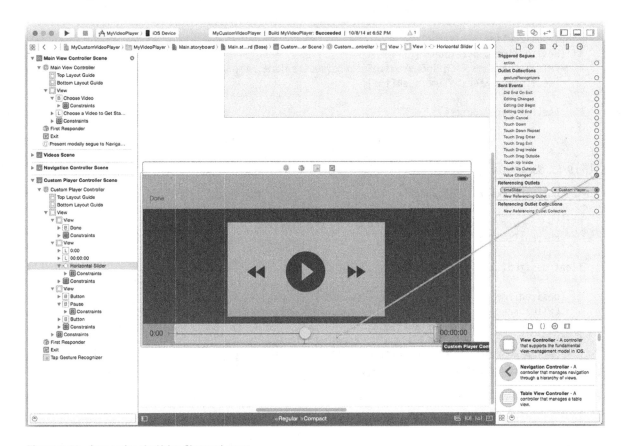

Figure 9-12. Connecting the Value Changed event

Now that you have the context of how to catch the event, you need to learn what to do with the event information. Video scrubbers allow users to skip to a desired time in the video. When you updated the user interface to show playback progress, you set the scrubber's position by calculating the *percent complete* of the video (current time / total time). Now that the user has a scrubber, you want to recalculate this time by using the new value. As shown in Listing 9-16, you can get the new value of the UISlider object from the value property.

Listing 9-16. Playback Scrubber Handler

```
-(IBAction)sliderChanged:(UISlider *)sender
{
    float progress = sender.value;
    NSInteger durationSeconds = CMTimeGetSeconds([self.playerItem duration]);
    float result = durationSeconds * progress;
    CMTime seekTime = CMTimeMakeWithSeconds(result, 1);


    [self.player seekToTime:seekTime];

}
```

The value property is a float between 0 and 1. By multiplying the video's *duration* by this value, you can find the new playback position. After seeking to the desired time, call the [self updateProgress] method to update the user interface immediately (users expect to see the new time they scrubbed to).

Dismissing the Playback Interface

To dismiss the playback controller, you need to send a message to its presenting view controller (your MainViewController object). To mimic the MPMoviePlayerController class, post a notification called customPlayerDidFinish when the user clicks the Done button, as shown in Listing 9-17.

Listing 9-17. Done Button Handler

```
-(IBAction)done:(id)sender
{
    NSDictionary *userDict = [NSDictionary dictionaryWithObject:@"user finished"
        forKey:@"reason"];
    [[NSNotificationCenter defaultCenter]
        postNotificationName:@"customPlayerDidFinish" object:userDict];
}
```

To handle this message, add an observer for the customPlayerDidFinish notification in the MainViewController class's [self viewDidLoad] method; similarly remove the observer in the [self dealloc] method. Your final view teardown and setup methods for the MainViewController class are shown in Listings 9-18 and 9-19.

Listing 9-18. MainViewController View Setup Method

```
- (void)viewDidLoad {
    [super viewDidLoad];
    // Do any additional setup after loading the view, typically from a nib.

    [[NSNotificationCenter defaultCenter] addObserver:self
        selector:@selector(playbackFinished:)
        name:@"customPlayerDidFinish"
        object:nil];
```

```
[[NSNotificationCenter defaultCenter] addObserver:self
    selector:@selector(loadStateChanged:)
    name:@"customPlayerLoadStateChanged" object:nil];
}
```

Listing 9-19. MainViewController View Teardown Method

```
- (void)dealloc
{
    [[NSNotificationCenter defaultCenter] removeObserver:self
        name:@"customPlayerDidFinish" object:nil];
    [[NSNotificationCenter defaultCenter] removeObserver:self
        name:@"customPlayerLoadStateChanged" object:nil];

}
```

In the notification's handler method, which Listing 9-19 specifies as [self playbackFinished:], make a call to [self dismissViewController:animated:]. To add error handling to this method, I have created an error entry in userDict, which you can use to check whether playback failed because of an error. The Playback Finished handler for the MainViewController class is provided in Listing 9-20.

Listing 9-20. Playback Finished Handler Method

```
-(void)playbackFinished:(NSNotification *) notification
{

    NSDictionary *userInfo = notification.userInfo;
    NSString *finishReason = [userInfo objectForKey:@"reason"];

    [self dismissViewControllerAnimated:YES completion:^{

        if ([finishReason isEqualToString:@"error"]) {
            NSError *error = [userInfo objectForKey:@"error"];
            NSString *errorString = [error description];

            UIAlertView *alert = [[UIAlertView alloc]
                initWithTitle:@"Error!" message:errorString
                delegate:nil cancelButtonTitle:@"OK"
                otherButtonTitles:nil];
            [alert show];
        }

    }];

}
```

Adding User-Interface Updates

To improve the user interface for the MyCustomVideoPlayer application, you should add user-interface updates to hide the playback controls and indicate the current playback progress, both of which can be accomplished through clever use of timers.

After the user has started playback, you should update the Current Time label and scrubber to indicate the current playback position. Also, after a couple of seconds of inactivity, you should hide the center playback control panel.

Updating Playback Progress

To update playback progress, you can reuse logic similar to that from the MyPlayer audio application in Chapter 6. Create a timer that will fire every second, and perform user-interface updates in its handler method. For the CustomPlayerController class, the user expects the progress slider (video scrubber) and progress label (to the left of the slider) to update every second.

Create a method called [self updateProgress] to contain this user-interface update code. To display progress, you need to know the total length of the video and the current playback position. You can query these via the duration and currentTime properties on the currently loaded AVPlayerItem object. For the CustomViewController class, this is the playerItem instance variable. For the progressLabel, you can simply display the currentTime after converting it to minutes and seconds. The scrubber is a bit more complicated—but not by much.

A video scrubber is an essential part of any video playback user interface. It allows the user to jump to a position in the video and see the current playback. It looks like a progress bar, because it is. To get the progress, you need to know how much of the video has been "watched," compared to how much is remaining. You can find this by dividing the current time by the duration. For instance, if a user has watched 30 seconds of a 60-second video, the progress should be 50%. After you have the new value in the form of a float between 0 and 1, you can apply it to a UISlider by setting the value property.

Listing 9-21 shows the [self updateProgress] method for the CustomViewController class, which updates the progress label and slider.

Listing 9-21. Updating the User Interface with Playback Progress

```
-(void)updateProgress
{

    NSInteger durationMinutes = CMTimeGetSeconds(
        [self.playerItem duration]) / 60;
    NSInteger durationSeconds = CMTimeGetSeconds(
        [self.playerItem duration])  - durationMinutes * 60;

    NSInteger currentTimeMinutes = CMTimeGetSeconds(
        [self.playerItem currentTime]) / 60;
    NSInteger currentTimeSeconds = CMTimeGetSeconds(
        [self.playerItem currentTime])  - currentTimeMinutes * 60;

    self.timeSlider.value = CMTimeGetSeconds(
        [self.playerItem currentTime])/CMTimeGetSeconds(
        [self.playerItem duration]) + 0.0f;
```

```
        self.progressLabel.text = [NSString stringWithFormat:@"%02ld:%02ld",
            currentTimeMinutes, currentTimeSeconds];
        self.totalTimeLabel.text = [NSString stringWithFormat:@"%02ld:%02ld",
            durationMinutes, durationSeconds];

}
```

Much like the MyPlayer application, you should update progress only when video playback is active. As shown in Listing 9-22, if the user is starting playback, create a timer that fires every second; otherwise, invalidate the existing timer to stop it.

Listing 9-22. Initiating Progress Updates

```
-(IBAction)togglePlayback:(id)sender
{
    if (self.isPlaying) {
        [self.player pause];

        [self.playbackButton setTitle:@"Play"
            forState:UIControlStateNormal];

        [self showControls:nil];

        [self.updateTimer invalidate];

    } else {
        [self.player play];

        [self.playbackButton setTitle:@"Pause"
            forState:UIControlStateNormal];

        self.updateTimer = [NSTimer scheduledTimerWithTimeInterval:1.0f
            target:self selector:@selector(updateProgress) userInfo:nil
            repeats:YES];
    }
    self.isPlaying = !self.isPlaying;
}
```

You will notice here that I called the [NSTimer scheduledTimerWithTimeInterval:target: selector:userInfo:repeats:] constructor to initialize the timer, instead of [NSTimer timerWithTime Interval:target:selector:userInfo:repeats:]. Since timer updates need to be caught on the main thread to execute, *scheduling* the timer is a good way to force this behavior.

Automatically Hiding the Playback Controls

While the playback controls are convenient to the user, they can be a nuisance if they remain on top of the player view. Several video applications (including Apple's) solve this problem by hiding the controls after a couple of seconds of inactivity. When a user clicks on the video area, you can usually correctly assume that the user is about to scrub the video or needs to toggle playback. Similarly, if 1 or 2 seconds goes by without the user touching any element, you can safely assume that user is done.

You detect such activity by adding a `UITapGestureRecognizer` to the playback view. *Gesture recognizers* are built into many `UIKit` classes, such as `UIButton`, and drive familiar events, such as *touch up inside*. Just as with any other event, you define the gesture to watch and which `IBAction` handler method you want to call when the event is caught. In Interface Builder, to add a gesture recognizer to any element, drag it out of the Object Library and drop it on your target. For the playback view, drag a *Tap gesture recognizer* onto the `CustomPlayerController`'s view property, as shown in Figure 9-13.

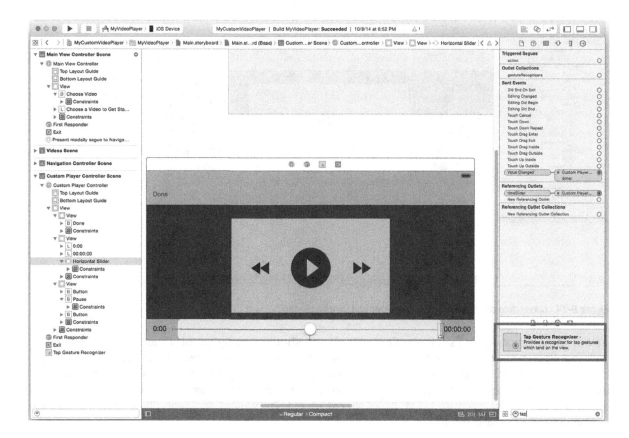

Figure 9-13. Adding a UITapGestureRecognizer to the CustomPlayerController class

For the handler method, create an `IBAction` method in your header file called `[self showControls:]`.

`-(IBAction)showControls:(id)sender;`

To connect the handler method to the gesture recognizer, hold down on the `selector` property under Sent Actions in the Connections Inspector, and drop it onto the `CustomPlayerController`, as shown in Figure 9-14. Select the `[self showControls:]` method from the drop-down menu.

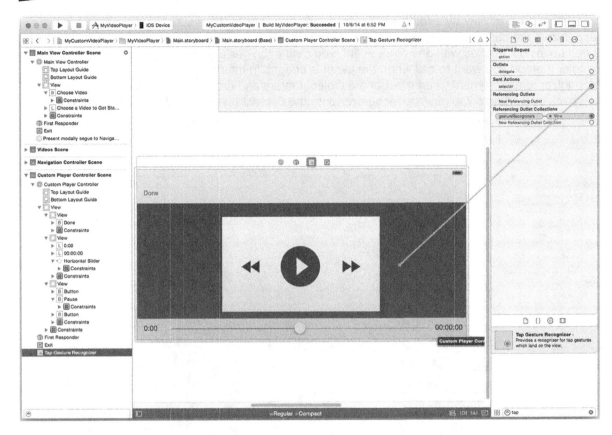

Figure 9-14. Connecting the UITapGestureRecognizer to a handler method

As the name suggests, in [self showControls:], you should display the playback controls. However, you should also start a timer to hide the controls after 2 seconds. As shown in Listing 9-23, to display the controls, bring the subview to the front (this will display it on top of the video) and enable user-interaction touch events. To hide the controls, create an instance variable called controlTimer and make its handler method, [self hideControllers:]. To prevent conflicting timer events, disable the previous timer if it is not nil.

Listing 9-23. Showing Controls upon a Tap Event

```
-(IBAction)showControls:(id)sender
{
    if (self.controlTimer != nil)
        [self.controlTimer invalidate];

    [self.view bringSubviewToFront:self.controlView];
    self.controlView.userInteractionEnabled = YES;
```

```
    if (sender != nil) {
        self.controlTimer = [NSTimer scheduledTimerWithTimeInterval:2.0f
            target:self selector:@selector(hideControls:) userInfo:nil
            repeats:NO];
    }
}
```

To hide the controls, reverse the process. Move the playback controls so they're behind the preview layer, and disable touch events so that you do not generate any false positives, as shown in Listing 9-24.

Listing 9-24. Hiding Controls After the Timer Fires

```
-(IBAction)hideControls:(id)sender
{
    [self.view sendSubviewToBack:self.controlView];
    self.controlView.userInteractionEnabled = NO;
}
```

You can use this same process to hide the bars at the top and bottom of the screen. Simply define them in your class and add them to the list of views that are hidden or shown by tap and timer events.

Summary

In this chapter, you saw how to build a custom playback controller by using the AVFoundation framework. You saw that by carefully using view positioning and auto-layout, you can build a user interface that matches a brand but that also has the flexibility to fit any number of screens.

To enable media playback, you learned how to load a file by using the AVPlayer class and how to observe status changes to determine whether it loaded successfully. Using this same object, you built playback controls that allowed the user to toggle playback, skip backward or forward a few seconds, and scrub to a desired position in the video.

Finally, to add that last little bit of magic to the application, you added user-interface updates to the application that hide the center playback controls when the user is not interacting with the app and update the current time label and scrubber with the current playback position.

Although the setup code for this user interface and playback stack was more involved than using the MPMoviePlayerController class directly, the result was a custom playback controller that can mimic the MPMoviePlayerController class both in functionality and its messaging system, while still allowing you to add your own branding on top.

Building a Custom Video-Recording Interface

To close out the unit on video, you will build your own video-recording interface "the hard way." As you have seen while working with other media features, Cocoa Touch provides a great built-in interface for video capture—but only if you are willing to accept its user interface and functionality limits. When you want to go beyond these limits, customizing the video-capture interface to better suit your workflow or brand, you need to build your own user interface. To do that, you need to hook into AVFoundation's low-level image-capture functionality.

If all this sounds familiar, that's because it is. By repeating many of the same steps you used to build a custom still-image interface in Chapter 4, you can build a custom video-capture interface. As you learned in Chapter 4, these are the major steps required to implement a still-image interface:

1. Discover and configure the camera hardware.

2. Build a user interface capable of displaying the live camera feed.

3. Modify the capture settings from the UI.

4. Save the image when the user presses the Take Picture button.

To adapt that workflow to video, you need to do the following:

1. Configure the capture session for video.

2. Add video-specific capture controls.

3. Display a preview interface when the user finishes recording.

4. Refactor the message-passing interface to handle larger files.

In this chapter, you will build a custom video-recording interface by implementing the MyCustomRecorder project (you can find the code in the Chapter 10 folder) that you first saw in Chapter 9, adding video-capture features accessible via a Record Video button. You will reuse the MyCustomPlayer project code for all video-playback functions. Users will be able to modify capture settings before video recording begins. After recording is complete, they will see a preview interface, where they can choose to accept or reject the video they just shot.

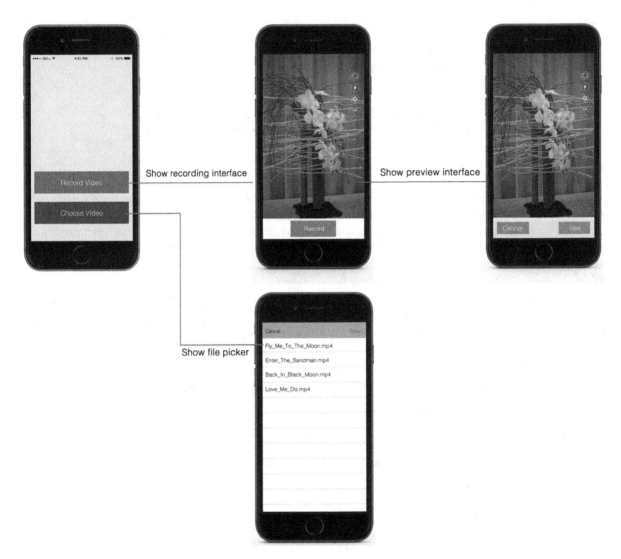

Figure 10-1. Mock-up for MyCustomRecorder project

In Figure 10-2, you can compare the MyCustomRecorder project to the MyCamera still-image capture project from Chapter 4. You can see that the general flow of the application is the same, with the exception of the preview interface and capture settings.

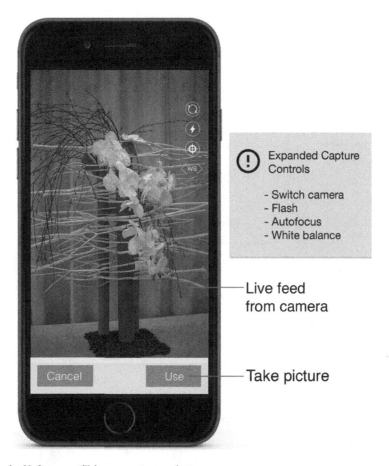

Figure 10-2. Mock-up for MyCamera still-image capture project

This chapter relies heavily on your knowledge of image capture using AVFoundation from Chapter 4. If you haven't mastered that topic, I recommend reviewing Chapter 4 before you proceed. This project reuses many of the image-capture code samples from Chapter 4, but my explanations of the core classes (such as AVCaptureInputDevice and AVCaptureSession) will not be as deep.

Getting Started

For this chapter, your primary focus is video capture. First, clone the MyCustomPlayer from Chapter 9 to get a base user interface and video-playback interface. You clone a project by making a copy of it in the Finder and then opening it in Xcode. As shown in Figure 10-3, remember that you can rename the project by clicking carefully inside the project file's name in the Project Navigator.

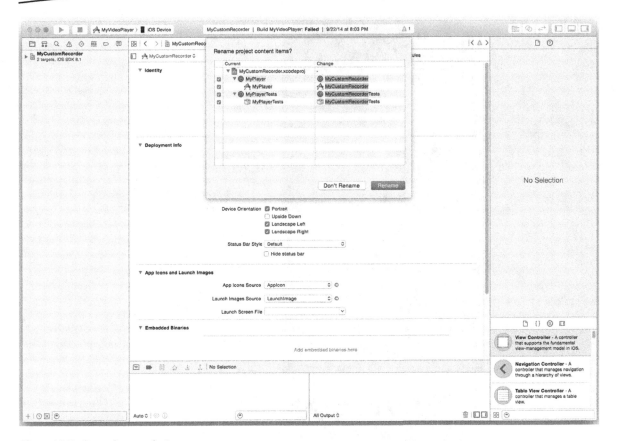

Figure 10-3. Renaming a project

To build a custom video-capture interface, you need to use the AVFoundation framework's image-capture classes. As in previous projects, add this framework to your project as a Linked Framework under your project's Settings. Your final set of included frameworks should look like the example in Figure 10-4.

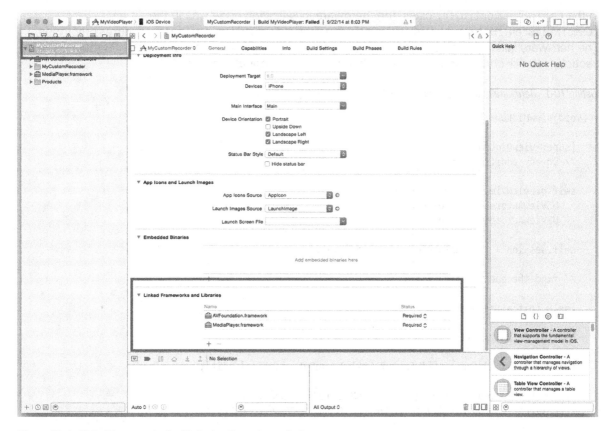

Figure 10-4. *List of frameworks for MyCustomRecorder project*

The device setup code, user interface, and protocol for the MyCamera project were encapsulated in the CameraViewController class. Because the user interface and protocol mimicked the UIImagePickerControllerView class closely, you should use these as a base for the MyCustomRecorder project. Copy these files over from the MyCamera project.

Setting Up the Hardware Interface

After including the base classes for the project, you can start modifying the CameraViewController class to support video capture. Before dealing with the user interface, you need to make sure the hardware interface to the camera is properly set up for video capture.

To review Chapter 4, the classes you configure to capture media are as follows:

AVCaptureDevice: Represents the hardware device you are going to access

AVCaptureInput: Represents the data stream you are accessing (for example, video stream for a camera, audio stream for a microphone)

AVCaptureOutput:Represents the data that is captured by your device (for example, a movie file)

AVCaptureSession: Manages the interface between the input data stream and the output

In the CameraViewController class, the hardware initialization code was in the [CameraViewController viewDidLoad] and [CameraViewController initializeCameras] methods. The hardware initialization code for still-image capture is highlighted in Listing 10-1. Throughout this section, you will change the settings so that they are appropriate for video.

Listing 10-1. Hardware Interface Settings for Still-Image Capture

```
- (void)viewDidLoad
{
    [super viewDidLoad];
    // Do any additional setup after loading the view.

    self.previewView.autoresizingMask =
        UIViewAutoresizingFlexibleWidth |
        UIViewAutoresizingFlexibleHeight;

    self.session = [[AVCaptureSession alloc] init];

    // find the back-facing camera

    [self initializeCameras];

    NSError *error = nil;

    self.stillImageOutput = [[AVCaptureStillImageOutput alloc] init];

     NSMutableDictionary *configDict = [NSMutableDictionary new];
     [configDict setObject:AVVideoCodecJPEG forKey:AVVideoCodecKey];

    [self.stillImageOutput setOutputSettings:configDict];

    if (error == nil && [self.session canAddInput:self.rearCameraInput]) {
        [self.session addInput:self.rearCameraInput];

        // set up our preview layer

        self.previewLayer = [[AVCaptureVideoPreviewLayer alloc]
                            initWithSession:self.session];

        CGRect layerRect = self.view.bounds;
        CGPoint layerCenter = CGPointMake(CGRectGetMidX(layerRect),
            CGRectGetMidY(layerRect));

        [self.previewLayer setBounds:layerRect];
        [self.previewLayer setPosition:layerCenter];

        [self.previewLayer setVideoGravity:AVLayerVideoGravityResize];

        [self.previewView.layer addSublayer:self.previewLayer];

        // set up our output
```

```objc
        if ([self.session canAddOutput:self.stillImageOutput]) {
            [self.session addOutput:self.stillImageOutput];
        }

        [self.view bringSubviewToFront:self.tapPosition];

    }
}

-(void)initializeCameras
{

    self.cameraArray = [AVCaptureDevice
                        devicesWithMediaType:AVMediaTypeVideo];

    NSError *error = nil;

    self.rearCamera = nil;
    self.frontCamera = nil;

    if ([self.cameraArray count] > 1) {

        for (AVCaptureDevice *camera in self.cameraArray) {
            if (camera.position == AVCaptureDevicePositionBack) {
                self.rearCamera = camera;
            } else if (camera.position == AVCaptureDevicePositionFront) {
                self.frontCamera = camera;
            }
        }

        self.rearCameraInput = [AVCaptureDeviceInput
            deviceInputWithDevice:self.rearCamera error:&error];
        self.frontCameraInput = [AVCaptureDeviceInput
            deviceInputWithDevice:self.frontCamera error:&error];

    } else {
        self.rearCamera = [AVCaptureDevice
            defaultDeviceWithMediaType:AVMediaTypeVideo];
        self.rearCameraInput = [AVCaptureDeviceInput
            deviceInputWithDevice:self.rearCamera error:&error];
    }

    self.currentDevice = self.rearCamera;
}
```

First, you need to make sure all of the AVCaptureDevice and AVCaptureInput objects for the hardware interfaces you want to use are correctly set up. In reviewing the [CameraViewController initializeCameras] method, you can see that still-image capture required you to find capture devices that were capable of capturing video (in order to display a live feed). That takes care of the visual aspect; however, to capture audio, you need to add an input device for the microphone. Listing 10-2 provides a modified version of the [CameraViewController initializeCameras] method that includes the audio input.

Listing 10-2. AVCaptureDevice and AVCaptureDeviceInput Settings for MyCustomRecorder Project, Including Audio

```
-(void)initializeCameras
{
    self.cameraArray = [AVCaptureDevice
                        devicesWithMediaType:AVMediaTypeVideo];

    NSError *error = nil;

    self.rearCamera = nil;
    self.frontCamera = nil;

    self.microphone = nil;

    if ([self.cameraArray count] > 1) {

        for (AVCaptureDevice *camera in self.cameraArray) {
            if (camera.position == AVCaptureDevicePositionBack) {
                self.rearCamera = camera;
            } else if (camera.position == AVCaptureDevicePositionFront) {
                self.frontCamera = camera;
            }
        }

        self.rearCameraInput = [AVCaptureDeviceInput
            deviceInputWithDevice:self.rearCamera error:&error];
        self.frontCameraInput = [AVCaptureDeviceInput
            deviceInputWithDevice:self.frontCamera error:&error];

    } else {
        self.rearCamera = [AVCaptureDevice
            defaultDeviceWithMediaType:AVMediaTypeVideo];
        self.rearCameraInput = [AVCaptureDeviceInput
            deviceInputWithDevice:self.rearCamera error:&error];
    }

    self.microphone = [[AVCaptureDevice
        devicesWithMediaType:AVMediaTypeAudio] objectAtIndex:0];
    self.audioInput = [AVCaptureDeviceInput
        deviceInputWithDevice:self.microphone error:&error];

    self.currentDevice = self.rearCamera;
}
```

Next, you need to make sure you have set up the correct AVCaptureOutput objects for your
media. For still-image capture, the AVCaptureOutput object for the class was represented by the
stillImageOutput property, which subclassed the AVCaptureStillImageOutput class. To capture
video, you need to generate a file that contains both the audio and video streams, in a format that
the MPMoviePlayerController class can play back. As a refresher, Table 10-1 repeats the list of
AVCaptureOutput types from Chapter 4. The most appropriate output type for recording a movie file
with both audio and video data is AVCaptureMovieFileOutput, which generates a valid QuickTime
movie file.

Table 10-1. AVCaptureOutput Types

Subclass	Capture Output
AVCaptureMovieFileOutput	QuickTime movie file
AVCaptureVideoDataOutput	Video frames—intended for processing
AVCaptureAudioFileOutput	Audio files supported by Core Audio (MP3, AIFF, WAV, AAC)
AVCaptureAudioDataOutput	Audio buffer— intended for processing
AVCaptureMetadataOutput	Media file metadata properties (for example, GPS location, exposure level)
AVCaptureStillImageOutput	Still images and metadata

You need to add a new property to your class to handle the movie output. In the MyVideoRecorder project, this property is called fileOutput:

```
@property (nonatomic, strong) AVCaptureMovieFileOutput *fileOutput;
```

So far, you have not configured the hardware interfaces to better suit your application. As with the simple video-recording example in Chapter 8 (the MyVideoRecorder project), at minimum you should specify dimensions for the video file and a maximum recording length. Additionally, for the AVCaptureMovieFileOutput class, you can implement the minFreeDiskSpaceLimit property to prevent recording from starting if the device does not have enough free disk space. Listing 10-3 shows a code snippet that initializes the fileOutput object with these changes. In your final code, this snippet will be part of the [CameraViewController viewDidLoad] method.

Listing 10-3. Initializing an AVCaptureMovieFileOutput Object

```
self.movieFileOutput = [[AVCaptureMovieFileOutput alloc] init];
self.movieFileOutput.minFreeDiskSpaceLimit = 200 * 1024; //200MB
self.movieFileOutput.maxRecordedDuration =
    CMTimeMakeWithSeconds(180, 1); //3 mins max

if ([self.session canAddOutput:self.movieFileOutput]) {
    [self.session addOutput:self.movieFileOutput];
} else {
    UIAlertView *alert = [[UIAlertView alloc] initWithTitle:@"Error!"
        message:@"Not enough disk space" delegate:self
        cancelButtonTitle:@"OK" otherButtonTitles:nil];
    [alert show];
}
```

Because video capture operates at a lower level than typical Cocoa Touch classes, the minFreeDiskSpaceLimit property uses the C type for a 64-bit integer, int64_t, and the maxRecordedDuration property uses Apple's lower-level struct (custom data type) for representing time: CMTime. As shown in the example, by casting, you can cleanly convert your input into types that the classes can work with.

Specifying the video resolution comes into play when you configure the final piece of the hardware interface: the AVCaptureSession object. The *session* functions much like a telephone operator for the hardware interface, connecting the input devices with the output streams. Looking back at Listing 10-2, remember that the basic steps for initializing an AVCaptureSession object are picking the appropriate constructor method and then adding *inputs*. While these steps are still true for video, there's an extra step: using a session preset to configure the session for video capture. Table 10-2 lists the preset options.

Table 10-2. AVCaptureSession Presets

Preset	Output Type
AVCaptureSessionPresetPhoto	High-quality still images
AVCaptureSessionPresetLow	Low-quality video and audio available on the device, suitable for transmitting over 3G cellular
AVCaptureSessionPresetMedium	Mid-range quality video and audio available on the device
AVCaptureSessionPresetHigh	Highest-quality video and audio available on the device (default)
AVCaptureSessionPreset1080x720	1080×720 (720p) video
AVCaptureSessionPreset1920x1080	1280×1080 (1080p) video
AVCaptureSessionPresetiFrame960x540	960×540 H.264 iFrame video (ideal for iMovie editing)
AVCaptureSessionPresetiFrame1280x720	1280×720 H.264 iFrame video (ideal for iMovie editing)
AVCaptureSessionPresetInputPriority	Raw video and audio streams, appropriate for advanced codecs or video processing

As with all applications, pick the preset that is best for your intended application and devices. If you're not sure, a safe bet for video capture is AVCaptureSessionPreset1920x1080. All iOS devices running iOS 6 or higher are capable of capturing 1080p video. To configure your session with a preset, simply set the property with your selected constant:

```
[self.session setSessionPreset:AVCaptureSessionPreset1920x1080];
```

Listing 10-4 shows the completed [CameraViewController viewDidLoad] and [CameraViewController initializeCameras] methods for the MyVideoRecorder project. As with the still-image sample in Listing 10-1, the hardware interface sections are in bold.

Listing 10-4. Completed Hardware Interface Code for MyCustomRecorder Project

```
- (void)viewDidLoad
{
    [super viewDidLoad];
    // Do any additional setup after loading the view.

    self.session = [[AVCaptureSession alloc] init];
```

```objc
    // find the back-facing camera

    [self initializeCameras];

    NSError *error = nil;

    if (error == nil && [self.session
        canAddInput:self.rearCameraInput]) {
        [self.session addInput:self.rearCameraInput];

        // set up our output

        self.movieFileOutput = [[AVCaptureMovieFileOutput alloc] init];
        self.movieFileOutput.minFreeDiskSpaceLimit = 200 * 1024; //200MB
        self.movieFileOutput.maxRecordedDuration =
            CMTimeMakeWithSeconds(180, 1); //3 mins max

        if ([self.session canAddOutput:self.movieFileOutput] &&
            [self.session
                canSetSessionPreset:AVCaptureSessionPreset1920x1080]) {
            [self.session
                setSessionPreset:AVCaptureSessionPreset1920x1080];
            [self.session addOutput:self.movieFileOutput];
        } else {
                UIAlertView *alert = [[UIAlertView alloc]
                initWithTitle:@"Error!" message:@"Camera Unavailable"
                delegate:self cancelButtonTitle:@"OK"
                otherButtonTitles:nil];
            [alert show];
        }

        [self.view bringSubviewToFront:self.tapPosition];
    }

}

-(void)initializeCameras
{
    self.cameraArray = [AVCaptureDevice
                        devicesWithMediaType:AVMediaTypeVideo];

    NSError *error = nil;

    self.rearCamera = nil;
    self.frontCamera = nil;

    self.microphone = nil;
```

```
if ([self.cameraArray count] > 1) {

    for (AVCaptureDevice *camera in self.cameraArray) {
        if (camera.position == AVCaptureDevicePositionBack) {
            self.rearCamera = camera;
        } else if (camera.position == AVCaptureDevicePositionFront) {
            self.frontCamera = camera;
        }
    }

    self.rearCameraInput = [AVCaptureDeviceInput
        deviceInputWithDevice:self.rearCamera error:&error];
    self.frontCameraInput = [AVCaptureDeviceInput
        deviceInputWithDevice:self.frontCamera error:&error];

} else {
    self.rearCamera = [AVCaptureDevice
        defaultDeviceWithMediaType:AVMediaTypeVideo];
    self.rearCameraInput = [AVCaptureDeviceInput
        deviceInputWithDevice:self.rearCamera error:&error];
}

self.microphone = [[AVCaptureDevice
    devicesWithMediaType:AVMediaTypeAudio] objectAtIndex:0];
self.audioInput = [AVCaptureDeviceInput
    deviceInputWithDevice:self.microphone error:&error];

self.currentDevice = self.rearCamera;
}
```

Building the User Interface

Having configured the hardware interface, you can start updating the user interface to support video capture. As with the hardware interface, you will not need to throw out all of the existing code to enable this; you will mostly need to make notifications to the existing code.

Similar to still-image capture, here are the major areas to target in your user interface:

- Display a live feed of the camera input.
- Expose controls for modifying capture settings.
- Expose controls for starting and stopping recording.

Unlike still images, you will need to change the user interface during recording. In addition to toggling the state of the Record button, you should display recording progress and hide some of the capture settings (users should not be able to change torch mode or low-light settings during recording; doing so produces a jarring effect). After recording is complete, users should enter a preview mode where they can accept or reject their recording.

This section focuses on the user-interface elements that initiate video recording and appear while recording is in progress. The process for completing a recording primarily consists of non-user-interface topics and is covered in the upcoming section, "Completing a Recording."

Setting Up the Video Layer

In the [CameraViewController viewDidLoad] method for the still-image capture project, you used an AVCaptureVideoPreviewLayer object to display the live feed from the camera. As shown in Listing 10-5, this layer was connected to the session object and configured to appear correctly in the parent view controller.

Listing 10-5. Video Preview Layer Initialization Code for MyCamera Project

```
self.previewLayer = [[AVCaptureVideoPreviewLayer alloc]
                        initWithSession:self.session];

// CGRect layerRect = self.previewView.bounds;
CGRect layerRect = self.view.bounds;
CGPoint layerCenter = CGPointMake(CGRectGetMidX(layerRect),
    CGRectGetMidY(layerRect));

[self.previewLayer setBounds:layerRect];
[self.previewLayer setPosition:layerCenter];

[self.previewLayer setVideoGravity:AVLayerVideoGravityResize];
// [self.previewLayer
//     setVideoGravity:AVLayerVideoGravityResizeAspectFill];

[self.previewView.layer addSublayer:self.previewLayer];
```

The good news is, for video capture, you need to make no changes at all to display live video in your code! You can reuse this code as is. While you needed to create an audio input object to manage audio capture in your hardware initialization code, the live preview should contain only video. The user will be able to preview audio after the video has completed recording, because previewing audio during recording causes a nasty feedback loop (echo).

Before moving on, I want to review a couple of configuration options you need to remember to give special attention to: setting the correct frame properties and starting the stream. From Chapter 4, you may remember that a layer is just a component you add to a view—like a part of an animation cel. To position a layer correctly, you need to give it the appropriate bounds and origin position. This is the same process you follow for a normal view, except you need to remember to explicitly define everything to correctly display a layer. Similarly, the concept of *auto-resizing* is not a default setting for video layers, so you need to make sure you specify AVLayerVideoGravityResize for the videoGravity property of the preview layer.

You may also remember that positioning the frame for the video layer did not automatically display the live feed on the target view. To display live video, you need to start your session. As with still-image capture, you can start a session by calling the [AVCaptureSession startRunning] method on your session object. This is applicable to most session preset types. An important distinction for the video-capture application is that starting the session is not the same as recording the file. You start or stop recordings through the AVCaptureMovieFileObject. You'll add that code to the handler for the Toggle Recording button later.

Listing 10-6 shows the final version of the [CameraViewController viewDidLoad] method for the MyCustomRecorder project. The video preview layer initialization code is highlighted in bold text.

Listing 10-6. Video Preview Layer Initialization Code for MyCustomRecorder Project

```
- (void)viewDidLoad
{
    [super viewDidLoad];
    // Do any additional setup after loading the view.

    self.previewView.autoresizingMask =
        UIViewAutoresizingFlexibleWidth |
        UIViewAutoresizingFlexibleHeight;

    self.session = [[AVCaptureSession alloc] init];

    // find the back-facing camera

    [self initializeCameras];

    NSError *error = nil;

    self.focusPoint = CGPointMake(0.5f, 0.5f);

    if (error == nil && [self.session
        canAddInput:self.rearCameraInput]) {
        [self.session addInput:self.rearCameraInput];

        // set up our preview layer
        self.previewLayer = [[AVCaptureVideoPreviewLayer alloc]
            initWithSession:self.session];

        CGRect layerRect = self.view.bounds;
        CGPoint layerCenter = CGPointMake(CGRectGetMidX(layerRect),
            CGRectGetMidY(layerRect));

        [self.previewLayer setBounds:layerRect];
        [self.previewLayer setPosition:layerCenter];

        [self.previewLayer setVideoGravity:AVLayerVideoGravityResize];

        [self.previewView.layer addSublayer:self.previewLayer];

        // set up our output

        self.movieFileOutput = [[AVCaptureMovieFileOutput alloc] init];
        self.movieFileOutput.minFreeDiskSpaceLimit =
            200 * 1024; //200MB
        self.movieFileOutput.maxRecordedDuration =
            CMTimeMakeWithSeconds(180, 1); //3 mins max
```

```
    if ([self.session canAddOutput:self.movieFileOutput] &&
        [self.session
            canSetSessionPreset:AVCaptureSessionPreset1920x1080]) {
        [self.session
            setSessionPreset:AVCaptureSessionPreset1920x1080];
        [self.session addOutput:self.movieFileOutput];
    } else {
        UIAlertView *alert = [[UIAlertView alloc]
            initWithTitle:@"Error!"
            message:@"Not enough disk space"
            delegate:self cancelButtonTitle:@"OK"
            otherButtonTitles:nil];
        [alert show];
    }

    [self.view bringSubviewToFront:self.tapPosition];
}

}
```

Adding Controls for Capture Settings

For the still-image capture project, you added a wide set of controls to modify the camera capture settings, such as exposure, flash, device selection, and autofocus control. While you can reuse the device selection and autofocus controls, you will need to pare down the list of controls for this project, because some concepts, such as exposure and flash, are applicable only when the camera's sensor is active, which is just for a moment. The good news is that you can implement features for video, such as torch mode, white balance, and low-light settings that provide similar functionality.

Looking at Apple's built-in camera interfaces in Figure 10-5, you can see that the only controls Apple exposes are Toggle Torch and Toggle Device.

Figure 10-5. Differences between Apple's still-image and video-capture interfaces

Because your application provides a user experience different from the default, you will add controls for torch mode and low-light settings, as shown in Figure 10-6.

Figure 10-6. Video capture interface for MyCustomRecorder project

For the MyCustomRecorder project, you will remove the exposure button and repurpose the flash button for torch mode. You will also add buttons for low-light settings and to start recording. After making these changes in Interface Builder, your storyboard should look like the one shown in Figure 10-7.

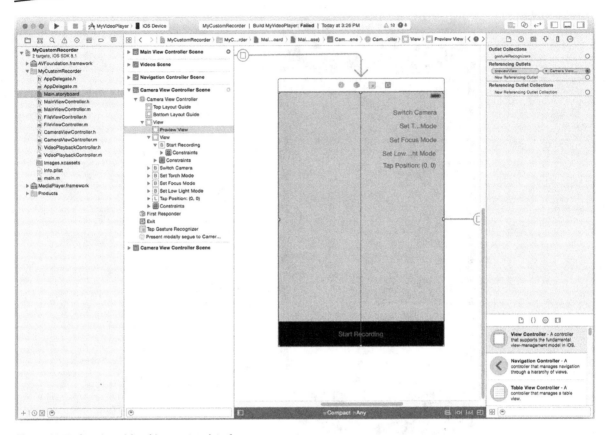

Figure 10-7. Storyboard for video-capture interface

With the new buttons in place, your `CameraViewController.h` file should look like the example
in Listing 10-7.

Listing 10-7. Modified Header File for CameraViewController, with New Controls

```
#import <UIKit/UIKit.h>
#import <AVFoundation/AVFoundation.h>

@protocol CameraDelegate <NSObject>

-(void)cancel;
-(void)didFinishWithImage:(UIImage *)image;

@end

@interface CameraViewController : UIViewController
    <UIActionSheetDelegate>

@property (nonatomic, strong) IBOutlet UIView *previewView;
@property (nonatomic, strong) IBOutlet UIButton *torchButton;
@property (nonatomic, strong) IBOutlet UIButton *lowLightButton;
@property (nonatomic, strong) IBOutlet UIButton *focusButton;
@property (nonatomic, strong) IBOutlet UIButton *cameraButton;
```

```
@property (nonatomic, strong) IBOutlet UILabel *tapPosition;

@property (nonatomic, strong) AVCaptureSession *session;
@property (nonatomic, strong) AVCaptureMovieFileOutput
    *movieFileOutput;

@property (nonatomic, strong) id <CameraDelegate> delegate;

-(IBAction)cancel:(id)sender;
-(IBAction)toggleRecording:(id)sender;

-(IBAction)torchMode:(id)sender;
-(IBAction)lowLightMode:(id)sender;
-(IBAction)focusMode:(id)sender;
-(IBAction)switchCamera:(id)sender;

-(IBAction)didTapPreview:(UIGestureRecognizer *)gestureRecognizer;

@end
```

For your reference, I have included the handlers for the autofocus and toggle device buttons in Listing 10-8. You don't need to modify these at all for video capture, and as always, they go in your `CameraViewController.m` file.

Listing 10-8. Button Handlers for Autofocus and Toggling Devices

```
-(void)switchToFocusWithIndex:(NSInteger)buttonIndex
{
    NSError *error = nil;

    AVCaptureFocusMode focusMode = 0;

    switch (buttonIndex) {
        case 0: {
            focusMode = AVCaptureFocusModeAutoFocus;
            self.focusButton.titleLabel.text = @"Focus: Auto";
            break;
        }
        case 1: {
            focusMode = AVCaptureFocusModeContinuousAutoFocus;
            self.focusButton.titleLabel.text = @"Focus: Cont";
            break;
        }
        case 2: {
            focusMode = AVCaptureFocusModeLocked;
            self.focusButton.titleLabel.text = @"Focus: Fixed";
            break;
        }
        default:
            break;
    }
```

```objc
    if ([self.currentDevice lockForConfiguration:&error] &&
        [self.currentDevice isFocusModeSupported:focusMode]) {

        self.currentDevice.focusMode = focusMode;

        [self.currentDevice unlockForConfiguration];
    } else {
        NSLog(@"could not set focus mode");
    }

}

-(void)switchToCameraWithIndex:(NSInteger)buttonIndex
{
    [self.session beginConfiguration];

    if (buttonIndex == 0) {

        [self.session removeInput:self.rearCameraInput];

        if ([self.session canAddInput:self.frontCameraInput]) {
            [self.session addInput:self.frontCameraInput];
        }

        self.cameraButton.titleLabel.text = @"Camera: Front";
        self.currentDevice = self.frontCamera;

    } else if (buttonIndex == 1) {

        [self.session removeInput:self.frontCameraInput];

        if ([self.session canAddInput:self.rearCameraInput]) {
            [self.session addInput:self.rearCameraInput];
        }

        self.cameraButton.titleLabel.text = @"Camera: Rear";
        self.currentDevice = self.frontCamera;
    }

    [self.session commitConfiguration];
}
```

Torch Mode

The idea of a flash in a camera is to provide a burst of light to brighten up a shot that would otherwise be too dark to be useful. Users frame their shot with the flash off, but when they press the capture button, the flash activates just long enough to illuminate the scene while the camera sensor is active. This concept does not translate to video, because the sensor is active for an extended period of time; however, by implementing torch mode, you can give users the ability to add light to a scene by keeping the flash LED active during recording.

To activate torch mode, you can reuse the Flash button from the MyCamera project. The functionality is different at a low level, but that difference is not apparent to users. In the MyCamera project, the handler for flash mode was the [CameraViewController flashMode:] method. Bring up your CameraViewController.h file and perform a secondary click (right-click or Option-click) on the method name to bring up the Refactor window, as shown in Figure 10-8. This will allow you to rename the method in every file in which it appears, including the Interface Builder files. Your new method should be named [CameraViewController torchMode:].

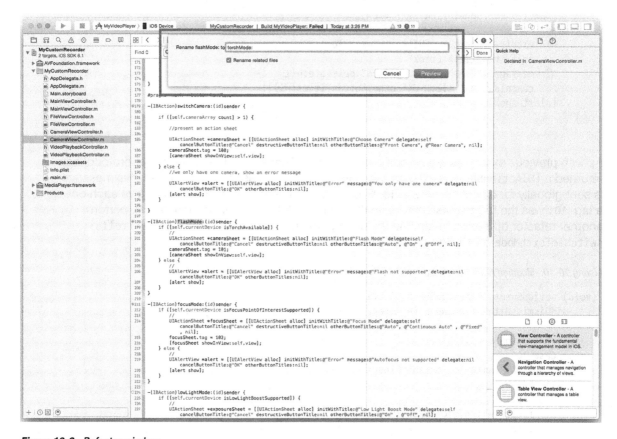

Figure 10-8. Refactor window

As you saw in Chapter 4, the general flow to modify a capture setting is to use the onscreen display button to show an action sheet of available modes, and then set the mode (if the device supports it). While almost all modern iOS devices these days have two cameras, it is important to note that the cameras are not equal. Generally, the rear-facing camera is more powerful, with support for high-resolution images, flash, and other features that improve picture quality (such as image stabilization for the iPhone 6 Plus). In contrast, the front-facing camera has lower resolution and a narrower set of capture controls.

The torchMode property controls torch mode on an AVCaptureDevice. Its configuration options are Off, On, and Auto, represented by the AVCaptureTorchModeOff, AVCaptureTorchModeOn, and AVCaptureTorchModeAuto constants, respectively. For the first step of the process, change your button handler to display these new values in the action sheet, as shown in Listing 10-9.

Listing 10-9. Button Handler for Torch Mode

```
-(IBAction)torchMode:(id)sender {
    if ([self.currentDevice isTorchAvailable]) {
        UIActionSheet *cameraSheet = [[UIActionSheet alloc]
            initWithTitle:@"Flash Mode" delegate:self
            cancelButtonTitle:@"Cancel" destructiveButtonTitle:nil
            otherButtonTitles:@"Auto", @"On" , @"Off", nil];
        cameraSheet.tag = 101;
        [cameraSheet showInView:self.view];
    } else {
        UIAlertView *alert = [[UIAlertView alloc]
            initWithTitle:@"Error"
            message:@"Flash not supported" delegate:nil
            cancelButtonTitle:@"OK" otherButtonTitles:nil];
        [alert show];
    }
}
```

As with previous examples, you modify the capture settings after the action sheet protocol has returned a [UIActionSheet didDismissWithButtonIndex:] message. Remember, this message is sent globally for all action sheets. To differentiate between action sheets, you give each one a tag (101 was the tag for flash mode). In the case block for torch mode (case 101), perform another refactor operation to rename the configuration method to [CameraViewController switchToTorchModeWithIndex:], as shown in Listing 10-10.

Listing 10-10. Modified Action Sheet Delegate for Torch Mode

```
-(void) actionSheet:(UIActionSheet *)actionSheet
    didDismissWithButtonIndex:(NSInteger)buttonIndex
{
    switch (actionSheet.tag) {
        case 100:
            [self switchToCameraWithIndex:buttonIndex];
            break;
        case 101:
            [self switchToTorchWithIndex:buttonIndex];
            break;
        case 102:
            [self switchToFocusWithIndex:buttonIndex];
            break;
        case 103:
            [self switchToExposureWithIndex:buttonIndex];
            break;
        default:
            break;
    }
}
```

The method you use to determine whether torch mode is available on an AVCaptureDevice is [AVCaptureDevice isTorchModeSupported:]. As shown in Listing 10-11, in your [CameraViewController switchToTorchModeWithIndex:] method, after locking the device for configuration, first check that torch mode is available, and then set it if applicable. After making your configuration change, unlock the device. If an error occurs while locking the device or attempting to make the change, show an error alert.

Listing 10-11. Method for Changing Torch Mode

```
-(void)switchToTorchWithIndex:(NSInteger)buttonIndex
{
    NSError *error = nil;

    AVCaptureTorchMode torchMode = 0;

    switch (buttonIndex) {
        case 0: {
            torchMode = AVCaptureTorchModeAuto;
            self.torchButton.titleLabel.text = @"Torch: Auto";
            break;
        }
        case 1: {
            torchMode = AVCaptureTorchModeOn;
            self.torchButton.titleLabel.text = @"Torch: On";
            break;
        }
        case 2: {
            torchMode = AVCaptureTorchModeOff;
            self.torchButton.titleLabel.text = @"Torch: Off";
            break;
        }
        default:
            break;
    }

    if ([self.currentDevice lockForConfiguration:&error]) {

        self.currentDevice.torchMode = torchMode;

        [self.currentDevice unlockForConfiguration];
    } else {
        NSLog(@"could not set torch mode");
    }

}
```

Following Apple's example, use AVCaptureTorchModeAuto as the default configuration setting for torch mode. You can define this by adding the torch mode setting to the [CameraViewController initializeCameras] method.

Low-Light Boost

With still images, you were able to use exposure as a way to modify the brightness or darkness of the captured image, without the need to involve the flash. As part of the framing process, you allowed users to specify whether they wanted the exposure to change automatically with changes in their focal point selection, or whether it should stay fixed based on a prior selection. In this way, when users readjust the focal point, they could see the image lighten/darken or maintain current brightness settings. Unfortunately, there is a trade-off to everything, and when you add or remove light to a picture, you are often adding or removing detail. This can result in a great amount of noise from the sensor, but you can often refocus the shot or change the exposure settings to compensate. When you are shooting video, however, you do not want to refocus or greatly change exposure settings while shooting, as either change will create unnatural effects that most people find distracting.

To compensate for changes in image quality during lighting adjustments in video, you will enable a control for low-light boost in your capture interface, in place of exposure modes. Low-light settings instruct the AVCaptureDevice class to automatically brighten or dim a scene based on its ambient light—unlike exposure modes, which change settings based on the current focal point. If the user chooses to disable low-light boosting, the camera will not adjust the lighting for the scene during recording.

You control low-light settings (boost on or off) for an AVCaptureDevice with the automaticallyEnablesLowLightBoostWhenAvailable method. As the name implies, the input is a BOOL, meaning users can only enable or disable the setting.

As with all capture settings, when committing changes, you need to lock the device and make sure the settings are supported by the hardware. To query whether low-light boost mode is supported on a device, use the lowLightSupported property. Listing 10-12 shows the handler for the Low-Light Mode button.

Listing 10-12. Handler for Low-Light Mode Button

```
-(IBAction)lowLightMode:(id)sender {
    if ([self.currentDevice isLowLightBoostSupported]) {
        //
        UIActionSheet *lowLightSheet = [[UIActionSheet alloc]
            initWithTitle:@"Low Light Boost Mode" delegate:self
            cancelButtonTitle:@"Cancel" destructiveButtonTitle:nil
            otherButtonTitles:@"On" , @"Off", nil];
        lowLightSheet.tag = 103;
        [lowLightSheet showInView:self.view];
    } else {
        //
        UIAlertView *alert = [[UIAlertView alloc]
            initWithTitle:@"Error"
            message:@"Low Light Boost not supported" delegate:nil
            cancelButtonTitle:@"OK" otherButtonTitles:nil];
        [alert show];
    }
}
```

```objc
-(void)switchToExposureWithIndex:(NSInteger)buttonIndex
{
    NSError *error = nil;

    BOOL boostOn;
    switch (buttonIndex) {
        case 0: {
            boostOn = YES;
            self.lowLightButton.titleLabel.text = @"LL Boost: On";
            break;
        }
        case 1: {
            boostOn = NO;
            self.lowLightButton.titleLabel.text = @"LL Boost: Off";
            break;
        }
        default:
            break;
    }

    if ([self.currentDevice lockForConfiguration:&error] &&
        [self.currentDevice isLowLightBoostSupported]) {

        self.currentDevice.
            automaticallyEnablesLowLightBoostWhenAvailable = boostOn;

        [self.currentDevice unlockForConfiguration];
    } else {
        NSLog(@"could not set exposure mode");
    }

}
```

Starting/Stopping Recording

Having set up the preview layer and capture controls for the video-capture interface, the only remaining user-interface task is to handle starting and stopping recording. Look at the Recording Active interface for Apple's Camera app, shown in Figure 10-9. Note that during recording, Apple changes the state of the Start button to Stop and displays the length of the current recording.

Figure 10-9. Recording Active interface for the Camera app

In the MyCustomRecorder app, you will go a step further by hiding the capture controls, because users should not be able to modify anything except the focal point during recording.

To display the recording time, add a UILabel to your storyboard and an NSTimer object to your CameraViewController class. In the MyCustomRecorder project, I named these timeLabel and recordingTimer, respectively:

```
@property (nonatomic, strong) IBOutlet UILabel *timeLabel;
@property (nonatomic, strong) NSTimer *recordingTimer;
```

In Interface Builder, use the Attributes Inspector to make the timeLabel hidden by default. You will show it when the user begins playback.

Before moving further, take a second to step back and review how you turned a captured image into an image file while building the still-image capture interface. Looking at Listing 10-13 for reference, you will see that in the handler for the Finish button, you called the [AVCaptureImageOutput captureS tillImageAsynchronouslyFromConnection:completionHandler:] method on your output to generate the image file. When the operation completed, you generated a UIImage object and passed it back to your delegate object.

Listing 10-13. Capturing an Image File from the Video Feed

```
-(IBAction)finish:(id)sender
{

    AVCaptureConnection *connection = [self.stillImageOutput
        connectionWithMediaType:AVMediaTypeVideo];

    [self.stillImageOutput
        captureStillImageAsynchronouslyFromConnection:connection
        completionHandler:^(CMSampleBufferRef imageDataSampleBuffer,
            NSError *error) {

        if (imageDataSampleBuffer != nil) {

            NSData *imageData = [AVCaptureStillImageOutput
             jpegStillImageNSDataRepresentation:imageDataSampleBuffer];

            UIImage *image = [UIImage imageWithData:imageData];

            [self.delegate didFinishWithImage:image];
        } else {

            NSLog(@"error description: %@", [error description]);

            [self.delegate cancel];
        }

    }];

}
```

For video capture, you want to toggle recording when the Record button is pressed. Similar to still-image capture, you need to perform this operation on the AVCaptureOutput object for the class, which is an AVCaptureMovieFileOutput object for video capture (AVCaptureMovieFileOutput is a subclass of AVCaptureFileOutput). Instead of calling one method to capture a still image, you instead want to start or stop recording. The methods to start and stop recording on an AVCaptureMovieFileOutput object are [AVCaptureFileOutput startRecordingToOutputFileURL:recordingDelegate:] and [AVCaptureFileOutput stopRecording].

Listing 10-14 shows the handler method for toggling recording, which was defined as [CameraViewController toggleRecording] in the CameraViewController.h file. In this method, you want to start or stop video capture based on the current state of the AVCaptureOutput object. You can query the recording state of an AVCaptureMovieFileOutput object by using the recording property.

Listing 10-14. Button Handler for Toggling Video Recording

```
-(IBAction)toggleRecording:(id)sender
{
    if ([self.movieFileOutput isRecording]) {

        NSArray *paths = NSSearchPathForDirectoriesInDomains(
            NSDocumentDirectory, NSUserDomainMask, YES);
        NSString *documentsDirectory = [paths objectAtIndex:0];
        NSString *relativePath = [documentsDirectory
            stringByAppendingPathComponent:@"movie.mov"];

        NSURL *fileURL = [NSURL fileURLWithPath:relativePath];

        [self.movieFileOutput startRecordingToOutputFileURL:fileURL
            recordingDelegate:self];
    } else {

        [self.movieFileOutput stopRecording];
    }
}
```

When you start recording a file, you need to specify the URL for the output file and a delegate for a protocol. The AVCaptureFileOutput class defines the AVCaptureFileOutputRecordingDelegate protocol for passing back the *complete* message for your movie file, so modify your CameraViewController's header file to indicate that you will be implementing that protocol:

```
@interface CameraViewController : UIViewController
    <UIActionSheetDelegate, AVCaptureFileOutputRecordingDelegate >
```

In the next section, "Completing a Recording," you will implement the delegate method to close the movie file.

As the final user-interface step, you should update your user interface after recording has started, by hiding the capture buttons and displaying recording progress. Luckily, hiding user-interface elements in Cocoa Touch is extremely easy: just set the isHidden property to YES. Setting this property to NO will show hidden elements. In Listing 10-15, I have added user-interface updates to the recording button handler.

Listing 10-15. Adding User Interface Updates to the Toggle Recording Button

```
-(IBAction)toggleRecording:(id)sender
{
    if ([self.movieFileOutput isRecording]) {

        NSArray *paths = NSSearchPathForDirectoriesInDomains(
            NSDocumentDirectory, NSUserDomainMask, YES);
        NSString *documentsDirectory = [paths objectAtIndex:0];
        NSString *relativePath = [documentsDirectory
            stringByAppendingPathComponent:@"movie.mov"];
```

```
        NSURL *fileURL = [NSURL fileURLWithPath:relativePath];

        self.torchButton.hidden = YES;
        self.focusButton.hidden = YES;
        self.cameraButton.hidden = YES;
        self.lowLightButton.hidden = YES;

        self.timeLabel.hidden = NO;

        [self.movieFileOutput startRecordingToOutputFileURL:fileURL
            recordingDelegate:self];

        self.recordingTimer = [NSTimer timerWithTimeInterval:1.0f
            target:self selector:@selector(updateProgress) userInfo:nil
            repeats:YES];
        self.duration = 0;
    } else {

        [self.movieFileOutput stopRecording];

        self.torchButton.hidden = NO;
        self.focusButton.hidden = NO;
        self.cameraButton.hidden = NO;
        self.lowLightButton.hidden = NO;

        self.timeLabel.hidden = YES;

        [self.recordingTimer invalidate];
      self.duration = 0;
    }
}
```

In addition to hiding or showing the user-interface elements, note that the recording button handler creates or invalidates the playbackTimer object. As with all timers, to update the status, you need to reinitialize the timer object with a handler method (selector). The only way to stop the timer is by destroying it. In Listing 10-16, you can find the selector method for the timer, [CameraViewController updateProgress], which updates the timeLabel with the current recording length.

Listing 10-16. Selector Method for Time Updates

```
-(void)updateProgress
{
    NSInteger durationMinutes = self.duration / 60;
    NSInteger durationSeconds = self.duration  - durationMinutes * 60;
    NSString *progressString = [NSString stringWithFormat:@"%d:%02d",
        durationMinutes, durationSeconds];
    self.timeLabel.text = progressString;
    self.duration++;
}
```

Completing a Recording

To finish the MyCustomRecorder project, you need to implement the code to complete the recording process. Although you called the [AVCaptureFileOutput stopRecording] method, this alone is not enough to generate a valid movie file that you can play back by using a MPMoviePlayerController subclass.

Because you are not using the UIImagePickerController class to record video, you need to present your own video player to preview the recorded file. As shown in Figure 10-10, this video player will expose limited playback controls, as well as buttons to let the user accept or reject the recorded video. To enable these limited controls, you will reuse the video player from the MyVideoPlayer project you built in Chapter 9.

Figure 10-10. Mock-up of video preview interface

Finally, to return results from the CameraViewController object, you need to use the CameraDelegate protocol, which you need to modify to handle video. Because video files are much larger than images, they cannot be passed back as parameters, so you need to find an alternative solution.

Saving Video Output

You may remember earlier discussions in the book, where I hinted that video files are more complex than image and audio files. Unlike image and audio files, which contain the binary information for one data stream, video files are *containers* that contain both audio and video data streams. This makes the requirement of having valid headers and footers (which indicate the termination points for the data) even more strict with video files. Combined with the increased sophistication of the algorithms required to compress video (codecs), you can start to see why the process is complex.

By calling the [AVCaptureFileOutput stopRecording] method from the [CameraViewController togglePlayback:] method, you instructed the AVCaptureMovieFileOutput class to kick off this process and close the file. After the File Close operation is complete, your output object calls the [AVCaptureFileOutputRecordingDelegate captureOutput:didFinishRecordingToOutput FileAtURL:fromConnections:error:] method on the object you declared as the delegate (for the MyCustomRecorder project—the CameraViewController class).

One of the key advantages of a protocol is that it strictly defines a set of messages it will send its delegates, down to the message name and parameter types. The didFinish protocol message sends back the following:

- An AVCaptureOutput object, identifying the output object that completed

- An NSURL object that indicates the URL for the file that successfully (or unsuccessfully) closed

- An NSArray of AVCaptureConnection objects that are associated with the session for the output

- An NSError object that returns a non-nil value if the file failed to close successfully

You can find the implementation for the CameraViewController class in Listing 10-17.

Listing 10-17. "Output Finished" Delegate Method for the CameraViewController Class

```
-(void)captureOutput:(AVCaptureFileOutput *)captureOutput
    didFinishRecordingToOutputFileAtURL:(NSURL *)outputFileURL
    fromConnections:(NSArray *)connections error:(NSError *)error
{
    if (error != nil)  {
        NSString *errorString = [error description];
        UIAlertView *alertView = [[UIAlertView alloc]
            initWithTitle:@"Error" message:errorString delegate:self
            cancelButtonTitle:@"OK" otherButtonTitles:nil];
        [alertView show];

    } else {
        VideoPlaybackController *playbackVC =
            [[VideoPlaybackController alloc]
            initWithURL:outputFileURL];
        playbackVC.delegate = self;
```

```
            [self presentViewController:playbackVC animated:YES
                completion:^{
                    [playbackVC prepareToPlay];
            }];
    }
}
```

This implementation uses the `error` object to check whether the operation was successful. If the operation was a failure, it displays an alert view with the human-readable `description` string from the `error` object. When the operation succeeds, it presents a `VideoPlaybackController` that has been initialized with the output file URL. The `VideoPlaybackController` is the customized subclass of the `MPMoviePlayerController` class that you will use in this project for the video preview.

> **Caution** Although the output file URL that is returned from the `AVCaptureFileOutputRecordingDelegate` protocol is the same as the one used to start the recording, you should not start playback until the delegate method has fired, because the file will not be valid until this message has been received.

Showing the Preview Interface

For your video preview interface, you will want to display a video player that allows users to accept or reject the video they just recorded. While you could simply return the recorded video as is, it is best to give users an opportunity to check their work before returning them to the main interface of the MyCustomRecorder application.

For the `VideoPlaybackController` class, you will want to take the basic video playback function of the `CustomVideoPlayer` class from the MyCustomPlayer project you built in Chapter 9 and modify the controls to toggle playback and to accept or reject the file. Subclassing is an object-oriented programming concept that allows you to inherit all of the properties and methods of a parent class while still retaining the ability to modify those properties and methods in your child class. Inheritance is a convenient way to expand the functionality of a class without destroying or affecting the original. In this case, you need to subclass to reuse the `CustomVideoPlayer` class for this app's full-screen video player.

First, copy the `CustomVideoPlayer.h` and `CustomVideoPlayer.m` files into your working directory and add them to your project. Next, from the File menu, choose New File. As shown in Figure 10-11, when you are asked to specify the parent class for your file, type **MyCustomPlayer**—doing so will cause Xcode to create a subclass template for you automatically.

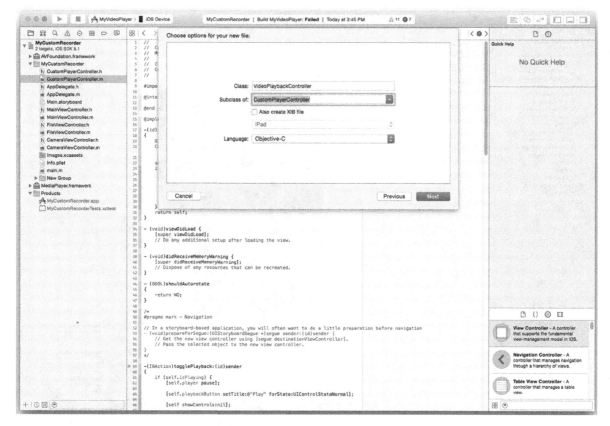

Figure 10-11. Specifying a parent class for a new file in Xcode

Next, you need to create the storyboard for the video player. The key difference between this new playback interface and the one you created for the MyCustomPlayer project is that instead of having a Done button in the navigation bar, you will have Accept and Reject buttons, both of which finish the video completion process. Using Figure 10-12 as a reference, add a layer for the video output and a button to control playback. Embed this view controller in a Navigation Controller so that you can add your buttons.

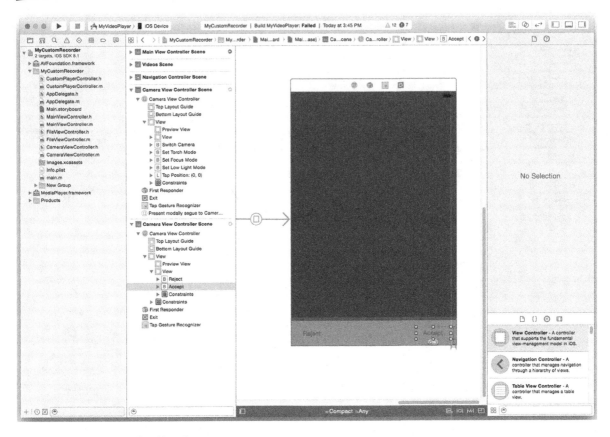

Figure 10-12. Storyboard for video player

The header file for the VideoPlaybackController class is in Listing 10-18. As with other projects, remember to tie your button handlers and properties to the storyboard.

Listing 10-18. Header File for VideoPlaybackController Class

```
#import <UIKit/UIKit.h>

@interface VideoPlaybackController : MyCustomPlayer

@property (nonatomic, strong) IBOutlet *const;

-(IBAction)accept:(id)sender;
-(IBAction)reject:(id)sender;

@end

@protocol CustomPlayerDelegate <NSObject>

-(void)didFinishWithSuccess:(BOOL)success;

@end
```

Because you are subclassing the CustomVideoPlayer class, you do not need to reimplement video playback. Simply tie your button to the togglePlayback button handler you defined in the CustomVideoPlayer class (methods from parent classes show up in Interface Builder just as if you had defined them in your class). For the video-recording process, you will need to focus on the Accept and Reject functionality.

When a user decides to accept the video just recorded, you should follow the same workflow as the UIImagePickerController and return the user to the main user interface. During this process, you will need to save the file and dismiss the video preview and capture interfaces. The Accept button handler for the VideoPlaybackController class is shown in Listing 10-19.

Listing 10-19. Accept Button Handler for VideoPlaybackController

```
-(IBAction)accept:(id)sender
{
    [self.mediaPlayer stop];
    [self.delegate didFinishWithSuccess:YES];
}
```

This button handler is very short—all it does is stop the player and call the [CustomPlayerDelegate didFinishWithSuccess:] method. The [ViewController dismissViewController:animated:] method dismisses only one modal controller at a time. To dismiss both the VideoPlaybackController and the CameraViewController, you need to dismiss each from the view controller that presented them. The CameraViewController was presented by the MainViewController, so you will need to dismiss it via the CameraDelegate protocol. Similarly, the VideoPlaybackController was presented by the CameraViewController, so you will need to dismiss it via the CustomPlayerDelegate protocol.

The Reject button handler is similarly straightforward. All you need to do is dismiss the playback controller and reset the video-recording interface. As part of the reset process, you should delete the current movie file. Listing 10-20 shows the Reject button handler method.

Listing 10-20. Reject Button Handler for VideoPlaybackController

```
-(IBAction)reject:(id)sender
{
    [self.mediaPlayer stop];
    [self.delegate didFinishWithSuccess:NO];
}
```

You may be wondering about the implementation of the [CustomPlayerDelegate didFinishWithSuccess:] method. In your CameraViewController class, if the success parameter is set to YES, then you know the user wanted to accept the video, so you can dismiss the modal view controller that represents the player and call the [CameraDelegate didFinishWithURL:] on your camera delegate object. If the success parameter was set to NO, then you know the user wanted to reject the video. The completed [CustomPlayerDelegate didFinishWithSuccess:] method for the CameraViewController class is provided in Listing 10-21.

Listing 10-21. "Playback Completed" Delegate Method for CameraViewController Class

```
-(void)didFinishWithSuccess:(BOOL)success
{
    NSURL *outputUrl = [self.movieFileOutput outputFileURL];

    if (success) {

        [self.delegate didFinishWithUrl:outputUrl];

        [self dismissViewControllerAnimated:YES completion:nil];

    } else {

        [self dismissViewControllerAnimated:YES completion:^{
            //delete old movie file

            [[NSFileManager defaultManager]
                removeItemAtPath:[outputUrl path] error:NULL];

        }];

    }
}
```

Next, you will learn more about the [CameraDelegate didFinishWithURL:] method, which is the message that allows you to pass back a video instead of an image.

Modifying Your Protocol for Video

To finish the Recording Complete process, you need to modify the CameraDelegate protocol to add an option that allows you to pass back a video. Looking at the implementation for still images in Listing 10-22, you can see that you specified a [CameraDelegate didFinishWithImage:] method, which returned the captured image as a UIImage object.

Listing 10-22. CameraDelegate Protocol Declaration for Still Images

```
@protocol CameraDelegate <NSObject>

-(void)cancel;
-(void)didFinishWithImage:(UIImage *)image;

@end
```

While this message-passing technique works for still images, which are a couple of megabytes at most, video files can easily be hundreds of megabytes in size. To effectively pass back a video, you should return the URL for the movie file generated by the AVCaptureMovieFileOutput. Listing 10-23 includes the modified declaration for the CameraDelegate protocol. The method for returning videos is named [CameraDelegate didFinishWithURL:].

Listing 10-23. CameraDelegate Protocol Declaration for Videos

```
@protocol CameraDelegate <NSObject>

-(void)cancel;
-(void)didFinishWithUrl:(NSURL *)url;

@end
```

> **Note** Remember, present the playback interface only after the AVCaptureFileOutputRecordingDelegate has completed. That way, you can be sure that the video file will be valid.

As with all other protocols, you need to implement the [CameraDelegate didFinishWithURL:] method in the class that was set as the delegate. For the MyCustomRecorder project, this was the MainViewController. All you need to do for your implementation is dismiss the video-capture interface and display a success alert view. Because you specified an output URL that was in the application's documents directory when you created your AVCaptureMovieFileOutput object, you do not need to do any extra work to save the video file. The final implementation for the MainViewController class is included in Listing 10-24.

Listing 10-24. "Did Finish with URL" Implementation for MainViewController Class

```
-(void)didFinishWithSuccess:(BOOL)success
{
    NSURL *outputUrl = [self.movieFileOutput outputFileURL];

    if (success) {

        [self.delegate didFinishWithUrl:outputUrl];

        [self dismissViewControllerAnimated:YES completion:nil];

    } else {

        [self dismissViewControllerAnimated:YES completion:^{
            //delete old movie file

            [[NSFileManager defaultManager]
                removeItemAtPath:[outputUrl path] error:NULL];

        }];

    }
}
```

Summary

In this chapter, you saw how to build a custom video-recording interface based on the AVFoundation framework's image-capture classes. To save time, you reused the CameraViewController class from Chapter 4 for the basic capture interface and the CustomPlayer class from Chapter 9 for the custom video-playback interface.

It's worth noting that you were able to reuse most of the code from the still-image capture project you built in Chapter 4, making only a few changes to handle movie file output and enable video-specific capture settings. To mimic the UIImagePickerController's preview interface, you added Accept and Reject controls to the CustomPlayer class. Finally, to accommodate the larger size of video files, you added a Did Finish with URL method to the CameraDelegate protocol.

As has been the pattern for so many other projects in this book, this custom video-recording project was primarily an exercise in modifying existing code to meet a new use case. As you continue as a media app developer (and engineer in general), you will find many other concepts that greatly overlap with what you already know. The key is to keep an open mind and take advantage of common patterns that you recognize.

iOS8 and Beyond

11

User Interface Development with Xcode 6

When I first started in iOS development, I had a very complicated relationship with Xcode and Interface Builder. I could lay things out, but they wouldn't connect the way I wanted them to, or I would get weird crashes that I couldn't debug. With a lot of hard work (and the release of storyboards), my frustration began to subside, and iOS user interface development started to become a more natural process. Fortunately, with the release of Xcode 6, Apple has continued to improve the development process by making it even easier to build and debug user interfaces.

In this chapter, you will see how to speed up your user interface development with adaptive user interfaces, how to add Quick Look live view debugging to any of your classes, and how to make your own classes fully compatible with Interface Builder's Attributes Inspector. These additions help you develop faster by reducing the steps required to see what's happening "right now" and by integrating with features that were previously limited solely to Apple-created classes.

> **Caution**   The topics covered in this chapter are available only in Xcode 6 with the iOS 8.0 SDK or greater.

Using Size Classes to Build Adaptive User Interfaces

For the first few years of its existence, iOS was limited to iPhones, which all had 3.5-inch screens. Subsequently, the device delivery options quickly grew to include 10-inch iPads, 8-inch iPad Minis, 4-inch Retina iPhones, 4.7-inch iPhones, and now (with the introduction of the iPhone 6 Plus), 5.5-inch iPhones When developers had to support only two screen sizes, they tended to use #ifdef statements and separate Interface Builder files to manage the two user interfaces. However, this approach broke down when Apple began introducing devices with higher pixel densities (the iPhone 4) and new aspect ratios (the iPhone 5). To help address the changing display requirements, Apple introduced *auto-layout* and *asset catalogs* in Xcode 5. To pave the way for future devices, Apple has introduced a design methodology for user interface development in Xcode 6 called *adaptive user interfaces*.

Apple's goal with adaptive user interfaces is to let you build one storyboard that can run on all devices. To accomplish this goal, Apple has introduced the concept of *size classes* to iOS 8: a new way of thinking of your layouts beyond "iPhone mode" and "iPad mode." Size classes in iOS encourage you to conceptualize user interfaces in terms of the space available to your view, rather than in terms of specific target devices (such as phone or tablet). To ensure a smooth transition, Apple has built support for this concept into various aspects of Interface Builder—including new constraint types, a new auto-layout preview interface, and a new simulator (the *resizable simulator*). To help you implement this feature programmatically, Apple has also introduced the UITraitCollection class, which brings together size classes and screen density (for example, Retina) into a robust alternative to the UIInterfaceIdiom macros for detecting device types.

This section focuses on how you can use size classes to build adaptive storyboards. You can learn more about the UITraitCollection class by checking Apple's Adaptive User Interfaces portal (https://developer.apple.com/design/adaptivity/).

As shown in Figure 11-1, if you were to compare the four major types of layouts for a user interface in iOS, your results would be iPhone portrait mode, iPhone landscape mode, iPad portrait mode, and iPad landscape mode.

iPhone (Landscape)   iPhone (Portrait)   iPad (Landscape)   iPad (Portrait)

Figure 11-1. Major layouts for iOS devices

In adaptive user interfaces, dimensions are expressed in terms of a vertical size class and a horizontal size class. The magnitude of these size classes is determined by the class of screen you are targeting: compact for phones or regular for tablets.

If you were to juxtapose the screens on top of one another, you would notice another interesting pattern, shown in Figure 11-2. The screens form an approximate 3×3 grid, with the widths forming the x axis, and the heights forming the y axis.

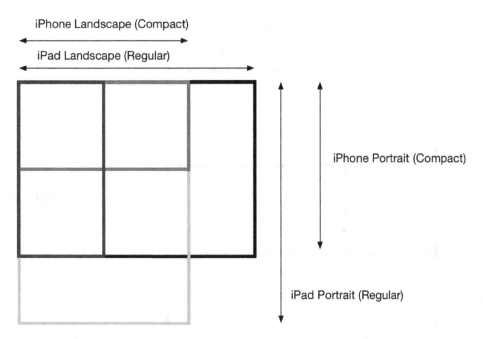

Figure 11-2. Juxtaposition of screen sizes

Although the attributes for the `compact` size classes sit nicely inside those of the `regular` size classes, you can see there is room to grow. For this reason, Apple provides the any size class, which is meant to serve as the default size class for your user interface. You should try to shrink items from an any size class to fit inside a `compact` size class, or increase their size/padding to make them fit in a `regular` size class.

A good way to visualize the possible combinations of size classes is by putting them in a 3×3 grid, arranging them by orientation and increasing size, as shown in Figure 11-3.

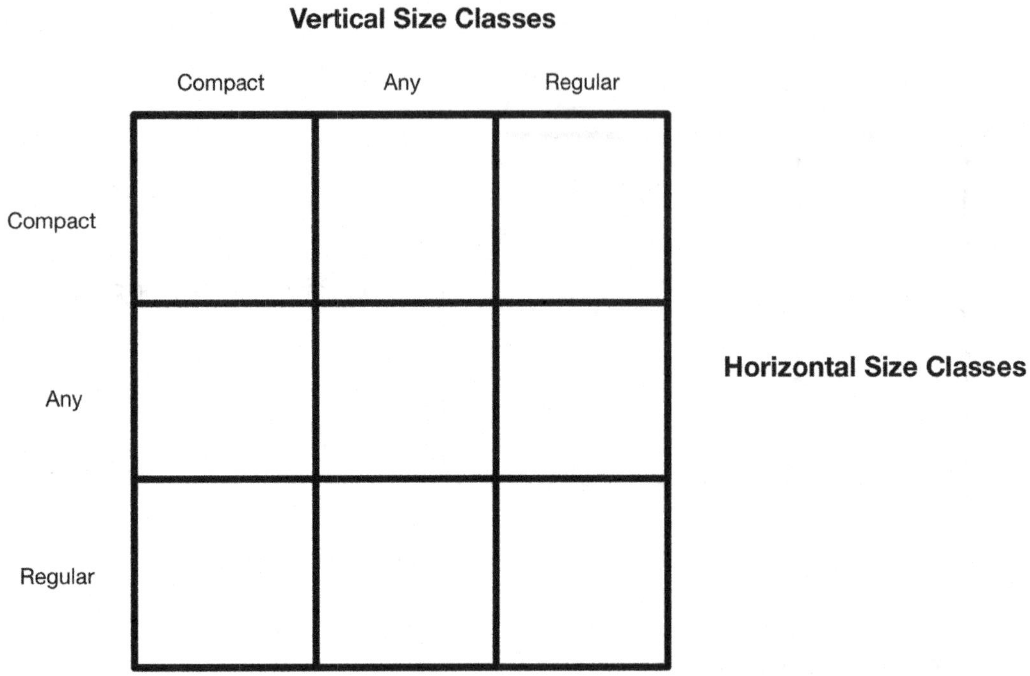

Vertical Size Classes

Figure 11-3. 3×3 grid of size classes

Tracing a line around the combination of boxes that correspond to the device you are targeting will give you an idea of the size classes you need to use to optimize your layout. For an iPad in landscape mode, you would use a regular horizontal size class, and an any vertical size class, as shown in Figure 11-4.

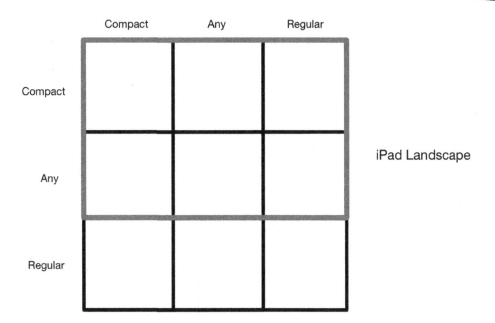

Figure 11-4. Size class combination for an iPad in landscape mode

Interface Builder allows you to seamlessly integrate size classes into your storyboards by giving you both a Size Class option in the Attributes Inspector, which lets you enable or disable size classes, and a new Auto-Layout preview toggle view, which allows you to switch between size class–specific versions of your storyboard.

You can toggle size class settings for your storyboard by selecting the File Inspector (the first tab in the rightmost pane of Interface Builder), as shown in Figure 11-5. If you created your project in Xcode 6 or greater, your storyboard will already have the Use Size Classes check box selected; otherwise, you will need to select it manually.

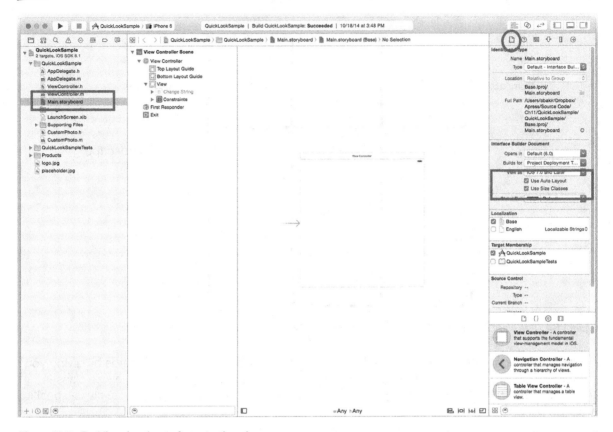

Figure 11-5. Enabling size classes for a storyboard

The first time you use size classes in your storyboard, the result will be quite jarring. As shown in Figure 11-6, your default storyboard preview will be square, corresponding to the any×any combination of size classes. The name of the selected combination for your storyboard is displayed in the center of the bottom pane of Interface Builder, outlined in red in Figure 11-6.

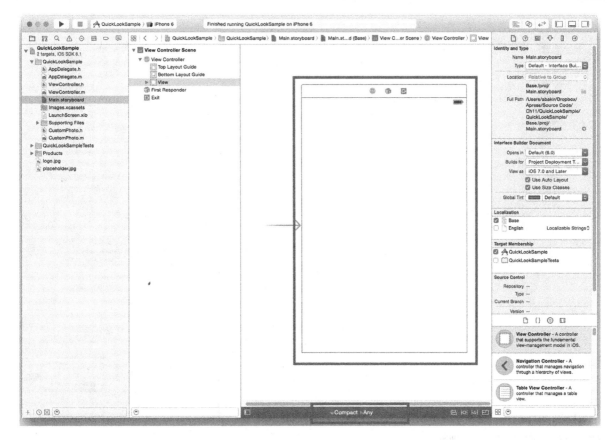

Figure 11-6. *Default storyboard and size class combination*

Clicking this label brings up a dimension picker, inside a popover, as shown in Figure 11-7. This picker uses the same table of size-class combinations as in Figure 11-1. Use the same logic of "tracing" your combination to select the appropriate combination for your device.

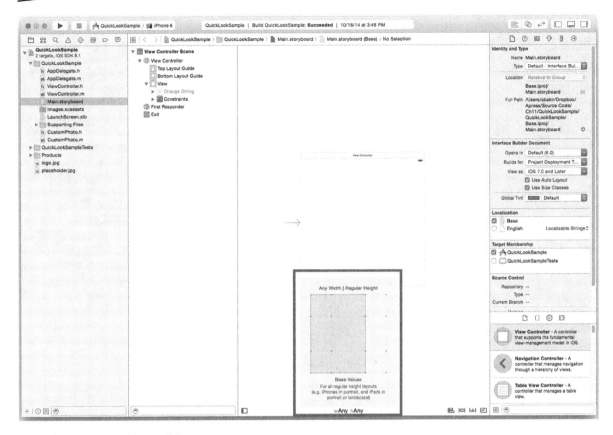

Figure 11-7. Storyboard layout picker

In Xcode 6, you are no longer forced to use the same set of auto-layout constraints for every version of your user interface. After switching layouts, all your constraint and positioning changes will apply to that layout only. Use this to your advantage by creating layouts that are most appropriate for your device size.

If you plan on using auto-layout constraints to position your items (such as keeping an item in the center of the screen), use the any×any layout as your base, and override your selections in other layouts (such as compact×regular).

Using Quick Look for Runtime Previews

Since version 5, Apple has provided a feature in Xcode called Quick Look. This feature allows you to hover over an object during debugging to see a preview of the contents, as shown in Figure 11-8. To do this, you need to use a Quick Look–compatible object. Prior to Xcode 6, Apple provided a limited set of classes (for example, UIView, NSString, CLLocation); however, starting with Xcode 6, you can extend Quick Look to any class by implementing the [NSObject debugQuickLookObject] method.

Figure 11-8. *Quick Look details for an object*

Table 11-1 lists the default Quick Look–compatible classes and their output. When you are building your Quick Look implementation, you will need to use one of these classes to display your debugging information.

Table 11-1. *Quick Look–Compatible Classes*

Class	Preview Type
UIView	A snapshot of your view and all its subviews
CLLocation	A map and legend showing the metadata for your CLLocation object
NSString	A plain-text printout of your string
NSAttributedString	A printout of your string, including all formatting (such as colors or bold)
UIColor	A swatch containing the selected color
UIImage	A preview of your image
NSURL	A preview of the content at your specified URL
NSData	A printout of the binary contents of your data

To access Quick Look, you must use a debugging session. After you have hit a breakpoint and execution is paused, you can bring up the Quick Look panel by hovering over any compatible object in your current scope (generally, the method that the debugger is paused in). Clicking the eye button, shown in Figure 11-9, brings up the Quick Look view with additional details for your object.

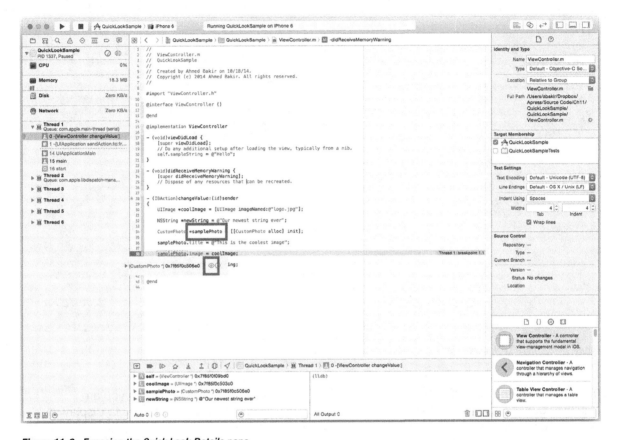

Figure 11-9. Exposing the Quick Look Details pane

To enable Quick Look in your applications, you need to implement the [NSObject debugQuickLookObject] method in your custom classes. Referring back to the Model View Controller design pattern, most of the classes for which you will need to implement Quick Look will be either *models* (representing data) or *views* (representing the visual layout of elements).

To help illustrate the subject, I have created a model class called CustomPhoto that represents an image and its associated metadata information, similar to the ALAsset class. You can find this sample code in the Chapter 11 folder of the source code bundle, under the QuickLookSample project. Listing 11-1 shows the header file for the CustomPhoto class.

Listing 11-1.   Header File for CustomPhoto Class

```
#import <Foundation/Foundation.h>
#import <UIKit/UIKit.h>

@interface CustomPhoto : NSObject

@property (nonatomic, strong) UIImage *image;
@property (nonatomic, strong) NSString *title;
@property (nonatomic, strong) NSString *location;

@end
```

It is natural to assume that a developer will want to be able to see a preview of the image and inspect the metadata properties when debugging a CustomPhoto object. Because you can return only one object from the [NSObject debugQuickLookObject] method, you need to pick a class that can hold the output from all the objects.

In the QuickLookSample project, I chose to create a UIView. Quick Look can paint a view fully in its preview pane, so adding subviews to a container UIView is a great way to display multiple items at once. As shown in Figure 11-10, for this example, I wanted to display the image in a UIImageView and the metadata attributes in UILabels.

Figure 11-10.   Mock-up of Quick Look output

The easiest way to build your UIView for Quick Look is to create and position all your subviews programmatically. Quick Look does not accept UIViewController subclasses as input, so it is not efficient to use a storyboard or XIB file to lay out your user interface. While it is more annoying to position your subviews manually, here are a couple of tricks about the CGRect that can help you build your subview faster:

- Use neighboring subviews as your reference for positioning. For instance, to position two elements at the same y position, use the CGRectMinY() convenience method on the frame of the first view.

- When creating UILabel objects, you can change the font by using the font property. The [UIFont systemFontWithSize:] method allows you to specify a pixel height for a font, which can serve as a helpful guide when you are trying to determine the height of your label. For instance, a 20-point font would be well served by 5 pixels of padding on the top and bottom—meaning you should specify a height of 30 pixels.

- When creating a UILabel, the default clipping behavior for text is to truncate the middle characters. You can make the text shrink to fit the UILabel by setting the adjustsFontSizeToFitWidth property to YES.

Listing 11-2 shows the code to create the UIView. In addition to the view-positioning code, you will see that I set a default value for each property. Because you are building a debugging view, you need to make it very clear to the user when the input is not set or invalid.

Listing 11-2. Enabling Quick Look for the CustomPhoto Class

```
-(id)debugQuickLookObject {
    UIView *quickLookView = [[UIView alloc] initWithFrame:CGRectMake(
        0, 0, 400, 400)];

    UIImageView *imageView = [[UIImageView alloc]
        initWithFrame:quickLookView.frame];

    imageView.image = (self.image == nil) ?
        [UIImage imageNamed:@"placeholder.jpg"]:
        imageView.image = self.image;

    CGFloat originX = CGRectGetMinX(quickLookView.frame) + 10;
    CGFloat originY = CGRectGetMaxY(quickLookView.frame) - 40;
    CGFloat width = quickLookView.frame.size.width;

    CGRect titleLabelFrame = CGRectMake(originX, originY, width, 20);
    CGRect locationLabelFrame = CGRectMake(originX, originY + 20,
        width, 20);

    UILabel *titleLabel = [[UILabel alloc] initWithFrame:titleLabelFrame];
    UILabel *locationLabel = [[UILabel alloc]
        initWithFrame:locationLabelFrame];

    titleLabel.text = (self.title == nil) ? @"No title" : self.title;
    locationLabel.text = (self.location == nil) ? @"No location" :
        self.location;
```

```
[quickLookView addSubview:imageView];
[quickLookView addSubview:titleLabel];
[quickLookView addSubview:locationLabel];


return quickLookView;
}
```

The output from the preceding method should look like the example in Figure 11-11.

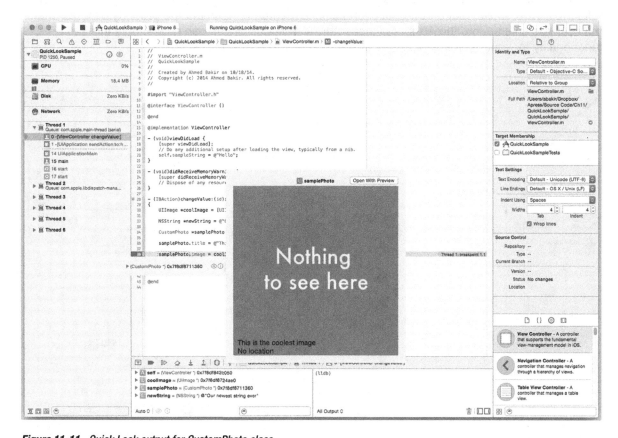

Figure 11-11. Quick Look output for CustomPhoto class

As an alternative to a UIView, you can build your output by using an NSAttributedString object. Attributed strings extend the NSString class by allowing you to specify formatting (such as colors and bold text) and additional input methods. For example, you can render HTML directly by using an NSAttributedString.

Adding Interface Builder Previews to Your Classes

Continuing on the theme of improved visual debugging for your user interfaces, Xcode 6 now allows you to preview and configure your own `UIView` subclasses within Interface Builder. Additionally, Interface Builder now provides a feature called *Debug Selected View*, which allows you to debug your views without running your application.

As with Quick Look, Apple has historically supported preview and configuration within Interface Builder for some of its own `UIView` subclasses, such as `UILabel` and `UIButton`. Looking at Figure 11-12 for reference, you can see that a `UIButton` changes its appearance to reflect the property changes that the user has entered into the Attributes Inspector. With Xcode 6, you can now enable this same functionality for your `UIView` subclasses by adding the `IB_DESIGNABLE` attribute.

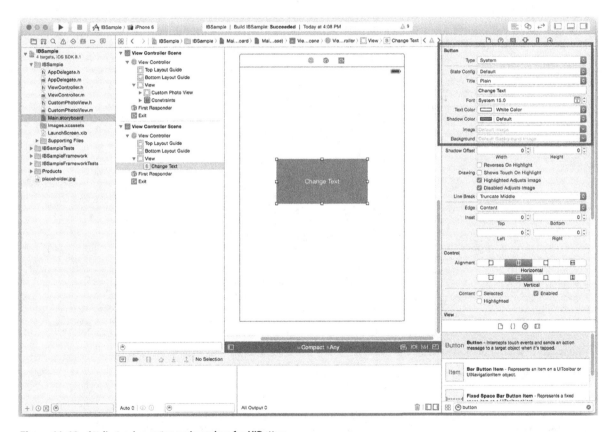

Figure 11-12. Attributes Inspector and preview for UIButton

To demonstrate this feature, you will create a single-view application that displays the content from the `CustomPhoto` class in a `UIView` subclass named `CustomPhotoView`. You'll find the code for this IBSample project in the Chapter 11 folder of the source code bundle.

For the `CustomPhotoView` class, you will display a `UIImage` and two `UILabel` objects representing metadata fields from the `CustomPhoto`, as shown in Figure 11-13. To aid with debugging, you want to let developers see live previews of these subviews in Interface Builder.

Figure 11-13. Mock-up of CustomPhotoView class

To get started, create the CustomPhotoView class as a subview of UIView. Add properties to represent the subviews in the mock-up, as shown in Listing 11-3.

Listing 11-3. Header File for CustomPhotoView Class

```
#import <UIKit/UIKit.h>

IB_DESIGNABLE

@interface CustomPhotoView : UIView

@property (nonatomic) UILabel *titleLabel;
@property (nonatomic) UILabel *locationLabel;
@property (nonatomic) UIImageView *imageView;

@end
```

To enable an Interface Builder preview of your view, add the IB_DESIGNABLE attribute to the line preceding the @interface declaration for your class. An *attribute* in Objective-C is a compiler directive (like a *macro*), which allows you to attach predefined behaviors to a variable declaration. The nonatomic attribute used in defining instance variables instructs the compilers to automatically create getters and setters for the object. Your modified header file should look like the example in Listing 11-4.

Listing 11-4. IB_DESIGNABLE-Compatible Header File for CustomPhotoView Class

```
#import <UIKit/UIKit.h>

IB_DESIGNABLE
```

```
@interface CustomPhotoView : UIView

@property (nonatomic) UILabel *titleLabel;
@property (nonatomic) UILabel *locationLabel;
@property (nonatomic) UIImageView *imageView;

@end
```

To visualize the `CustomPhotoView` class, you need to add it to your storyboard. Select your project's `Main.storyboard` file and drag a View object onto the View Controller Scene. Use the Identity Inspector (third tab in Interface Builder) to associate the view to the `CustomPhotoView` class, as shown in Figure 11-14. To make the view easier to see, give it a nonwhite background color by using the Attributes Inspector.

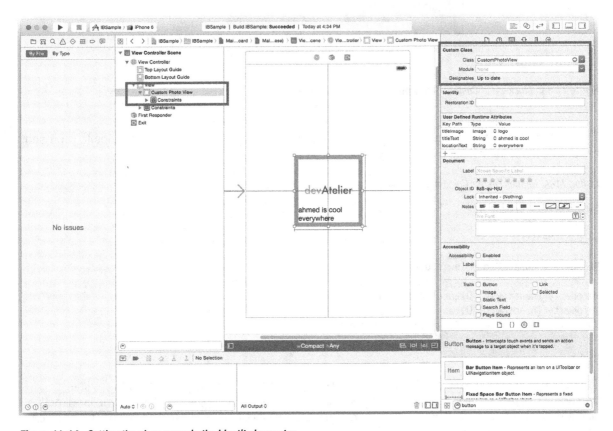

Figure 11-14. Setting the class name in the Identity Inspector

To take full advantage of Interface Builder previews, you need to lay out your view programmatically (similar to Quick Look). Normally, to lay out a view programmatically, you would use the [`UIView initWithFrame:`] constructor method. Unfortunately, by their very nature, previews need to be dynamic. Since the core of the functionality is built on subviews, you need to use a method that will be called whenever the view is instructed to reload its subviews. Because of this design restriction, the best method to use is [`UIView layoutSubviews`].

> **Note**   If you have any code for drawing elements in your UIView, such as adding a border, place it in your [UIView drawRect] method.

In your [UIView layoutSubviews] method, add the initialization code for your subviews. The UIImageView should fill the entire visible area of the UIView (meaning it should use the same frame), and the UILabels should sit at the bottom of the view. Similar to the Quick Look example, use neighboring frames to position elements. After initializing your subviews with sample data, your result should look like Listing 11-5.

Listing 11-5. Initializing the CustomPhotoView Class

```
-(void)layoutSubviews
{
    [super layoutSubviews];

    CGFloat padding = 10.0f;
    CGFloat labelHeight = 20.0f;
    CGFloat viewWidth = self.frame.size.width;
    CGFloat viewHeight = self.frame.size.height;

    CGRect insideFrame = CGRectMake(padding, padding,
        viewWidth - padding * 2, viewHeight - padding * 2);
    CGRect label1Frame = CGRectMake(padding,
        CGRectGetMaxY(insideFrame) - 40, viewWidth, labelHeight);
    CGRect label2Frame = CGRectMake(padding,
        CGRectGetMinY(label1Frame) + 20,  viewWidth, labelHeight);

    self.imageView = [[UIImageView alloc] initWithFrame:insideFrame];
    [self addSubview:self.imageView];

    self.titleLabel = [[UILabel alloc] initWithFrame:label1Frame];
    [self addSubview:self.titleLabel];
    self.titleLabel.text = @"No title";

    self.locationLabel = [[UILabel alloc] initWithFrame:label2Frame];
    [self addSubview:self.locationLabel];
    self.LocationLabel.text = @"No location";

}
```

To preview the CustomPhotoView in Interface Builder, select your storyboard file. You should see your placeholder text inside the view, as shown in Figure 11-15. Unfortunately, you still need to do a little more work to be able to preview the image.

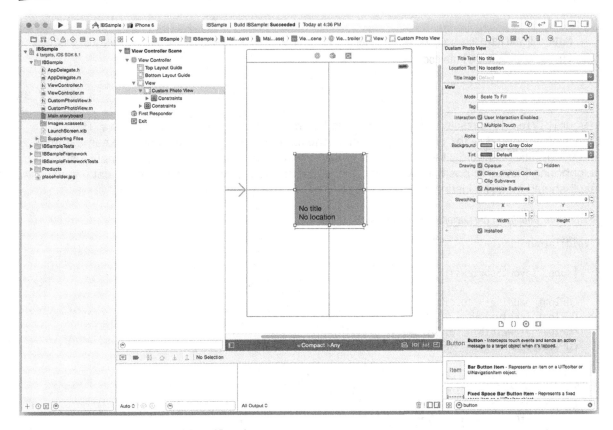

Figure 11-15. Previewing the CustomPhotoView class

As exciting as it is to see placeholder text, it is more exciting (and useful) for developers to be able to see the results of changing the image and text on-the-fly, from within Interface Builder. Xcode 6 allows you to expose a limited set of classes as editable properties in Interface Builder via the IBInspectable attribute. This attribute works much like the IBOutlet attribute: adding the necessary code to your declaration allows the property to show up in Interface Builder. You can find a list of supported classes in Table 11-2.

Table 11-2. IBInspectable-Compatible Classes

Class	Purpose
UIImage	Allows you to select an image from your app bundle or asset catalog
UIColor	Allows you to select a color by using the OS X color picker
NSString	Allows you to type in a string
NSInteger	Allows you to type in an integer value
CGFloat	Allows you to type in a float value
CGRect	Allows you to type in four float values, corresponding to a frame's x, y, width, and height values

To create IBInspectable-compatible objects, add properties to the CustomPhotoView class representing the image, title, and location properties from the CustomPhoto class, as shown in Listing 11-6.

Listing 11-6. Adding IBInspectable Properties to the CustomPhotoView Class

```
#import <UIKit/UIKit.h>

IB_DESIGNABLE

@interface CustomPhotoView : UIView

@property (nonatomic) UILabel *titleLabel;
@property (nonatomic, strong) IBInspectable NSString *titleText;
@property (nonatomic) UILabel *locationLabel;
@property (nonatomic, strong) IBInspectable NSString *locationText;

@property (nonatomic) UIImageView *imageView;
@property (nonatomic, strong) IBInspectable UIImage *titleImage;

@end
```

To verify that Interface Builder recognizes your properties, select your view in the storyboard. At the top of the Attributes Inspector, you will see a section containing your properties, as shown in Figure 11-16.

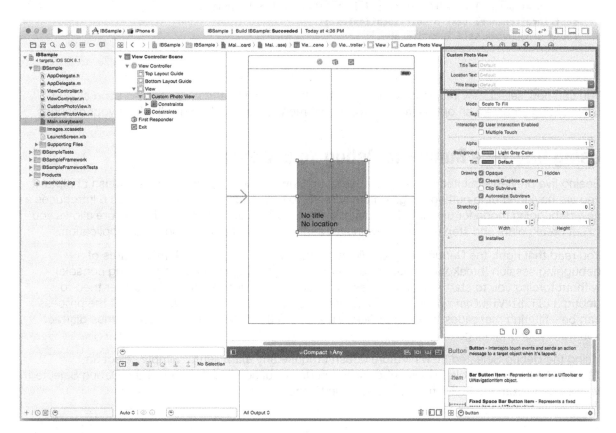

Figure 11-16. Viewing IBInspectable properties in Interface Builder

To make the user's input affect the preview, you need to connect these properties to your subviews in the [`UIView layoutSubviews`] method. As shown in Listing 11-7, by replacing your placeholder values with references to your `IBInspectable`-compatible properties, you can enable live previews for your properties.

Listing 11-7. Adding Live Updates

```
-(void)layoutSubviews
{
    [super layoutSubviews];

    ...

    self.imageView = [[UIImageView alloc] initWithFrame:insideFrame];
    self.imageView.image = self.titleImage;

    [self addSubview:self.imageView];

    self.titleLabel = [[UILabel alloc] initWithFrame:label1Frame];
    self.titleLabel.text = self.titleText;
    [self addSubview:self.titleLabel];


    self.locationLabel = [[UILabel alloc] initWithFrame:label2Frame];
    self.locationLabel.text = self.locationText;
    [self addSubview:self.locationLabel];

}
```

You can now select new values for your properties from within Interface Builder. As soon as you finish typing (or select an option from a drop-down menu), the storyboard will reflect your changes.

Using Interface Builder to Debug Your Views

Seeing live previews in Interface Builder speeds up view debugging considerably, but isn't helpful if you are having trouble putting things on the screen. To help address this need, Xcode 6 introduces a new debugging mode for user interface developers: Debug Selected Views. This feature allows you to set breakpoints and step through view initialization code without executing your application.

You read that right: the Debug Selected Views feature lets you perform all the features of a debugging session (breakpoints, stepping over code, and using the LLDB debugging console) without forcing you to start a debugging session for your application. If you have ever tried to debug a `UITableViewController`, you are already intimately familiar with how difficult the process can be—filtering messages for each `UITableViewCell` in the data source can sometimes distract you from your original goal.

Using the Debug Selected Views feature doesn't require any extra setup. Simply select an `IB_DESIGNABLE`-compatible `UIView` subclass in Interface Builder, and then select the Debug Selected Views option from the Editor menu, as shown in Figure 11-17.

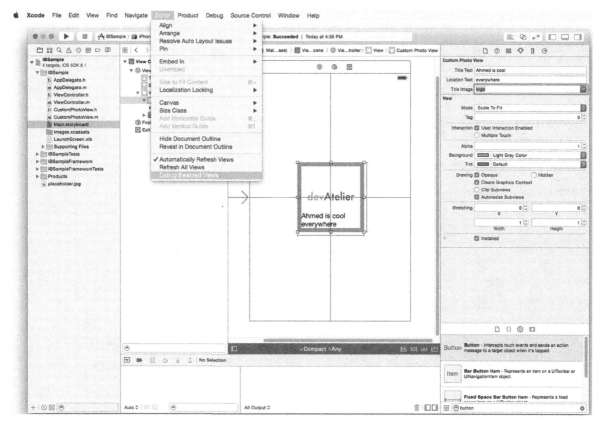

Figure 11-17. Enabling Debug Selected Views

Make sure you set breakpoints in your UIView subclass; otherwise, the debugger will have nothing to inspect. When the debugger hits a breakpoint, you will see the familiar LLDB debugging interface, as shown in Figure 11-18. You can use these extra panes to inspect the stack, set additional breakpoints, and even send instructions to the LLDB debugger.

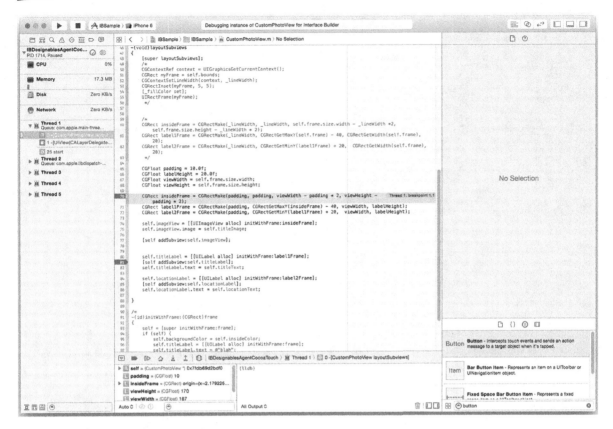

Figure 11-18. *Debugging interface*

Unlike a normal debugging session, view debugging does not launch the iOS simulator. To debug your views, open Interface Builder in a separate tab or as a companion view in Xcode (the Venn Diagram icon). Because you have enabled the IB_DESIGNABLE attribute for your class, you will be able to view live previews in Interface Builder as you step through your code.

Summary

In this chapter, you explored several of the new features in Xcode 6 that can help you build and debug user interfaces faster and more intelligently. First, size classes can help you build a single storyboard that you can use across all devices. Next, you saw how to add Quick Look–compatible output to any class, making snapshots of your classes available from within the Xcode debugging interface. Finally, to help you make reusable user interface elements, you saw how to add Interface Builder compatibility to any UIView subclass with the IB_DESIGNABLE attribute. The goal of any integrated development environment should be to speed up your workflow. All of these features certainly help with that goal, giving you better ways of debugging your user interfaces than constantly restarting debugging sessions.

Chapter 12

Using the AVKit Framework for Media Playback

While iOS 7 brought a seismic shift in design sensibilities to the Apple mobile application world, iOS 8 promises to shift mobile app development yet again with its emphasis on new functionality and streamlining of old features. The changes extend into media playback, with the introduction of yet another media playback framework—AVKit!

The AVKit framework is intended to be a drop-in replacement for the media playback features of the MediaPlayer framework. As shown in Figure 12-1, this framework provides a playback interface via the AVPlayerViewController class that is almost exactly the same as the one provided by the MPMediaPlayerController class that you have been using throughout the book.

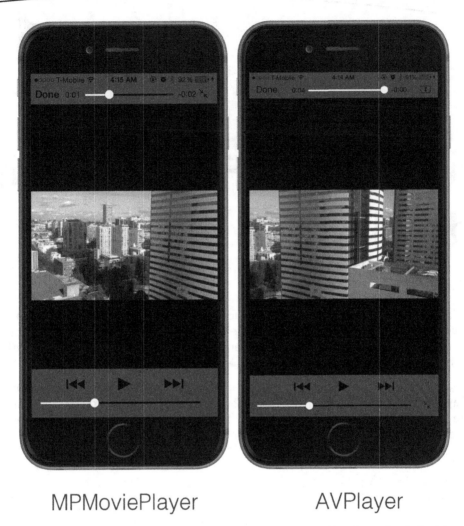

MPMoviePlayer   AVPlayer

Figure 12-1. *The familiar MPMoviePlayerController playback interface vs. the new AVPlayerController playback interface*

From the user interface perspective, not much has changed, aside from the addition of a tiny Expand button in the control bar. For some videos, you may also see a Dialog button, which exposes an audio and subtitle track picker, as shown in Figure 12-2.

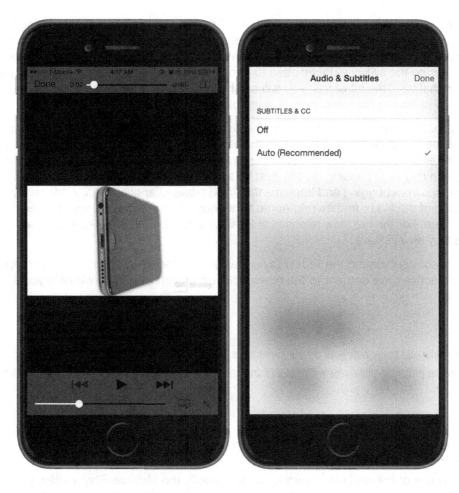

Home Screen   Subtitle Menu

Figure 12-2. Audio and subtitle picker for AVPlayerController class

This new feature is driven by the key difference between the AVKit and MediaPlayer frameworks at a software-architecture level; the AVKit framework is designed to be a media playback that operates closer to the AVFoundation framework. From the video chapters (Chapters 8–10), you may remember that you used the MediaPlayer framework to present the iOS built-in media playback interface, but that you had to drop down to the AVFoundation level to override controls or to create your own recording interface.

Similarly, from the audio chapters (Chapters 5–7), you may remember that AVFoundation allowed you to control playback—as long as you built your own playback interface. The AVKit framework tries to bridge this gap by providing a playback interface that operates on AVAssetItem objects (the class AVFoundation uses to represent media). Thus it can perform more-advanced operations with less "glue" code. This makes it easier for you to work with media files and even lets you perform video effects on-the-fly—such as adding watermarks or color filters.

In this chapter, you will see how to take advantage of the AVKit framework by modifying the MyVideoPlayer video player application from Chapter 9 to use the AVPlayerController class for media playback. Additionally, you will learn about AVKit's tighter integration with the AVFoundation framework by using the AVQueuePlayer class to effortlessly load a playlist into your video player. Finally, to add that last little bit of flair, you will see how to add a watermark to your player—a convenient way of adding branding to your video playback interface.

At this point, you may be wondering whether the MediaPlayer framework will be around and whether your knowledge will stay relevant for the next few years. The answer is yes, absolutely! The AVPlayerViewController class is meant to mimic the MPMoviePlayerController class in its functionality and message passing, so the MediaPlayer framework knowledge you have will reduce any speed bumps in debugging and implementing AVKit-based applications. Additionally, despite the introduction of the AVKit framework, Apple announced that the MediaPlayer framework is *not* being deprecated. For the next few releases at least, you can expect MediaPlayer-based apps to work just as they always have.

While Apple is not deprecating the MediaPlayer framework, their general trend with competing APIs is to shift active development to the newer one; getting started early will help you stand out from the crowd.

> **Caution**   You need to upgrade your development tools to Xcode 6 and the iOS 8 SDK before attempting to implement the project in this chapter. The AVKit framework is not available in SDK versions prior to iOS 8.

Getting Started

To illustrate the use of the AVKit framework, you will modify the MyVideoPlayer video playback application from Chapter 9 to use the AVPlayerViewController class for media playback, and you will add support for watermarking and queue playback (playlists). The new project will be called MyAVPlayer and can be found in the Chapter 13 folder of the source code bundle.

The MyVideoPlayer project presented a windowed video player. Users could choose a media file to play from the app's documents folder. As shown in Figure 12-3, the only graphical interface changes apparent to users in the MyAVPlayer project are the watermark, which appears over the player, and an additional Play All button that begins playing all the media files in the documents folder.

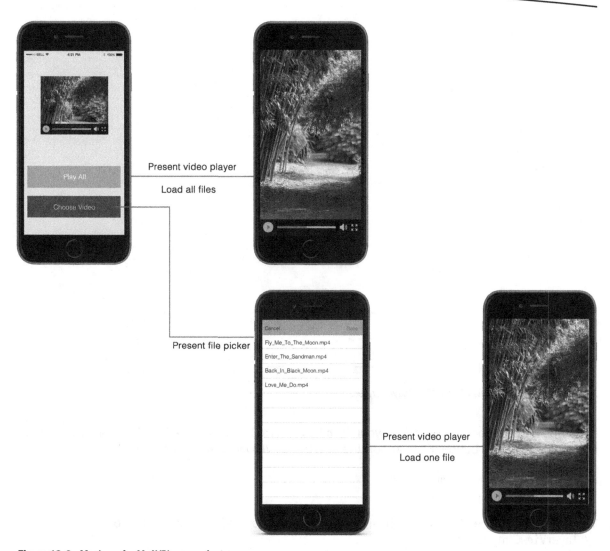

Figure 12-3. Mock-up for MyAVPlayer project

Following the same process you used in Chapter 8 to create the MyVideoPlayer project from a copy of the MyPod project, create a copy of the folder containing the MyVideoPlayer project and then rename it to **MyAVPlayer** in Xcode.

To use the AVKit framework, you must make sure that both it and the AVFoundation framework are included in your project. If you are using Xcode 6 and the iOS 8 SDK (or greater), both will appear in the Framework Browser. Because you are using AVKit as a drop-in replacement for the MediaPlayer framework in this project, remove the MediaPlayer framework from your project. Your final list of frameworks should look like the example in Figure 12-4.

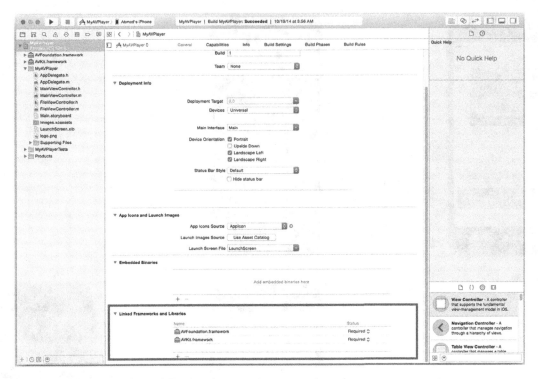

Figure 12-4. List of frameworks for MyAVPlayer project

Next, you need to update the code in your MainViewController class to reflect the AVKit framework and the new Play All button. First, import the AVKit and AVFoundation frameworks:

```
#import <AVFoundation/AVFoundation.h>
#import <AVKit/AVKit.h>
```

Then change the type of the moviePlayer property from MPMoviePlayerController to AVPlayerViewController:

```
@property (nonatomic, strong) AVPlayerViewController *moviePlayer;
```

Finally, add a UIButton property representing the Play All button:

```
@property (nonatomic, strong) IBOutlet UIButton *playAllButton;
```

Your header file for the MainViewController class should look like the example in in Listing 12-1.

Listing 12-1. Header File for MainViewController Class

```
#import <UIKit/UIKit.h>
#import <AVFoundation/AVFoundation.h>
#import <AVKit/AVKit.h>
#import "FileViewController.h"
```

```
@interface MainViewController : UIViewController <FileControllerDelegate>

@property (nonatomic, strong) IBOutlet UIView *playerViewContainer;
@property (nonatomic, strong) IBOutlet UIButton *chooseFileButton;
@property (nonatomic, strong) IBOutlet UIButton *playAllButton;
@property (nonatomic, strong) AVPlayerViewController *moviePlayer;

-(IBAction)playAll:(id)sender;

@end
```

To wrap things up, add your Play All button to the storyboard for the project, and tie it to the property you just added. Your intermediate storyboard should look like the example in Figure 12-5.

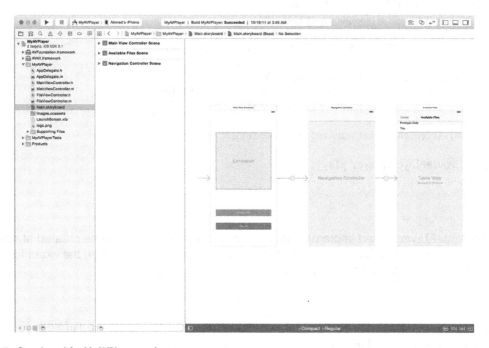

Figure 12-5. Storyboard for MyAVPlayer project

Using the AVPlayer Class to Play a Media File

Just as with the MPMediaPlayerController class, to initialize an AVPlayerViewController object, you need to provide it with a media file or content URL to use as an input. The AVPlayer class handles the playback functions of the AVPlayerViewController class. The AVPlayer class uses AVPlayerItem objects, a subclass of AVAsset, to represent media items. Unlike an MPMediaItem object, an AVAsset can represent media files in *container* formats, can include multiple subtitle and audio tracks, and can represent AVComposition objects—special objects that add time-based effects such as filters and transitions to assets.

You initialize an AVPlayer object with a single media file by using the [AVPlayer playerWithURL:] method. Doing so automatically converts your content URL to an AVPlayerItem object. As with the MyVideoPlayer application, you should initialize your AVPlayer after the user has selected a file from the file picker. Place your initialization code in the handler method for the FileControllerDelegate protocol, [FileControllerDelegate didFinishWithFile:], as shown in Listing 12-2. This will replace your previous MPMoviePlayerController initialization code.

Listing 12-2. Loading a Media File into an AVPlayer Object

```
-(void)didFinishWithFile:(NSString *)filePath
{
    NSArray *paths = NSSearchPathForDirectoriesInDomains(
        NSDocumentDirectory, NSUserDomainMask, YES);
    NSString *documentsDirectory = [paths objectAtIndex:0];
    NSString *relativePath = [documentsDirectory
        stringByAppendingPathComponent:filePath];

    NSURL *fileURL = [NSURL fileURLWithPath:relativePath];

    self.moviePlayer.player = [AVPlayer playerWithURL:fileURL];
    [self.moviePlayer.player addObserver:self forKeyPath:@"status"
                            options:0 context:nil];

    [self dismissViewControllerAnimated:YES completion:^{

        [self.moviePlayer.player play];
    }];

}
```

As with the MediaPlayer-based implementation, your content URL needs to be created at runtime, to correctly determine the location of your app's documents directory (remember, the exact location is tied to a UUID that is auto-generated by iOS).

> **Note** If you want to load an AVComposition or AVPlayerItem directly, you can use the [AVPlayer playerWithPlayerItem:] method.

After an AVPlayer object has been initialized, a user can click the Play button to start file playback. However, to fully implement the workflow of the MyVideoPlayer project, you need to add two final steps:

1. Present the AVPlayerViewController.

2. Define media playback events, (for example, preloading the media so it will load faster).

Presenting the AVPlayerViewController

From a user interface perspective, AVPlayerViewController has two major advantages over MPMoviePlayerController: it provides *adaptive* controls that respond to both the size of the window and to the type of content being played, and it provides an object representation you use in Interface Builder, as shown in Figure 12-6.

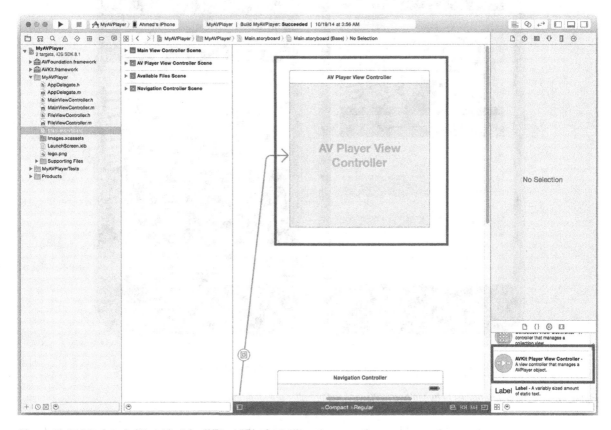

Figure 12-6. Interface Builder object for AVPlayerViewController

As shown in Figure 12-7, the AVPlayerViewController class will automatically switch the control types based on the presentation style (windowed or full-screen). In contrast, the MPMoviePlayerController required users to specify their control style.

Windowed Controls   Fullscreen Controls

Figure 12-7. Control differences between two AVPlayerViewController presentation styles

As with the `MPMoviePlayerController` class, users can click the Expand control in the embedded player to toggle between windowed and full-screen playback.

> **Note** You can still hide the `AVPlayerViewController` controls completely by using the `showsPlaybackControls` property.

Similarly, the controls change based on whether the user is playing a local media file or a streaming one. As shown in Figure 12-8, local playback exposes a Play button and Forward/Back buttons so users can navigate through a playlist, while streaming playback exposes a Play button and a Repeat button. As with control style, the `AVPlayerViewController` class does all of this automatically.

Local File   Streaming URL

Figure 12-8. AVPlayerViewController control differences between local and streaming files

Although the user interface for the MyAVPlayer project should replicate the MyVideoPlayer project, you need to change the view initialization code. The AVPlayer class is responsible for controlling media playback while the AVPlayerViewController acts as a wrapper for the user interface. To present an AVPlayerViewController in windowed mode, use a container view to contain the AVPlayerViewController object.

To place the AVPlayerViewController on the MainViewController class, drag and drop Container View and AVPlayer View Controller objects from the Interface Builder Object Library onto your storyboard, as shown in Figure 12-9.

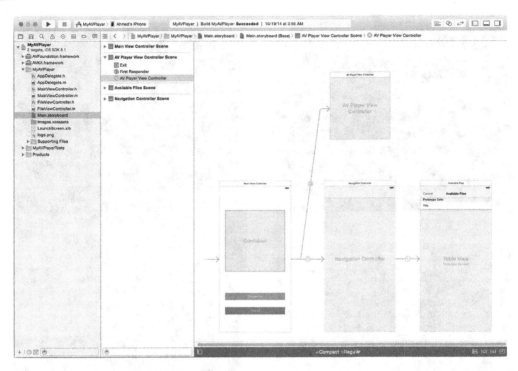

Figure 12-9. Completed storyboard for MyAVPlayer project

Attach the container view to the `playerView` property in your `MainViewController` class. To initialize the view, create an *embed* segue named `setPlayer`. The system will call this segue only once—after the view has loaded. As with all segues, add this to the `[MainViewController prepareForSegue:sender:]` method, as shown in Listing 12-3.

Listing 12-3. Initializing an AVPlayerViewController object from a segue

```
-(void)prepareForSegue:(UIStoryboardSegue *)segue sender:(id)sender
{
    if ([segue.identifier isEqualToString:@"setPlayerContent"]) {
        AVPlayerViewController *playerVC = (AVPlayerViewController *)
            segue.destinationViewController;
        self.moviePlayer = playerVC;

    } else if ([segue.identifier isEqualToString:@"showFilePicker"]) {
        NSMutableArray *videoArray = [NSMutableArray new];

        NSArray *paths = NSSearchPathForDirectoriesInDomains(
            NSDocumentDirectory, NSUserDomainMask, YES);
        NSString *documentsDirectory = [paths objectAtIndex:0];
        NSError *error = nil;

        NSArray *allFiles = [[NSFileManager defaultManager]
            contentsOfDirectoryAtPath:documentsDirectory error:&error];
```

```
    if (error == nil) {

        for (NSString *file in allFiles) {
            NSString *fileExtension = [
                [file pathExtension] lowercaseString];
            if ([fileExtension isEqualToString:@"m4v"] ||
                [fileExtension isEqualToString:@"mov"]) {
                    [videoArray addObject:file];
            }
        }

    UINavigationController *navigationController =
        (UINavigationController *) segue.destinationViewController;
    FileViewController *fileVC =
      (FileViewController *)navigationController.topViewController;
    fileVC.delegate = self;
    fileVC.fileArray = videoArray;
    } else {
        NSLog(@"error looking up files: %@", [error description]);
    }

    }
}
```

With segues, the primary method for accessing the *destination* view controller is through the destinationViewController property. Because the setPlayer segue identifier is used only once in your storyboard, you know that the destinationViewController object points to the AVPlayerViewController you placed there. After casting, you have a valid object that you can use to set the moviePlayer property of the MainViewController class. (Remember, objects placed on a storyboard are initialized by their default constructor when loaded).

Because you initialized the AVPlayer object in the [FileViewDelegate didFinishWithFile:] method (after the user selected a file from the file picker), your video player is now ready to use. When the user selects a media file, your video player will load the first frame of the video and the control bar for the player, indicating that it is ready for playback.

Using the AVQueuePlayer Class to Play a Playlist

Another advantage of the AVKit framework over the MediaPlayer framework is that it allows you to initialize a media player with a playlist, using the AVQueuePlayer class. In addition to being able to load multiple files at once, using AVQueuePlayer as the player property for your AVPlayerController will automatically add controls and handler methods so that users can navigate between items in the playlist.

You might be thinking, "This is pretty standard functionality; shouldn't all of the media player classes have it?" Unfortunately, the primary classes you have used for media playback, AVAudioPlayer (for audio) and MPMediaPlayerController (for video), cannot be initialized with a playlist. The way most applications implement playlist-like functionality with these classes is by initializing a media player with the "next file" in the playlist when the app receives the event for *playback completed*. Prior to AVKit, the only media player class that could handle a playlist natively was the

MPMusicPlayerController class, which you used for iPod music playback—but remember, you had to implement your own user interface to use this class. The AVQueuePlayer class kills two birds with one stone by providing both the user interface and transition logic from one object.

Just as the AVPlayerViewController class is intended to be a drop-in replacement for the MPMediaPlayerController class, you can use the AVQueuePlayer class as a drop-in replacement for the AVPlayer class. The key difference between the two classes is that instead of initializing an AVQueuePlayer with a single media asset, you pass it an array of AVPlayerItem objects:

```
AVQueuePlayer *queuePlayer = [[AVQueuePlayer alloc]
                              initWithItems:playerItemArray];
```

The requirement to use AVPlayerItem objects means that you cannot use a single content URL to initialize your player. However, you can create AVPlayerItem objects from content URLs by using the [AVPlayerItem playerItemWithURL:] method:

```
AVPlayerItem *item1 = [AVPlayerItem playerItemWithURL:@"goodDoge.mp4"];
```

This method allows you to use either a local file URL or a remote content URL. As always, remember to calculate your local file URL at runtime in order to properly load it:

```
NSString *relativePath = [documentsDirectory
    stringByAppendingPathComponent:@"goodDoge.mp4"];
NSURL *fileURL = [NSURL fileURLWithPath:relativePath];
AVPlayerItem *item1 = [AVPlayerItem playerItemWithURL:fileURL];
```

Because the AVQueuePlayer class is a subclass of AVPlayer, all you need to do to is pass an AVQueuePlayer object to your AVPlayerViewController's player property:

```
self.moviePlayer.player = queuePlayer;
```

As mentioned at the beginning of the chapter, in the MyAVPlayer project, you want to let the user play a single file by using the Choose File button, or load all available files when they use the Play All button. To do this, initialize the AVPlayerViewController with an AVPlayer when the user selects the Choose File button, and an AVQueuePlayer when the user selects the Play All button.

To retain single-file playback, you should leave the Choose File handler (the file picker delegate) untouched. Instead, make a new method, [MainViewController playAll:], which will act as the handler for the Play All button. As shown in Listing 12-4, use this method to set the player property for the shared AVPlayerViewController object.

Listing 12-4. Initializing an AVPlayerViewController with an AVQueuePlayer

```
-(IBAction)playAll:(id)sender
{

    NSString *relativePath = [documentsDirectory
        stringByAppendingPathComponent:@"goodDoge.mp4"];
    NSURL *fileURL = [NSURL fileURLWithPath:relativePath];
    AVPlayerItem *item1 = [AVPlayerItem playerItemWithURL:fileURL];
```

```
NSString *relativePath2 = [documentsDirectory
    stringByAppendingPathComponent:@"badDoge.mp4"];
NSURL *fileURL2 = [NSURL fileURLWithPath:relativePath2];

AVPlayerItem *item2 = [AVPlayerItem
    playerItemWithURL:@"http://www.devatelier.com/commercial.mov"];
NSArrray *playerItemArray = [NSArray arrayWithObjects: item1, item2];

self.moviePlayer.player = [[AVQueuePlayer alloc]
    initWithItems:playerItemArray];

[self.moviePlayer.player addObserver:self forKeyPath:@"status"
    options:0 context:nil];

[self.moviePlayer.player play];

}
```

To get this code to compile, you need to define the inputPlaylist object. Because the goal is to play all files, you can duplicate the scanning logic from the file picker (the FileViewController) class. Scan for all files in the documents directory and add them to an NSMutableArray. When that process completes, attach it to your AVPlayerViewController. Listing 12-5 shows the completed initialization method.

Listing 12-5. Completed Initialization Code for AVQueuePlayer

```
-(IBAction)playAll:(id)sender
{
    NSArray *paths = NSSearchPathForDirectoriesInDomains(
        NSDocumentDirectory, NSUserDomainMask, YES);
    NSString *documentsDirectory = [paths objectAtIndex:0];
    NSError *error = nil;

    NSArray *allFiles = [[NSFileManager defaultManager]
        contentsOfDirectoryAtPath:documentsDirectory error:&error];

    NSMutableArray *playerItemArray = [NSMutableArray new];

    for (NSString *file in allFiles) {

        if ([[file pathExtension] isEqualToString:@"mp4"] ||
            [[file pathExtension] isEqualToString:@"mov"] ||
             [[file pathExtension] isEqualToString:@"MOV"]) {
            NSString *relativePath = [documentsDirectory
                stringByAppendingPathComponent:file];

            NSURL *fileURL = [NSURL fileURLWithPath:relativePath];

            AVPlayerItem *playerItem = [AVPlayerItem
                playerItemWithURL:fileURL];
```

```
            [playerItem addObserver:self forKeyPath:@"status"
                options:nil context:nil];

            [playerItemArray addObject:playerItem];
        }

    }

    self.moviePlayer.player = [[AVQueuePlayer alloc]
        initWithItems:playerItemArray];

    [self.moviePlayer.player addObserver:self forKeyPath:@"status"
        options:0 context:nil];

    [self.moviePlayer.player play];

}
```

Working with Media Playback Events

One of the few features from the `MPMediaPlayerController` class that was not ported directly to the `AVPlayerViewController` class was reporting playback state changes through notifications. The good news is that you implement similar functionality in `AVPlayerViewController` by using key-value observers. Notifications still exist for some playback events, such as *playback finished* and similar events.

USING KEY-VALUE OBSERVERS

Like notifications, key-value observing (KVO) is a subscription-based message-passing system, meaning a class does not receive any messages until it declares it is *observing* them. While notifications require you to define and use a notification "name" to pass and receive messages through a central service (the notification center), key-value observers are decentralized.

Key-value observer messages are triggered when the content (value) of a property (key) changes on an object. In KVO, a class declares itself an observer of messages for an object, and specifies a handler method—just as with notifications. Any object or property can be observed, giving you the flexibility to define handling of events that are not tied to notifications or delegate methods—at the cost of reuse (your implementation will be class-specific and less portable).

The process of creating and using a key-value observer is quite similar to that of creating a notification (with the major exception being its object-specific nature): Declare your class as observing a property on an object.

1. Implement handler code for the KVO event.

2. Remove your observer when it's no longer needed (to prevent crashing).

The API for registering a key-value observer is [`NSObject addObserver:forKeyPath:options:context`]. If you wanted to observe when an array's length changed, your registration code would look like this:

```
[self.peopleArray addObserver:self forKeyPath:@"count" options:nil
    context:nil];
```

The *receiver* (calling class) for this message is the object that needs to be observed; in this case, the array itself. The *observer* is the class that acts like a delegate and receives messages based on the indicated value change. `key path` is the property of the object that you want to observe; the name is passed as a case-sensitive string. The `options` parameter lets you specify how information should be sent to the handler method. For example, you can pare down the frequency of messages (the default value of `nil` is sufficient for most beginning applications). The `context` parameter lets you to specify an "original value" to compare against in your handler method. Once again, `nil` is sufficient for most beginning applications.

Unlike a notification, the NSObject method handles all key-value observers by using [NSObject observeValueFor KeyPath:ofObject:change:context]. For the array example, your handler method would look like this:

```
-(void)observeValueForKeyPath:(NSString *)keyPath
    ofObject:(id)object change:(NSDictionary *)change
    context:(void *)context
{
    if ((object == self.peopleArray) &&
        [keyPath isEqualToString:@"count"] ) {
            NSLog(@"new count!", [self.peopleArray count]);
    }
}
```

The parameters for handling a KVO message correspond in a one-to-one relationship with the parameters you used to declare your observer. The unfamiliar part should be the handling logic. Because one method handles all the messages, you need to check that the message originated from the object you specified. If you are using an instance variable, you would compare the object directly; if you wanted to use a local variable, you could compare the object type. Additionally, you need to check that the message corresponds to the expected property (because you can observe multiple properties on the same object).

Finally, to remove an observer, you call the [NSObject removeObserver:forKeyPath] method on the receiving object, during the tear-down process for your class. For the array example, it would look like this:

```
-(void)dealloc
{
    [self.peopleArray removeObserver:self forKeyPath:@"count"];
}
```

Just as with notifications, a KVO message could fire after you have torn down your class; cleaning up your observer will prevent crashes. If you are reinitializing an instance variable at runtime, it is wise to remove the observer as part of your reset step.

Loading Complete Event

As you may remember from Chapter 8, after selecting a media file, you immediately called the [MPMediaPlayer prepareToPlay] method to start loading it. After the file was loaded, the MPMoviePlayerLoadStateChanged notification fired, indicating the file was ready for playback. Upon receipt of this notification, you called the [MPMediaPlayer play] function. The AVPlayer object status property retrieves the loading state of a video. In your FileViewController delegate method, add an observer after initializing your player object, as shown in Listing 12-6.

Listing 12-6. Adding a Key-Value Observer for Video Loading State

```
-(IBAction)playAll:(id)sender
{
    NSArray *paths = NSSearchPathForDirectoriesInDomains(
        NSDocumentDirectory, NSUserDomainMask, YES);
    NSString *documentsDirectory = [paths objectAtIndex:0];
    NSError *error = nil;

    NSArray *allFiles = [[NSFileManager defaultManager]
        contentsOfDirectoryAtPath:documentsDirectory error:&error];

    if (error == nil) {
        NSMutableArray *playerItemArray = [NSMutableArray new];

      for (NSString *file in allFiles) {
        NSString *fileExtension = [file pathExtension];
        if ([[fileExtension lowercaseString] isEqualToString:@"mp4"] ||
            [[fileExtension lowercaseString] isEqualToString:@"mov"]) {

                NSString *relativePath = [documentsDirectory
                    stringByAppendingPathComponent:file];

                NSURL *fileURL = [NSURL fileURLWithPath:relativePath];

                AVPlayerItem *playerItem = [AVPlayerItem
                    playerItemWithURL:fileURL];

                [playerItem addObserver:self forKeyPath:@"status"
                    options:NSKeyValueObservingOptionNew context:nil];

                [playerItemArray addObject:playerItem];
        }

    }
}
```

```
    self.moviePlayer.player = [[AVQueuePlayer alloc] initWithItems:playerItemArray];

    [self.moviePlayer.player addObserver:self forKeyPath:@"status" options:0 context:nil];

    [self.moviePlayer.player play];


  } else {
      NSLog(@"no files found");
  }
}
```

Referring back to the "Using Key-Value Observers" sidebar, in your [MainViewController observeValueForKeyPath:] method, place your handler logic in an if block that checks to make sure the observed object was your player and that the observed keyPath was status. If an error occurs, display an alert view; otherwise, start playing the video file immediately, as shown in Listing 12-7. Your handler method should execute only when both comparisons are successful.

Listing 12-7. Handler method for Video Loading State Key-Value Observer

```
-(void)observeValueForKeyPath:(NSString *)keyPath ofObject:(id)object
    change:(NSDictionary *)change context:(void *)context
{
    if ((object == self.moviePlayer.player) && [keyPath
        isEqualToString:@"status"] ) {

        UIImage *image = [UIImage imageNamed:@"devat"];
        UIImageView *imageView = [[UIImageView alloc]
            initWithImage:image];
        imageView.frame = self.moviePlayer.videoBounds;
        imageView.contentMode = UIViewContentModeBottomRight;
        imageView.autoresizingMask = UIViewAutoresizingFlexibleHeight |
            UIViewAutoresizingFlexibleWidth;

        if ([self.moviePlayer.contentOverlayView.subviews count] == 0) {
            [self.moviePlayer.contentOverlayView addSubview:imageView];
        }

        [object removeObserver:self forKeyPath:@"status"];

    } else if ([object isKindOfClass:[AVPlayerItem class]]) {

        AVPlayerItem *currentItem = (AVPlayerItem *)object;

        if (currentItem.status == AVPlayerItemStatusFailed) {
            NSString *errorString = [currentItem.error description];
            NSLog(@"item failed: %@", errorString);
```

```
        if ([self.moviePlayer.player
            isKindOfClass:[AVQueuePlayer class]]) {
            AVQueuePlayer *queuePlayer =
                (AVQueuePlayer *)self.moviePlayer.player;
            [queuePlayer advanceToNextItem];
        } else {
            UIAlertView *alert = [[UIAlertView alloc]
                initWithTitle:@"Error" message:errorString
                delegate:self cancelButtonTitle:@"OK"
                otherButtonTitles:nil];
            [alert show];
        }
    } else {
        [object removeObserver:self forKeyPath:@"status"];
    }
  }
}
}
```

Remember, the goal of key-value observing is to filter your messages down to exactly what you need (for example, a specific media player object, a specific property). You do not need to add in error-handling logic since the delegate method is shared by the entire class (every KVO object will send a message to this class).

Also note that the last line of Listing 12-7 removes the observer after catching it. This prevents crashes from occurring the next time the user starts playing a video. At this point, your original AVPlayer object has been freed from memory.

Playback Complete Event

In the MyVideoPlayer app, you showed an alert view when media playback completed, by observing the MPMoviePlayerPlaybackDidFinishNotification notification. To catch the equivalent notification for the AVKit framework, add an observer for the AVPlayerItemDidPlayToEndTimeNotification notification, as shown in Listing 12-8.

Listing 12-8. Adding an Observer for AVPlayer's "Playback Completed" Notification

```
- (void)viewDidLoad {
    [super viewDidLoad];
    [[NSNotificationCenter defaultCenter] addObserver:self
        selector:@selector(playbackFinished:)
        name:AVPlayerItemDidPlayToEndTimeNotification object:nil];
}
```

Many video applications commonly dismiss the video playback interface automatically when playback has completed. You can implement this behavior by calling the [self dismissViewController:anima ted:] method in your callback method, as shown in Listing 12-9.

Listing 12-9. Callback Method for "Playback Completed" Notification

```
-(void)playbackFinished:(NSNotification *) notification
{
    NSDictionary *userInfo = notification.userInfo;

    if ([self.moviePlayer.player isKindOfClass:[AVPlayer class]]) {
        [self dismissViewControllerAnimated:YES completion:nil];
    } else {
        //do nothing
    }

}
```

With the Playback Completed notification, be careful to check the type of the AVPlayer object that is currently loaded before dismissing the AVPlayerViewController entirely. For an AVQueuePlayer, you will need to create a variable that maintains the queue position before dismissing the AVPlayerViewController. Unfortunately, there is no API for this yet.

Error Handling

When you are playing one media file, it is good form to display an error message if the file failed to load. When you are playing multiple files, it is critical to have a recovery strategy, such as skipping the bad item and continuing with the next one. The *playback state* observer handled this error when you were playing a single file using the AVPlayer class. For the AVQueuePlayer, you will need something a little bit more advanced.

You can enable item error handling for the AVQueuePlayer class by observing the status variable on each AVPlayerItem that you add to the queue. As shown in Listing 12-10, modify your [MainViewController playAll:] method to add an observer for each AVPlayerItem you create. While the same observer method can service all the items, unless you register them individually, their events will be ignored.

Listing 12-10. Adding Key-Value Observers for AVPlayerItem Objects

```
-(IBAction)playAll:(id)sender
{
    NSArray *paths =
        NSSearchPathForDirectoriesInDomains(NSDocumentDirectory,
        NSUserDomainMask, YES);
    NSString *documentsDirectory = [paths objectAtIndex:0];
    NSError *error = nil;

    NSArray *allFiles = [[NSFileManager defaultManager]
        contentsOfDirectoryAtPath:documentsDirectory error:&error];

    NSMutableArray *playerItemArray = [NSMutableArray new];
```

```objc
    if (error == nil) {

        for (NSString *file in allFiles) {
            NSString *fileExtension =           [[file pathExtension] lowercaseString];
                if ([fileExtension isEqualToString:@"m4v"] ||
                    [fileExtension isEqualToString:@"mov"]) {

                        NSString *relativePath = [documentsDirectory
                                stringByAppendingPathComponent:file];

                    NSURL *fileURL = [NSURL fileURLWithPath:relativePath];

                    AVPlayerItem *playerItem = [AVPlayerItem
                            playerItemWithURL:fileURL];

                    [playerItem addObserver:self forKeyPath:@"status"
                    options:NSKeyValueObservingOptionNew context:nil];

                    [playerItemArray addObject:playerItem];
                }
        }

    self.moviePlayer.player = [[AVQueuePlayer alloc]
    initWithItems:playerItemArray];

    [self.moviePlayer.player addObserver:self forKeyPath:@"status"
    options:0 context:nil];

    [self.moviePlayer.player play];

}
```

Because the objects you are observing were created on-the-fly, in the [MainViewController observeValueForKeyPath:] method, you will need to check the incoming object for class type, rather than doing a direct pointer comparison. In Cocoa Touch, you can check the type of any object by using the method [NSObject kindOfClass:]. Compare your incoming object to the class property of the target class. In the KVO handler method, comparing against the AVPlayerItem class would look like this:

```objc
if ([object isKindOfClass:[AVPlayerItem class]])
```

After passing the type comparison, you can query the status property of the incoming object to see if it is in the AVPlayerItemStatusFailed state. As shown in Listing 12-11, if the player is an AVQueuePlayer, log the error and advance to the next item; otherwise, display an alert view.

Listing 12-11. Key-Value Observer for Item State

```
-(void)observeValueForKeyPath:(NSString *)keyPath ofObject:(id)object
    change:(NSDictionary *)change context:(void *)context
{
    if ((object == self.moviePlayer.player) && [keyPath
        isEqualToString:@"status"] ) {

        UIImage *image = [UIImage imageNamed:@"logo.png"];
        UIImageView *imageView = [[UIImageView alloc]
            initWithImage:image];
        imageView.frame = self.moviePlayer.videoBounds;
        imageView.contentMode = UIViewContentModeBottomRight;
        imageView.autoresizingMask = UIViewAutoresizingFlexibleHeight |
            UIViewAutoresizingFlexibleWidth;

        if ([self.moviePlayer.contentOverlayView.subviews count] == 0) {
            [self.moviePlayer.contentOverlayView addSubview:imageView];
        }

        [object removeObserver:self forKeyPath:@"status"];

    } else if ([object isKindOfClass:[AVPlayerItem class]]) {

        AVPlayerItem *currentItem = (AVPlayerItem *)object;

        if (currentItem.status == AVPlayerItemStatusFailed) {
            NSString *errorString = [currentItem.error description];
            NSLog(@"item failed: %@", errorString);

            if ([self.moviePlayer.player
                isKindOfClass:[AVQueuePlayer class]]) {
                AVQueuePlayer *queuePlayer =
                    (AVQueuePlayer *)self.moviePlayer.player;
                [queuePlayer advanceToNextItem];
            } else {
                UIAlertView *alert = [[UIAlertView alloc]
                    initWithTitle:@"Error" message:errorString
                    delegate:self cancelButtonTitle:@"OK"
                    otherButtonTitles:nil];
                [alert show];
            }
        } else {
            [object removeObserver:self forKeyPath:@"status"];
        }
    }
}
```

What you have seen is just a taste of the playback state events you can handle for the AVPlayer class. For the complete list, check Apple's Developer Library documentation for the AVPlayer class (https://developer.apple.com/Library/ios/documentation/AVFoundation/Reference/AVPlayer_Class/index.html). Remember, if a notification does not exist for the event you are trying to observe—create a key-value observer!

Adding an Overlay View (Watermark)

Another added convenience of the AVPlayerViewController class is its ability to let you add a *content overlay view*. Overlay views let you display static or live content on top of your video layer, without the hassle of writing complicated low-level code to intercept the video layer. For example, if you need to display annotations, live status indicators, or even a watermark, content overlay views are a quick way to enable such features. One famous example of overlay behavior is the YouTube Advertising view, as shown in Figure 12-10, which allows you to click on a highlighted area to visit an advertiser's site.

Figure 12-10. YouTube Ad functionality

In this section, you will learn how to add a watermark to your video—a great way to add branding to your app. This example uses a static image for the watermark, but you can display anything you want in the overlay view—as long as it subclasses the UIView class.

> **Caution**   Avoid placing highly interactive elements in your content overlay view, because they could conflict with the control bar.

To get started, import an image into your project. If you want your watermark to have some transparency, use a PNG image with a transparency layer; otherwise, use a JPEG or opaque PNG image file. I prefer to use images that are approximately 50 pixels in height, so that the image does not distract viewers from the content. Try to build in at least 10 pixels of padding on all edges into the image. Create a UIImage object with this image. In the MyAVPlayer project, the file is named logo.png:

```
UIImage *image = [UIImage imageNamed:@"logo.png"];
```

To display the image on the content overlay view, you need to wrap it in a subclass of UIView, so initialize a UIImageView object with the UIImage object you just created:

```
UIImageView *imageView = [[UIImageView alloc] initWithImage:image];
```

Remember that the process of creating a `UIView` is not the same as sizing and placing it. To imitate a television broadcast, most video applications like to place their watermark at the bottom-right or top-right corner of the video. By setting the `contentMode` property of the `UIImageView` class to `UIViewContentModeBottomRight`, you can instruct the `UIImageView` class to place the image in the bottom-right corner, while retaining its original dimensions:

```
imageView.contentMode = UIViewContentModeBottomRight;
```

Similarly, you will want the image to stay in the video playback area. Unfortunately, the size of the video player changes with the presentation style of the `AVPlayerViewController` (windowed or full-screen). However, you can account for this by setting the size of your overlay equal to the *bounding frame* of the video playback area, and adding *flexible* width and height resizing masks:

```
imageView.frame = self.moviePlayer.videoBounds;
imageView.autoresizingMask = UIViewAutoresizingFlexibleHeight |
    UIViewAutoresizingFlexibleWidth;
```

After you have initialized and positioned the `UIImageView`, add it as a subview on top of the `contentOverlayView`:

```
[self.moviePlayer.contentOverlayView addSubview:imageView];
```

Now for the most important question, "Where?" As mentioned, one of the requirements for placing the `contentOverlayView` on top of the video layer is information about the dimensions of the video layer. Unfortunately, this value is not valid until the video is loaded. Luckily, this is the same event that you built a key-value observer for, to find out when an item was loaded. Create a new `if` block for the overlay, as shown in Listing 12-12.

Listing 12-12. Adding a Watermark to Your "Loading Complete" Key-Value Observer

```
-(void)observeValueForKeyPath:(NSString *)keyPath ofObject:(id)object
     change:(NSDictionary *)change context:(void *)context
{
    if ((object == self.moviePlayer.player) && [keyPath
        isEqualToString:@"status"] ) {

        UIImage *image = [UIImage imageNamed:@"logo.png"];
        UIImageView *imageView = [[UIImageView alloc]
            initWithImage:image];
        imageView.frame = self.moviePlayer.videoBounds;
        imageView.contentMode = UIViewContentModeBottomRight;
        imageView.autoresizingMask = UIViewAutoresizingFlexibleHeight |
                            UIViewAutoresizingFlexibleWidth;

        if ([self.moviePlayer.contentOverlayView.subviews count] == 0) {
            [self.moviePlayer.contentOverlayView addSubview:imageView];
        }
```

```
        [object removeObserver:self forKeyPath:@"status"];

    } else if ([object isKindOfClass:[AVPlayerItem class]]) {

        AVPlayerItem *currentItem = (AVPlayerItem *)object;

        if (currentItem.status == AVPlayerItemStatusFailed) {
            NSString *errorString = [currentItem.error description];
            NSLog(@"item failed: %@", errorString);

            if ([self.moviePlayer.player
                isKindOfClass:[AVQueuePlayer class]]) {
                AVQueuePlayer *queuePlayer =
                    (AVQueuePlayer *)self.moviePlayer.player;
                [queuePlayer advanceToNextItem];
            } else {
                UIAlertView *alert = [[UIAlertView alloc]
                    initWithTitle:@"Error" message:errorString
                    delegate:self cancelButtonTitle:@"OK"
                    otherButtonTitles:nil];
                [alert show];
            }
        } else {
            [object removeObserver:self forKeyPath:@"status"];
        }
    }
}
```

As a final note, the contentOverlayValue property is read-only, meaning you cannot remove subviews from it; you can only add views. For this reason, in Listing 12-12, I checked the number of subviews before adding the watermark—you should have only one watermark, no matter how many times the user selects a video!

Summary

In this chapter, you saw how to use the AVKit framework and its media playback classes, AVPlayer and AVQueuePlayer, as a drop-in replacement for the MediaPlayer framework. Through the MyAVPlayer project, you integrated a playlist-based media and overlay view, taking advantage of AVKit's tighter integration with the AVFoundation framework. During the integration process, you saw that many of the design patterns of the framework mimic those used in MediaPlayer closely, but required slightly different implementations.

Remember, although Apple is not retiring the MediaPlayer framework immediately, employing it sooner rather than later gives you access to a new feature set that you would otherwise have had to develop yourself.

Tracking Fitness with HealthKit and Core Motion

Of all the features that were announced at this year's Apple Worldwide Developers Conference, the one that took everyone by surprise was HealthKit—Apple's platform for health and fitness tracking. While health and fitness are two of the largest segments of the App Store, Apple had always taken a backseat in the process, providing APIs and hardware interfaces, but never getting too involved in the software side (aside from developing companion apps for the Nike+ pedometers). HealthKit changes all that, by providing a repository for health data that all developers are encouraged to integrate with, and the Health app, which comes bundled with iOS 8, that allows users to view their stored data.

Although you can find apps that provide everything from step counting to highly specialized coaching, it has been extremely difficult to sync or share information between applications. For instance, you might have one app that does an amazing job of helping you through your morning run, and another that encourages you to stay active throughout the day, but combining the data from the two applications is nearly impossible. The proliferation of Bluetooth and WiFi-connected devices has only exacerbated this problem. Nearly every health accessory has required its own custom companion app that communicates with the accessory and logs its data. Until HealthKit, there has been no good way to see everything in one place.

To help expand health and fitness even further, Apple has built the M-series of motion coprocessors into every new iOS device since the iPhone 5S, including the iPad Air, iPhone 6, and iPhone 6 Plus. M-series chips provide a highly advanced set of sensors that reduce the need for external accessories that provide the same functionality. Additionally, the M-series are extremely low-power, so they're a practical alternative for sensing motion. According to Apple, the M-series chips are 100 times more power efficient than the chips Apple previously used for motion sensing. Starting with iOS 7, Apple has built support for the M-series coprocessors into their motion-sensing framework, Core Motion, and has now made it even easier to quantify this data.

In this chapter, you will see how to take advantage of the two frameworks by adding motion tracking and logging to the MyPod application. The new application will be called MyFitnessPod and is provided in the Chapter 13 folder of the source code bundle. As shown in Figure 13-1, you will reuse the media playback and playlist selection features of the MyPod app, but you will also add workout controls and status information. The toggle playback button is missing, because it is tied to the workout controls: when the user starts, pauses, or ends a workout, so will playback.

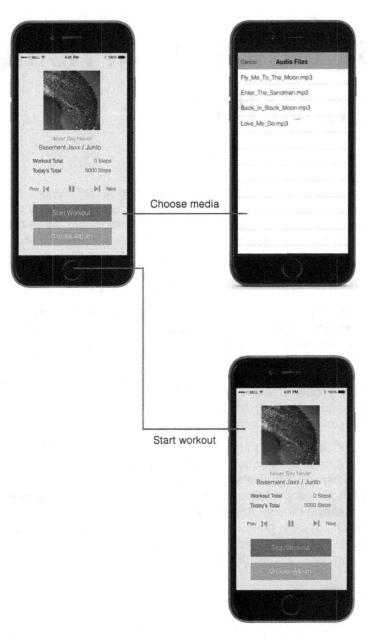

Figure 13-1. Mock-up for MyFitnessPod project

You may be wondering how this ties into HealthKit and Core Motion. When users begin their workouts, the MyFitnessPod app will begin tracking their activity by using the Core Motion framework. Similarly, when users complete their activity, you will close it out using Core Motion and log the activity data to HealthKit. While the activity is in progress, you will monitor from both frameworks to display daily steps and current workout progress.

> **Caution**   This chapter requires iOS 8 and a device with an M-series motion coprocessor (iPhone 5S or newer) to fully implement. The Core Motion features will not run on an incompatible device, and HealthKit is not available in SDK versions prior to iOS 8.0.

Getting Started

As with prior projects, this one takes advantage of your previous work. Begin by cloning the MyPod project from Chapter 7 and renaming it to **MyFitnessPod**. If you are still unsure how to rename a project, refer back to the "Getting Started" section of Chapter 8.

Next, you need to add the requisite frameworks. In Xcode 6, you will find both the CoreMotion and HealthKit frameworks in the Framework Browser. Your final framework set should look like the example in Figure 13-2.

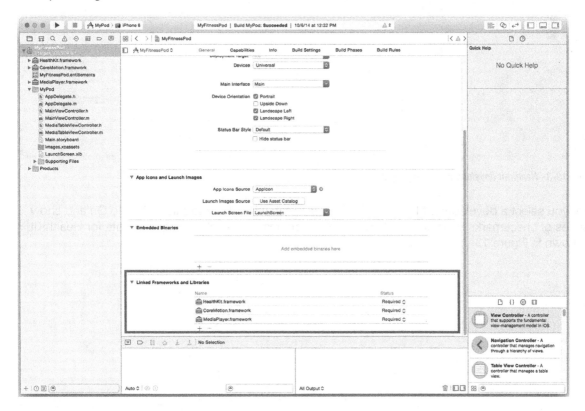

Figure 13-2. Frameworks used by MyFitnessPod project

Because HealthKit accesses sensitive user information, and some users may want to opt out, you need to add HealthKit access to your list of application capabilities. As with previous capability changes, navigate to the Capabilities tab of your project settings. Scroll down to HealthKit and click the toggle switch. You will be presented with a dialog box asking you to select a Development Team to associate the application with, as shown in Figure 13-3.

Figure 13-3. HealthKit development team prompt

After you select a development team, the Capabilities tab will set the toggle switch to On and show a series of checkmarks indicating that your application has met all of the requirements for HealthKit, as shown in Figure 13-4.

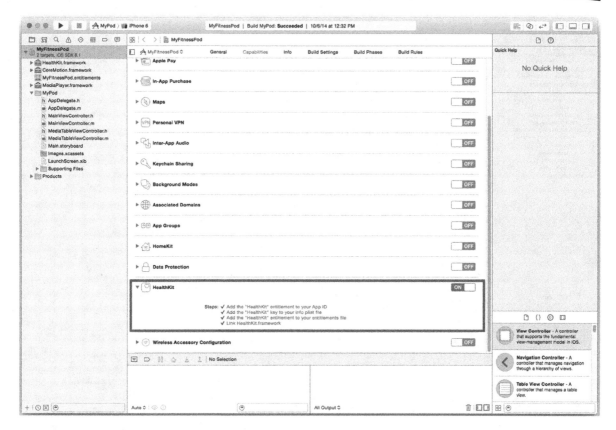

Figure 13-4. Successful HealthKit configuration

Because many users set their devices to sleep during a workout, you should also turn on the Audio and AirPlay background mode, as shown in Figure 13-5.

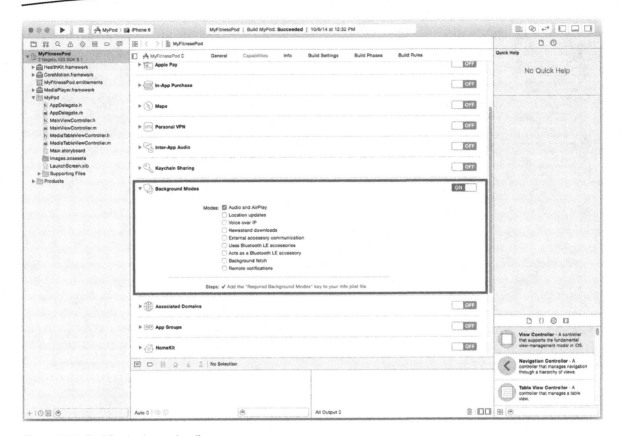

Figure 13-5. Enabling background audio

Note   The final version of the code included in the MyFitnessPod project includes the background audio control features from Chapter 9. That code is not listed here to save space. If you are porting the examples yourself, be careful to use MPMusicPlayerController playback messages, instead of those for the AVAudioPlayer class.

Now that the project has been configured for HealthKit and Core Motion, you can begin modifying the user interface to add the workout controls and status labels. Figure 13-6 shows a screenshot of the storyboard for the MyFitnessPod project. Note that there are no new view controllers, only additional labels and buttons on the MainViewController.

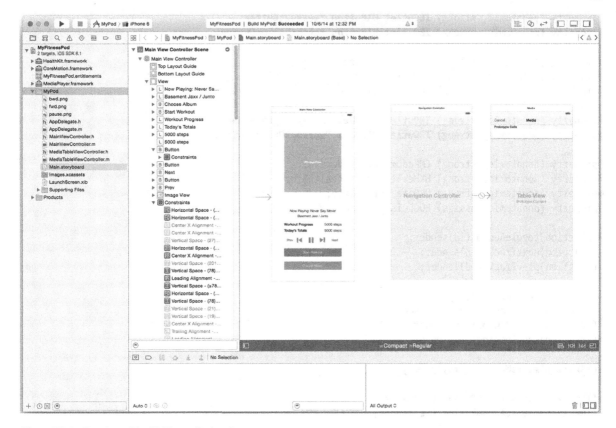

Figure 13-6. Storyboard for MyFitnessPod project

To connect these user-interface elements, as always, you need to add IBOutlet properties and IBAction handler methods for each item. Listing 13-1 shows the header file for the MainViewController class, with the new items highlighted in bold. Use these to connect your storyboard to the code.

Listing 13-1. Header File for MainViewController Class

```
#import <UIKit/UIKit.h>
#import <MediaPlayer/MediaPlayer.h>
#import "MediaTableViewController.h"
#import <CoreMotion/CoreMotion.h>
#import <HealthKit/HealthKit.h>

@interface MainViewController : UIViewController <MediaTableDelegate>

@property (nonatomic, strong) MPMusicPlayerController *musicPlayer;

@property (nonatomic, strong) IBOutlet UIButton *playButton;
@property (nonatomic, strong) IBOutlet UIButton *rewindButton;
@property (nonatomic, strong) IBOutlet UIButton *forwardButton;
@property (nonatomic, strong) IBOutlet UIButton *prevButton;
@property (nonatomic, strong) IBOutlet UIButton *nextButton;
```

```
@property (nonatomic, strong) IBOutlet UIButton *workoutButton;
@property (nonatomic, strong) IBOutlet UIButton *chooseAlbumButton;

@property (nonatomic, strong) IBOutlet UILabel *titleLabel;
@property (nonatomic, strong) IBOutlet UILabel *albumLabel;
@property (nonatomic, strong) IBOutlet UIImageView *albumImageView;

@property (nonatomic, strong) IBOutlet UILabel *dailyProgressLabel;
@property (nonatomic, strong) IBOutlet UILabel *workoutProgressLabel;

@property (nonatomic, strong) CMPedometer *pedometer;
@property (nonatomic, strong) HKHealthStore *healthStore;
@property (nonatomic, strong) NSDate *startDate;
@property (nonatomic, assign) BOOL isWorkoutActive;

-(IBAction)toggleAudio:(id)sender;
-(IBAction)nextTrack:(id)sender;
-(IBAction)prevTrack:(id)sender;

-(IBAction)seekForward:(id)sender;
-(IBAction)startFastForward:(id)sender;
-(IBAction)startRewind:(id)sender;
-(IBAction)stopSeeking:(id)sender;

-(IBAction)startWorkout:(id)sender;

-(IBAction)chooseTrackButton:(id)sender;
-(IBAction)chooseAlbumButton:(id)sender;

@end
```

Using Core Motion to Track Activity

Core Motion has been iOS's motion-sensing framework since iOS 4. Developers have been using it for years to access the built-in accelerator and gyroscope (enabling thousands of racing games ever since). However, until the M-series of motion coprocessors, there was never an easy way to access step data. You could use the accelerator to detect when the device experienced a "bump" in movement, but you had to develop your own code to define a "step." Similarly, you could use GPS to determine how far a user moved, but doing so would drain the battery quickly.

Although iOS 7 added an interface to the M-series motion coprocessor to the Core Motion framework, iOS 8 has fully unlocked it, allowing you to retrieve data directly as *steps* and *activity types*. Core Motion takes care of all the work to define what a step is, what it corresponds to in terms of distance, and what the user was doing when the step was registered (for example, running or walking).

Now that you know what Core Motion can do, you can discover how to enable it. For the MyFitnessPod app, you will want to use Core Motion to start logging the user's step and echo the display to the user interface. To do this, you prepare the application to accept motion data, a task that includes the following:

1. Requesting permission to use the hardware (if it is available)

2. Registering your class for motion updates

3. Implementing handler methods for these updates

The Core Motion framework depends heavily on completion handlers (blocks) for message-passing. If you are still unsure of how to use blocks, refer back to the "Quick Guide to Blocks" sidebar in Chapter 4.

Requesting Motion Activity Permission

Because health data is one of the most sensitive pieces of information you can collect about a user, before you can get started accessing the M-series motion coprocessor hardware, you need to make sure your application has permission from the user to access *motion activity* data. As with the photo-based applications you developed earlier, you cannot override the user's decision, but you can catch the response and initialize your application appropriately.

The Core Motion class that manages motion events and the motion activity permission is CMMotionActivityManager. Strictly speaking, a *motion activity* is defined as an event that corresponds to the type of movement the user is currently engaged in, whether that is walking, running, or even driving. Although handling these events is not within the scope of the MyFitnessPod project, Apple uses motion activity as the permission level for Core Motion, so you need to include it in your project.

You query for motion activity status by calling the public method [CMMotionActivity isActivityAvailable]. This method returns a BOOL value, indicating whether the user has given your app permission to access motion activity . As shown in Figure 13-7, calling this method for the first time exposes the system's permission action sheet. Privacy permissions are keyed by *application identifier*, meaning subsequent launches (or reinstalls) of your application will not prompt the user to select the permission level again. (Users can change their permission level at any time by selecting the Privacy option in the iOS Settings application.)

Figure 13-7. Motion activity permission prompt

Note   You can reset all application permissions on a device by choosing General ä Reset ä Reset Privacy & Location in the iOS Settings application.

Because the action sheet needs to be visible for the user to respond to it, you need to make the call from a user-initiated action (instead of using the [self viewDidLoad] method). For the MyFitnessPod application, the primary user-initiated action that requires motion data is the Start Workout button, so place your permission call in that button's handler method, defined as [MainViewController toggleWorkout] in the header file from Listing 13-1. As shown in Listing 13-2, after determining whether the user is about to start a workout, you should immediately check for motion activity permission. If the user has given your app permission, you can begin updating the user interface and start setting up the pedometer; otherwise, you should show an alert, letting the user know that your app requires the motion activity permission.

Listing 13-2. Checking for Motion Activity Permission

```
-(IBAction)toggleWorkout:(id)sender
{
    if (self.isWorkoutActive) {
        //stop workout
        self.isWorkoutActive = NO;

    } else {
        //start workout

        if ([CMMotionActivityManager isActivityAvailable])
          {
            self.isWorkoutActive = YES;

        } else {
            UIAlertView *errorAlert = [[UIAlertView alloc]
                initWithTitle:@"Error"
                message:@"Motion permission required"
                delegate:self
                cancelButtonTitle:@"OK" otherButtonTitles:nil];
            [errorAlert show];
        }
    }

}
```

After you have determined that your app is allowed to access motion activity, you need to make a second check—to determine whether the device has an M-series motion coprocessor with step tracking. The Core Motion class that retrieves step data from the M-series motion coprocessor is CMPedometer. This class lets you to query the hardware for updates and returns values by using the CMPedometerData class, which automatically abstracts accelerometer and altimeter data into step counts, distance, and "floors" ascended or descended. The public method to query pedometer availability is [CMPedometer isStepTrackingAvailable]. As shown in Listing 13-3, add this as a second condition before updating the user interface, so that a workout cannot start unless both the permission and hardware are available. After determining that the hardware is available, you can initialize a CMPedometer object to maintain an interface to the hardware.

Listing 13-3. Checking for and Initializing a Pedometer

```
-(IBAction)toggleWorkout:(id)sender
{
    if (self.isWorkoutActive) {
        //stop workout

    } else {
        //start workout
```

```objc
            if ([CMMotionActivityManager isActivityAvailable] &&
                [CMPedometer isStepCountingAvailable]) {
                self.pedometer = [[CMPedometer alloc] init];
                self.isWorkoutActive = YES;}
            else {
                UIAlertView *errorAlert = [[UIAlertView alloc]
                    initWithTitle:@"Error"
                    message:@"Motion permission required"
                    delegate:self
                    cancelButtonTitle:@"OK"
                    otherButtonTitles:nil];
                [errorAlert show];
            }
        }

}
```

Although Core Motion uses blocks for message passing, you should maintain an instance variable for your `CMPedometer` object so that you can handle background updates. In the `MainViewController` class, this object is represented by the pedometer property:

```objc
@property (nonatomic, strong) CMPedometer *pedometer;
```

> **Note**   Distance and altimeter data are not available on all devices, so call the `[CMPedometer isDistanceAvailable]` and `[CMPedometer isFloorCountingAvailable]` public methods if you are planning on using either in your applications.

Starting a Workout

Having determined that your application has a valid pedometer to work with, you are now ready to implement the code required to start a workout. Figure 13-8 shows a subset of Figure 13-1, highlighting the start transition for the application.

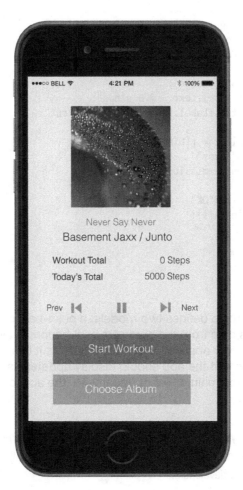

Figure 13-8. *Mock-up for Start Workout screen*

When a user hits the Start Workout button, you want to start music playback, change the text of the button to Stop Workout, and begin displaying live feedback indicating the user's workout progress. As shown in Listing 13-4, playing music playback and updating the user interface are simple: you just make calls to methods you have already defined. However, getting pedometer progress updates is a bit more complicated.

Listing 13-4. Updating the User Interface When Starting a Workout

```
-(IBAction)toggleWorkout:(id)sender
{
    if (self.isWorkoutActive) {
        //stop workout

    } else {
        //start workout
```

```
        if ([CMMotionActivityManager isActivityAvailable] &&
            [CMPedometer isStepCountingAvailable]) {
            self.pedometer = [[CMPedometer alloc] init];
            self.isWorkoutActive = YES;
            self.startDate = [NSDate date];
            self.workoutProgressLabel.text = @"0 steps";
            self.workoutButton.titleLabel.text = @"Stop Workout";
        } else {
            UIAlertView *errorAlert = [[UIAlertView alloc]
                initWithTitle:@"Error"
                message:@"Motion permission required"
                delegate:self
                cancelButtonTitle:@"OK"
                otherButtonTitles:nil];
            [errorAlert show];
        }
    }
}
```

For pedometer data updates, Apple defines two models: a push-based model, where your application constantly receives data from the hardware as it becomes available (every 2.5 seconds), and a pull-based model where your application requests data as it is needed. The mock-up for the MyFitnessPod project indicates that the app should display updates as they are available, so you should use the push model as the main driver of updates for the application.

> **Caution**   A push-based delivery model is a software design pattern, whereas *push notifications* are a very specific iOS feature (where notifications are "pushed" directly to your device). Be very careful not to confuse the two when you talking to other developers.

To receive push updates, call the [CMPedometer startPedometerUpdatesFromDate:withHandler] method on your CMPedometer object. As the signature implies, the input parameters are a completion handler that receives the updates, and a start time that acts as the baseline for pedometer updates. Core Motion will transmit updates containing the events that have occurred since that starting time. For the MyFitnessPod application, the start time is when the user presses the Start Workout button. Programmatically, you obtain this by simply getting the *current time* using the [NSDate date] method. Listing 13-5 provides the [CMPedometer startPedometerUpdatesFromDate:withHandler] call for the MyFitnessPod project.

Listing 13-5. Setting up the MainViewController Class for Pedometer Updates

```
-(IBAction)toggleWorkout:(id)sender
{
    if (self.isWorkoutActive) {
        //stop workout
        if (self.pedometer != nil) {
            [self.pedometer stopPedometerUpdates];
        }
```

```objc
        [self.musicPlayer stop];
        self.isWorkoutActive = NO;
        self.workoutButton.titleLabel.text = @"Start Workout";

    } else {
        //start workout
        if ([CMMotionActivityManager isActivityAvailable] &&
            [CMPedometer isStepCountingAvailable]) {
            self.pedometer = [[CMPedometer alloc] init];
            self.isWorkoutActive = YES;
            self.startDate = [NSDate date];
            self.workoutProgressLabel.text = @"0 steps";
            self.workoutButton.titleLabel.text = @"Stop Workout";

            [self.pedometer
                startPedometerUpdatesFromDate:self.startDate
                withHandler:^(CMPedometerData *pedometerData,
                NSError *error) {


                ...
            }];

        } else {
            UIAlertView *errorAlert = [[UIAlertView alloc]
                initWithTitle:@"Error"
                message:@"Motion permission required"
                delegate:self cancelButtonTitle:@"OK"
                otherButtonTitles:nil];
            [errorAlert show];
        }
    }

}
```

When your app receives an update, you should display the updated step count in the Workout Progress label. The CMPedometerData class, which represents pedometer events, makes this easy, by declaring the numberOfSteps property as an NSNumber object. You display this value by calling the [NSNumber intValue] method to get the value as an int and then including it in a string:

```objc
NSString *workoutProgressString = [NSString string withFormatter:"%ld steps",
    [pedometerData.numberOfSteps intValue]];
self.workoutProgressLabel.text = workoutProgressString;
```

Before adding this to your handler method, you need to account for one complication: blocks always execute in the *background*, while the user interface always executes on the main thread. To close this gap, use the dispatch_async (dispatch_queue_t queue, dispatch_block_t block) method to update the workProgressLabel object on the main queue. The first parameter of dispatch_async()

takes a queue object, and the second parameter takes a block. By passing `dispatch_get_main_queue()` as your queue, you can automatically retrieve a pointer to the main queue of execution:

```
dispatch_async(dispatch_get_main_queue(), ^{
    self.workoutProgressLabel.text =
    [NSString stringWithFormat:@"%ld steps",
    [pedometerData.numberOfSteps integerValue]];
    });
```

You can find the complete implementation for the MyFitnessPod project in Listing 13-6.

Listing 13-6. Pedometer Update Block, Including User Interface Changes

```
-(IBAction)toggleWorkout:(id)sender
{
    if (self.isWorkoutActive) {
        //stop workout

    } else {
        //start workout

        if ([CMMotionActivityManager isActivityAvailable] &&
            [CMPedometer isStepCountingAvailable]) {
            self.pedometer = [[CMPedometer alloc] init];
            self.isWorkoutActive = YES;
            self.startDate = [NSDate date];
            self.workoutProgressLabel.text = @"0 steps";
            self.workoutButton.titleLabel.text = @"Stop Workout";
            [self.pedometer
                startPedometerUpdatesFromDate:self.startDate
                withHandler:^(CMPedometerData *pedometerData,
                NSError *error) {

                NSLog(@"number of steps: %ld",
                    [pedometerData.numberOfSteps integerValue]);
                dispatch_async(dispatch_get_main_queue(), ^{
                    self.workoutProgressLabel.text =
                    [NSString stringWithFormat:@"%ld steps",
                    [pedometerData.numberOfSteps integerValue]];
                });
            }];

        } else {
            UIAlertView *errorAlert = [[UIAlertView alloc]
                initWithTitle:@"Error"
                message:@"Motion permission required"
                delegate:self
                cancelButtonTitle:@"OK"
                otherButtonTitles:nil];
            [errorAlert show];
        }
    }

}
```

Integrating Background Updates

The 800-pound gorilla of any app is its background functionality. With workout apps, this becomes even more critical, because users are likely to be busy for 30 minutes or longer (well beyond the sleep setting for most iOS devices). The good news is that, because you initialize the [CMPedometer startPedometerUpdatesFromDate:withHandler] method with a start time, backgrounding your application will not prevent the method from returning accurate information when it returns to the foreground (the updates will still be compared to the original time you provided).

The issue you run into with background updates is one of user-interface initialization. It does not make sense to update the user interface while the application is backgrounded, because users will never see that information. However, at the same time, you don't want users to come back to the application and still see their old workout progress on the screen (as it would be until the next update). To solve this problem, use the pull mechanism of the CMPedometer class to retrieve the user's steps as soon as the application returns to the foreground.

For the MainViewController class, you can use the [self viewDidAppear:] method to handle this event. The [self viewDidAppear:] event gets called whenever the view appears, regardless of whether the appearance results from the app returning from the background, from being initialized for the first time, or from another view disappearing. As shown in Listing 13-7, by checking whether the workout is already active, you can query for these updates only after a workout has started.

Listing 13-7. Preparing for Background Updates

```
- (void)viewDidAppear:(BOOL)animated
{
    if (self.isWorkoutActive) {
        [self.pedometer queryPedometerDataFromDate:self.startDate
            toDate:[NSDate date] withHandler:^(CMPedometerData
            *pedometerData, NSError *error) {

                NSLog(@"number of steps: %ld", [pedometerData.numberOfSteps integerValue]);
            dispatch_async(dispatch_get_main_queue(), ^{

                self.workoutProgressLabel.text = [NSString
                    stringWithFormat:@"%ld steps",
                    [pedometerData.numberOfSteps integerValue]];
            });
        }];
    }
}
```

The pull method for the CMPedometer class is [CMPedometer queryPedometerDataFromDate:toDate: withHandler:], which takes two dates and a completion handler as its inputs. For the *start date*, use the start time for the pedometer, For the *end date*, use the current time—the time when the application is returning to the foreground. To maintain the start date, add an instance variable to your class:

```
@property (nonatomic, strong) NSDate *startDate;
```

Next, when you click the Start Workout button, add an extra step to save the startDate, as shown in Listing 13-8.

Listing 13-8. Saving the Start Date of a Workout

```
-(IBAction)toggleWorkout:(id)sender
{
    if (self.isWorkoutActive) {
        //stop workout

    } else {
        //start workout

        if ([CMMotionActivityManager isActivityAvailable] &&
            [CMPedometer isStepCountingAvailable]) {
            self.pedometer = [[CMPedometer alloc] init];
            self.isWorkoutActive = YES;
            self.startDate = [NSDate date];
            self.workoutProgressLabel.text = @"0 steps";
            self.workoutButton.titleLabel.text = @"Stop Workout";
            [self.pedometer startPedometerUpdatesFromDate:self.startDate
                withHandler:^(CMPedometerData *pedometerData,
                NSError *error) {

                NSLog(@"number of steps: %ld",
                    [pedometerData.numberOfSteps integerValue]);
                dispatch_async(dispatch_get_main_queue(), ^{
                    self.workoutProgressLabel.text =
                    [NSString stringWithFormat:@"%ld steps",
                    [pedometerData.numberOfSteps integerValue]];
                });
            }];

        } else {
            UIAlertView *errorAlert = [[UIAlertView alloc]
                initWithTitle:@"Error"
                message:@"Motion permission required"
                delegate:self
                cancelButtonTitle:@"OK"
                otherButtonTitles:nil];
            [errorAlert show];
        }
    }

}
```

You can now use your startDate instance variable as the baseline for your pull query. For your completion handler, perform the exact same logic as in your push handler—update the user interface on the main thread to display the number of steps received. Listing 13-9 shows the completed [self viewDidAppear] method for the MyFitnessPod project.

Listing 13-9. Updating the User Interface After Returning to the Foreground

```
- (void)viewDidAppear:(BOOL)animated
{
    if (self.isWorkoutActive) {
        [self.pedometer queryPedometerDataFromDate:self.startDate
            toDate:[NSDate date]
            withHandler:^(CMPedometerData *pedometerData,
            NSError *error) {

            NSLog(@"number of steps: %ld",
                [pedometerData.numberOfSteps integerValue]);
            dispatch_async(dispatch_get_main_queue(), ^{
                self.workoutProgressLabel.text =
                [NSString stringWithFormat:@"%ld steps",
                [pedometerData.numberOfSteps integerValue]];
            });
        }];
    }
}
```

Stopping a Workout

Eventually, all workouts must come to an end, and so should the pedometer updates. By calling the [CMPedometer stopPedometerUpdates] method on your CMPedometer object, let Core Motion know that it should stop sending pedometer events to the completion handler you defined previously.

For the MyFitnessPod application, place this logic in the user-initiated event for stopping the workout: the handler for the Stop Workout button. As shown in Listing 13-10, after determining that the workout is active, call the [CMPedometer stopPedometerUpdates] method and reset the user interface to its original state, by stopping music playback and resetting the title of the workout button. You do not need to reset the number of steps, because most users expect to see their totals at the end of a workout.

Listing 13-10. Stopping Updates and Resetting the User Interface

```
-(IBAction)toggleWorkout:(id)sender
{
    if (self.isWorkoutActive) {
        //stop workout

        if (self.pedometer != nil) {
            [self.pedometer stopPedometerUpdates];
        }
        [self.musicPlayer stop];
        self.isWorkoutActive = NO;
        self.workoutButton.titleLabel.text = @"Start Workout";
    } else {
        //start workout
```

```
        if ([CMMotionActivityManager isActivityAvailable] &&
            [CMPedometer isStepCountingAvailable]) {
            self.pedometer = [[CMPedometer alloc] init];
            /*
             if (queue loaded) {
                 play queue
             } else {
                 load default playlist
             }
             */

            self.isWorkoutActive = YES;
            self.startDate = [NSDate date];
            self.workoutProgressLabel.text = @"0 steps";
            self.workoutButton.titleLabel.text = @"Stop Workout";
            [self.pedometer startPedometerUpdatesFromDate:self.startDate
                withHandler:^(CMPedometerData *pedometerData,
                NSError *error) {

                NSLog(@"number of steps: %ld",
                    [pedometerData.numberOfSteps integerValue]);
                dispatch_async(dispatch_get_main_queue(), ^{
                    self.workoutProgressLabel.text =
                    [NSString stringWithFormat:@"%ld steps",
                    [pedometerData.numberOfSteps integerValue]];
                });
            }];

        } else {
            UIAlertView *errorAlert = [[UIAlertView alloc]
                initWithTitle:@"Error"
                message:@"Motion permission required"
                delegate:self cancelButtonTitle:@"OK"
                otherButtonTitles:nil];
            [errorAlert show];
        }
    }

}
```

Using HealthKit to Sync Data

At this point, the MyFitnessPod app is able to take advantage of the M-series motion coprocessor, so it is time to make it a "responsible data citizen" by using HealthKit as the back end for posting and retrieving the workout data the app collects. As mentioned at the beginning of the chapter, HealthKit allows you to skip the unnecessary step of building your own data-logging interface, by giving all apps a central location where they can store (and retrieve) health and fitness data. Additionally, the Health app gives users windows into this data profile, allowing them to monitor such things as step information, caloric intake, weight, blood pressure, and countless other health metrics, all in one place. Users can even create their own dashboards to get a historical snapshot. You can view my dashboard from when I wrote this chapter in Figure 13-9.

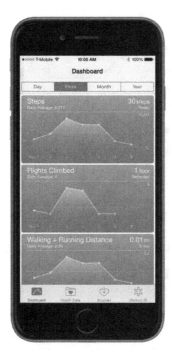

Figure 13-9. The author's Health app dashboard

In this section, you will learn how to take advantage of HealthKit to log workouts, retrieve past workout activity, and receive real-time data updates. This allows your users to share their data between apps, and will complete the user interface by implementing the Today's Totals label and populating it with accurate data.

Although HealthKit is a completely separate framework from Core Motion, the good news is that it shares a lot of design similarities, such as the idea of push- and pull-based data queries. HealthKit also exposes data types that provide rich information for each type of stored activity. The fundamental steps you need to implement to use HealthKit are as follows:

1. Request permission for an object type (read, write, or both).

2. Implement a query and handler method to retrieve data as it becomes available.

3. Create a properly formatted object to store data.

Requesting Permission to Use HealthKit

As with Core Motion, before you can perform any kind of operation with HealthKit, you need to request the correct permissions. Again, because health data is sensitive personal information, the permission levels are extremely granular, resulting in a detailed modal view that the users can review before providing permission, as shown in Figure 13-10.

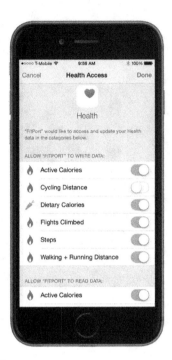

Figure 13-10. HealthKit Permissions modal view

You will notice that this modal view presents read and write permissions for each type of health data an application wishes to access. Every operation in HealthKit is tied to an *object type*, represented by the HKObject class. Just like the CMPedometerData class, the HKObject class stores a rich set of properties for each type of health data that is being stored, including quantity (or characteristic), time of measurement, and the measurement source. The set of properties varies for each object type. There are two high-level types of object types to remember: *quantities*, which are measured with quantitative units (such as weight), and *characteristics*, which are represented by qualitative observations (such a poor sleep quality). The user will be prompted to opt into permissions for every object type you try to operate on.

To request HealthKit permissions, you need to call the [HKHealthStore requestAuthorization ToShareTypes:readTypes:completion:] method, on an HKHealthStore object. The HKHealthStore class represents an interface to HealthKit for data operations, similar to how a managed object context provides an interface to a database in Core Data. Just as with a database, it does not make sense to create a health store for every data operation you want to perform, so declare one as an instance variable. For the MainViewController class, this property is called healthStore:

```
@property (nonatomic, strong) HKHealthStore *healthStore;
```

To request permissions, you need to specify an NSSet of object types that represent the type of data you want to request. For the MyFitnessPod project, you only need to read and write step counts, so initialize your permission set with the NSQuantityTypeIdentifierStepCount constant:

```
NSSet *dataTypes =
    [NSSet setWithObject:HKQuantityTypeIdentifierStepCount];
```

When you requested motion activity, you needed to make the call to obtain status after the view was visible, due to the nature of the request (a simple yes or no). Because HealthKit permissions are more complicated, the [HKHealthStore requestAuthorizationToShareTypes:readTypes:comple tion:] method lets you specify a completion handler that returns a success variable that indicates whether or not the user has given your app all the permissions it requested. This allows you to place your initialization code in the [self viewDidLoad] method. Listing 13-11 shows the [self viewDidLoad] method for the MainViewController class, including the HealthKit initialization.

Listing 13-11. Requesting Step Count Permission from HealthKit

```
- (void)viewDidLoad {
    [super viewDidLoad];
    // Do any additional setup after loading the view,
    // typically from a nib.

    self.musicPlayer = [MPMusicPlayerController applicationMusicPlayer];

....
    self.isWorkoutActive = NO;

    if ([HKHealthStore isHealthDataAvailable]) {
        NSSet *dataTypes =
            [NSSet setWithObject:HKQuantityTypeIdentifierStepCount];
        [self.healthStore requestAuthorizationToShareTypes:dataTypes
            readTypes:dataTypes
            completion:^(BOOL success, NSError *error) {
            if (success) {

            } else {

                UIAlertView *alert = [[UIAlertView alloc]
                    initWithTitle:@"Error"
                    message:@"MyFitnessPod requires step count access!"
                    otherButtonTitles:nil];
                [alert show];
            }
        }];
    }
}
```

Note that the beginning of the permission block contains a call to [HKHealthStore isHealthDataAvailable]. This is another easy way to check whether a device is HealthKit-enabled (iOS 8 or greater), and prevents crashes on older devices (you cannot access a class that is not defined!).

If the completion handler returns success, your HKHealthStore will be ready to use, requiring no additional initialization on your part. If the permission request failed, you should present an error message to the user. If the user has already set permissions for your app, the completion handler will be called immediately with the result.

Retrieving Data from HealthKit

In keeping with its design similarities to Core Motion, HealthKit provides push- and pull-based queries for retrieving data. Like Core Motion, the push-based method returns a result every time an event is logged, while the pull-based method returns a result just once, after being initiated. HealthKit's push-based mechanism is very unusual for database-like systems, where manually initiating an action helps increase performance, but it is valuable given the shared nature of the resource, because it allows apps to react to updates coming from other applications. For example, if you background one app to get a blood-pressure reading in another app, when you return to the original app, you could receive an update.

Two steps are involved in executing a query with HealthKit:

1. Define an HKQuery object with a type matching the result type (such as statistics, samples, cloud-backed data, and so on) and the desired execution method (push or pull).

2. Perform the query on your HKHealthStore object to get results.

HKQuery is an abstract class that defines the general rules for initializing a query and specifying what it should return, without specifying the behavior or return types. To perform a query, you must select a subclass of HKQuery that matches the type of results you are looking for (for example, a collection of data or a single item) and the execution behavior you need (push or pull based). Table 13-1 lists the major HKQuery subclasses, including the result type and execution behavior of each.

Table 13-1. Result Types and Execution Behaviors for Major HKQuery Subclasses

Subclass	Result Type	Execution Behavior
HKSampleQuery	A set of sample objects (containing sample time and quantity)	Pull (generates one event)
HKStatisticsQuery	Statistical results (for example, average, sum) for a set of sample objects	Pull
HKStatisticsCollectionQuery	A set of statistical results for a sample type (appropriate for building a graph)	Pull
HKObserverQuery	Changes to a quantity object (such as step count)	Push (generates events until stopped)
HKAnchoredObjectQuery	The most recent object matching a sample type	Pull

For the MyFitnessPod application, use an HKStatisticsQuery to determine the total number of steps (sum) for the Today's Progress label, and an HKObserverQuery to monitor when the step count changes.

To create a statistics query, create a new HKStatisticsQuery object and initialize it using the [HKStatisticsQuery initWithQuantityType:quantitySamplePredicate:options:completionHandler:] method. For the quantity type, you need to use an HKQuantityType object that matches the type of data you wish to retrieve. There is a convenience constructor for the HKQuantityType class, [HKQuantityType quantityTypeForIdentifier:], that allows you to create an object based on a constant matching a predefined constant. The constant for step count is HKQuantityTypeIdentierStepCount:

```
HKQuantityType *quantityType = [HKQuantityType
    quantityTypeForIdentifier: HKQuantityTypeIdentierStepCount];
```

The sample predicate used to initialize the HKStatisticsQuery is an NSPredicate, similar to the one you used in the MyPod project from Chapter 7 to limit album selection by letting users choose from the media picker. NSPredicate objects need to be very specific to filter data types properly, but to assist you, the HKQuery class comes with convenience constructors. To filter sample objects by date, use the public method [HKQuery predicateForSamplesWithStartDate:endDate:options:]. For your start and end dates, use midnight (00:00) and 11:59 PM (23:59) for the current date, as shown in Listing 13-12.

Listing 13-12. Building a Date-Based Sample Predicate

```
-(NSPredicate *)getCurrentDatePredicate {
    NSCalendar *calendar = [NSCalendar currentCalendar];
    NSDate *now = [NSDate date];
    NSDate *startDate = [calendar dateBySettingHour:0 minute:0 second:0
        ofDate:now options:0];
    NSDate *endDate = [calendar dateBySettingHour:0 minute:0 second:0
        ofDate:now options:0];
    NSPredicate *datePredicate = [HKQuery
        predicateForSamplesWithStartDate:startDate
        endDate:endDate options:0];
    return datePredicate;
}
```

For your query options, you should specify HKStatisticsCumulativeSum to indicate that you want to retrieve the sum of your sample set.

For the completion handler, you will use the sumQuantity of the query's result object to extract today's steps, and use that value to construct the string for the Today's Progress label. To execute the query, call the [HKHealthStore executeQuery:] method on your HKHealthStore object.

The code to trigger the total steps query for the MainViewController class is included in Listing 13-13. It is encapsulated in a method because you don't want to have to duplicate this code every time you query the total step status.

Listing 13-13. Statistics Query for Step Count

```
-(void)updateTotalStepCount
{
    NSPredicate *datePredicate =
        [self getCurrentDatePredicate];

    HKUnit *countUnit = [HKUnit unitFromString:@"count"];

    HKQuantityType *quantityType = [HKQuantityType
        quantityTypeForIdentifier:HKQuantityTypeIdentifierStepCount];
```

```
HKStatisticsQuery *statisticsQuery = [[HKStatisticsQuery alloc]
    initWithQuantityType:quantityType
    quantitySamplePredicate:datePredicate
    options:HKStatisticsOptionCumulativeSum
    completionHandler:^(HKStatisticsQuery *query,
                        HKStatistics *result,
    NSError *error) {

    HKQuantity *sumQuantity = result.sumQuantity;
    dispatch_async(dispatch_get_main_queue(), ^{
        self.dailyProgressLabel.text =
            [NSString stringWithFormat:@"%l steps",
            [sumQuantity doubleValueForUnit:countUnit]];
    });

}];
[self.healthStore executeQuery:statisticsQuery];
}
```

To get the total number of steps, you need to use the results property, which represents an HKQuantity object containing the results of the query. The sumQuantity property represents the sum value. Calling [HKQuantity doubleValueForUnit:] returns a double value that you can display in a string.

In Listing 13-14, you can see that I call the [MainViewController updateTotalStepCount] method in the [self viewDidLoad:] method—right after confirming HealthKit permissions—in order to initialize the Today's Progress label.

Listing 13-14. Making the First Query

```
- (void)viewDidLoad {
    [super viewDidLoad];
    // Do any additional setup after loading the view,
    // typically from a nib.

    ...

    self.isWorkoutActive = NO;

    if ([HKHealthStore isHealthDataAvailable]) {
        NSSet *dataTypes =
            [NSSet setWithObject:HKQuantityTypeIdentifierStepCount];
        [self.healthStore requestAuthorizationToShareTypes:dataTypes
            readTypes:dataTypes
            completion:^(BOOL success, NSError *error) {
            if (success) {
                [self updateTotalStepCount];
            } else {
                UIAlertView *alert = [[UIAlertView alloc]
                    initWithTitle:@"Error" message:@"MyFitnessPod " +
                        "requires step count access for total progress!"
```

```
                delegate:self cancelButtonTitle:@"OK"
                otherButtonTitles:nil];
            [alert show];
        }
    }];
    }
}
```

Getting Real-Time Updates

To get real-time updates during a workout, you need to trigger the [MainViewController updateTotalStepCount] method from an HKObserverQuery, which checks whether the total step count has been updated. Unfortunately, there is no query that kills both birds with one stone (determining both the change event and the new quantity), because an HKObserverQuery notifies the observer of events, but does not return any data about them.

Because push queries need to be stopped, define your HKObserverQuery as an instance variable:

```
@property (nonatomic, strong) HKObserverQuery *observerQuery;
```

To initialize an HKObserverQuery, use the method [HKObserverQuery initWithSampleType:predi cate:updateHandler]. For the sample type, you will once again use the HKQuantityType object corresponding to step count (all HKQuantityType objects are subclasses of HKSampleType):

```
HKQuantityType *quantityType = [HKQuantityType
    quantityTypeForIdentifier:HKQuantityTypeIdentierStepCount];
```

You do not need to specify a predicate for the query, because you do not need to filter the events. Every change to the step count will be an addition.

In the completion handler, now that you know the step count has changed, you can call the [MainViewController updateTotalStepCount] method to retrieve the latest totals.

In Listing 13-15, you can see that I have added this query to the [MainViewController viewDidLoad] method, as the user should be able to see total step count updates as long as the app is open.

Listing 13-15. Statistics Query for Step Count

```
- (void)viewDidLoad {
    [super viewDidLoad];
    // Do any additional setup after loading the view,
    // typically from a nib.

    ...

    self.isWorkoutActive = NO;
```

```
if ([HKHealthStore isHealthDataAvailable]) {
    NSSet *dataTypes =
        [NSSet setWithObject:HKQuantityTypeIdentifierStepCount];
    [self.healthStore requestAuthorizationToShareTypes:dataTypes
        readTypes:dataTypes
        completion:^(BOOL success, NSError *error) {
        if (success) {
            [self updateTotalStepCount];

            HKQuantityType *quantityType = [HKQuantityType
                quantityTypeForIdentifier:
                HKQuantityTypeIdentifierStepCount];

            self.observerQuery = [[HKObserverQuery alloc]
                initWithSampleType:quantityType predicate:nil
                updateHandler:^(HKObserverQuery *query,
                                HKObserverQueryCompletionHandler
                                completionHandler, NSError *error) {
                if (!error) {
                    [self updateTotalStepCount];
                } else {
                        NSLog(@"Unable to retrieve step count.");
                }
            }];

        } else {
            UIAlertView *alert = [[UIAlertView alloc]
                initWithTitle:@"Error"
                message:@"MyFitnessPod requires step count access " +
                    "for total progress!"
                delegate:self cancelButtonTitle:@"OK"
                otherButtonTitles:nil];
            [alert show];
        }

    }];
    }
}
```

For all long-running queries, you need to call the [HKHealthStore stopQuery:] method to stop receiving updates. As shown in Listing 13-16, I make this call in the [MainViewController dealloc] method, to indicate that the application should stop receiving updates when it exits.

Listing 13-16. Stopping an HKObserverQuery

```
-(void)dealloc
{
    [self.healthStore stopQuery:self.oberverQuery];
    [super dealloc];
}
```

Logging an Activity

To enable other applications to use the data from the MyFitnessPod app, you need to save the results of your workouts to HealthKit. To save a workout to HealthKit, you need to create an HKSample object when your workout completes, and save it to your HKHeathStore object by using the [HKHealthStore saveObject:withCompletion:] method.

An HKSample object in HealthKit represents a piece of data and the time span over which it was collected. The HKQuantitySample subclass extends this to allow you to store quantity data, such as step count. This should all sound very familiar, because when you retrieved data from the CMPedometer class, you received a quantity (a number of steps), based on a date range. As shown in Listing 13-17, by fetching the final pedometer reading when users end their workouts, you can create an HKQuantitySample object that you can save to HealthKit.

Listing 13-17. Creating an HKQuantitySample from Pedometer Data

```
self.pedometer queryPedometerDataFromDate:self.startDate
    toDate:[NSDate date] withHandler:^(CMPedometerData *pedometerData,
    NSError *error) {

        NSLog(@"number of steps: %ld", [pedometerData.numberOfSteps
            integerValue]);
        __block double stepCount = 0;
        dispatch_async(dispatch_get_main_queue(), ^{
            stepCount = [pedometerData.numberOfSteps doubleValue];

            HKUnit *countUnit = [HKUnit unitFromString:@"count"];
            HKQuantity *stepQuantity = [HKQuantity
                quantityWithUnit:countUnit doubleValue:stepCount];
            HKQuantitySample *exerciseSample = [HKQuantitySample
                quantitySampleWithType:HKQuantityTypeIdentifierStepCount
                quantity:stepQuantity startDate:self.startDate
                endDate:[NSDate date]];
```

> **Caution**   Remember, you always need to use the __block keyword whenever you are relying on a variable that gets mutated by a block.

An HKQuantity object requires a value and a *unit*, represented by the HKUnit class. This allows it to provide context to the value and automatically perform unit conversion (depending on the user's region). Because *count* is a universally understood unit, use the count string to initialize your HKUnit object.

Now that you have a valid HKQuantitySample object based on your pedometer data, you can save it to your health store. As shown in Listing 13-18, this should happen in the [MainViewController togglePlayback:] method. In your completion handler, display an error if the save fails.

Listing 13-18. Saving an HKQuantitySample to HealthKit

```objc
-(IBAction)toggleWorkout:(id)sender
{
    if (self.isWorkoutActive) {
        //stop workout

        if (self.pedometer != nil) {
            [self.pedometer stopPedometerUpdates];
        }

        [self.musicPlayer stop];

        self.isWorkoutActive = NO;

        self.workoutButton.titleLabel.text = @"Start Workout";

        __block double stepCount = 0;
        [self.pedometer queryPedometerDataFromDate:self.startDate
            toDate:[NSDate date]
            withHandler:^(CMPedometerData *pedometerData,
                NSError *error) {

            NSLog(@"number of steps: %ld",
                [pedometerData.numberOfSteps integerValue]);
            dispatch_async(dispatch_get_main_queue(), ^{
                stepCount = [pedometerData.numberOfSteps doubleValue];

                HKUnit *countUnit = [HKUnit unitFromString:@"count"];
                HKQuantity *stepQuantity = [HKQuantity
                    quantityWithUnit:countUnit doubleValue:stepCount];
                HKQuantitySample *exerciseSample = [HKQuantitySample
                  quantitySampleWithType:HKQuantityTypeIdentifierStepCount
                  quantity:stepQuantity startDate:self.startDate
                  endDate:[NSDate date]];

                [self.healthStore saveObject:exerciseSample
                    withCompletion:^(BOOL success, NSError *error){
                    if (success) {
                        [self updateTotalStepCount];
                    } else {
                        NSLog(@"error saving steps");
                    }
                }];

            });
        }];

    } else {
        ...
    }

}
```

You do not need to manually refresh total step count after saving your workout results, because that is handled by the HKObserverQuery you set up earlier.

Summary

In this chapter, you saw how to repurpose the MyPod application, turning it from a simple iPod-based music player to a powerful HealthKit-connected workout fitness application. By integrating Core Motion into the application, you were able to create an accessory-less interface to the M-series motion coprocessor on the user's device, and you were able to query pedometer data directly as a step count. To make your application work well with other fitness apps, and to obtain a total snapshot of the user's daily activity, you integrated HealthKit into the app as the repository for health information. Along the way, you learned how design similarities in the two frameworks allow you to quickly convert data types and use similar design patterns for retrieving data.

Chapter 14

Getting Started with Swift

It is very hard to end an iOS book written after June 2, 2014 without a mention of one of the most earthshaking announcements in recent years: Swift. *Swift* is Apple's brand-new programming language, intended to lower the barrier to entry to iOS and OS X. For many developers, Objective-C's unique blend of C and Smalltalk syntax is extremely daunting. It is rare for universities to have a purely C-based computer science curriculum these days, because the jobs that rely on it typically involve either extremely low-level programming or legacy code. While Smalltalk was one of the first pure object-oriented programming (OOP) languages, its syntax is unlike any other popular language, and the language rarely sees adoption nowadays outside the realm of teaching concepts.

To address this problem, Apple hopes to use Swift to marry the design concepts of Objective-C with the best syntax features of newer programming languages, such as Java, Python, and Haskell. To give the language legs, Apple has announced that Xcode, Cocoa, and Cocoa Touch are fully compatible with Swift, allowing you to build apps entirely in Swift. That compatibility also means that developers who are still learning the language can mix Objective-C and Swift in their projects.

In this chapter, you will see how to get started with Swift by converting the MyAVPlayer project from Chapter 9 from Objective-C to Swift. Along the way, I will cover Swift syntax as you port different parts of the project, discuss how you can integrate Swift with your existing Objective-C code, and highlight how you need to modify your Xcode workflow for Swift.

This chapter is intended only as a very high-level overview of the Swift programming language. For a more in-depth discussion of the language, I recommend *Beginning iPhone Development with Swift* by David Mark et al. (Apress, 2014), as well as Apple's own guide to the language, *The Swift Programming Language*, available from the iBooks Store.

Getting Started

In this chapter, you will port the MyAVPlayer project to Swift. The resulting project will be called SwiftAVPlayer and is included in the Chapter 14 folder of the source code bundle. Before getting started, it's worth reviewing the mock-up of the MyAVPlayer project from Chapter 1, provided in Figure 14-1.

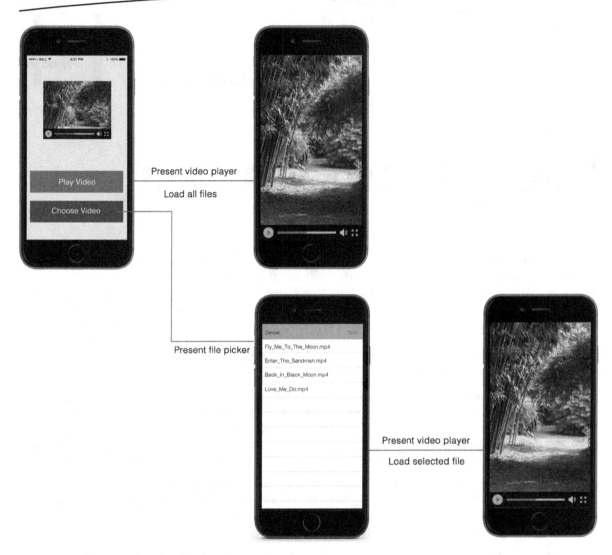

Figure 14-1. Mock-up of MyAVPlayer project

In the MyAVPlayer project, the goal was to create a media playback app using the AVKit framework. Users could initiate playback by clicking the Choose File and Play All buttons at the bottom of the main view controller, which let them manually select a file to play or automatically play (respectively) all of the files available in the app's documents directory. The SwiftAVPlayer project will retain this functionality.

Creating a New Project

As with Objective-C projects, the first step in creating a Swift project is to select New ä Project from Xcode's File menu. You will see the familiar project wizard that you saw in the Objective-C projects you have created throughout this book. However, to create a Swift project, select Swift in the Language drop-down, as shown in Figure 14-2. To target both iPhone and iPad, select Universal for your Device type.

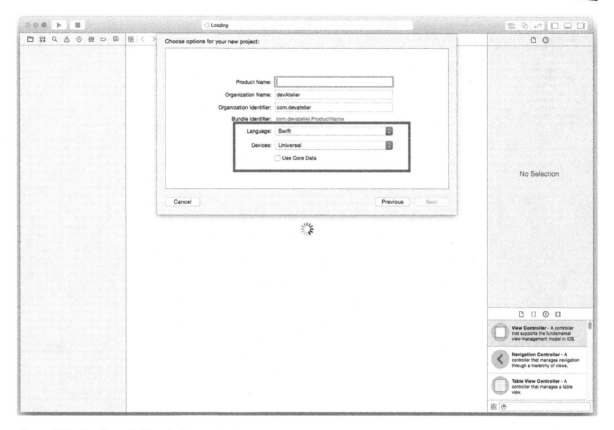

Figure 14-2. *Creating a Swift project*

When your project has been created successfully, you will see the project hierarchy shown in Figure 14-3. Your project will be pre-populated with a ViewController class (called ViewController.swift), an AppDelegate class (called AppDelegate.swift), a storyboard file (called Main.storyboard), and default Xcode project settings, based on your wizard selections.

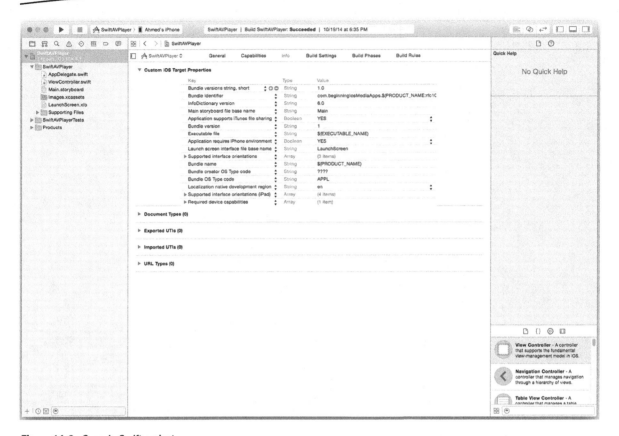

Figure 14-3. Sample Swift project

This project hierarchy is similar to the one you would receive when creating an Objective-C project. The major differences are that your project's base compilation language is set to Swift and the default classes are provided in Swift. All the Xcode project settings screens and Interface Builder screens work exactly the same way as they do for an Objective-C project, because there are no major changes to the file formats. Because the MyAVPlayer project depended on the app's documents directory for its files, you need to enable iTunes file sharing in your project. As with an Objective-C project, enable this by clicking the Info tab for your project and selecting Application Supports ciTunes File Sharing, as shown in Figure 14-4. Make sure the value for the key is set to Yes to enable file sharing.

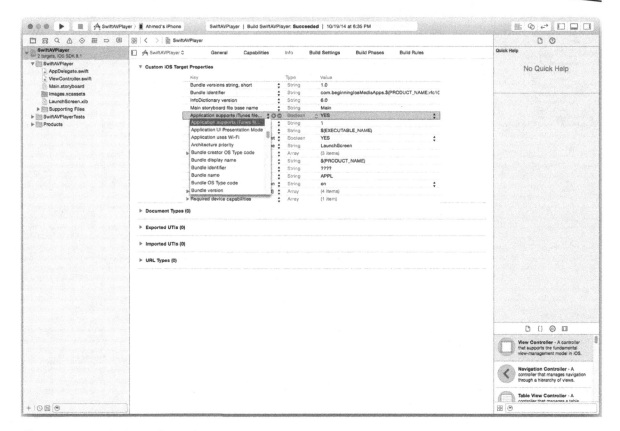

Figure 14-4. Enabling iTunes file-sharing support

Importing Objective-C Classes into Your Project

Before moving on to building the storyboard, I should discuss the 800-pound gorilla in the room: Swift compatibility with Objective-C. Swift lets you import classes written in Objective-C and call Objective-C methods. This import capability is extremely valuable, because you can import any of the existing Cocoa Touch APIs or your existing Objective-C code.

To illustrate this, rather than rewriting the entire MyAVPlayer project in Swift, you will rewrite only the MainViewController class in Swift, and you will import the FileViewController (file picker) as an Objective-C class.

To add an Objective-C class to your Swift project, follow the same process you would use for an Objective-C project: drag and drop the files onto the Project Navigator, or select Add Files to <Project Name> from the File menu. The first time you import Objective-C classes into a Swift project, you will be asked to create an Objective-C bridging header, as shown in Figure 14-5. Select Yes to continue.

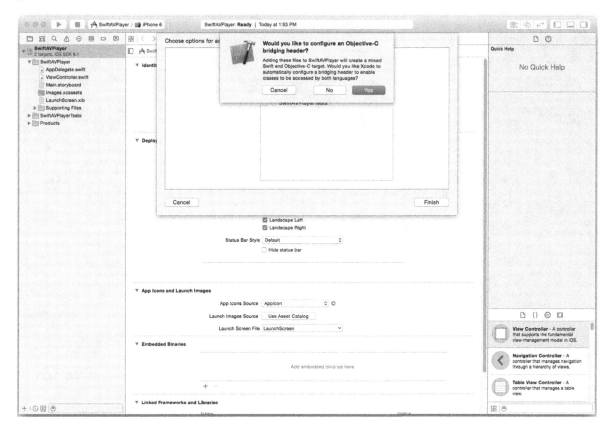

Figure 14-5. *Objective-C bridging header prompt*

An *Objective-C bridging header* is a special header file that gives the compiler a list of Objective-C header files to expose to Swift classes. This works as a universal header file, similar to a PCH (precompiled header) file. Add classes by #importing them. For the SwiftAVPlayer project, the only class you need to import is FileViewController. Add the following #import statement to the SwiftAVPlayer-Bridging-Header.h file in your project:

```
#import "FileViewController.h"
```

If you wanted to import more Objective-C classes (including third-party components) into your project, you would follow the same steps, making sure you add all of the classes to your bridging header file. You do not need to add any Cocoa Touch classes to this bridging header file, because Apple has already taken care of this for you.

Building a Storyboard

The process of building a storyboard for a Swift-based project is exactly the same as that of building a storyboard for a project based on Objective-C, except that you need some additional configuration to use imported Objective-C classes. All the Interface Builder features you are already familiar with, including the Attributes Editor, Object Library, and View Hierarchy, are available for your Swift-based projects.

For the MySwiftAVPlayer project, build the storyboard shown in Figure 14-6.

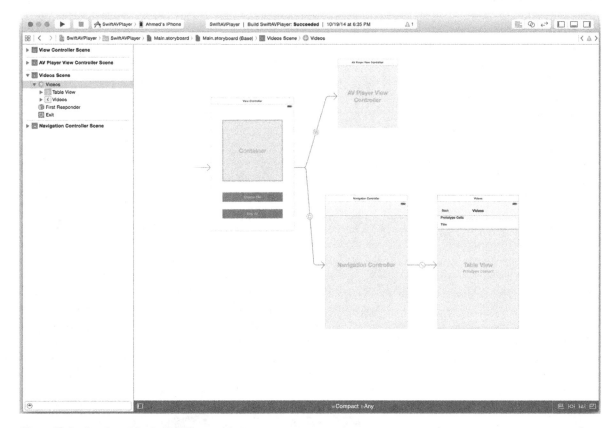

Figure 14-6. Storyboard for SwiftAVPlayer project

The key components of this storyboard are as follows:

- An AVKit player view controller that will represent the media player for the project

- A container view that holds the media player, and an Embed segue named setPlayerContent that is used to initialize the media player

- A UITableViewController subclass that will be used for the file picker

- A UINavigationController that embeds the file picker, and that connects to the Choose File option via a Present Modally segue named showFilePicker

For more details on how to build each component of this storyboard, review Chapter 9.

To connect the file picker on the storyboard to its parent class, FileViewController.h, use the Identity Inspector in Interface Builder, just as you would in an Objective-C based project. To allow Interface Builder to recognize an Objective-C–based class, you need to select a parent class and a *module*. Modules are another way of adding Swift compatibility to Objective-C classes. For a basic project, you do not need to define a module; however, you need to click inside the Module drop-down in the Identity Inspector to make Interface Builder recognize your Objective-C class.

As shown in Figure 14-7, after entering `FileViewController` as your class, click inside the empty Module drop-down in order to save your selection.

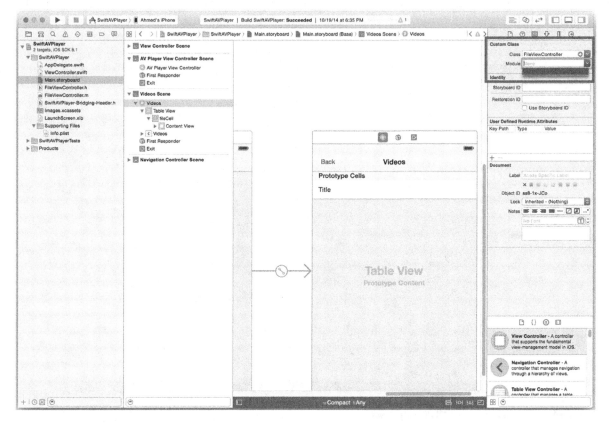

Figure 14-7. Selecting an empty module for an Objective-C based class

Caution   This step is a limitation of Xcode 6 and is required to use Objective-C classes with your storyboard.

In the next section, you will see how to make connections to your `IBOutlets` and `IBActions` in Swift.

Basic Swift Syntax

Before jumping in, I want to introduce some basic Swift syntax concepts to help you become comfortable with the language. To help make the transitions clear, I will preface each Swift code example with the corresponding Objective-C code. The code in this section is not meant to be used directly in the final project, so feel free to experiment while working the examples.

Calling Methods (Hello World)

In Objective-C, to print "Hello World" on the console, you would use the `NSLog()` method:

```
NSLog(@"Hello World");
```

In Swift, the equivalent is as follows:

```
println("Hello World")
```

You should notice a couple of big differences:

> *No semicolons*: Swift uses the `newline` character to separate lines.
>
> *No @ symbol*: Swift has its own `String` class, which is implemented as a simple character array.
>
> *println*: Swift uses this familiar method name from C and Java to allow you to print a line directly to the console.

Calling a method with multiple parameters in Objective-C looks like this:

```
NSInteger finalSum = [self calculateSumOf:5 andValue:5];
```

In Swift, you call methods with multiple parameters by adding them to a comma-delimited list within the parentheses (as you would in C or Java):

```
var finalSum = calculateSum(5, 5)
```

If the method defines labels for its parameters, add the labels in front of the values:

```
var finalSum = calculateSum(firstValue: 5, secondValue: 5)
```

Defining Variables

After "Hello World," every programming lesson must continue with a discussion of variables.

In Objective-C, you created variables by declaring the type, variable, and value:

```
NSInteger count = 5;
```

In Swift, you declare variables by specifying their name and mutability (`var` or `let`), and optionally, the data type and initialization value:

```
var count : Int = 5
```

All variables defined with `var` in Swift are *mutable*, meaning you can change their values without re-initializing the variable—for example, `NSMutableString` or `NSMutableArray`.

The `let` keyword is similar to `const` in Objective-C and C; this is a *constant* value that is not meant to change.

Swift infers data types, so if you prefer, you can omit the type from your declaration:

```
var count = 5
```

Instantiating Objects

In Objective-C, you would instantiate an object by allocating it in memory and then calling its constructor method:

```
NSMutableArray *fileArray = [[NSMutableArray alloc] init];
```

Things are a bit easier in Swift. Swift automatically allocates memory, removing the `alloc` step. Additionally, the default constructor for a class in Swift is the class name with an empty set of parentheses appended to the end:

```
var fileArray = NSMutableArray()
```

If the class you are initializing takes parameters in its constructor, call the constructor as you would any other method:

```
var myView = UIView(frame: myFrame)
```

If you are instantiating an object from an Objective-C class, you need to call its constructor as a method:

```
var mutableArray = NSMutableArray()
```

Accessing Properties and Methods (Including Objective-C)

In Swift, you can access a property or method of an object by using dot-notation, as you would in C or Java. This includes classes that were defined in Objective-C.

In Objective-C, you accessed the `lastPathComponent` property of a string by using the following code:

```
NSString *extension = [fileName lastPathComponent];
```

The Swift equivalent is as follows:

```
var extension = fileName.lastPathComponent
```

To call the `reloadSubviews` method on a `UIView` object in Objective-C, you would make a call like the following:

```
[myView reloadSubviews];
```

In Swift, the same line of code would look like this:

```
myView.reloadSubviews()
```

Casting

In Objective-C, to cast an object from one class to another, you would prepend the class name and optionally an asterisk, identifying your pointer:

```
UINavigationController *navigatonController = (UINavigationController *)segue.destinationController;
```

In Swift, casting is as easy as using the as keyword:

```
let navigationController = segue.destinationController as UINavigatonController
```

Simply add the as keyword and the class name to the result, and the compiler will do the rest for you. You can even insert this keyword inline, wherever you would normally use your object:

```
for (file as String in fileArray) {}
```

Using String Formatters

In Objective-C, when you wanted to insert a value from an object into a string, you had to use a string formatter to build a custom string:

```
NSString *summaryString = [NSString
    stringWithFormat:@"value 1: %d value 2: %d", value1, value2];
```

For each value you wanted to insert into the string, you needed to use a substitution character representing its type.

In Swift, this is a thing of the past. You can insert a value into a string by placing the variable's name in parentheses, prepended by a forward slash:

```
let value1 = 5
let value2 = 10
var summaryString = "value 1: \(value1) value2: \(value2)"
```

Using Arrays

In Objective-C, you used the NSArray class to represent arrays. Arrays in Objective-C contained objects only, and could be initialized with several convenience constructor methods, including [NSArray arrayWithObjects:]:

```
NSArray *stringArray = [NSArray arrayWithObjects:@"string 1",
    @"string 2", @"string 3"]
```

In Swift, you can declare an array by providing its values in square brackets when you define the variable:

```
var stringArray = ["string 1", "string 2", "string 3"]
```

Swift does not place the same restriction on the contents of an array, so you can initialize it with scalar values (such as Ints):

```
var intArray = [1, 3, 5]
```

If you do not want to initialize your array with values, declare a variable type for the input by placing the type name in square brackets:

```
var intArray : [Int]
```

You can also use subscript notation to read or change values in a Swift array:

```
var sampleString = stringArray[3]
```

If you define your array as a mutable variable, you can use the plus (+) operator to append values to the array:

```
stringArray += "string4"
```

Using Conditional Logic

In Objective-C, you implemented the most basic kind of conditional logic by placing a comparison in braces, as part of an if statement:

```
if (currentValue < maximumValue) {
}
```

In Swift, this syntax is largely unchanged, except the requirement for parentheses is gone:

```
if currentValue < maximumValue
```

An if-else statement retains this rule as well:

```
if currentValue < maximumValue {
    //Do something
} else if currentValue == 3 {
    //Do something else
}
```

> **Note**   All the comparison operators you are familiar with from Objective-C are still valid in Swift.

When you wanted to check against multiple values in Objective-C, you used a `switch` statement, with a `case` block for each value:

```
switch(currentValue) {
    case 1: NSLog("value 1");
        break;
    case 2: NSLog("value 2");
        break;
    case 3: NSLog("value 3");
        break;
}
```

The good news is the `switch` statement is also available in Swift, with a few changes:

- `switch` statements in Swift allow you to compare objects. The Objective-C requirement for comparing only values has been eliminated in Swift.

- `switch` statements in Swift no longer fall through by default. This means you do not have to add a `break;` statement at the end of each `case`.

- `switch` statements in Swift need to be exhaustive (meaning they must either cover all values or include a `default` case). This requirement is a best practice for code security and prevents unexpected comparisons.

In Swift, the earlier `switch` statement would look like this:

```
switch currentValue {
    case 1: println("value 1")
    case 2: NSLog("value 2")
    case 3: NSLog("value 3")
    default: NSLog("other value")
}
```

Using Loops

The syntax for all of the major types of loops (`for`, `for-each`, `do`, `do-while`) are largely unchanged in Swift. Two major changes are that you do not need to declare your type, and parentheses are once again optional:

```
for name in nameArray {
    println("name = \(name)")
}
```

Swift includes a major addition that can improve your loops: *ranges*. Ranges in Swift allow you to specify a set of values that you can use to iterate a loop or as part of comparison.

There are two major types of ranges in Swift:

- *Closed ranges*, expressed as x...y, create a range that starts at x and includes all values including y. (Note: *three* dots!)

- *Half-open ranges*, expressed as x..y , create a range that starts at x and includes all values up to y. (Note: *two* dots!)

You could use a range in a for-each loop as follows:

```
for i in 1..5 {
    println(i)
}
```

This would print the numbers 1–4.

Defining Methods

Before defining a method in Swift, let's investigate a method signature in Objective-C:

```
-(BOOL)compareValue1:(NSInteger)value1 toValue2:(NSInteger)value2;
```

In this line of code, you can see that the return type comes before the method name and that each of the parameters is provided after a colon. You add labels to every parameter after the first one, to increase readability.

In Swift, you declare a method by placing the func keyword in front of the method name and then including the input parameters and output parameters in parentheses:

```
func compareValues(value1: Int, value2: Int) -> (result: Bool)
```

Swift uses -> to separate the input parameters and return parameters.

As with variables in Swift, you indicate the type of each parameter by appending the type name with a colon.

If your method does not return anything, you can omit the return parameters and ->:

```
func isValidName(name: String) {
}
```

Calling Enumerated Types

In Swift, you can build an enumerated type by specifying its name, type, and values:

```
enum PlaybackStates : Int {
    case .Failed = -1, case .Loading, case .Success
}
```

Unlike Objective-C, to denote values in an enum, you need to place a period before the constant name. When comparing against an enum value, retain the period:

```
if playbackState == .Success {
    println("Success!")
```

Using Unusual Punctuation (Question Mark and Exclamation Mark Operators)

For anyone coming from a C-based language, one of the most jarring aspects of Swift is how it uses the question mark and exclamation mark operators.

In Swift, the question mark operator (?) is used to denote an optional variable. An *optional variable* is one that can hold either a value or nil. You may be wondering why this is important. In other languages, an object can be nil, but a scalar variable (such as an int) always stores a value. Optional variables in Swift remove this restriction, allowing anything to store a nil value.

You declare a variable as optional by appending a question mark to the end of its type:

```
var myString : String?
```

This also applies if you are initializing an object with a value:

```
var myString : String? = "Ahmed is cool"
```

Because Swift infers variable types, optionals are extremely important when you need to pass an object (such as an NSError) by reference.

> **Note**   You still use a question mark to denote a ternary operation in Swift.

The exclamation mark operator in Swift allows you to *unwrap* an optional variable. This is the equivalent of dereferencing a pointer in Objective-C or another C-based language. Unwrapping allows you to extract an optional variable's properties (or nil if the variable has not been initialized).

To unwrap a variable, append an exclamation mark to the end of its variable name:

```
var errorString = error!.description
```

> **Caution**   Do not omit the period after the exclamation mark in dot-notation. Both are required to unwrap a variable.

Building a Class

Unlike Objective-C, Swift does not have a concept of interface files (.h) and implementation files (.m). In Swift, your entire class is declared within a .swift file.

In Objective-C, a class declaration consisted of the following:

- Class name
- Parent class
- Property declarations (in interface file)
- Method definitions (in implementation file)

As a basis of comparison, refer to the class declaration for the MyAVPlayer project, shown in Listing 14-1. In the MyAVPlayer project, you can find this in the MainViewController.h file.

Listing 14-1. Header File for Main View Controller Class

```
#import <UIKit/UIKit.h>
#import <AVKit/AVKit.h>
#import "FileViewController.h"
@interface MainViewController : UIViewController <FileControllerDelegate>

@property (nonatomic, strong) IBOutlet UIView *playerViewContainer;
@property (nonatomic, strong) IBOutlet UIButton *chooseFileButton;
@property (nonatomic, strong) IBOutlet UIButton *playAllButton;
@property (nonatomic, strong) AVPlayerViewController *moviePlayer;

-(IBAction)playAll:(id)sender;

@end
```

To import classes in Swift, use the import keyword and specify the name of the class. Unlike Objective-C, you do not need to indicate the path for the header file:

```
import UIKit
import AVKit
import FileViewController
```

In Swift, you define a class similar to a variable: by specifying the class name after the class keyword, and specifying the parent class name after the colon (as you would specify the type for a variable). Add curly braces after the parent class name to indicate a block of code:

```
class ViewController : UIViewController {
}
```

Since Swift does not separate its interface and implementation files, you need to declare your properties and methods inside your class definition.

A property in Swift is declared like any other variable, except its scope is at the top level of the class:

```swift
class ViewController : UIViewController {
    var playAllButton : UIButton!
    var chooseFileButton : UIButton!
    var playAllButton : UIButton!
    var moviePlayer : AVPlayerViewController!
}
```

Similarly, to define a method, place it at the top level of your class:

```swift
class ViewController : UIViewController {
    var playAllButton : UIButton!
    var chooseFileButton : UIButton!
    var playAllButton : UIButton!
    var moviePlayer : AVPlayerViewController!
    func playAll() {

    }
}
```

In Listing 14-2, you can find the Swift file for the ViewController class, which includes the viewDidLoad and didReceiveMemoryWarning methods from the UIViewController class. When you override methods from your parent class, you need to add the override keyword in front of your method definition.

Listing 14-2. Modified Swift File for ViewController Class

```swift
import UIKit
import AVFoundation
import AVKit

class ViewController: UIViewController, FileControllerDelegate {

    var chooseFileButton : UIButton!
    var playAllButton : UIButton!
    var moviePlayer : AVPlayerViewController!

    override func viewDidLoad() {
        super.viewDidLoad()
        // Do any additional setup after loading the view,
        // typically from a nib.
    }

    override func didReceiveMemoryWarning() {
        super.didReceiveMemoryWarning()
        // Dispose of any resources that can be recreated.
    }

}
```

Connecting Items to Interface Builder

Just as with Objective-C, to make your user-interface elements and handler methods visible to Interface Builder, you need to add the @IBOutlet attribute to your property declarations and @IBAction for your methods.

In the Objective-C version of the MainViewController class, you declared an element as an *outlet* for Interface Builder by adding the @IBOutlet keyword in front of your class name:

@property (nonatomic, strong) IBOutlet UIButton *playAllButton;

In Swift, you can declare an object as an outlet by adding the @IBOutlet keyword to the front of the variable declaration:

@IBOutlet var chooseFileButton : UIButton!

To declare a method as an Interface Builder *action* in Objective-C, you changed the return type to IBAction and used an id object to represent the sender of the event:

-(IBAction)playAll:(id)sender;

In Swift, you implement the same logic by adding the @IBAction attribute in front of your method signature and by taking the sender object as an input:

@IBAction func playAll:(sender: AnyObject)

A big difference you will notice is that the generic object type for Swift is AnyObject instead of id. The id keyword does not compile in Swift, so do not attempt to use it.

After adding these attributes, you can link your properties and handlers in Interface Builder.

Listing 14-3 shows the Objective-C version of the handler for the Play All button. In this method, you built an array of AVPlayerItem objects based on the files available in the documents directory. After constructing the list, you started playback on the media player.

Listing 14-3. Objective-C Handler for Play All Button

```
-(IBAction)playAll:(id)sender
{
    NSArray *paths =
        NSSearchPathForDirectoriesInDomains(NSDocumentDirectory,
        NSUserDomainMask, YES);
    NSString *documentsDirectory = [paths objectAtIndex:0];
    NSError *error = nil;

    NSArray *allFiles = [[NSFileManager defaultManager]
        contentsOfDirectoryAtPath:documentsDirectory error:&error];

    NSMutableArray *playerItemArray = [NSMutableArray new];
```

```
    if (error == nil) {
        for (NSString *file in allFiles) {
            NSString *extensionString = [[file pathExtension]
                lowercaseString];
            if ([extensionString isEqualToString:@"mp4"] ||
                [extensionString isEqualToString:@"mov"]) {

                NSString *relativePath = [documentsDirectory
                    stringByAppendingPathComponent:file];

                NSURL *fileURL = [NSURL
                    fileURLWithPath:relativePath];

                AVPlayerItem *playerItem = [AVPlayerItem
                    playerItemWithURL:fileURL];

                [playerItem addObserver:self forKeyPath:@"status"
                    options:NSKeyValueObservingOptionNew context:nil];

                [playerItemArray addObject:playerItem];
            }
        }
    } else {
        NSLog ("could not load files");
    }

    self.moviePlayer.player = [[AVQueuePlayer alloc]
        initWithItems:playerItemArray];

    [self.moviePlayer.player addObserver:self forKeyPath:@"status"
        options:0 context:nil];

    [self.moviePlayer.player play];

}
```

Listing 14-4 shows the Swift version of the handler for the Play All button.

Listing 14-4. Swift Handler for Play All Button

```
@IBAction func playAll(sender : AnyObject) {

    var error : NSError? //optional variable (can be nil)

    let paths =
        NSSearchPathForDirectoriesInDomains(.DocumentDirectory,
        .UserDomainMask, true) // dot syntax for enums values
    let documentsDirectory = paths[0] as String
```

```swift
    let allFiles =
        NSFileManager.defaultManager().contentsOfDirectoryAtPath(
        documentsDirectory, error: &error) as [String]

    if error != nil {
        let errorString = error!.description //extract value
        // print error string
        println("error loading files: \(errorString)")

    } else {
        var playerItemArray  = NSMutableArray()
        for file in allFiles {
            let fileExtension = file.pathExtension.lowercaseString
            if fileExtension == "m4v" || fileExtension == "mov" {
                let relativePath = documentsDirectory.
                    stringByAppendingPathComponent(file)
                let fileURL = NSURL(fileURLWithPath: relativePath)
                let playerItem = AVPlayerItem(URL: fileURL)

                playerItem.addObserver(self, forKeyPath: "status",
                    options:nil, context: nil)

                playerItemArray.addObject(playerItem)

            }
        }

        moviePlayer.player = AVQueuePlayer(items: playerItemArray)
        moviePlayer.player.addObserver(self, forKeyPath: "status",
            options: nil, context: nil)

        moviePlayer.player.play()
    }

}
```

Adding Delegate Support

In Objective-C, to declare your class as a delegate of a protocol, you needed to add the protocol name to your class signature and implement the @required delegate methods in your class. In Swift, you follow the same process, but the syntax is different.

In Objective-C, you would declare your class as a protocol by adding the protocol name(s) in carets after your parent class name:

```
@interface MainViewController : UIViewController <FileControllerDelegate>
```

But in Swift, the syntax is to add your protocol names as a comma-delimited list, after your parent class name:

```
class ViewController: UIViewController, FileControllerDelegate {
```

In the MyAVPlayer project, you needed to use the `FileControllerDelegate` protocol to handle the user interface events when the user decided to close the file picker or select a file. You can find the Objective-C versions of these methods in Listing 14-5.

Listing 14-5. Objective-C Delegate Methods

```objc
-(void)cancel
{
    //Dismisses the file picker
    [self dismissViewControllerAnimated:YES completion:nil];
}

-(void)didFinishWithFile:(NSString *)filePath
{
    NSArray *paths = NSSearchPathForDirectoriesInDomains(
        NSDocumentDirectory, NSUserDomainMask, YES);
    NSString *documentsDirectory = [paths objectAtIndex:0];
    NSString *relativePath = [documentsDirectory
        stringByAppendingPathComponent:filePath];

    NSURL *fileURL = [NSURL fileURLWithPath:relativePath];

    self.moviePlayer.player = [AVPlayer playerWithURL:fileURL];
    [self.moviePlayer.player addObserver:self forKeyPath:@"status"
        options:0 context:nil];

    [self dismissViewControllerAnimated:YES completion:^{

        [self.moviePlayer.player play];
    }];

}
```

In [`FileControllerdelegate didFinishWithFile:`], you initialized the movie player with a URL based on the user's selection and then began playback. In the [`FileControllerdelegate cancel`] method, you simply dismissed the file picker without a media selection.

The Swift versions of these methods are shown in Listing 14-6.

Listing 14-6. Swift Delegate Methods

```swift
func cancel() {
    dismissViewControllerAnimated(true, completion: nil)
}

func didFinishWithFile(filePath: String!) {

    let paths = NSSearchPathForDirectoriesInDomains(
        .DocumentDirectory,.UserDomainMask, tru-e)
    let documentsDirectory = paths[0] as String
    let relativePath = documentsDirectory.
        stringByAppendingPathComponent(filePath)
```

```
    let fileURL = NSURL(fileURLWithPath: relativePath)
    moviePlayer.player = AVPlayer(URL: fileURL)

    moviePlayer.player.addObserver(self, forKeyPath: "status",
    options: nil, context: nil)

    dismissViewControllerAnimated(true, completion: { () -> Void in
        self.moviePlayer.player.play()
    })

}
```

Because you are not overriding the delegate methods from your parent class, you do not need to add the override keyword in front of your method signature. You will notice here that several of the local variables are declared as constants by using let; because I am using the variables to access properties, I do not need the variables to be mutable.

The () -> Void snippet in the dismissViewControllerAnimated method call indicates a completion handler. Blocks in Swift are treated like methods without names; to implement a completion handler in Swift, for your parameter, use the set of input and output parameters for the block (or two sets of empty parentheses if it does not need parameters):

```
() -> () {
//do something
}
```

Adding Key-Value Observer Support

In the MyAVPlayer project, you used key-value observing to auto-advance items during playback of a queue and to automatically dismiss the full-screen media player when playback completed. To re-create this behavior, you need to implement key-value observing in Swift.

As a general rule, Swift tries to move away from key-value observing and instead prefers to use a new concept called *property observers*. As shown in Listing 14-7, property observers allow you to implement blocks for when a variable is about to change (willSet) and after it has changed (didSet). You can access the values via the oldValue and newValue constants that are available in these blocks.

Listing 14-7. Property Observers

```
var count : Int {
    willSet
    {
        println("old value \(oldValue)")
    }
    didSet
    {
        println("new value \(newValue)")
    }
}
```

Unfortunately, property observers need to be implemented when you define a property or local variable. For a property of an existing class, you can continue to use the Objective-C method for adding an observer: [NSObject addObserver:forKeyPath:options:context:], except you need to call it by using Swift-method syntax:

```
moviePlayer.player.addObserver(self, forKeyPath: "status", options: nil,
    context: nil)
```

For your reference, you can find the Objective-C version of the KVO handler method in Listing 14-8. If the incoming object was an AVPlayer, you would add an image as an overlay view. If it was an AVPlayerItem, you would auto-advance to the next item in the AVQueuePlayer.

Listing 14-8. Objective-C Handler Method for KVO

```
-(void)observeValueForKeyPath:(NSString *)keyPath ofObject:(id)object
    change:(NSDictionary *)change context:(void *)context
{
    if ((object == self.moviePlayer.player) &&
        [keyPath isEqualToString:@"status"] ) {

        UIImage *image = [UIImage imageNamed:@"logo.png"];
        UIImageView *imageView = [[UIImageView alloc]
            initWithImage:image];
        imageView.frame = self.moviePlayer.videoBounds;
        imageView.contentMode = UIViewContentModeBottomRight;
        imageView.autoresizingMask = UIViewAutoresizingFlexibleHeight |
                                     UIViewAutoresizingFlexibleWidth;

        if ([self.moviePlayer.contentOverlayView.subviews count] == 0) {
            [self.moviePlayer.contentOverlayView addSubview:imageView];
        }

        [object removeObserver:self forKeyPath:@"status"];

    } else if ([object isKindOfClass:[AVPlayerItem class]]) {

        AVPlayerItem *currentItem = (AVPlayerItem *)object;

        if (currentItem.status == AVPlayerItemStatusFailed) {
            NSString *errorString = [currentItem.error description];
            NSLog(@"item failed: %@", errorString);

            if ([self.moviePlayer.player
                isKindOfClass:[AVQueuePlayer class]]) {
                    AVQueuePlayer *queuePlayer =
                        (AVQueuePlayer *)self.moviePlayer.player;
                [queuePlayer advanceToNextItem];
            } else {
                UIAlertView *alert = [[UIAlertView alloc]
                    initWithTitle:@"Error" message:errorString
                    delegate:self cancelButtonTitle:@"OK"
```

```
                        otherButtonTitles:nil];
                    [alert show];
                }
            } else {
                [object removeObserver:self forKeyPath:@"status"];
            }
        }
    }
```

The Swift version of the handler method for the observer is shown in Listing 14-9. As it is an inherited method, remember to add the override keyword to your method signature.

Listing 14-9. Swift Handler Method for KVO

```
override func observeValueForKeyPath(keyPath: String, ofObject
    object: AnyObject, change: [NSObject : AnyObject],
    context: UnsafeMutablePointer<Void>) {
        if object.isKindOfClass(AVPlayer) && keyPath == "status" {
            let overlayImage = UIImage(named: "logo.png")
            let imageView = UIImageView(image: overlayImage)
            imageView.frame = moviePlayer.videoBounds
            imageView.contentMode = .BottomRight
            imageView.autoresizingMask = .FlexibleHeight | .FlexibleWidth

            if moviePlayer.contentOverlayView.subviews.count == 0 {
                self.moviePlayer.contentOverlayView.addSubview(imageView)
            }

            object.removeObserver(self, forKeyPath: "status")

        } else if object.isKindOfClass(AVPlayerItem) {
            let currentItem = object as AVPlayerItem

            if currentItem.status == .Failed {
                let errorString = currentItem.error.description
                println("error playing item: \(errorString)")

                if (moviePlayer.player.isKindOfClass(AVQueuePlayer)) {
                    let queuePlayer = moviePlayer.player as AVQueuePlayer
                    queuePlayer.advanceToNextItem()
                } else {
                    let alert = UIAlertView(title: "Error",
                        message: errorString, delegate: self,
                        cancelButtonTitle: "OK")
                    alert.show()
                }
            } else {
                object.removeObserver(self, forKeyPath: "status")
            }
        }
}
```

In this method, you will find two interesting changes from the Objective-C implementation. First, when you check the type of the incoming object, you can call the `isKindOfClass()` method on the name of your class directly. Additionally, when you check the incoming message string, you perform a comparison on the value directly, instead of calling the `isEqualToString()` method.

Adding Notification Support

Notifications are fully supported in Swift, with the caveat that you must implement the Objective-C methods for posting and observing notifications.

In Objective-C, you set up the main view controller class for Playback Complete notifications by declaring a selector method for `AVPlayerItemDidPlayToEndTimeNotification`:

```
[[NSNotificationCenter defaultCenter] addObserver:self
    selector:@selector(playbackFinished:)
    name:AVPlayerItemDidPlayToEndTimeNotification object:nil];
```

You can use the same method in Swift to add an observer, being careful to convert it to Swift-style syntax:

```
var notificationCenter = NSNotificationCenter.defaultCenter()
notificationCenter.addObserver(self, selector: "playbackFinished:",
    name: AVPlayerItemDidPlayToEndTimeNotification, object: nil)
```

The Objective-C notification handler is shown in Listing 14-10. In this method, you would dismiss the full-screen media player upon receiving the notification that playback had finished.

Listing 14-10. Notification Handler in Objective-C

```
-(void)playbackFinished:(NSNotification *) notification
{
    NSDictionary *userInfo = notification.userInfo;

    if ([self.moviePlayer.player isKindOfClass:[AVPlayer class]]) {
        [self dismissViewControllerAnimated:YES completion:nil];
    } else {
        //do nothing
    }

}
```

For your Swift handler method, remember to set the incoming notification as your input parameter, as shown in Listing 14-11.

Listing 14-11. Notification Handler in Swift

```
func playbackFinished(notification : NSNotification) {

    let userInfo = notification.userInfo

    if moviePlayer.player.isKindOfClass(AVPlayer) {
        dismissViewControllerAnimated(true, completion: nil)
    } else {
        //do nothing
    }
}
```

Summary

In this chapter, you experienced your first taste of Swift by porting the MyAVPlayer project. After seeing how to set up a Swift project and import existing Objective-C classes, a crash course on the syntax of the Swift language gave you the basics to apply your new knowledge to rewrite the ViewController class in Swift. While Swift brings significant syntax changes to iOS development, its methods are designed to work like Objective-C. For the most part, by using Swift method syntax, you can call any Objective-C Cocoa Touch method from Swift. In instances where this is not possible, check Apple's Developer Library for alternate methods.

Index

Q

R

Get the eBook for only $10!

Now you can take the weightless companion with you anywhere, anytime. Your purchase of this book entitles you to 3 electronic versions for only $10.

This Apress title will prove so indispensible that you'll want to carry it with you everywhere, which is why we are offering the eBook in 3 formats for only $10 if you have already purchased the print book.

Convenient and fully searchable, the PDF version enables you to easily find and copy code—or perform examples by quickly toggling between instructions and applications. The MOBI format is ideal for your Kindle, while the ePUB can be utilized on a variety of mobile devices.

Go to www.apress.com/promo/tendollars to purchase your companion eBook.